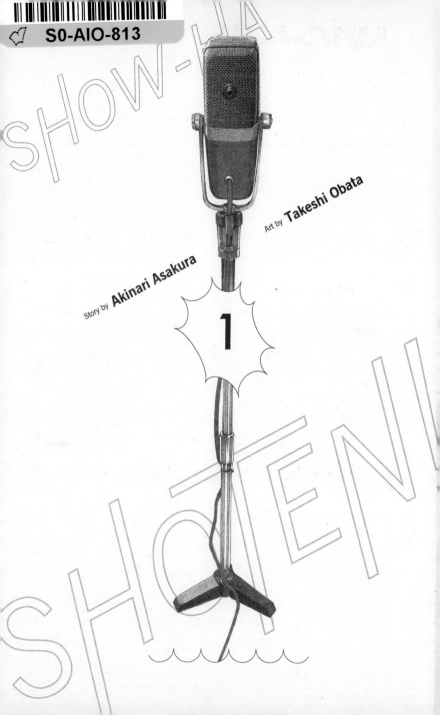

Story by **Akinari Asakura**

Art by **Takeshi Obata**

1

Contents 1

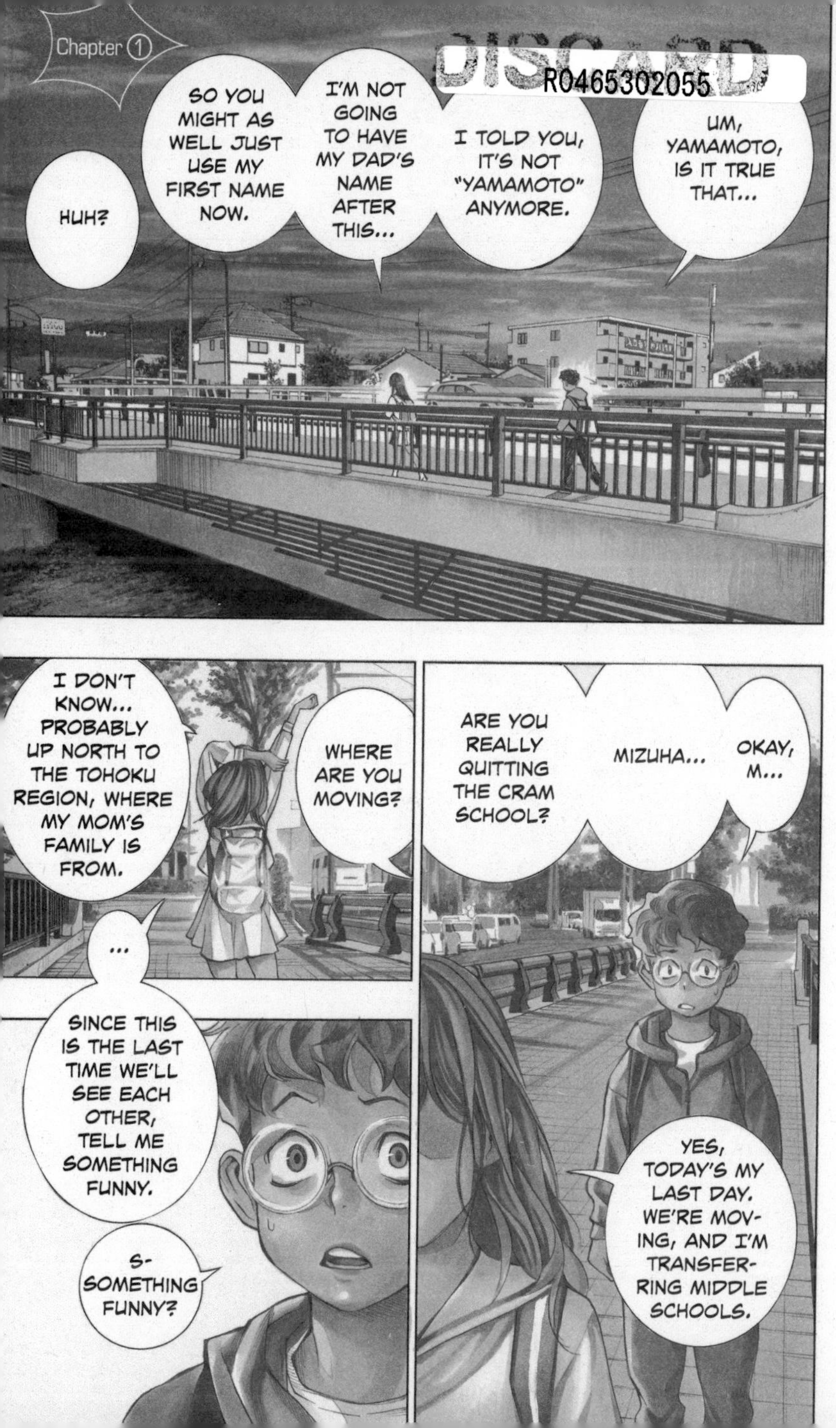
Chapter 1
UM, YAMAMOTO, IS IT TRUE THAT...
I TOLD YOU, IT'S NOT "YAMAMOTO" ANYMORE.
I'M NOT GOING TO HAVE MY DAD'S NAME AFTER THIS...
SO YOU MIGHT AS WELL JUST USE MY FIRST NAME NOW.
HUH?
OKAY, M...
MIZUHA...
ARE YOU REALLY QUITTING THE CRAM SCHOOL?
YES, TODAY'S MY LAST DAY. WE'RE MOVING, AND I'M TRANSFERRING MIDDLE SCHOOLS.
WHERE ARE YOU MOVING?
I DON'T KNOW... PROBABLY UP NORTH TO THE TOHOKU REGION, WHERE MY MOM'S FAMILY IS FROM.
...
SINCE THIS IS THE LAST TIME WE'LL SEE EACH OTHER, TELL ME SOMETHING FUNNY.
S-SOMETHING FUNNY?

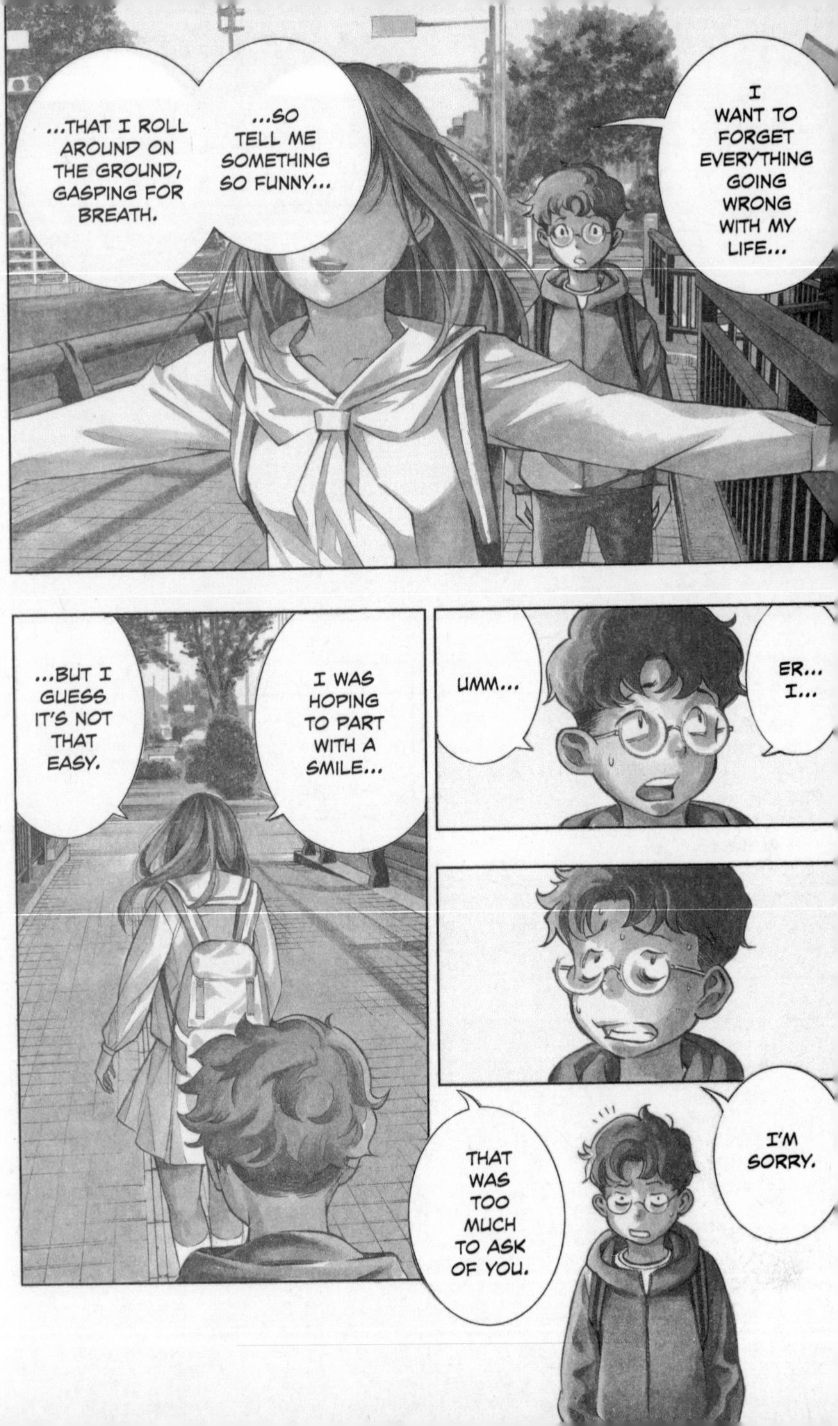
I WANT TO FORGET EVERYTHING GOING WRONG WITH MY LIFE...
...SO TELL ME SOMETHING SO FUNNY...
...THAT I ROLL AROUND ON THE GROUND, GASPING FOR BREATH.
ER... I...
UMM...
I'M SORRY.
THAT WAS TOO MUCH TO ASK OF YOU.
I WAS HOPING TO PART WITH A SMILE...
...BUT I GUESS IT'S NOT THAT EASY.

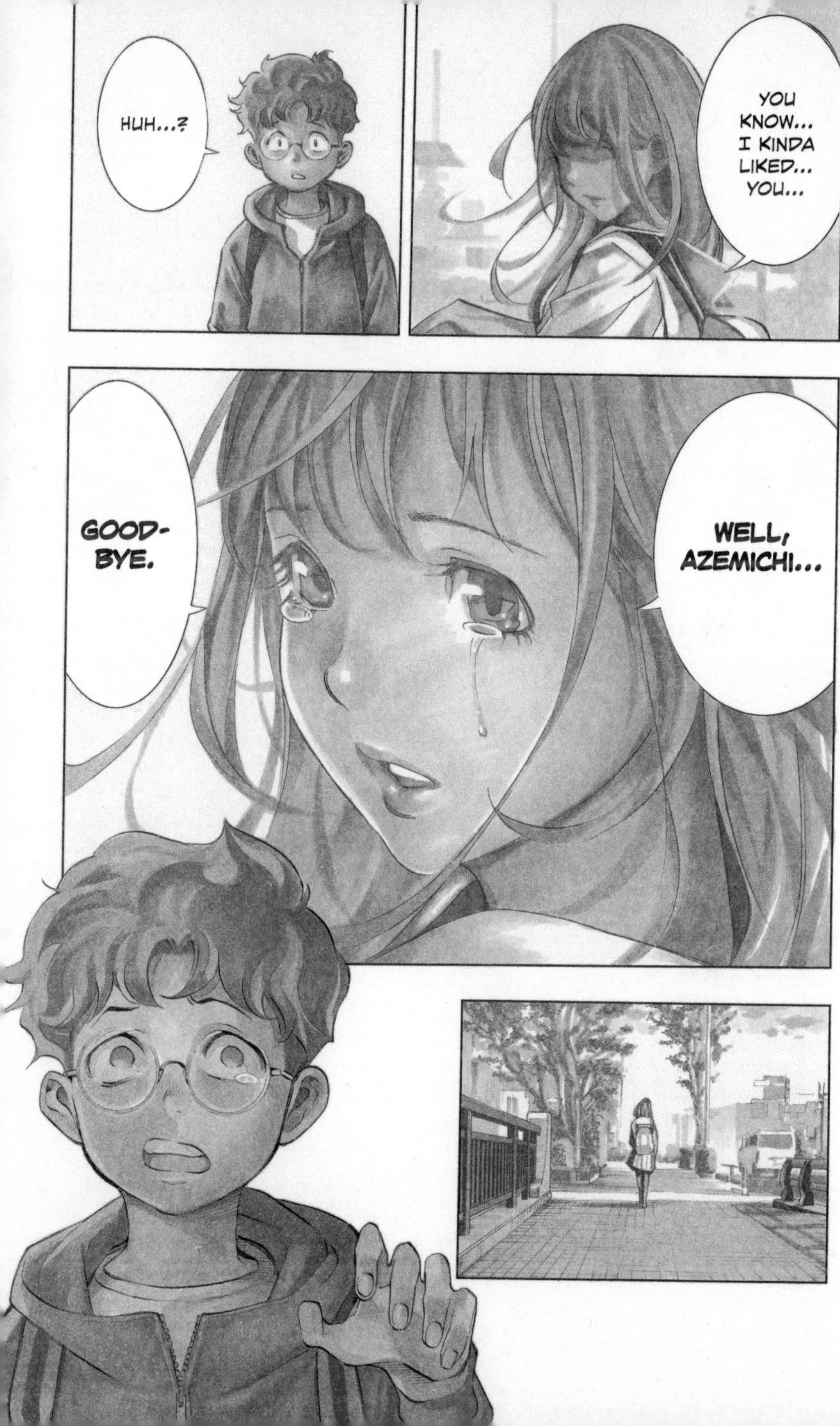
YOU KNOW... I KINDA LIKED... YOU...
HUH...?
WELL, AZEMICHI...
GOOD-BYE.

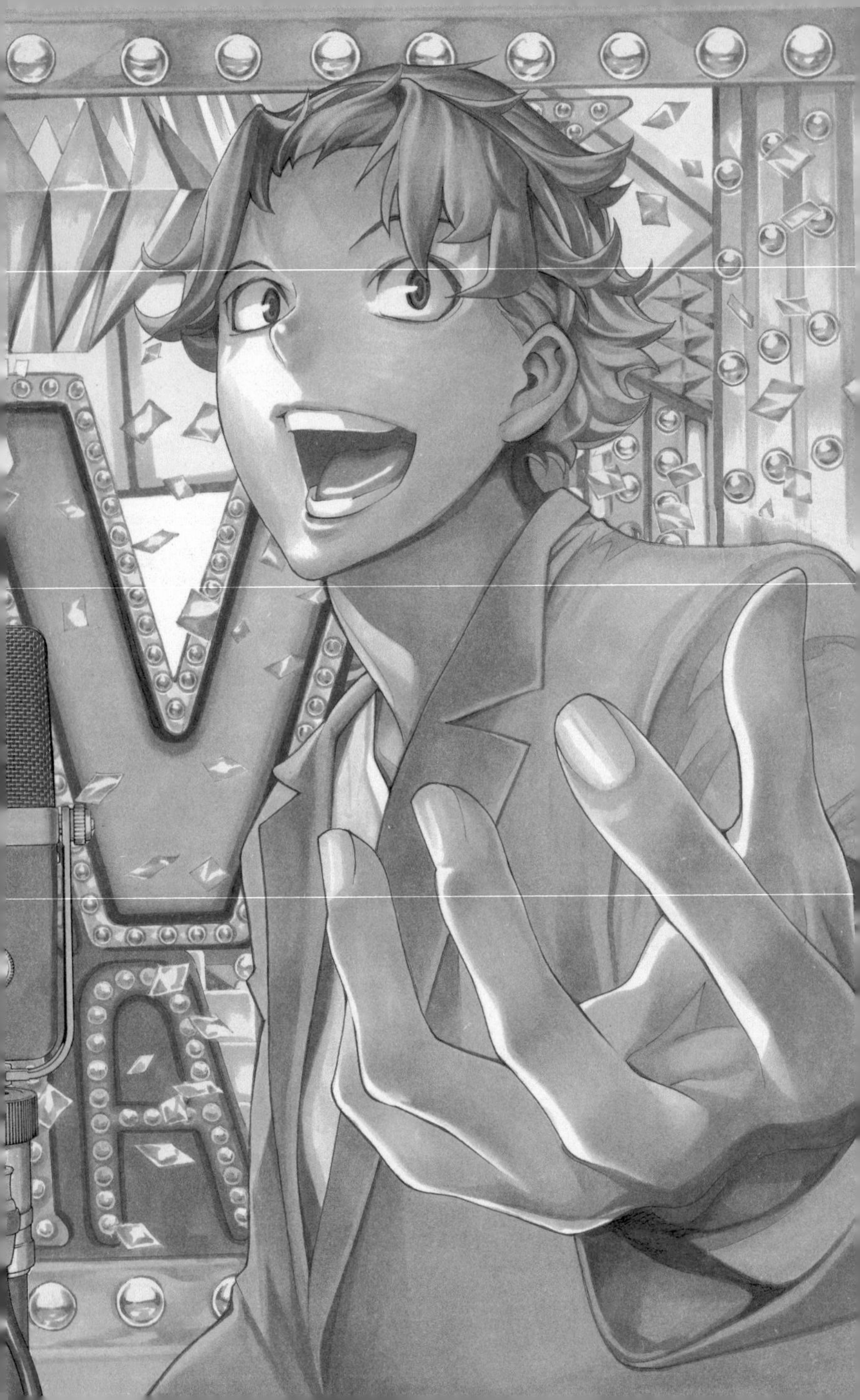

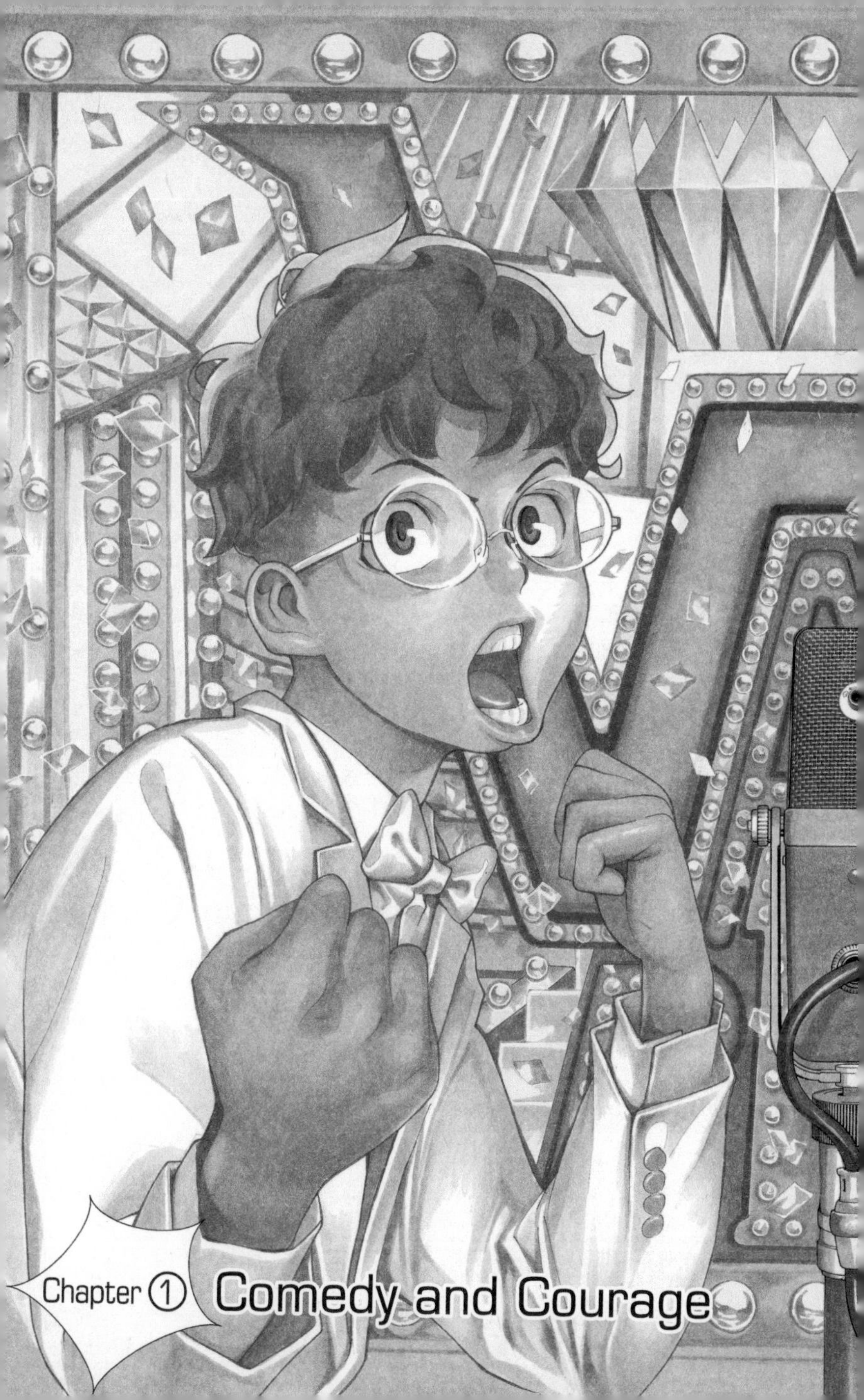
Chapter 1 Comedy and Courage

Show-ha Shoten!

SHOW-HA SHOTEN!

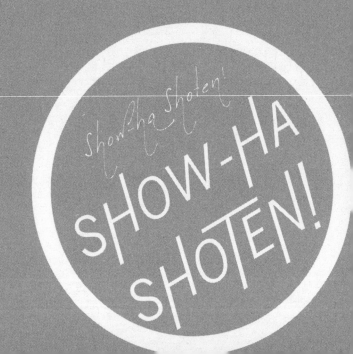

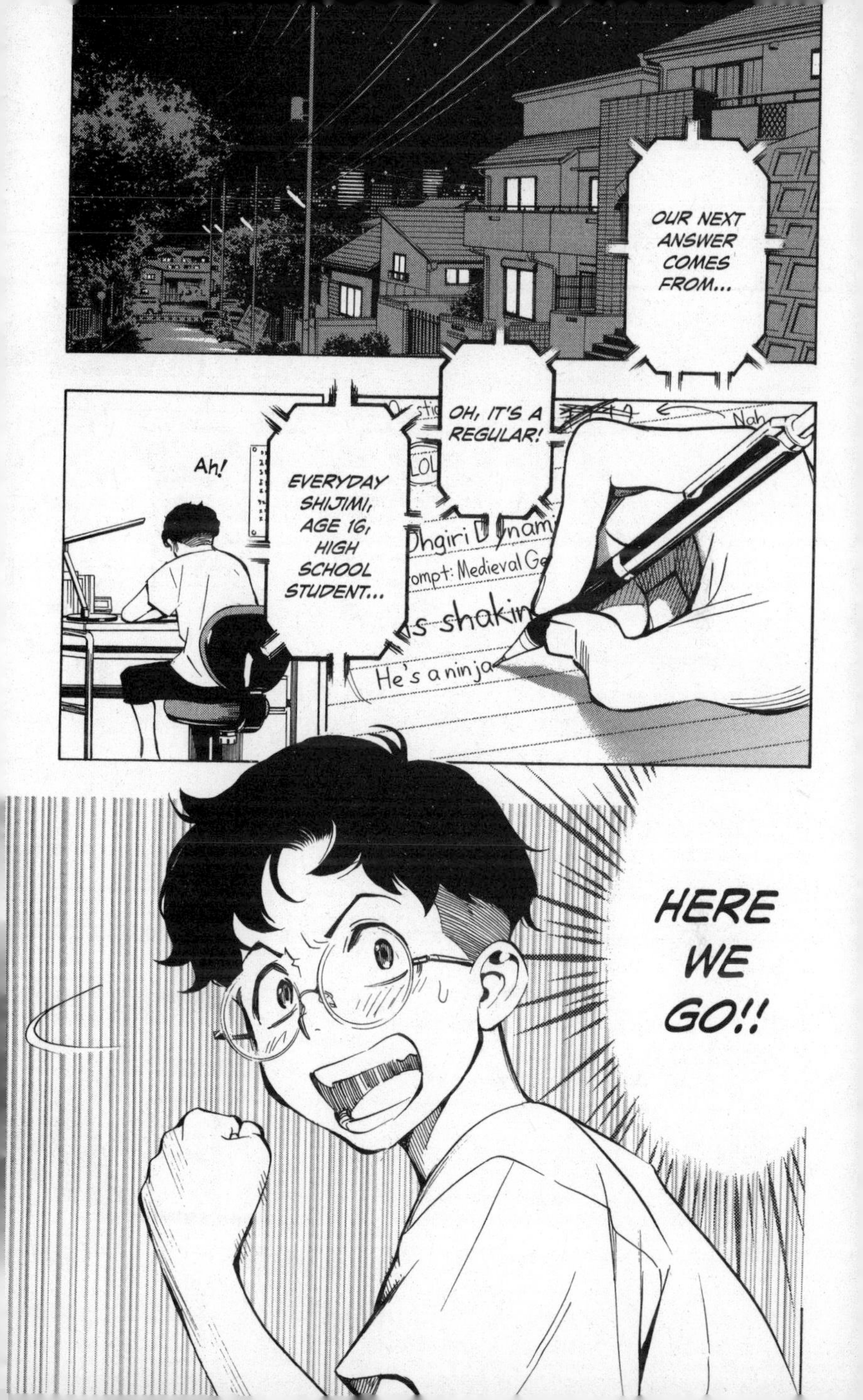
OUR NEXT ANSWER COMES FROM...
OH, IT'S A REGULAR!
EVERYDAY SHIJIMI, AGE 16, HIGH SCHOOL STUDENT...
Nah
LOL
He's a ninja
Ah!
HERE WE GO!!

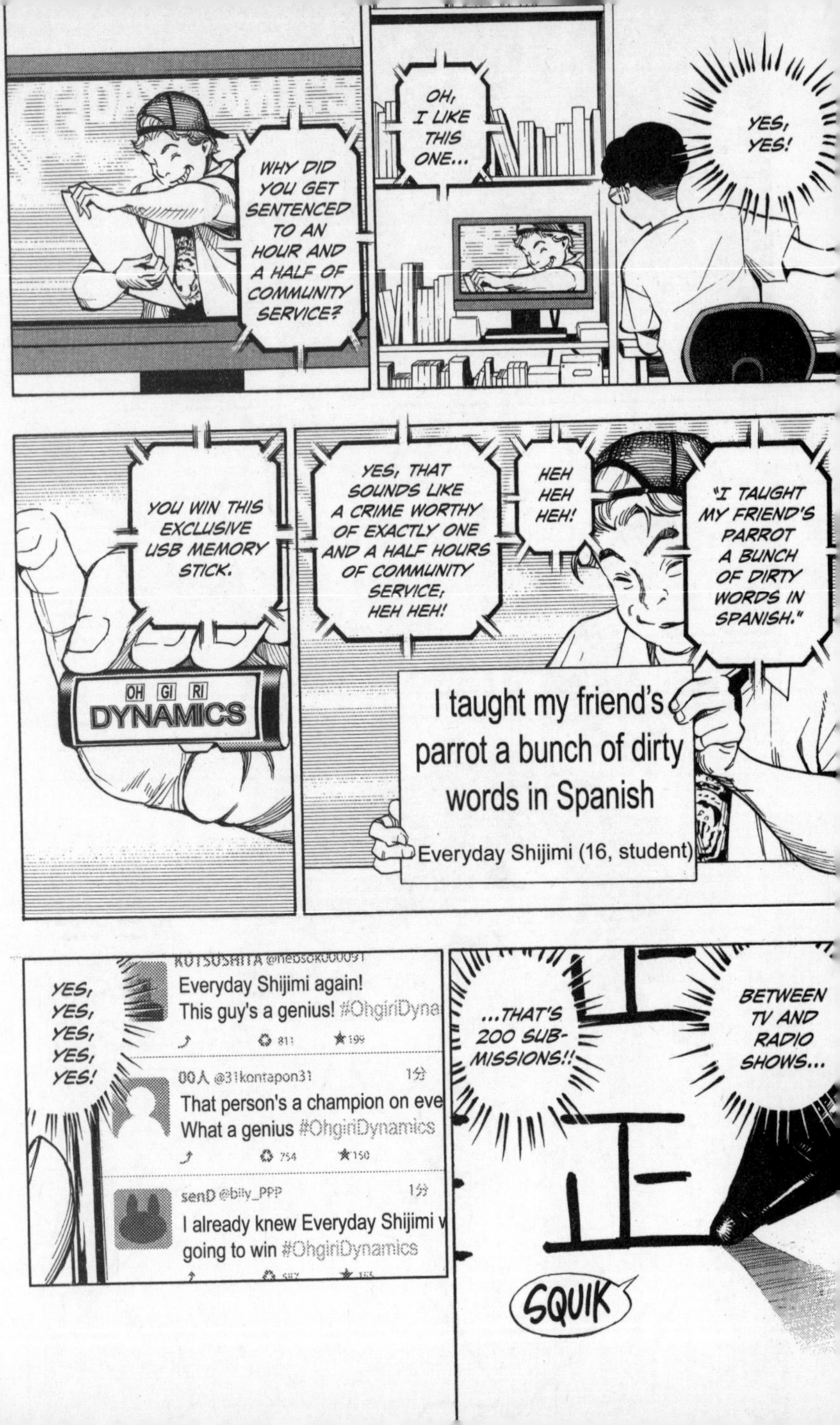
YES, YES!
OH, I LIKE THIS ONE...
WHY DID YOU GET SENTENCED TO AN HOUR AND A HALF OF COMMUNITY SERVICE?
"I TAUGHT MY FRIEND'S PARROT A BUNCH OF DIRTY WORDS IN SPANISH."
HEH HEH HEH!
YES, THAT SOUNDS LIKE A CRIME WORTHY OF EXACTLY ONE AND A HALF HOURS OF COMMUNITY SERVICE, HEH HEH!
I taught my friend's parrot a bunch of dirty words in Spanish
Everyday Shijimi (16, student)
YOU WIN THIS EXCLUSIVE USB MEMORY STICK.
OH GI RI DYNAMICS
BETWEEN TV AND RADIO SHOWS...
...THAT'S 200 SUBMISSIONS!!
SQUIK
Everyday Shijimi again!
This guy's a genius! #OhgiriDyna
811 199
00人 @31kontapon31 1分
That person's a champion on eve
What a genius #OhgiriDynamics
754 150
senD @bily_PPP 1分
I already knew Everyday Shijimi v
going to win #OhgiriDynamics
YES, YES, YES, YES, YES!

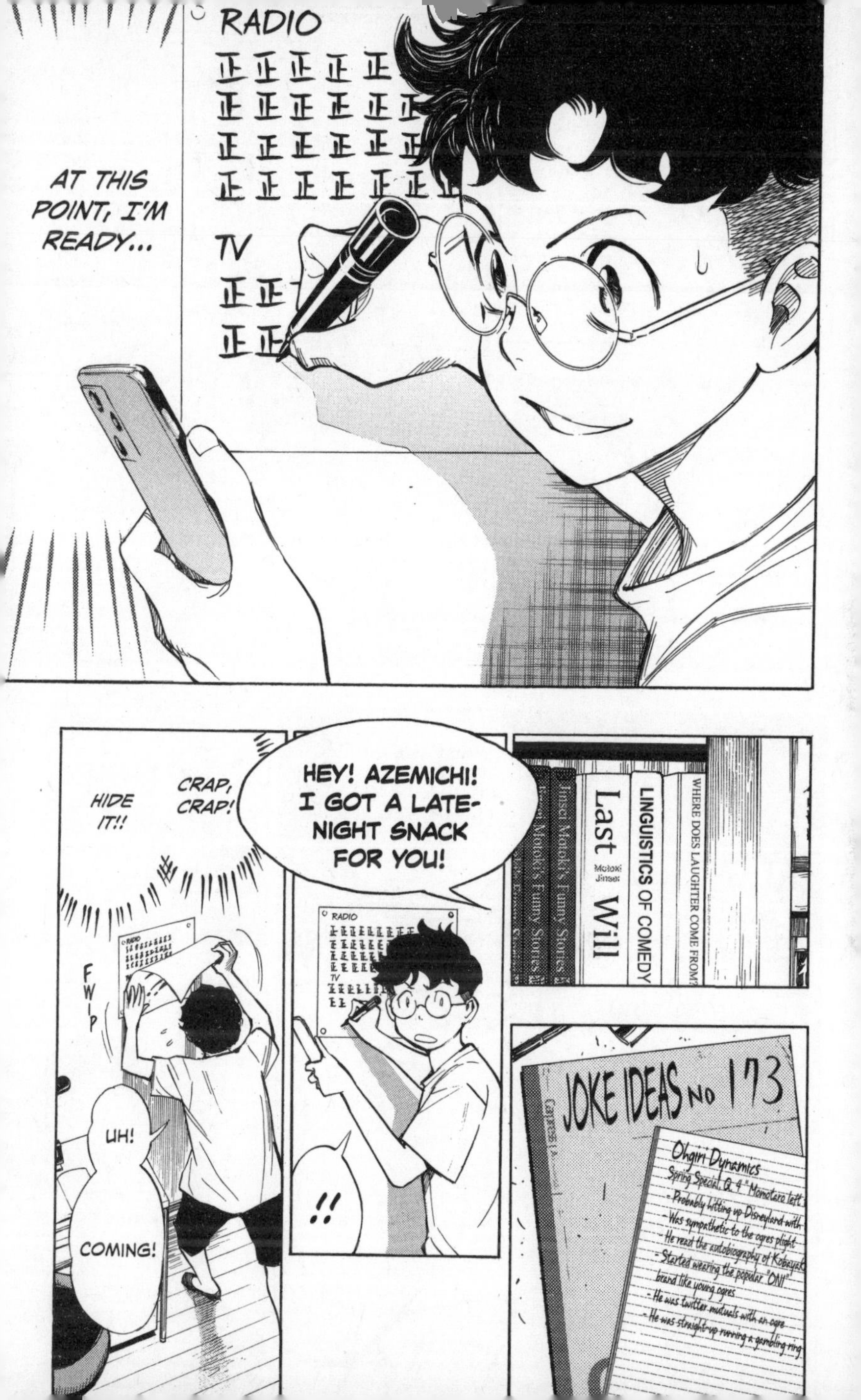

RADIO
TV
AT THIS POINT, I'M READY...
Jinsei Motoki's Funny Stories
Last Will
Motoki Jinsei
LINGUISTICS OF COMEDY
WHERE DOES LAUGHTER COME FROM?
JOKE IDEAS No 173
Ohgiri Dynamics
Spring Special, Q 4 "Momotaro left
- Probably hitting up Disneyland with
- Was sympathetic to the ogres plight
- He read the autobiography of Kobayak
- Started wearing the popular "ONI" brand like young ogres
- He was twitter mutuals with an ogre
- He was straight-up running a gambling ring
HEY! AZEMICHI! I GOT A LATE-NIGHT SNACK FOR YOU!
!!
CRAP, CRAP!
HIDE IT!!
FWIP
UH!
COMING!

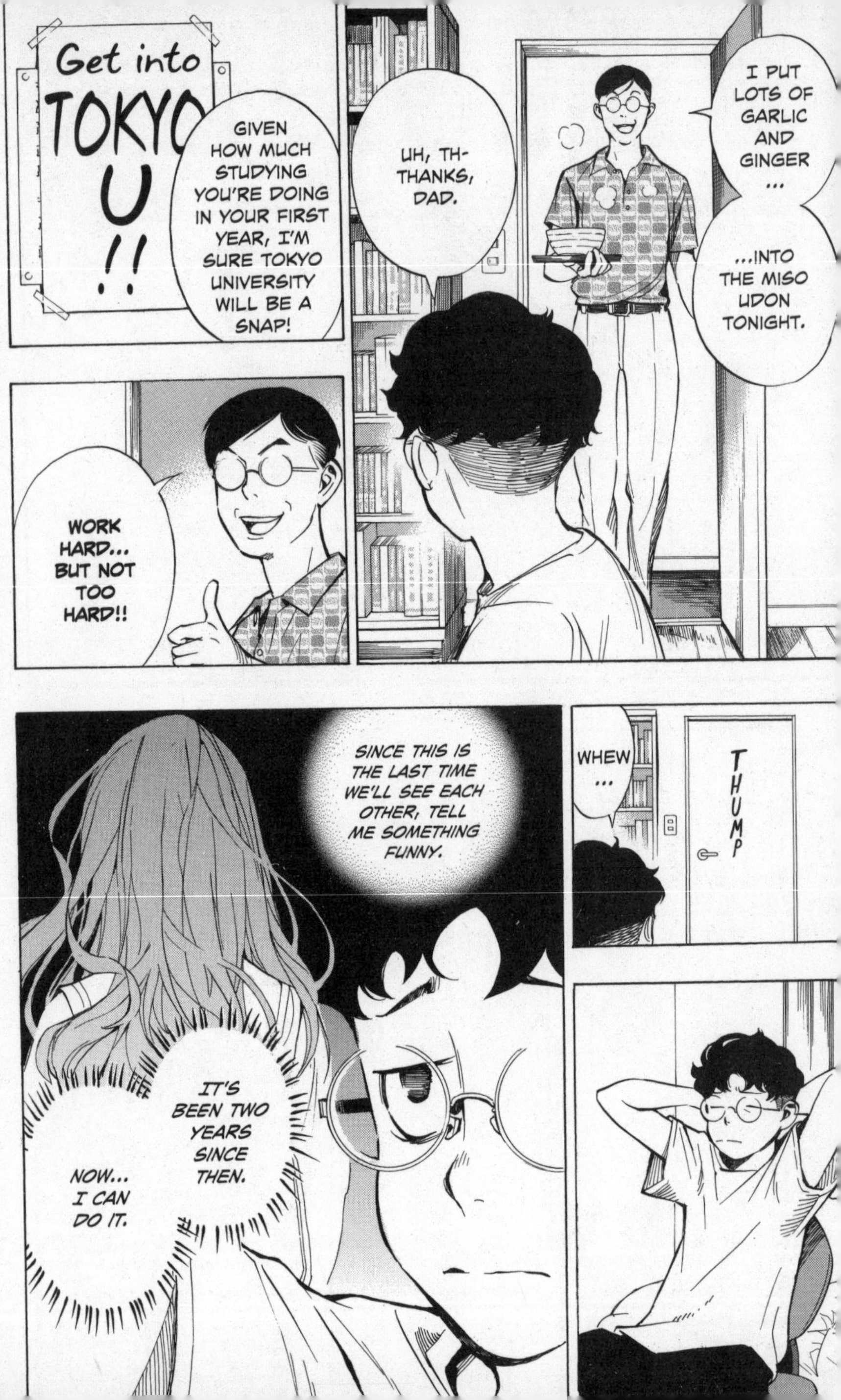
I PUT LOTS OF GARLIC AND GINGER ...
...INTO THE MISO UDON TONIGHT.
UH, TH-THANKS, DAD.
Get into TOKYO U!!
GIVEN HOW MUCH STUDYING YOU'RE DOING IN YOUR FIRST YEAR, I'M SURE TOKYO UNIVERSITY WILL BE A SNAP!
WORK HARD... BUT NOT TOO HARD!!
THUMP
WHEW ...
SINCE THIS IS THE LAST TIME WE'LL SEE EACH OTHER, TELL ME SOMETHING FUNNY.
IT'S BEEN TWO YEARS SINCE THEN.
NOW... I CAN DO IT.

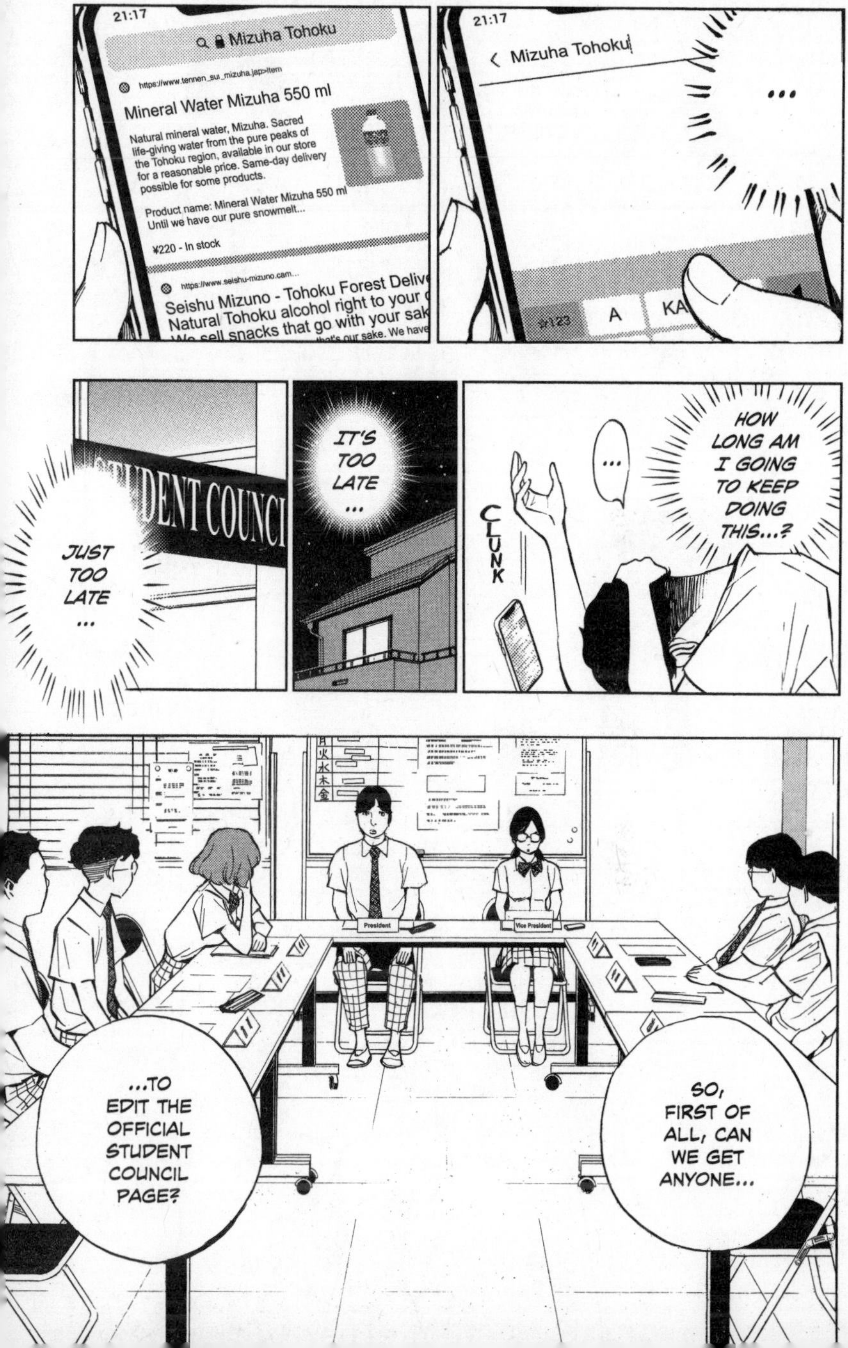
21:17
Mizuha Tohoku
...
A
KA
21:17
Mizuha Tohoku
https://www.tennen_sui_mizuha.jap>item
Mineral Water Mizuha 550 ml
Natural mineral water, Mizuha. Sacred life-giving water from the pure peaks of the Tohoku region, available in our store for a reasonable price. Same-day delivery possible for some products.
Product name: Mineral Water Mizuha 550 ml
Until we have our pure snowmelt...
¥220 - In stock
https://www.seishu-mizuno.cam...
Seishu Mizuno - Tohoku Forest Delive
Natural Tohoku alcohol right to your
HOW LONG AM I GOING TO KEEP DOING THIS...?
...
CLUNK
IT'S TOO LATE...
JUST TOO LATE...
DENT COUNCI
President
Vice President
SO, FIRST OF ALL, CAN WE GET ANYONE...
...TO EDIT THE OFFICIAL STUDENT COUNCIL PAGE?

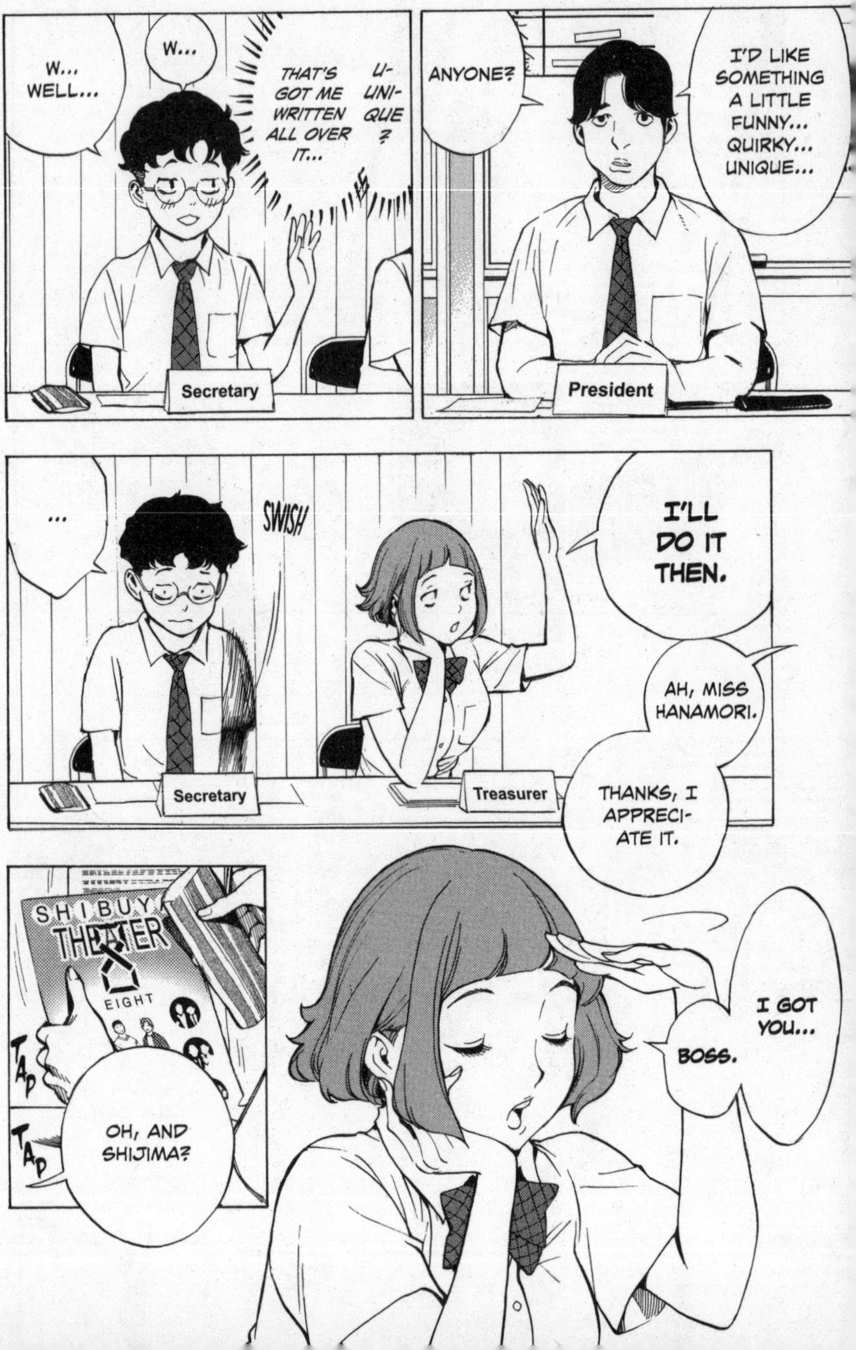
I'D LIKE SOMETHING A LITTLE FUNNY... QUIRKY... UNIQUE...
ANYONE?
President
U-UNI-QUE?
THAT'S GOT ME WRITTEN ALL OVER IT...
W...
W... WELL...
Secretary
I'LL DO IT THEN.
SWISH
...
Treasurer
Secretary
AH, MISS HANAMORI.
THANKS, I APPRECIATE IT.
I GOT YOU...
BOSS.
EIGHT
TAP
TAP
OH, AND SHIJIMA?

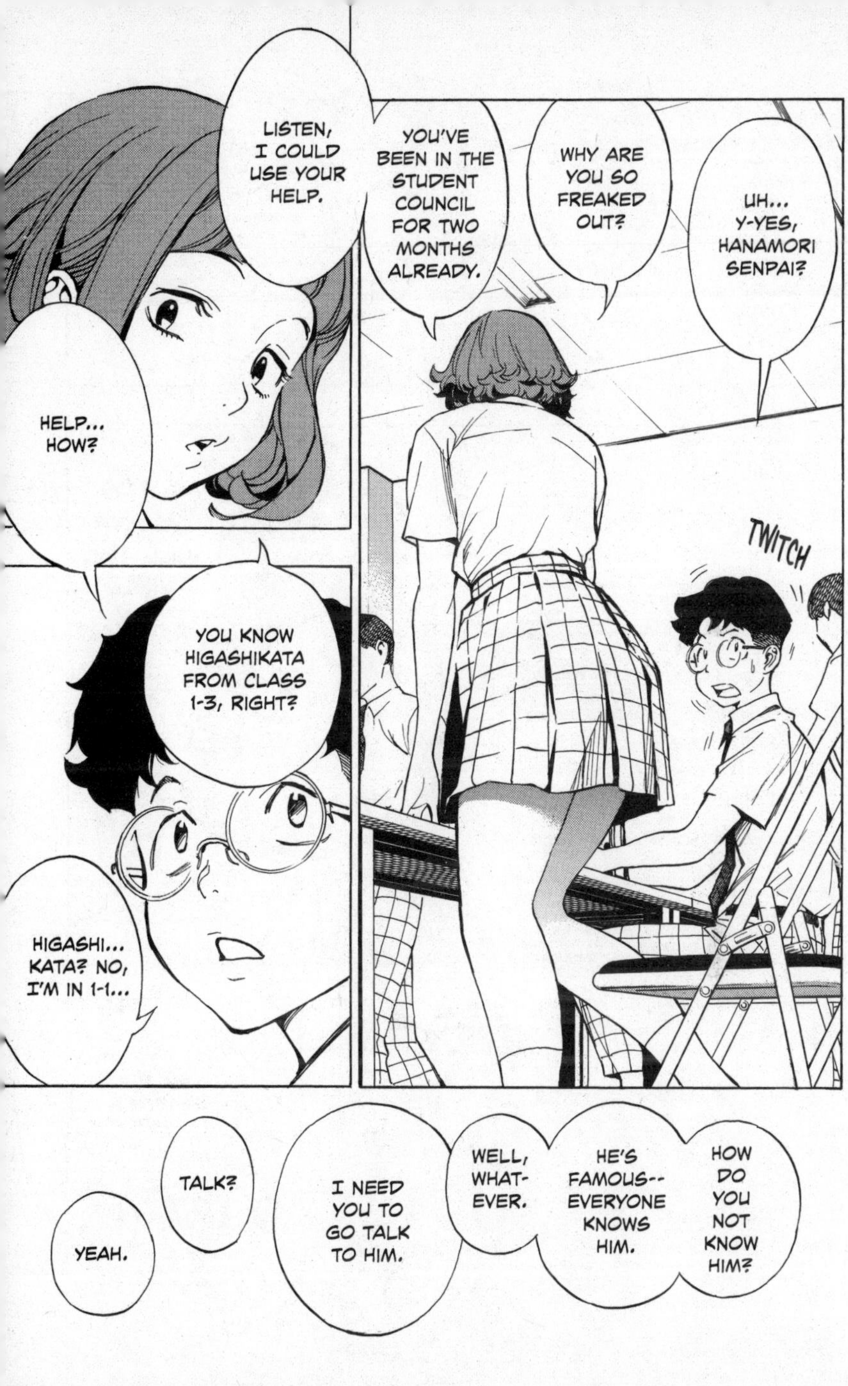

UH... Y-YES, HANAMORI SENPAI?
WHY ARE YOU SO FREAKED OUT?
YOU'VE BEEN IN THE STUDENT COUNCIL FOR TWO MONTHS ALREADY.
TWITCH
LISTEN, I COULD USE YOUR HELP.
HELP... HOW?
YOU KNOW HIGASHIKATA FROM CLASS 1-3, RIGHT?
HIGASHI... KATA? NO, I'M IN 1-1...
HOW DO YOU NOT KNOW HIM?
HE'S FAMOUS-- EVERYONE KNOWS HIM.
WELL, WHATEVER.
I NEED YOU TO GO TALK TO HIM.
TALK?
YEAH.

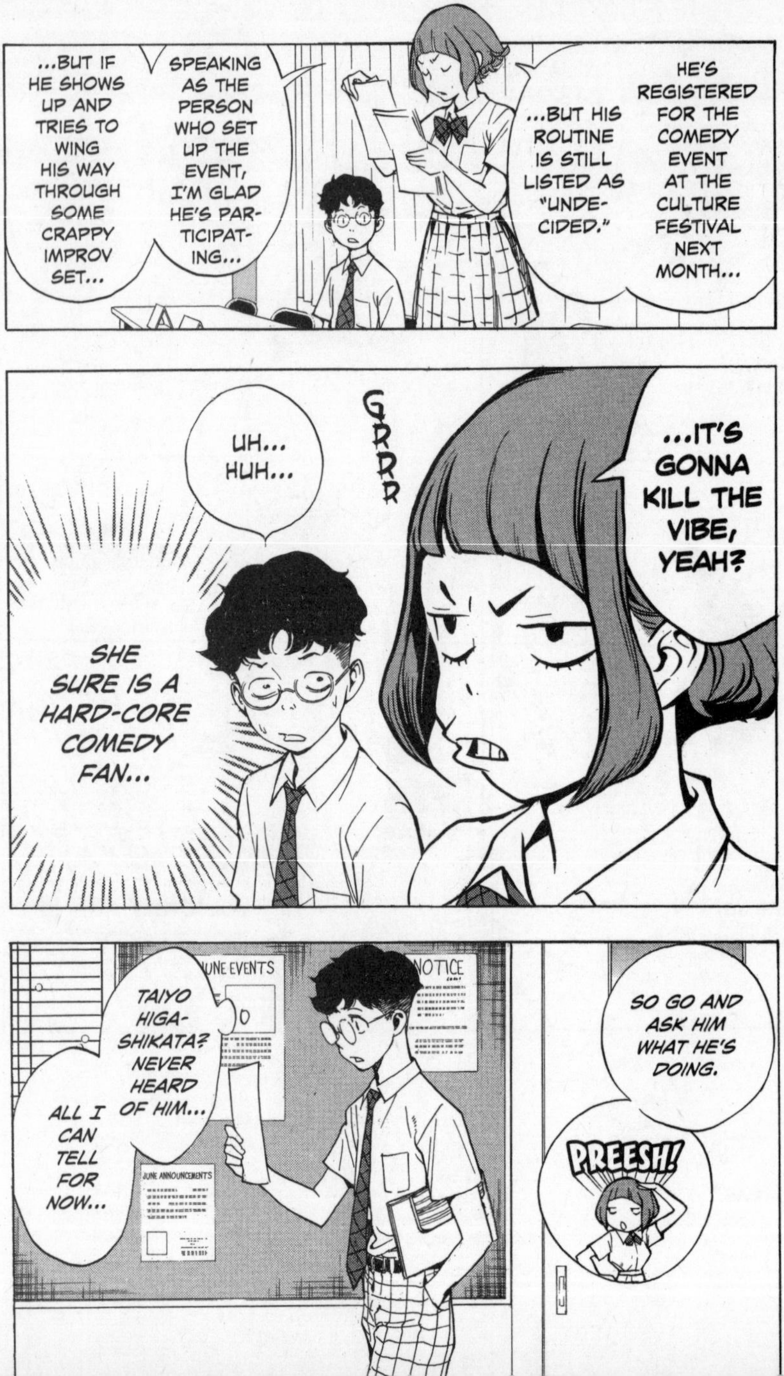
HE'S REGISTERED FOR THE COMEDY EVENT AT THE CULTURE FESTIVAL NEXT MONTH...
...BUT HIS ROUTINE IS STILL LISTED AS "UNDECIDED."
SPEAKING AS THE PERSON WHO SET UP THE EVENT, I'M GLAD HE'S PARTICIPATING...
...BUT IF HE SHOWS UP AND TRIES TO WING HIS WAY THROUGH SOME CRAPPY IMPROV SET...
...IT'S GONNA KILL THE VIBE, YEAH?
GRRR
UH... HUH...
SHE SURE IS A HARD-CORE COMEDY FAN...
SO GO AND ASK HIM WHAT HE'S DOING.
PREESH!
NOTICE
JUNE EVENTS
TAIYO HIGASHIKATA? NEVER HEARD OF HIM...
ALL I CAN TELL FOR NOW...
JUNE ANNOUNCEMENTS

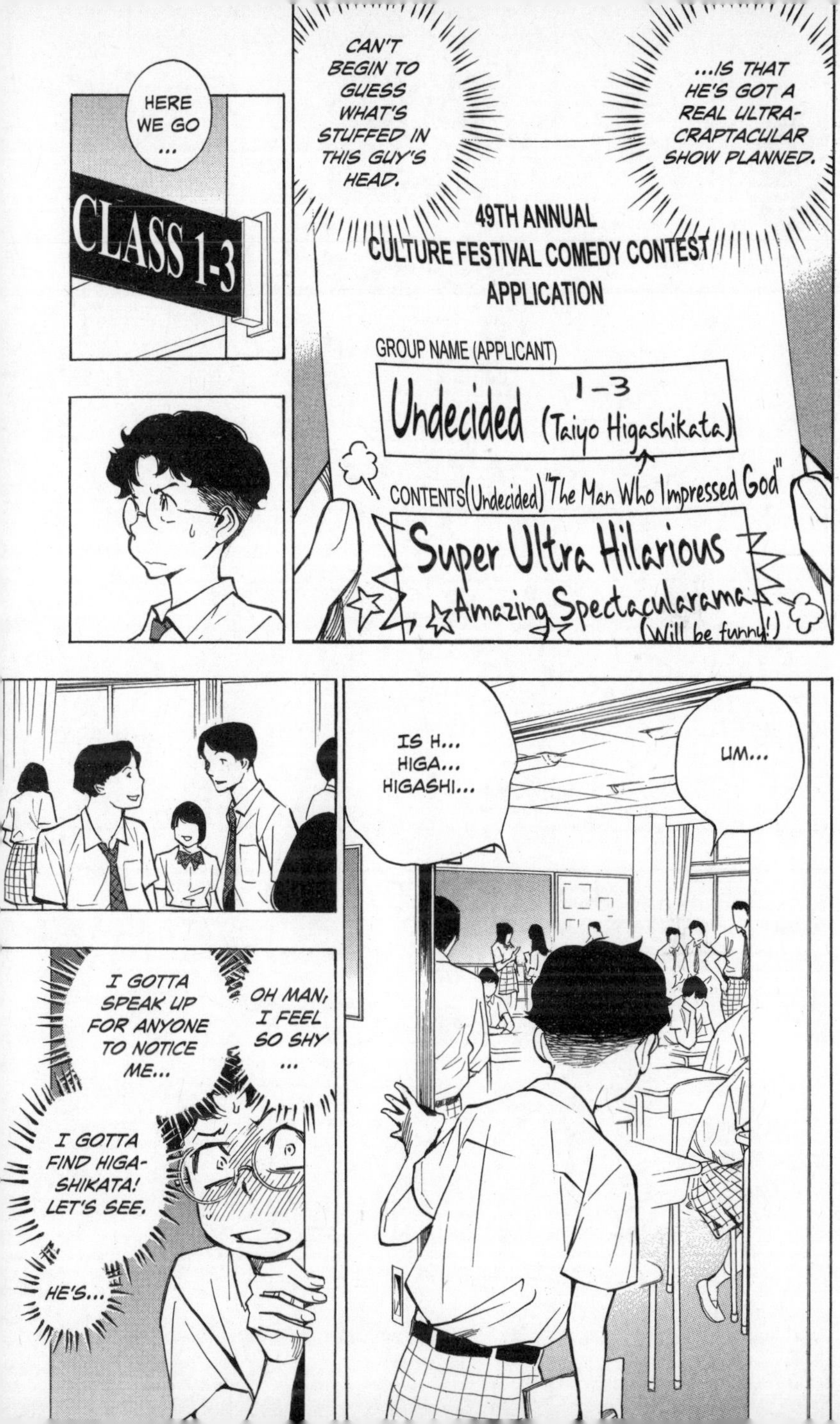
...IS THAT HE'S GOT A REAL ULTRA-CRAPTACULAR SHOW PLANNED.
CAN'T BEGIN TO GUESS WHAT'S STUFFED IN THIS GUY'S HEAD.
49TH ANNUAL CULTURE FESTIVAL COMEDY CONTEST APPLICATION
GROUP NAME (APPLICANT)
Undecided 1-3 (Taiyo Higashikata)
CONTENTS (Undecided) "The Man Who Impressed God"
Super Ultra Hilarious Amazing Spectacularama
(Will be funny!)
HERE WE GO...
CLASS 1-3
UM...
IS H... HIGA... HIGASHI...
OH MAN, I FEEL SO SHY...
I GOTTA SPEAK UP FOR ANYONE TO NOTICE ME...
I GOTTA FIND HIGA-SHIKATA! LET'S SEE.
HE'S...

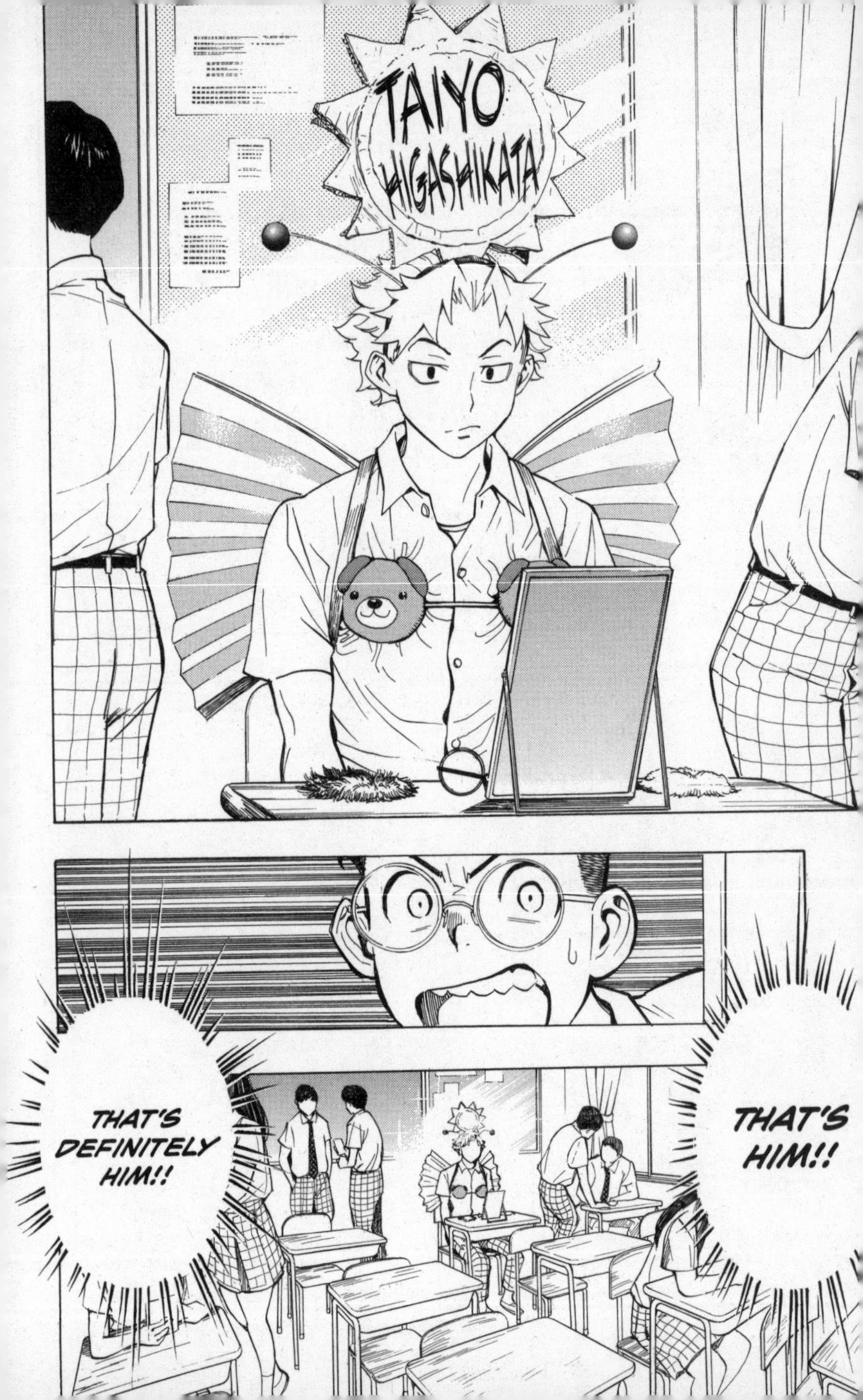
TAIYO HIGASHIKATA
THAT'S HIM!!
THAT'S DEFINITELY HIM!!

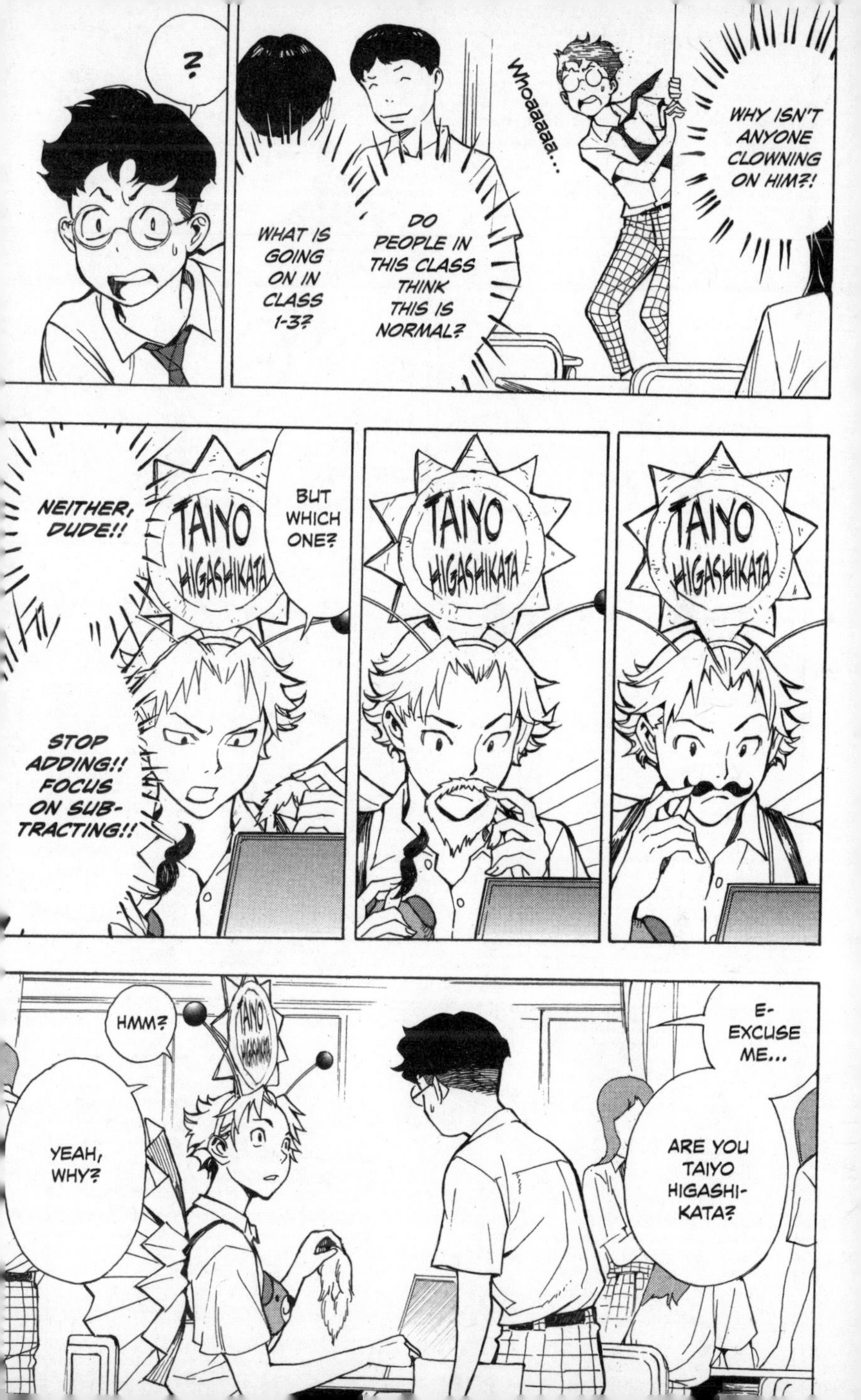

WHY ISN'T ANYONE CLOWNING ON HIM?!
Whoaaaaa...
DO PEOPLE IN THIS CLASS THINK THIS IS NORMAL?
WHAT IS GOING ON IN CLASS 1-3?
?
TAIYO HIGASHIKATA
TAIYO HIGASHIKATA
TAIYO HIGASHIKATA
BUT WHICH ONE?
NEITHER, DUDE!!
STOP ADDING!! FOCUS ON SUB-TRACTING!!
E-EXCUSE ME...
ARE YOU TAIYO HIGASHI-KATA?
HMM?
YEAH, WHY?

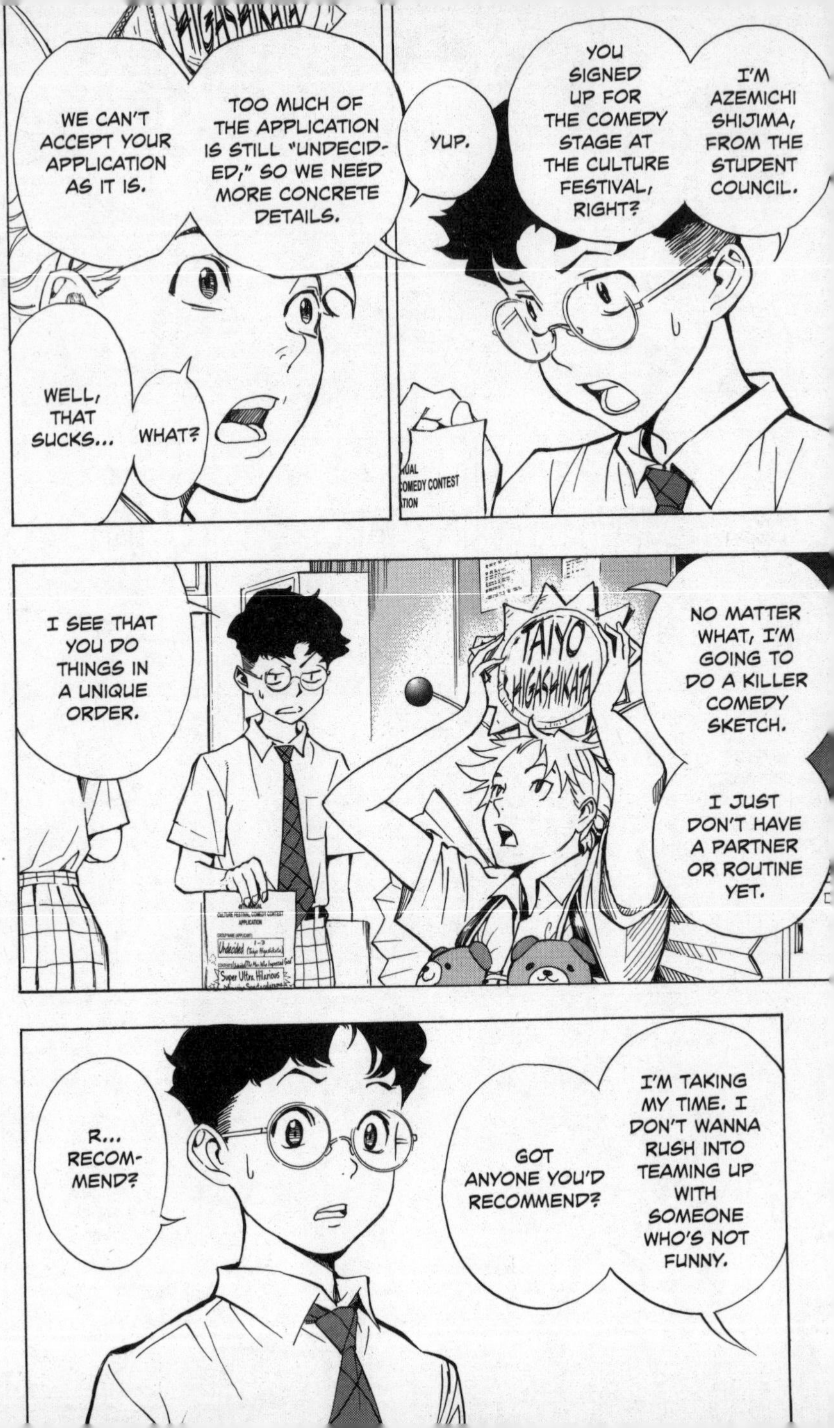
HIGASHIKATA
I'M AZEMICHI SHIJIMA, FROM THE STUDENT COUNCIL.
YOU SIGNED UP FOR THE COMEDY STAGE AT THE CULTURE FESTIVAL, RIGHT?
YUP.
TOO MUCH OF THE APPLICATION IS STILL "UNDECIDED," SO WE NEED MORE CONCRETE DETAILS.
WE CAN'T ACCEPT YOUR APPLICATION AS IT IS.
WHAT?
WELL, THAT SUCKS...
TAIYO HIGASHIKATA
NO MATTER WHAT, I'M GOING TO DO A KILLER COMEDY SKETCH.
I JUST DON'T HAVE A PARTNER OR ROUTINE YET.
I SEE THAT YOU DO THINGS IN A UNIQUE ORDER.
Undecided
Super Ultra Hilarious
I'M TAKING MY TIME. I DON'T WANNA RUSH INTO TEAMING UP WITH SOMEONE WHO'S NOT FUNNY.
GOT ANYONE YOU'D RECOMMEND?
R... RECOMMEND?

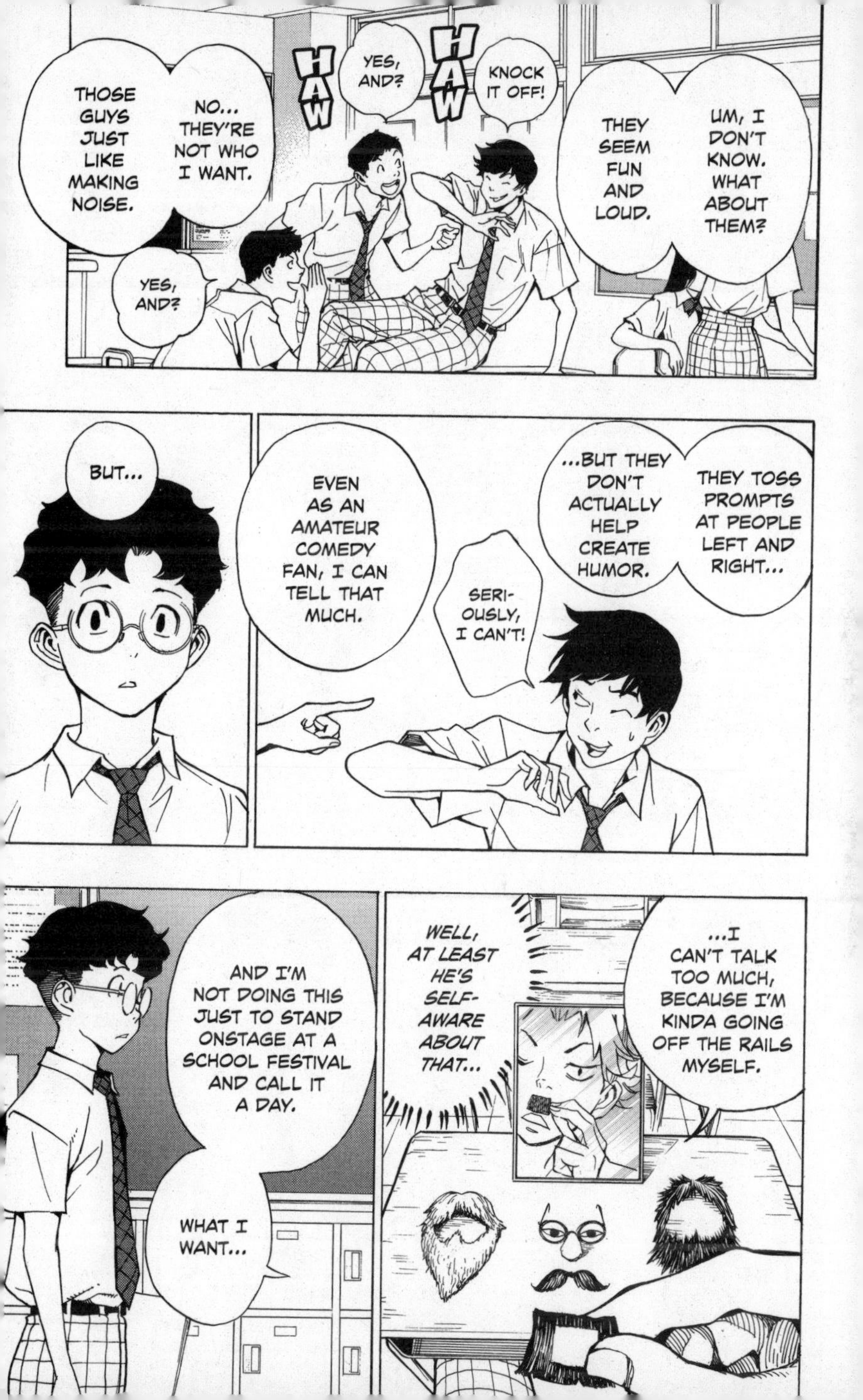
UM, I DON'T KNOW. WHAT ABOUT THEM?
THEY SEEM FUN AND LOUD.
KNOCK IT OFF!
HAW
YES, AND?
HAW
NO... THEY'RE NOT WHO I WANT.
THOSE GUYS JUST LIKE MAKING NOISE.
YES, AND?
THEY TOSS PROMPTS AT PEOPLE LEFT AND RIGHT...
...BUT THEY DON'T ACTUALLY HELP CREATE HUMOR.
SERIOUSLY, I CAN'T!
EVEN AS AN AMATEUR COMEDY FAN, I CAN TELL THAT MUCH.
BUT...
...I CAN'T TALK TOO MUCH, BECAUSE I'M KINDA GOING OFF THE RAILS MYSELF.
WELL, AT LEAST HE'S SELF-AWARE ABOUT THAT...
AND I'M NOT DOING THIS JUST TO STAND ONSTAGE AT A SCHOOL FESTIVAL AND CALL IT A DAY.
WHAT I WANT...

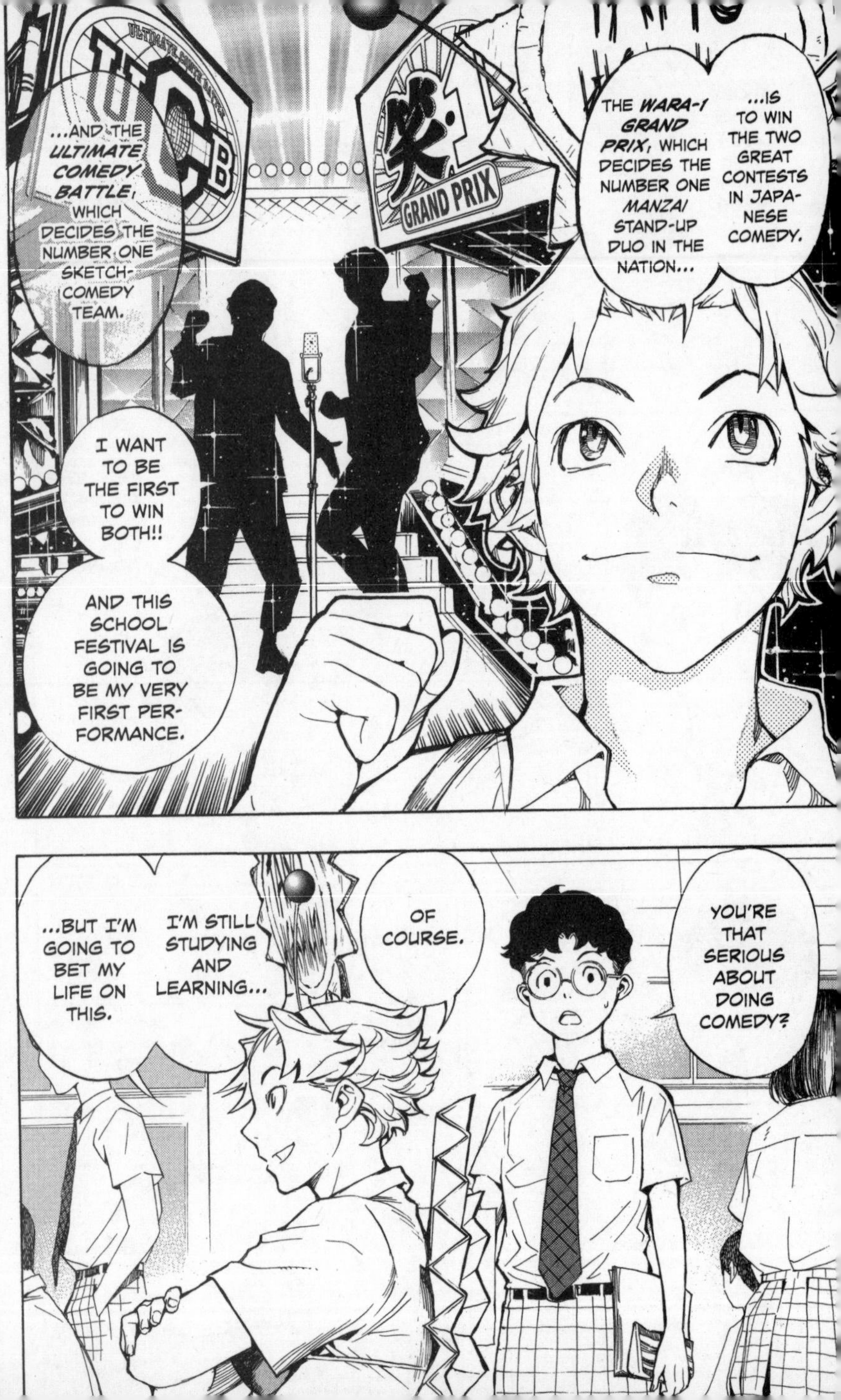
...IS TO WIN THE TWO GREAT CONTESTS IN JAPANESE COMEDY.
THE *WARA-1 GRAND PRIX*, WHICH DECIDES THE NUMBER ONE *MANZAI* STAND-UP DUO IN THE NATION...
GRAND PRIX
ULTIMATE CONTE BATTLE
UCB
...AND THE *ULTIMATE COMEDY BATTLE*, WHICH DECIDES THE NUMBER ONE SKETCH-COMEDY TEAM.
I WANT TO BE THE FIRST TO WIN BOTH!!
AND THIS SCHOOL FESTIVAL IS GOING TO BE MY VERY FIRST PERFORMANCE.
YOU'RE THAT SERIOUS ABOUT DOING COMEDY?
OF COURSE.
I'M STILL STUDYING AND LEARNING...
...BUT I'M GOING TO BET MY LIFE ON THIS.

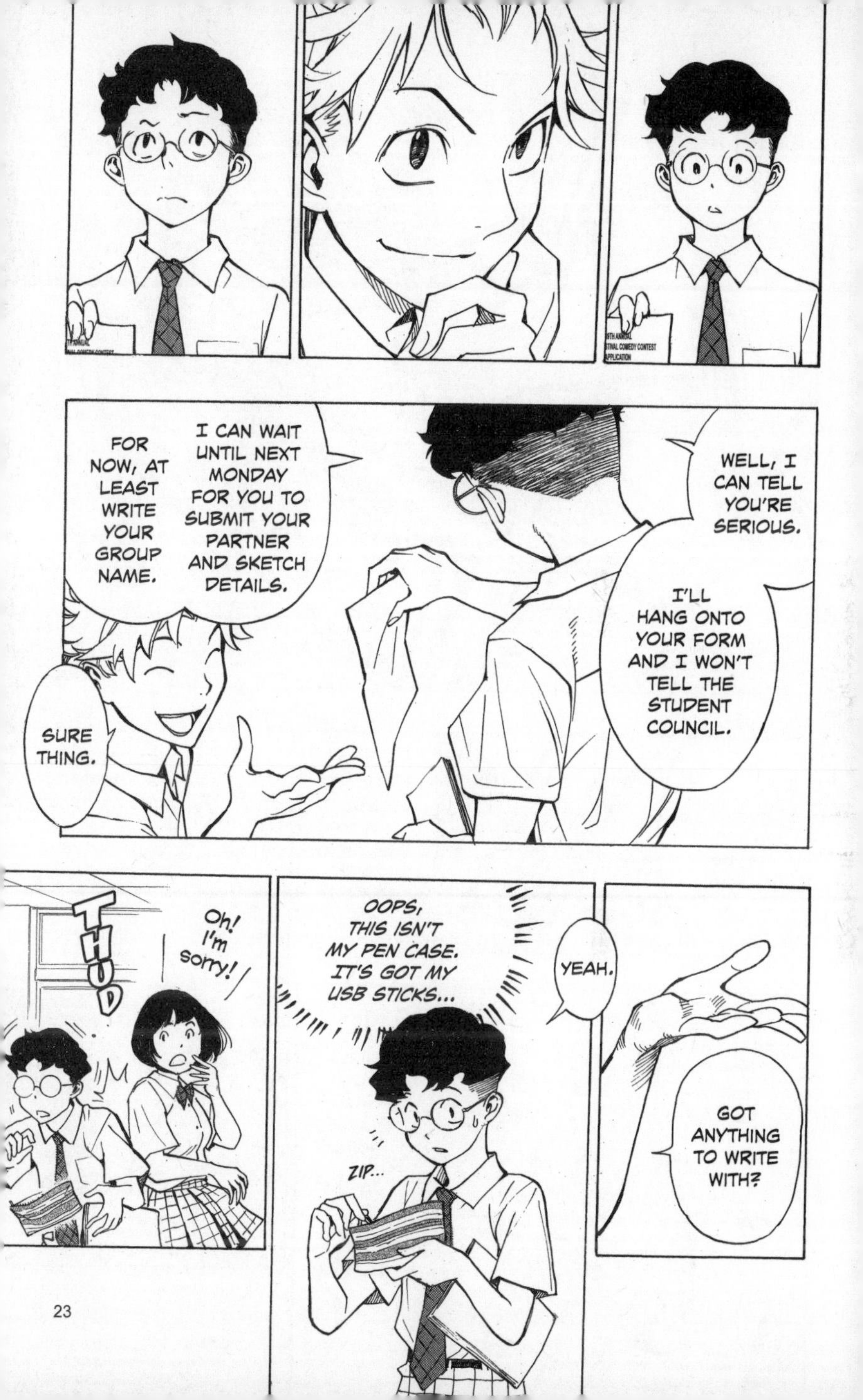
WELL, I CAN TELL YOU'RE SERIOUS.
I'LL HANG ONTO YOUR FORM AND I WON'T TELL THE STUDENT COUNCIL.
I CAN WAIT UNTIL NEXT MONDAY FOR YOU TO SUBMIT YOUR PARTNER AND SKETCH DETAILS.
FOR NOW, AT LEAST WRITE YOUR GROUP NAME.
SURE THING.
GOT ANYTHING TO WRITE WITH?
YEAH.
OOPS, THIS ISN'T MY PEN CASE. IT'S GOT MY USB STICKS...
ZIP...
Oh! I'm sorry!
THUD

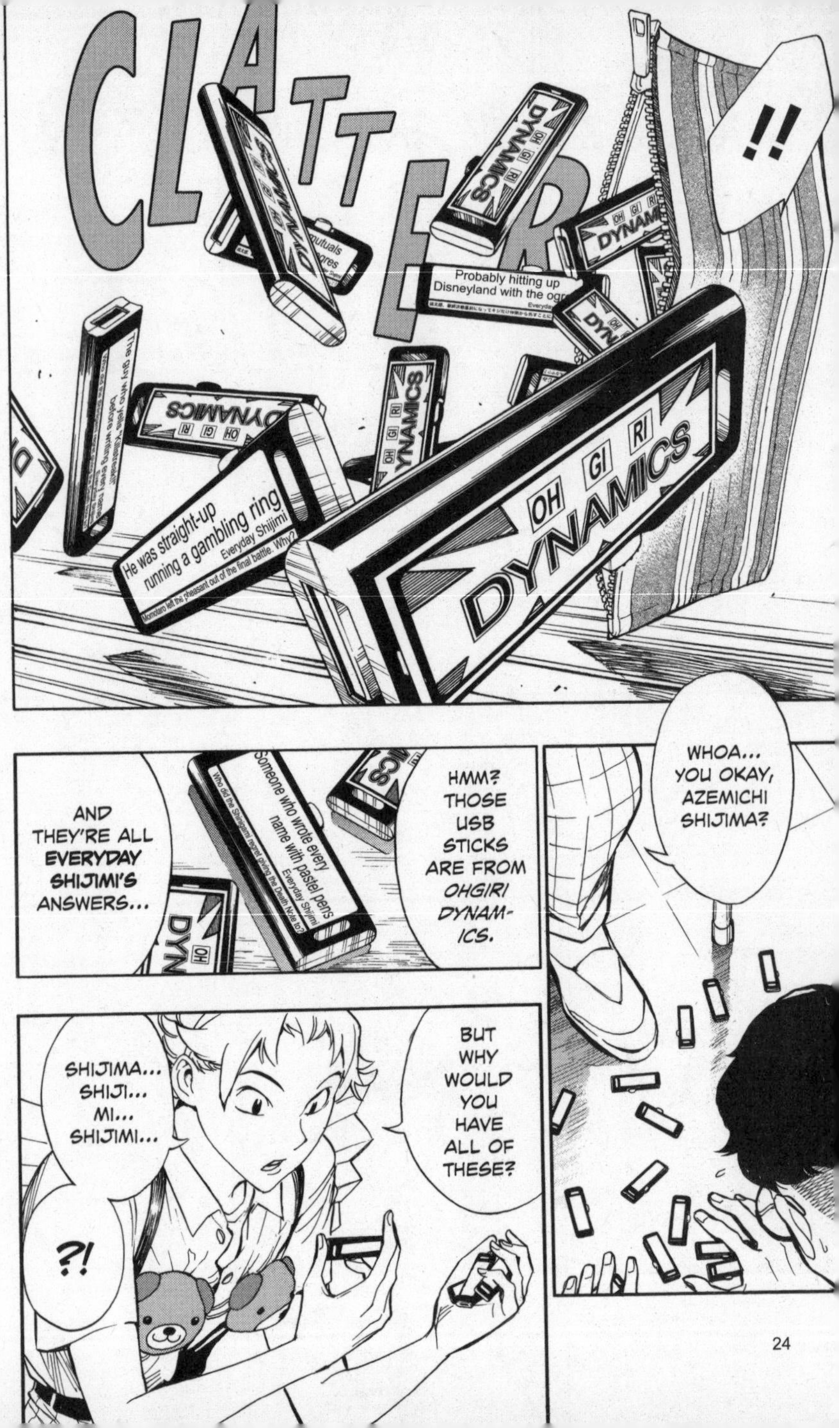
CLATTER
!!
OH GI RI DYNAMICS
Probably hitting up Disneyland with the ogr
He was straight-up running a gambling ring
Everyday Shijimi
Momotaro left the pheasant out of the final battle. Why?
WHOA... YOU OKAY, AZEMICHI SHIJIMA?
HMM? THOSE USB STICKS ARE FROM *OHGIRI DYNAMICS*.
Someone who wrote every name with pastel pens
Everyday Shijimi
Who did the Shinigami regret giving the Death Note to?
AND THEY'RE ALL **EVERYDAY SHIJIMI'S** ANSWERS...
BUT WHY WOULD YOU HAVE ALL OF THESE?
SHIJIMA... SHIJI... MI... SHIJIMI...
?!

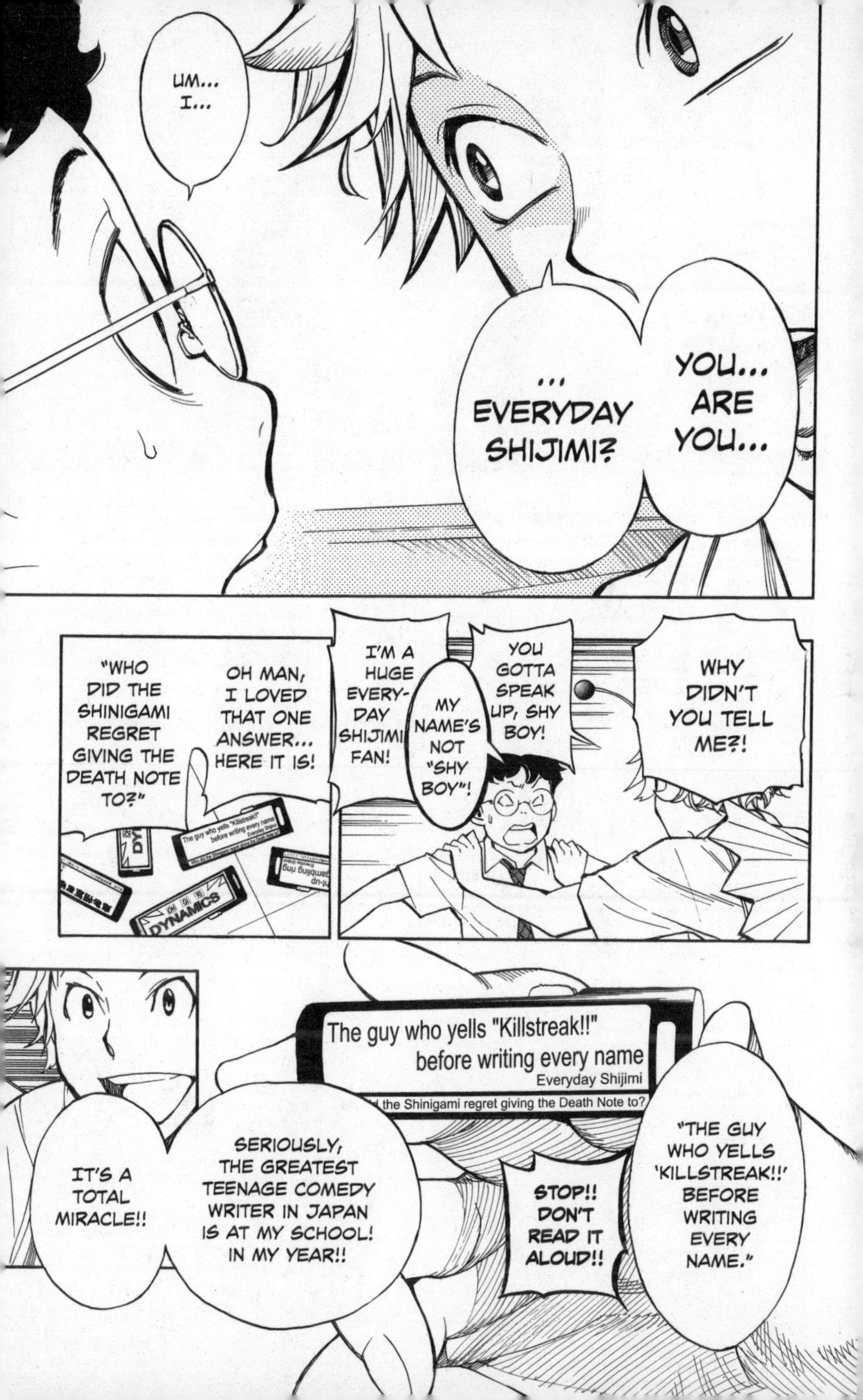
YOU... ARE YOU...
... EVERYDAY SHIJIMI?
UM... I...
WHY DIDN'T YOU TELL ME?!
YOU GOTTA SPEAK UP, SHY BOY!
MY NAME'S NOT "SHY BOY"!
I'M A HUGE EVERY-DAY SHIJIMI FAN!
OH MAN, I LOVED THAT ONE ANSWER... HERE IT IS!
"WHO DID THE SHINIGAMI REGRET GIVING THE DEATH NOTE TO?"
DYNAMICS
The guy who yells "Killstreak!!" before writing every name
Everyday Shijimi
the Shinigami regret giving the Death Note to?
"THE GUY WHO YELLS 'KILLSTREAK!!' BEFORE WRITING EVERY NAME."
STOP!! DON'T READ IT ALOUD!!
SERIOUSLY, THE GREATEST TEENAGE COMEDY WRITER IN JAPAN IS AT MY SCHOOL! IN MY YEAR!!
IT'S A TOTAL MIRACLE!!

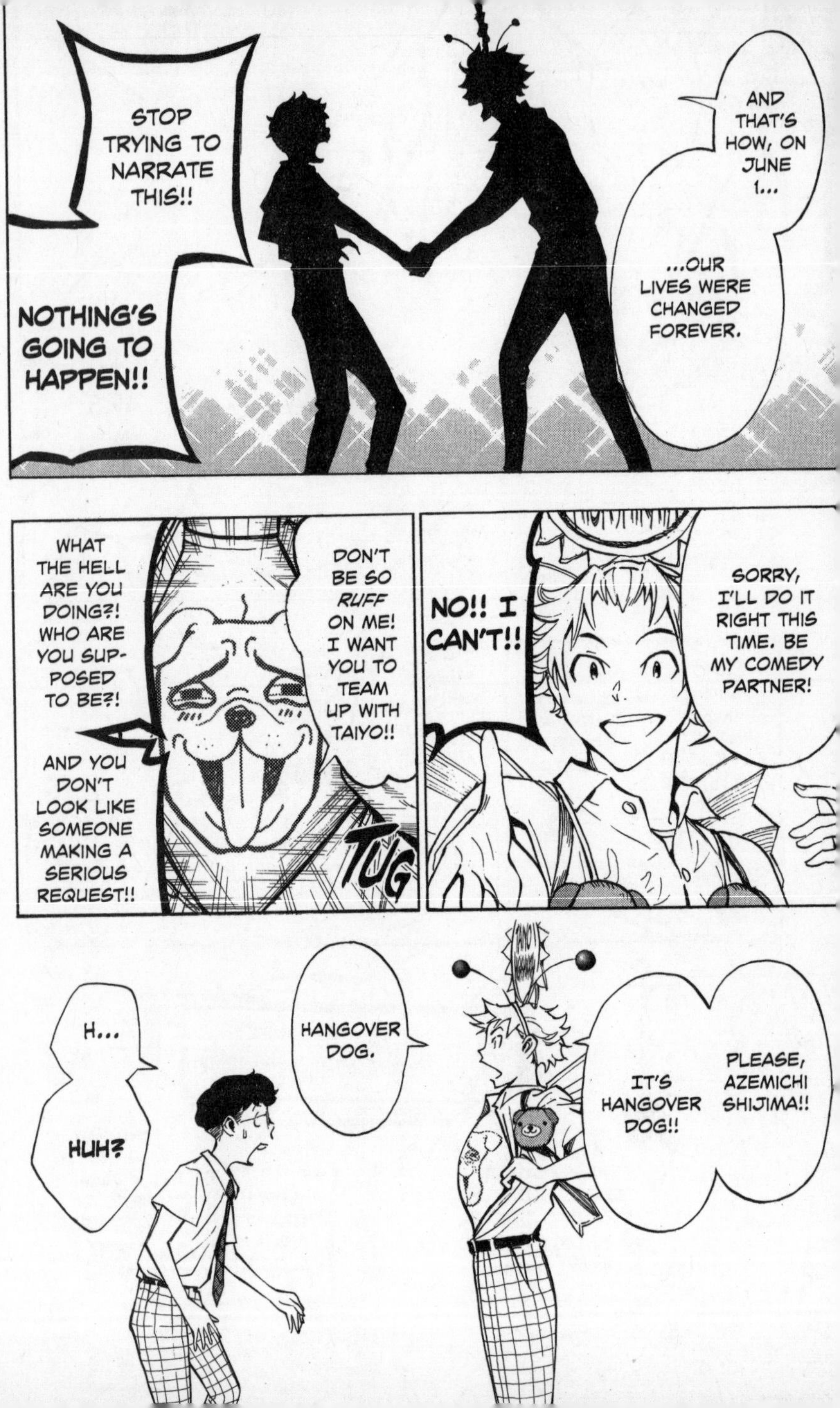
AND THAT'S HOW, ON JUNE 1...
...OUR LIVES WERE CHANGED FOREVER.
STOP TRYING TO NARRATE THIS!!
NOTHING'S GOING TO HAPPEN!!
SORRY, I'LL DO IT RIGHT THIS TIME. BE MY COMEDY PARTNER!
NO!! I CAN'T!!
DON'T BE SO *RUFF* ON ME! I WANT YOU TO TEAM UP WITH TAIYO!!
WHAT THE HELL ARE YOU DOING?! WHO ARE YOU SUPPOSED TO BE?!
AND YOU DON'T LOOK LIKE SOMEONE MAKING A SERIOUS REQUEST!!
TUG
PLEASE, AZEMICHI SHIJIMA!!
IT'S HANGOVER DOG!!
HANGOVER DOG.
H...
HUH?

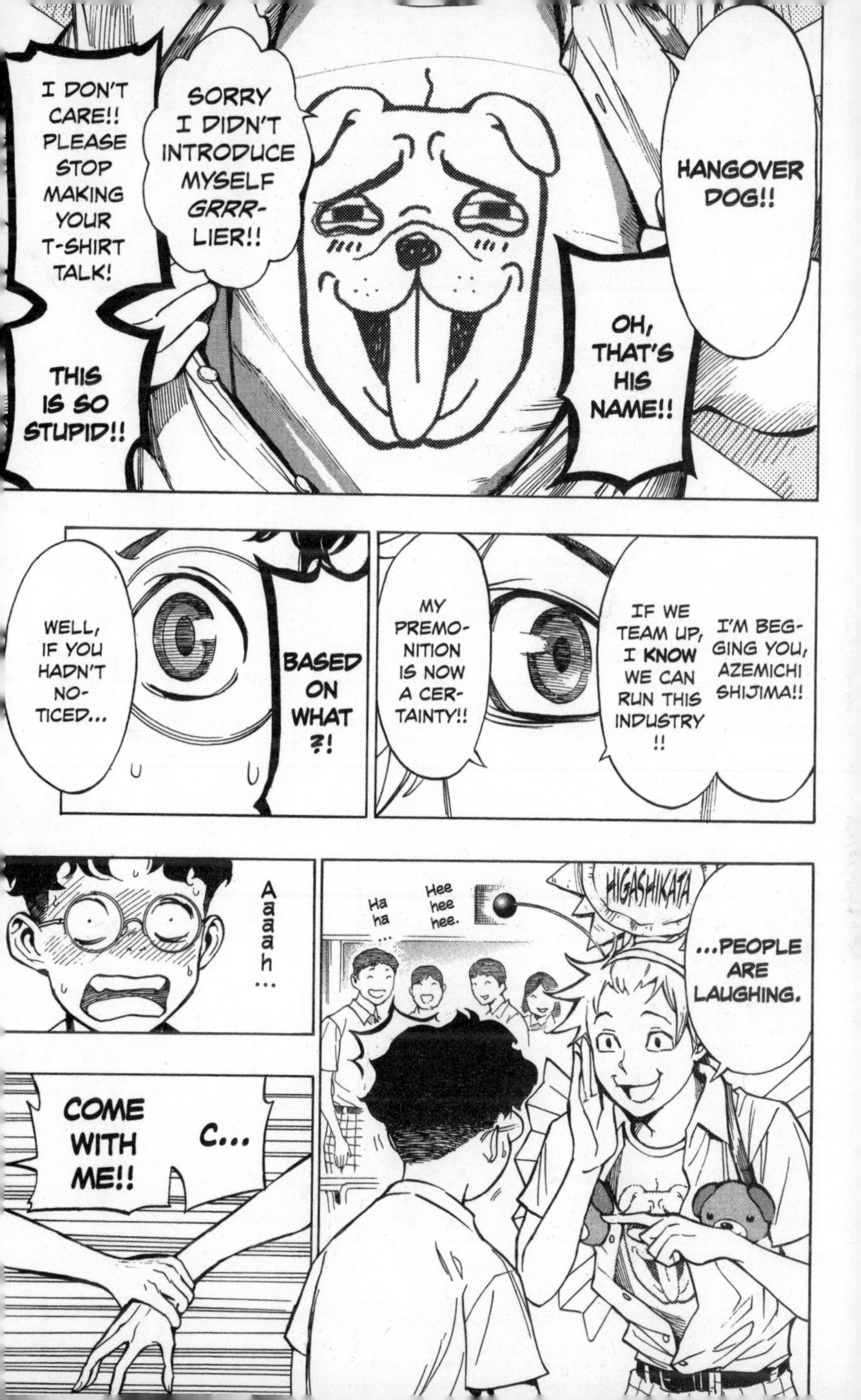
HANGOVER DOG!!
OH, THAT'S HIS NAME!!
SORRY I DIDN'T INTRODUCE MYSELF GRRR-LIER!!
I DON'T CARE!! PLEASE STOP MAKING YOUR T-SHIRT TALK!
THIS IS SO STUPID!!
I'M BEG-GING YOU, AZEMICHI SHIJIMA!!
IF WE TEAM UP, I KNOW WE CAN RUN THIS INDUSTRY!!
MY PREMO-NITION IS NOW A CER-TAINTY!!
BASED ON WHAT?!
WELL, IF YOU HADN'T NO-TICED...
HIGASHIKATA
...PEOPLE ARE LAUGHING.
Hee hee hee.
Ha ha ...
Aaaah...
C...
COME WITH ME!!

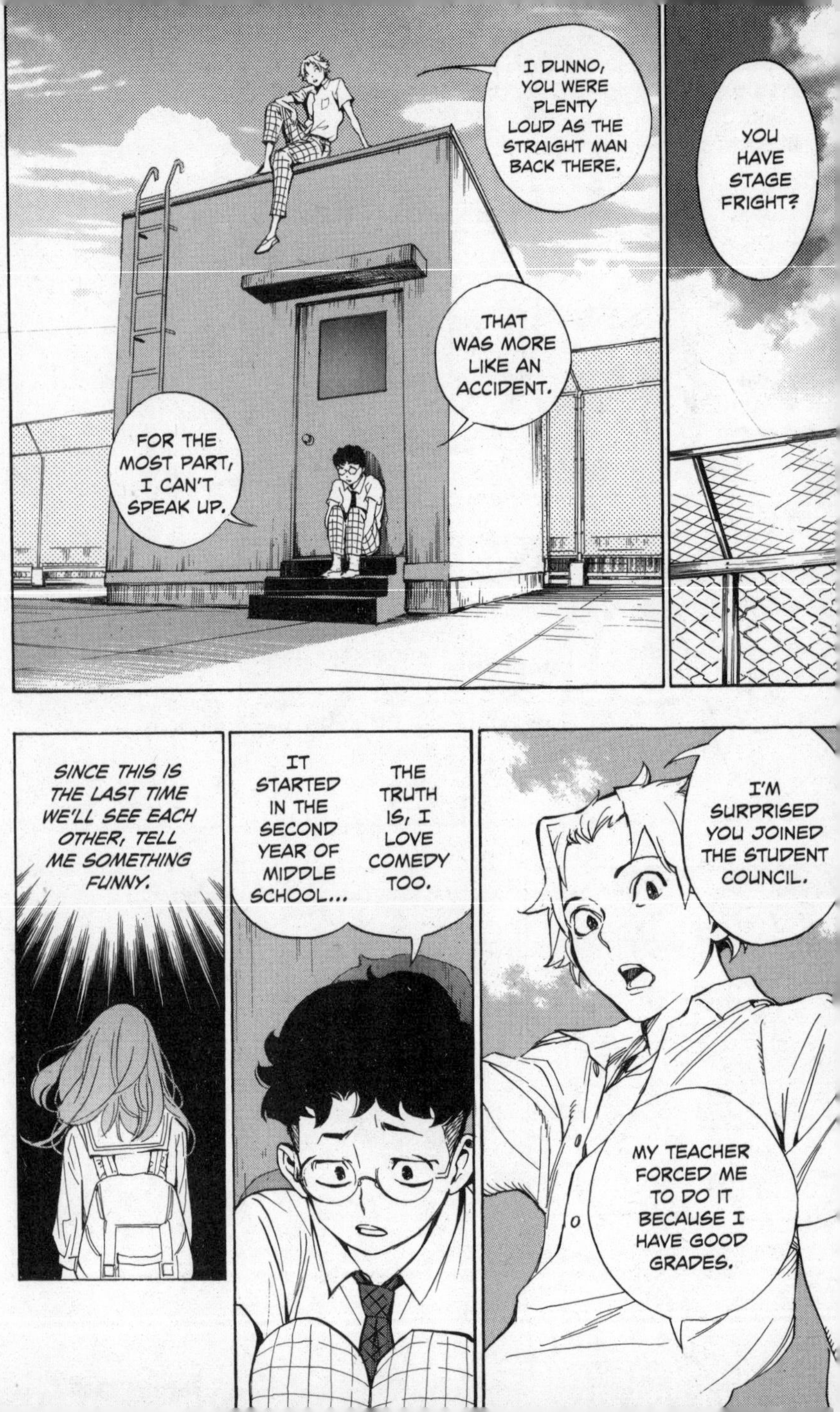
YOU HAVE STAGE FRIGHT?
I DUNNO, YOU WERE PLENTY LOUD AS THE STRAIGHT MAN BACK THERE.
THAT WAS MORE LIKE AN ACCIDENT.
FOR THE MOST PART, I CAN'T SPEAK UP.
I'M SURPRISED YOU JOINED THE STUDENT COUNCIL.
MY TEACHER FORCED ME TO DO IT BECAUSE I HAVE GOOD GRADES.
THE TRUTH IS, I LOVE COMEDY TOO.
IT STARTED IN THE SECOND YEAR OF MIDDLE SCHOOL...
SINCE THIS IS THE LAST TIME WE'LL SEE EACH OTHER, TELL ME SOMETHING FUNNY.

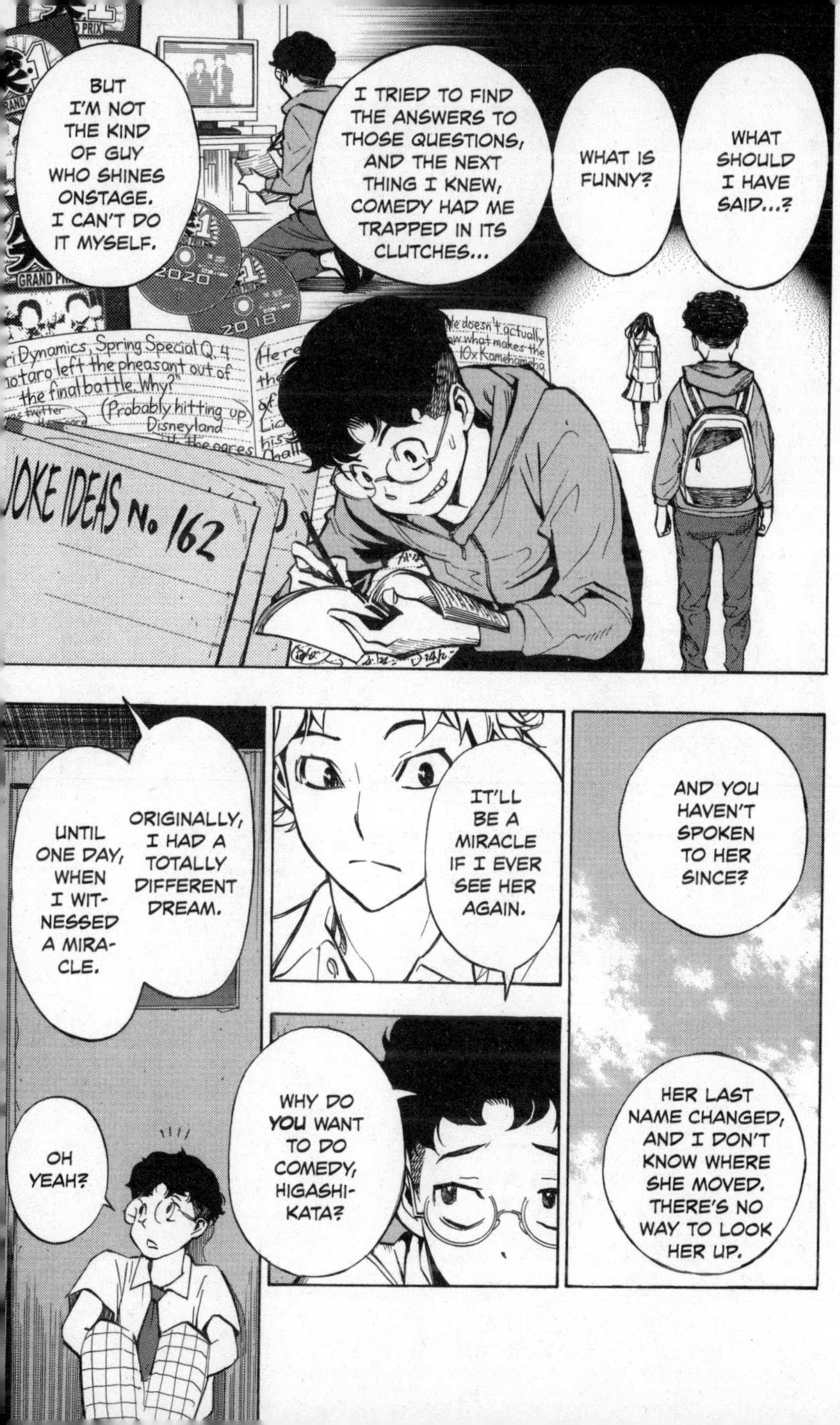
WHAT SHOULD I HAVE SAID...?
WHAT IS FUNNY?
I TRIED TO FIND THE ANSWERS TO THOSE QUESTIONS, AND THE NEXT THING I KNEW, COMEDY HAD ME TRAPPED IN ITS CLUTCHES...
BUT I'M NOT THE KIND OF GUY WHO SHINES ONSTAGE. I CAN'T DO IT MYSELF.
JOKE IDEAS No. 162
(Probably hitting up Disneyland
AND YOU HAVEN'T SPOKEN TO HER SINCE?
HER LAST NAME CHANGED, AND I DON'T KNOW WHERE SHE MOVED. THERE'S NO WAY TO LOOK HER UP.
IT'LL BE A MIRACLE IF I EVER SEE HER AGAIN.
WHY DO **YOU** WANT TO DO COMEDY, HIGASHIKATA?
ORIGINALLY, I HAD A TOTALLY DIFFERENT DREAM.
UNTIL ONE DAY, WHEN I WITNESSED A MIRACLE.
OH YEAH?

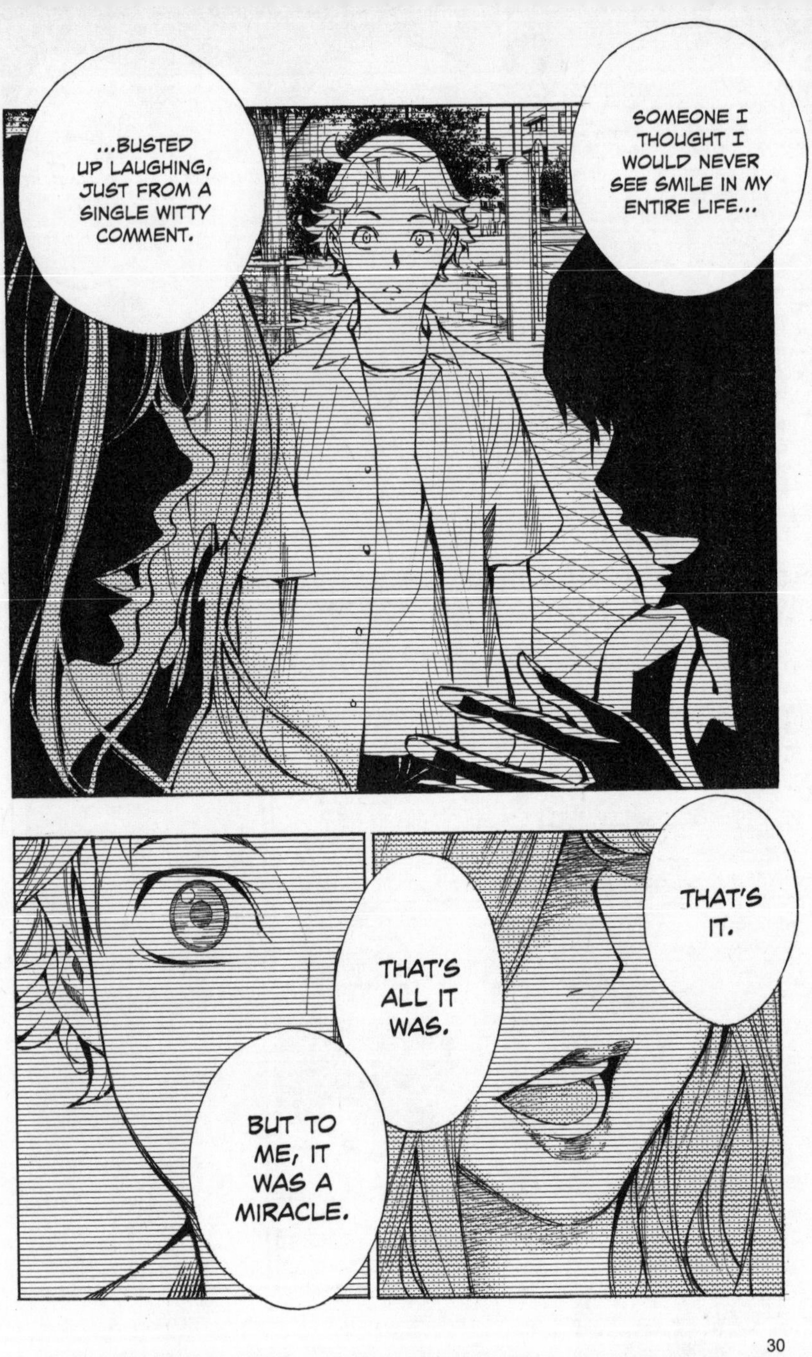
SOMEONE I THOUGHT I WOULD NEVER SEE SMILE IN MY ENTIRE LIFE...
...BUSTED UP LAUGHING, JUST FROM A SINGLE WITTY COMMENT.
THAT'S IT.
THAT'S ALL IT WAS.
BUT TO ME, IT WAS A MIRACLE.

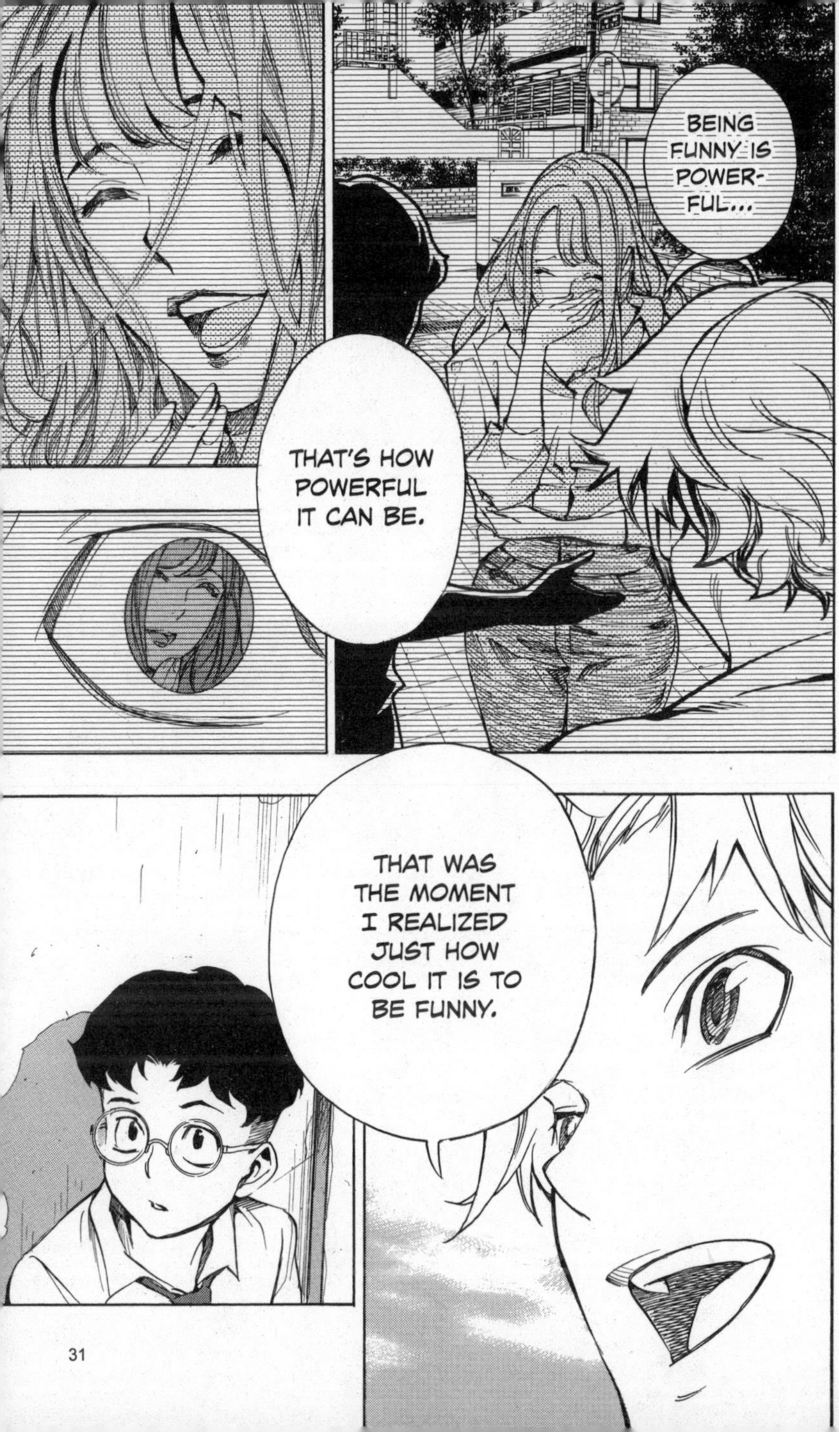
BEING FUNNY IS POWER-FUL...
THAT'S HOW POWERFUL IT CAN BE.
THAT WAS THE MOMENT I REALIZED JUST HOW COOL IT IS TO BE FUNNY.

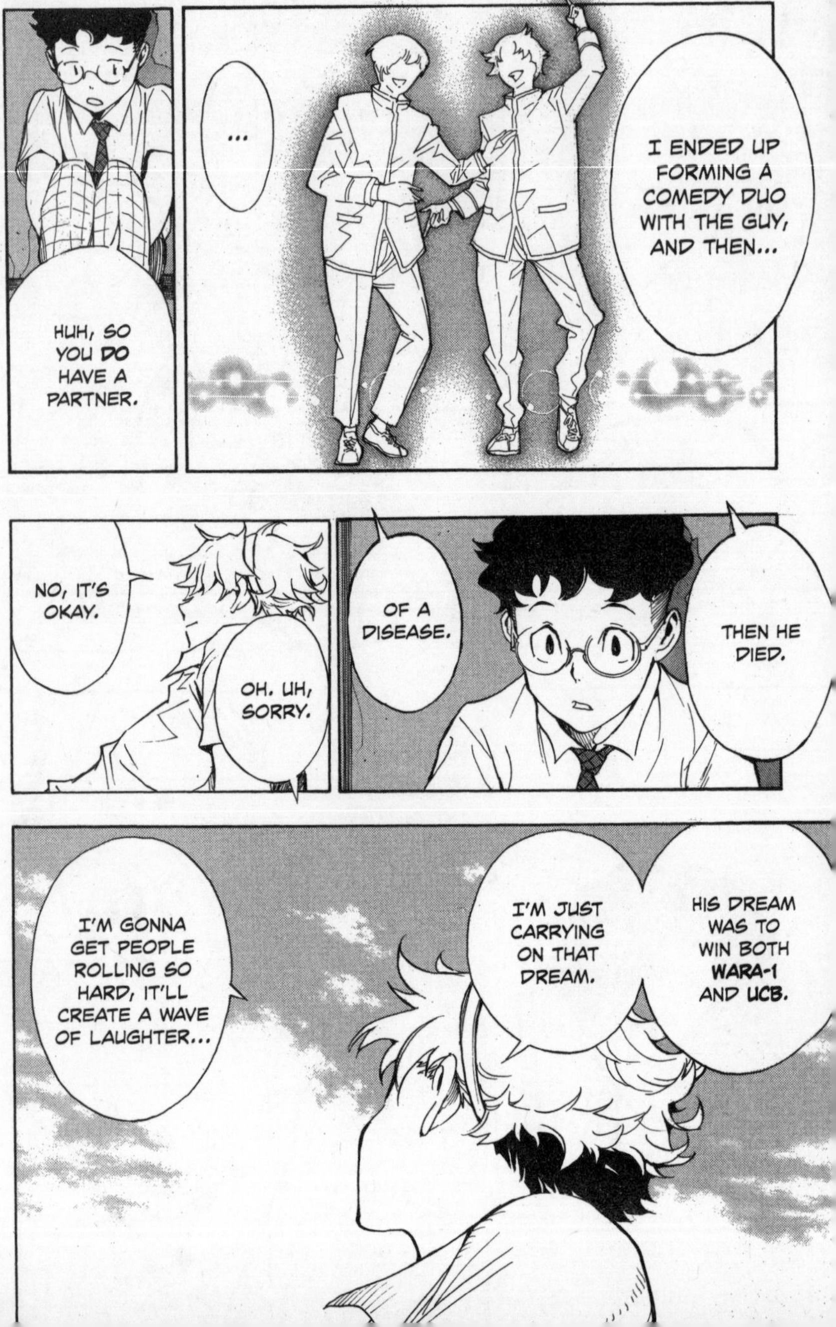
I ENDED UP FORMING A COMEDY DUO WITH THE GUY, AND THEN...
...
HUH, SO YOU **DO** HAVE A PARTNER.
THEN HE DIED.
OF A DISEASE.
OH. UH, SORRY.
NO, IT'S OKAY.
HIS DREAM WAS TO WIN BOTH **WARA-1** AND **UCB**.
I'M JUST CARRYING ON THAT DREAM.
I'M GONNA GET PEOPLE ROLLING SO HARD, IT'LL CREATE A WAVE OF LAUGHTER...

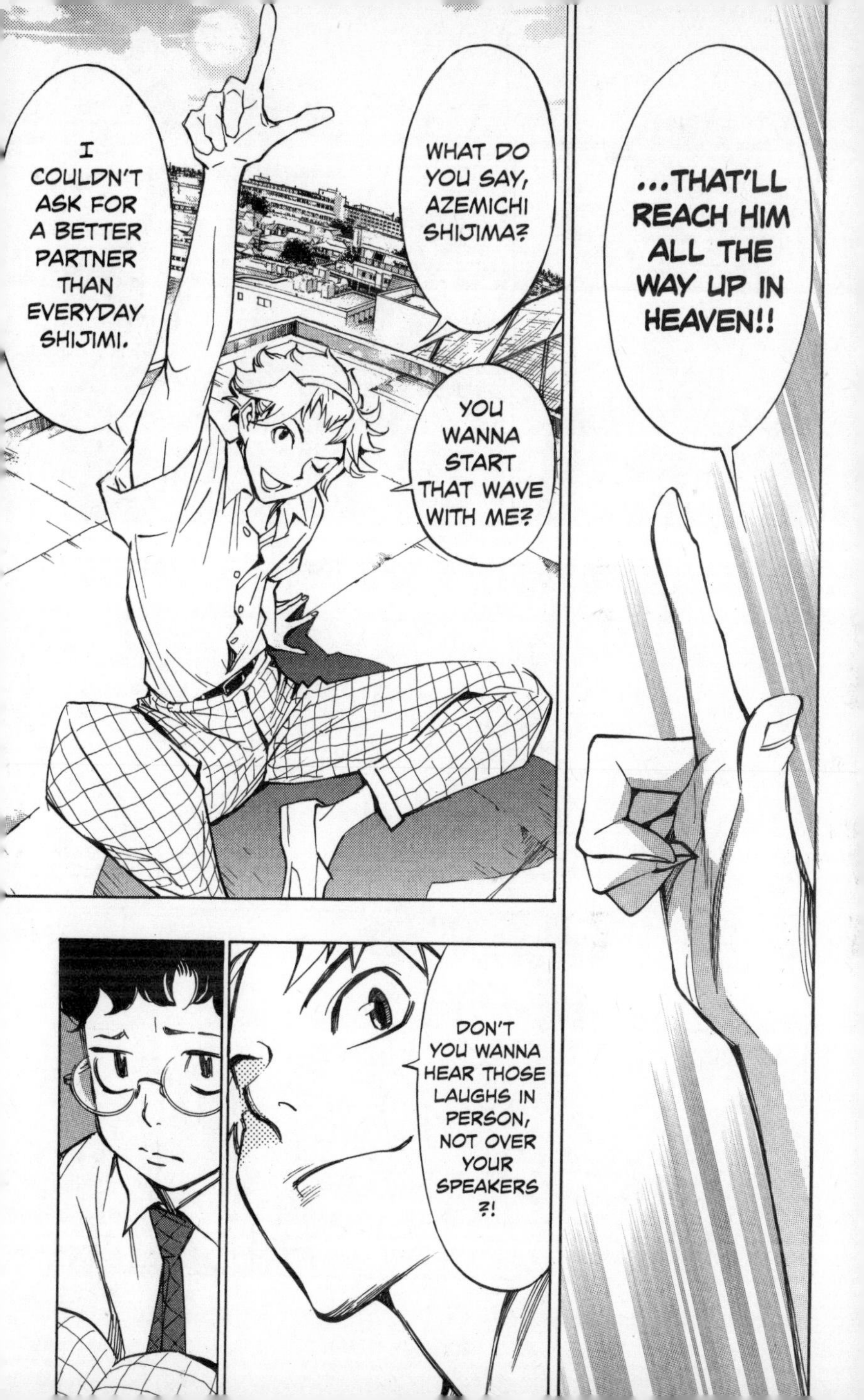
...THAT'LL REACH HIM ALL THE WAY UP IN HEAVEN!!
WHAT DO YOU SAY, AZEMICHI SHIJIMA?
I COULDN'T ASK FOR A BETTER PARTNER THAN EVERYDAY SHIJIMI.
YOU WANNA START THAT WAVE WITH ME?
DON'T YOU WANNA HEAR THOSE LAUGHS IN PERSON, NOT OVER YOUR SPEAKERS?!

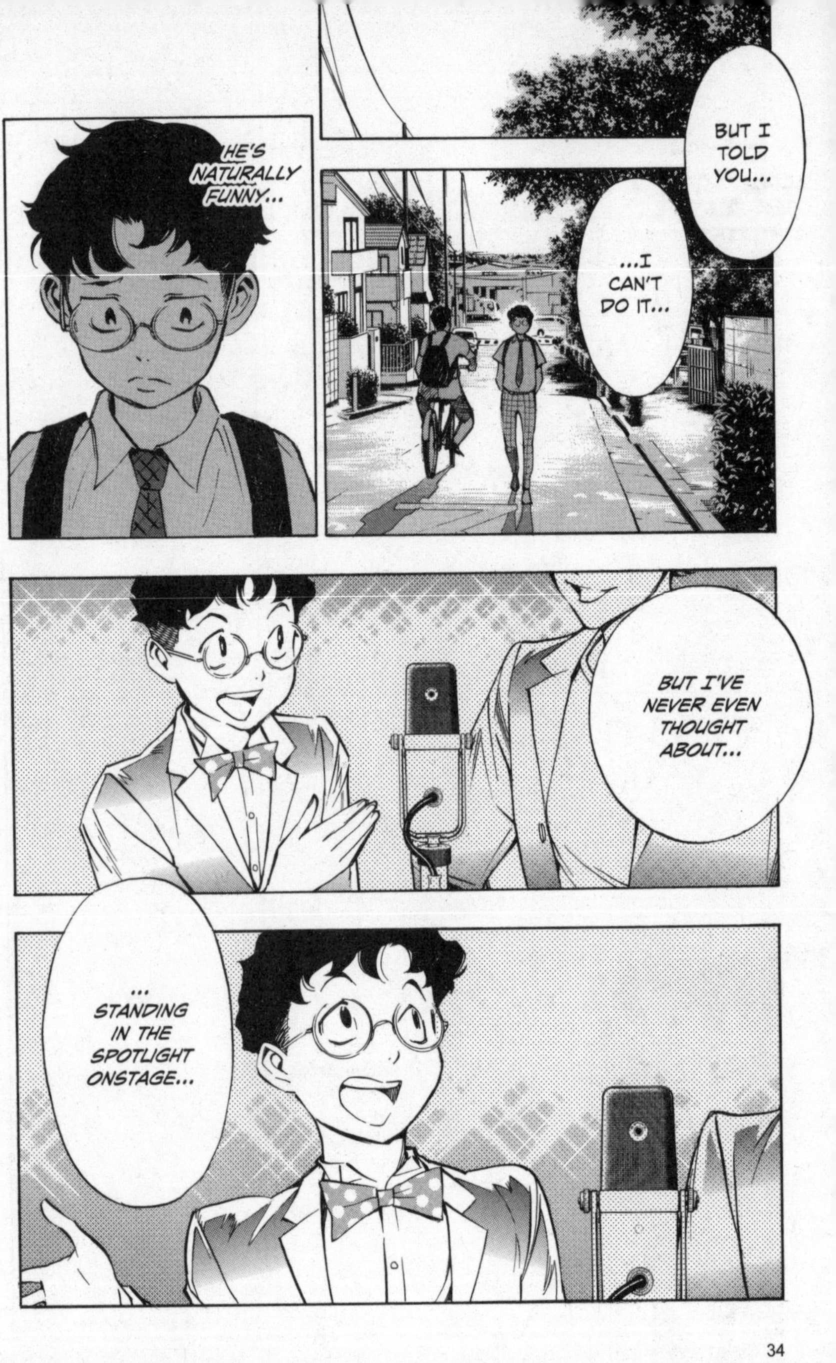
BUT I TOLD YOU...
...I CAN'T DO IT...
HE'S NATURALLY FUNNY...
BUT I'VE NEVER EVEN THOUGHT ABOUT...
... STANDING IN THE SPOTLIGHT ONSTAGE...

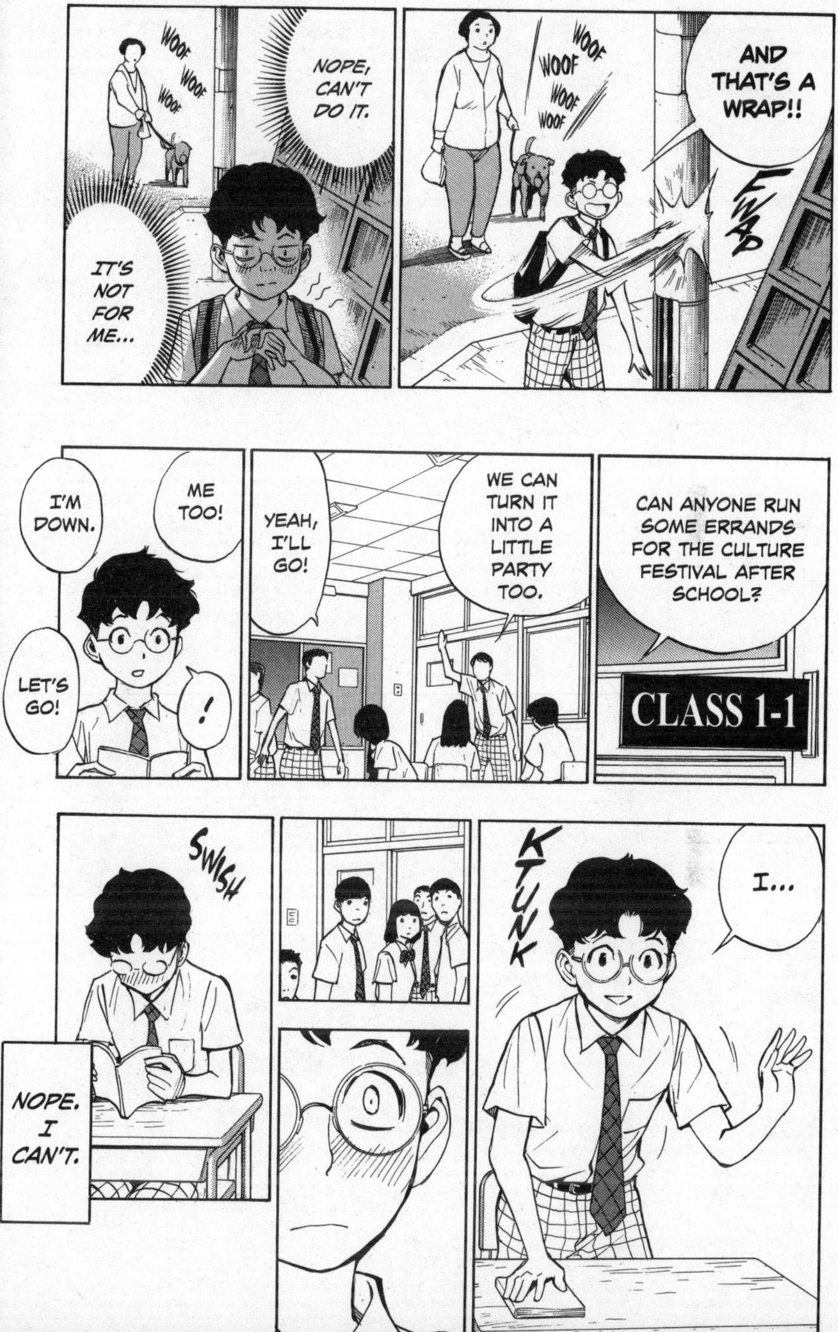
AND THAT'S A WRAP!!
WOOF
WOOF
WOOF
WOOF
FWAP
NOPE, CAN'T DO IT.
WOOF
WOOF
WOOF
IT'S NOT FOR ME...
CAN ANYONE RUN SOME ERRANDS FOR THE CULTURE FESTIVAL AFTER SCHOOL?
CLASS 1-1
WE CAN TURN IT INTO A LITTLE PARTY TOO.
YEAH, I'LL GO!
ME TOO!
I'M DOWN.
!
LET'S GO!
I...
KTUNK
SWISH
NOPE. I CAN'T.

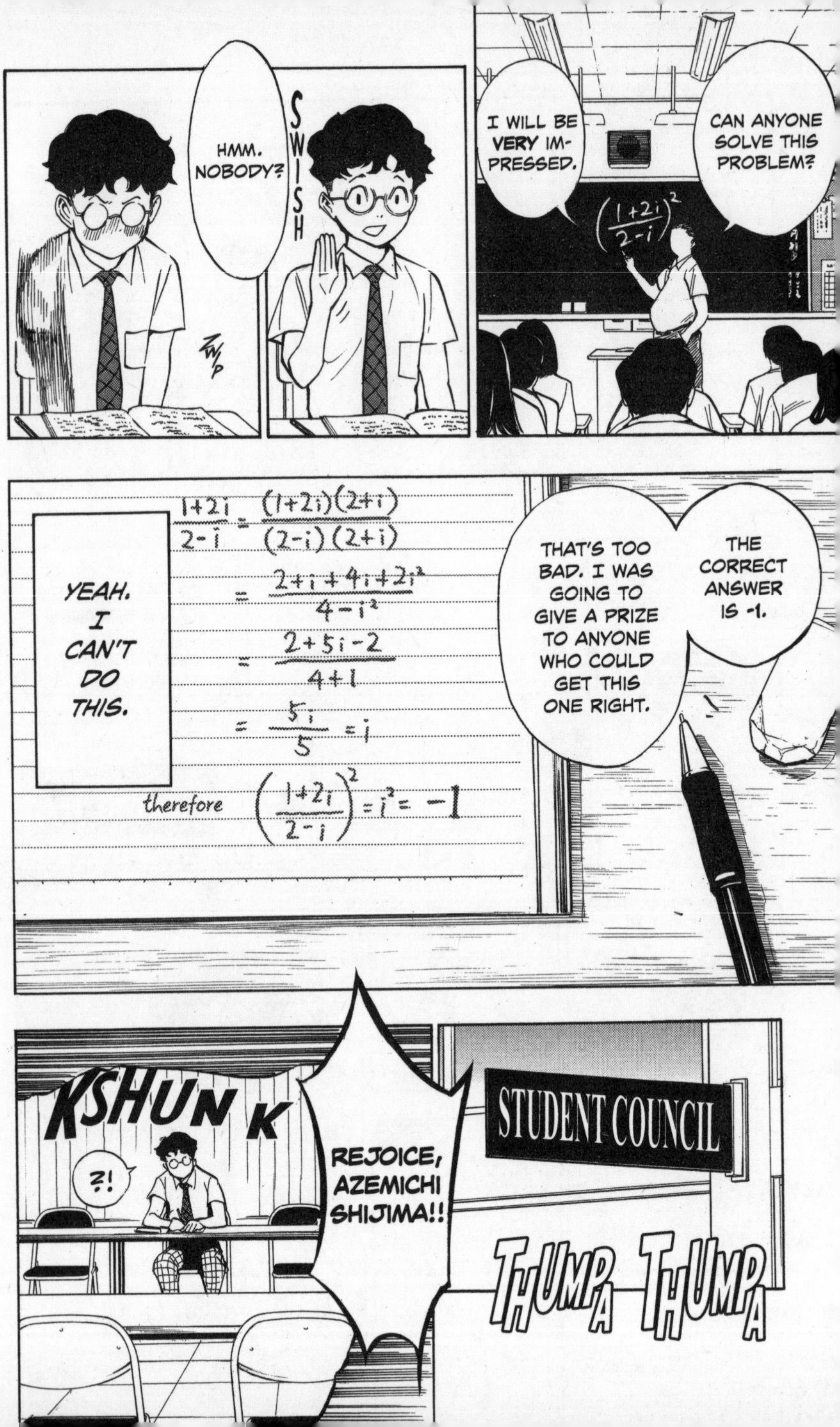
CAN ANYONE SOLVE THIS PROBLEM?
I WILL BE VERY IMPRESSED.
(1+2i / 2-i)²
SWISH
HMM. NOBODY?
ZWIP
THE CORRECT ANSWER IS -1.
THAT'S TOO BAD. I WAS GOING TO GIVE A PRIZE TO ANYONE WHO COULD GET THIS ONE RIGHT.
YEAH. I CAN'T DO THIS.
1+2i / 2-i = (1+2i)(2+i) / (2-i)(2+i)
= 2+i+4i+2i² / 4-i²
= 2+5i-2 / 4+1
= 5i / 5 = i
therefore (1+2i / 2-i)² = i² = -1
STUDENT COUNCIL
THUMPA THUMPA
REJOICE, AZEMICHI SHIJIMA!!
KSHUNK
?!

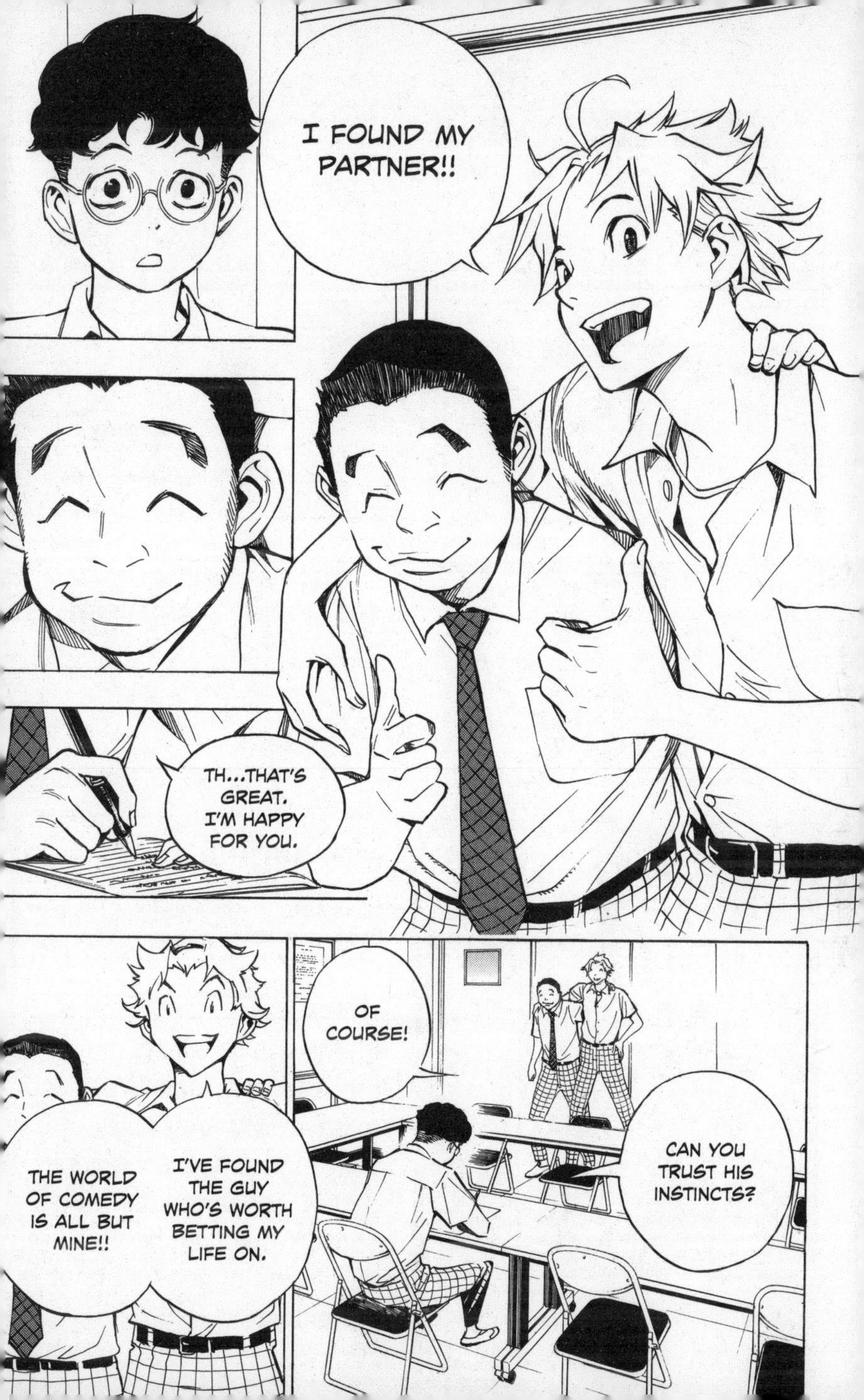
I FOUND MY PARTNER!!
TH...THAT'S GREAT. I'M HAPPY FOR YOU.
CAN YOU TRUST HIS INSTINCTS?
OF COURSE!
I'VE FOUND THE GUY WHO'S WORTH BETTING MY LIFE ON.
THE WORLD OF COMEDY IS ALL BUT MINE!!

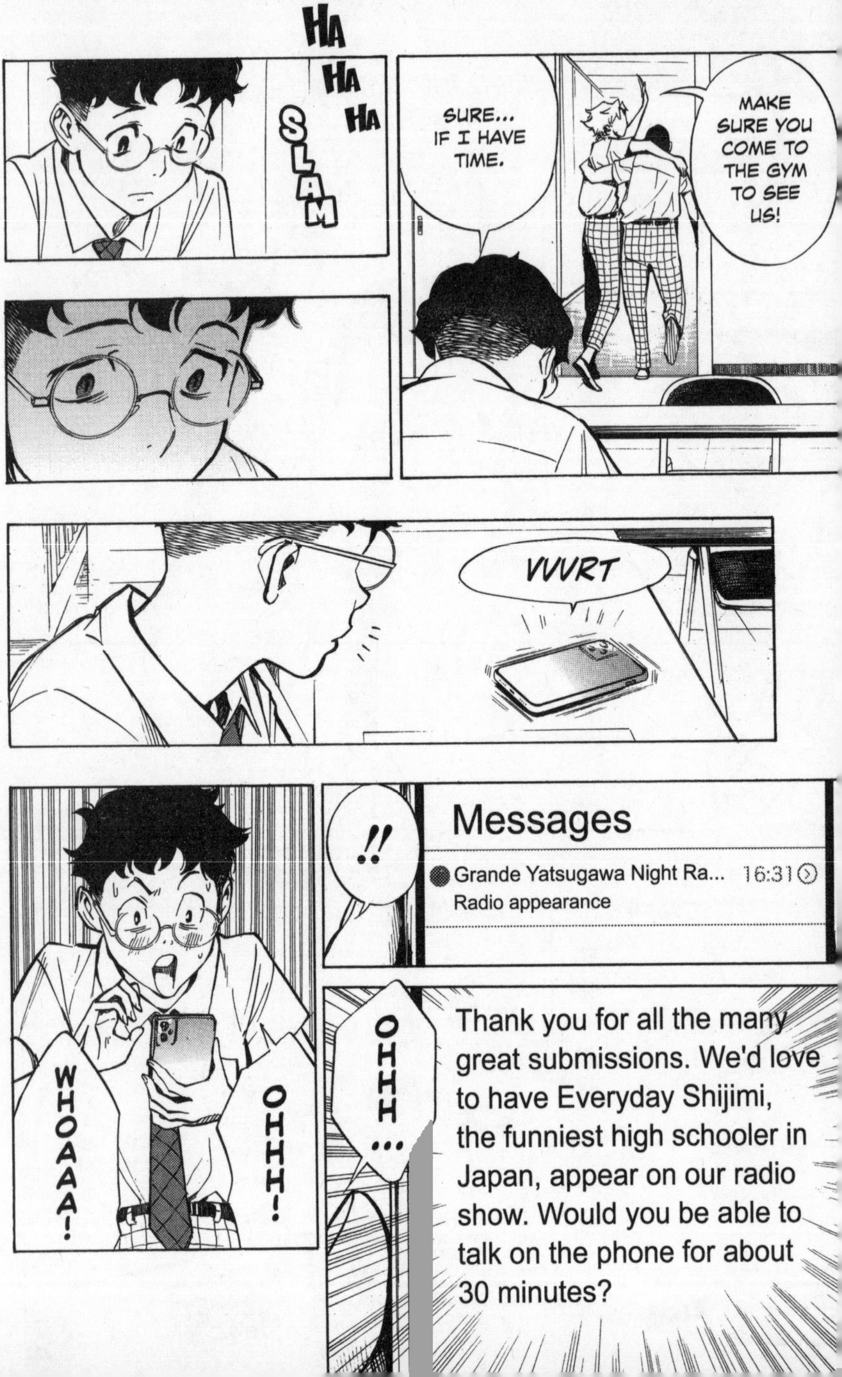
MAKE SURE YOU COME TO THE GYM TO SEE US!
SURE... IF I HAVE TIME.
HA HA HA
SLAM
VVURT
Messages
!!
Grande Yatsugawa Night Ra... 16:31
Radio appearance
Thank you for all the many great submissions. We'd love to have Everyday Shijimi, the funniest high schooler in Japan, appear on our radio show. Would you be able to talk on the phone for about 30 minutes?
OHHH...
OHHH!
WHOAAA!

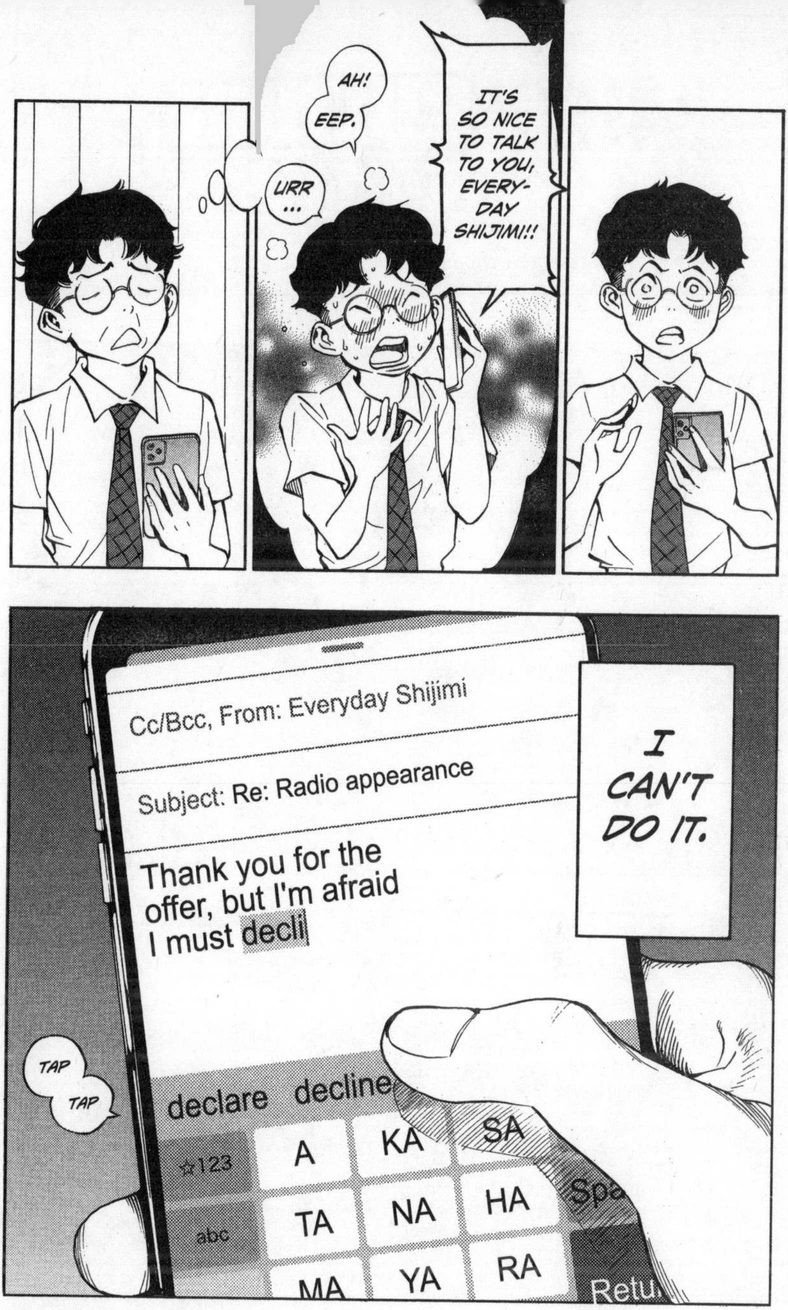
IT'S SO NICE TO TALK TO YOU, EVERY-DAY SHIJIMI!!
AH! EEP.
URR...
I CAN'T DO IT.
Cc/Bcc, From: Everyday Shijimi
Subject: Re: Radio appearance
Thank you for the offer, but I'm afraid I must decli
declare decline
☆123
abc
A
KA
SA
TA
NA
HA
MA
YA
RA
TAP TAP

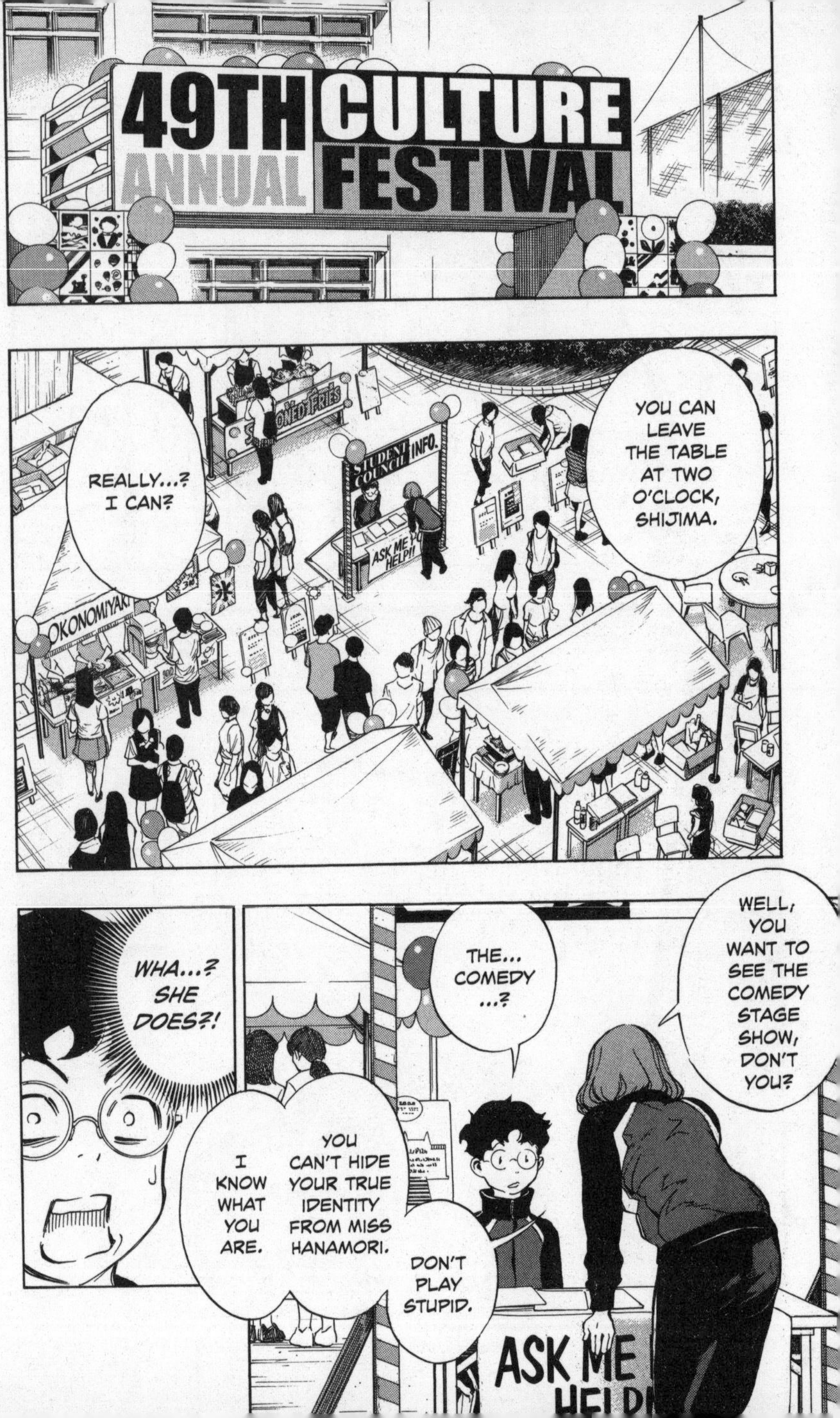
49TH ANNUAL CULTURE FESTIVAL
STUDENT COUNCIL INFO.
ASK ME HELP!!
OKONOMIYAKI
YOU CAN LEAVE THE TABLE AT TWO O'CLOCK, SHIJIMA.
REALLY...? I CAN?
WELL, YOU WANT TO SEE THE COMEDY STAGE SHOW, DON'T YOU?
THE... COMEDY...?
YOU CAN'T HIDE YOUR TRUE IDENTITY FROM MISS HANAMORI.
I KNOW WHAT YOU ARE.
DON'T PLAY STUPID.
ASK ME
WHA...? SHE DOES?!

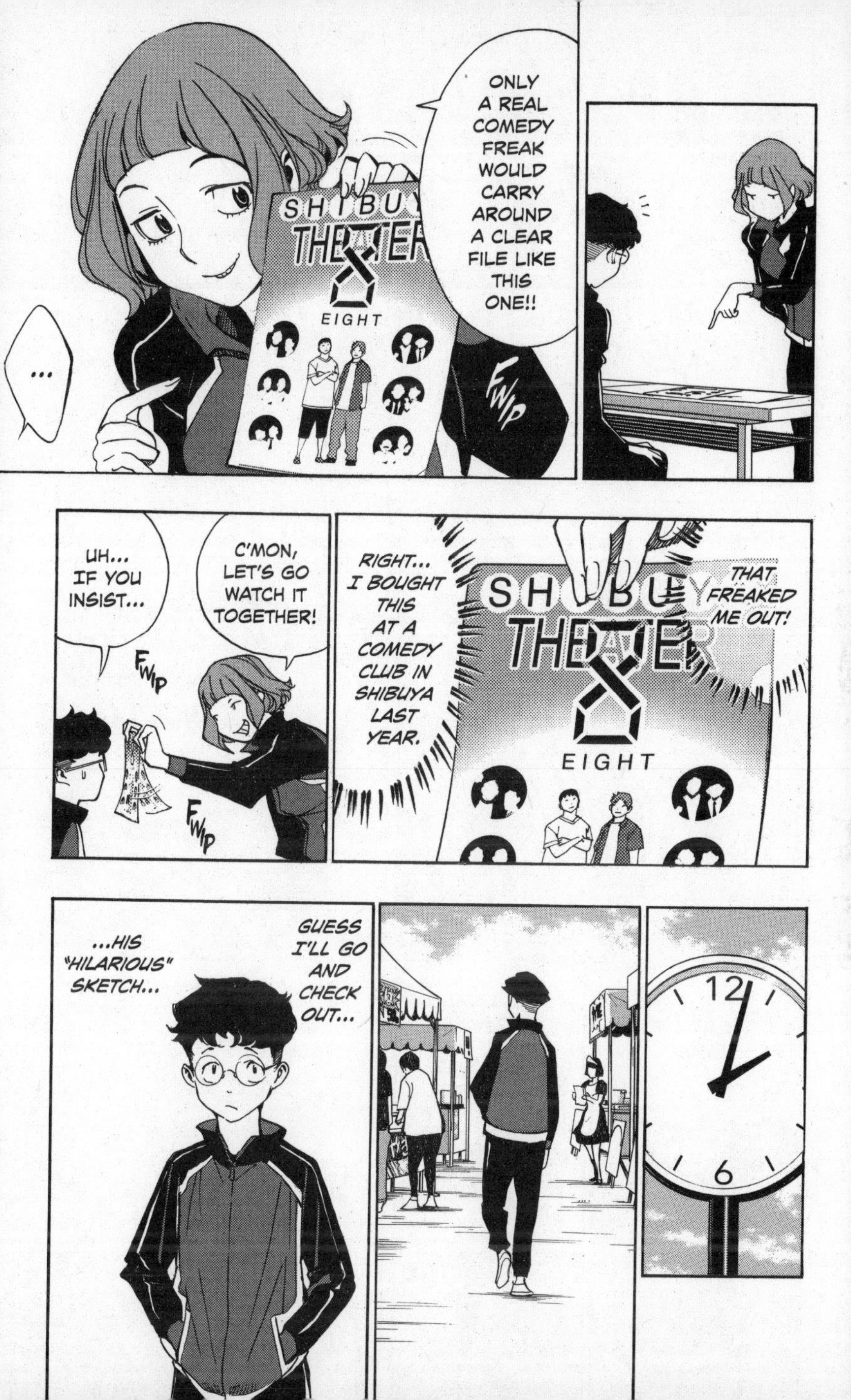
ONLY A REAL COMEDY FREAK WOULD CARRY AROUND A CLEAR FILE LIKE THIS ONE!!
EIGHT
FWIP
...
THAT FREAKED ME OUT!
RIGHT... I BOUGHT THIS AT A COMEDY CLUB IN SHIBUYA LAST YEAR.
EIGHT
C'MON, LET'S GO WATCH IT TOGETHER!
FWIP
UH... IF YOU INSIST...
FWIP
GUESS I'LL GO AND CHECK OUT...
...HIS "HILARIOUS" SKETCH...

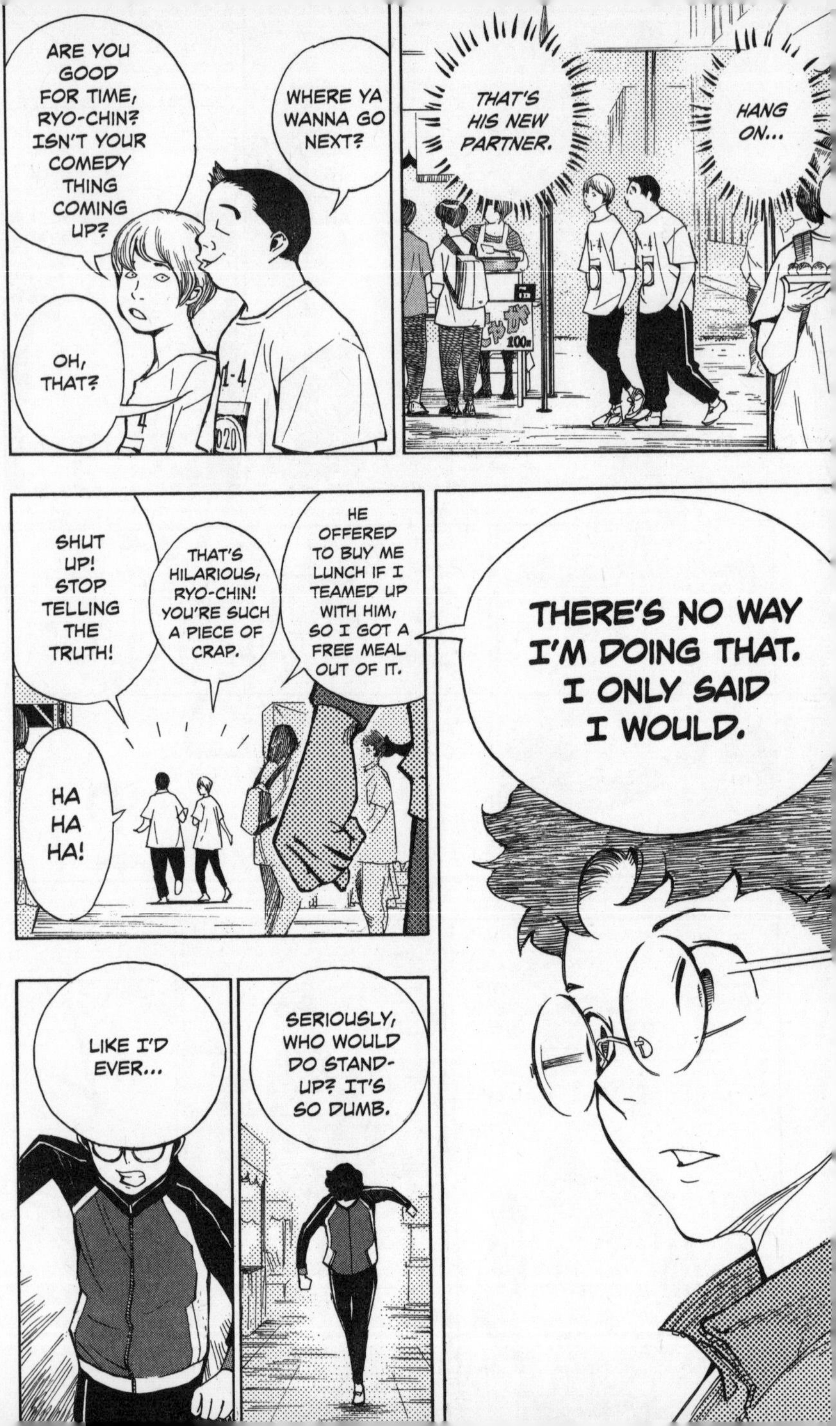
HANG ON...
THAT'S HIS NEW PARTNER.
WHERE YA WANNA GO NEXT?
ARE YOU GOOD FOR TIME, RYO-CHIN? ISN'T YOUR COMEDY THING COMING UP?
OH, THAT?
THERE'S NO WAY I'M DOING THAT. I ONLY SAID I WOULD.
HE OFFERED TO BUY ME LUNCH IF I TEAMED UP WITH HIM, SO I GOT A FREE MEAL OUT OF IT.
THAT'S HILARIOUS, RYO-CHIN! YOU'RE SUCH A PIECE OF CRAP.
SHUT UP! STOP TELLING THE TRUTH!
HA HA HA!
SERIOUSLY, WHO WOULD DO STAND-UP? IT'S SO DUMB.
LIKE I'D EVER...

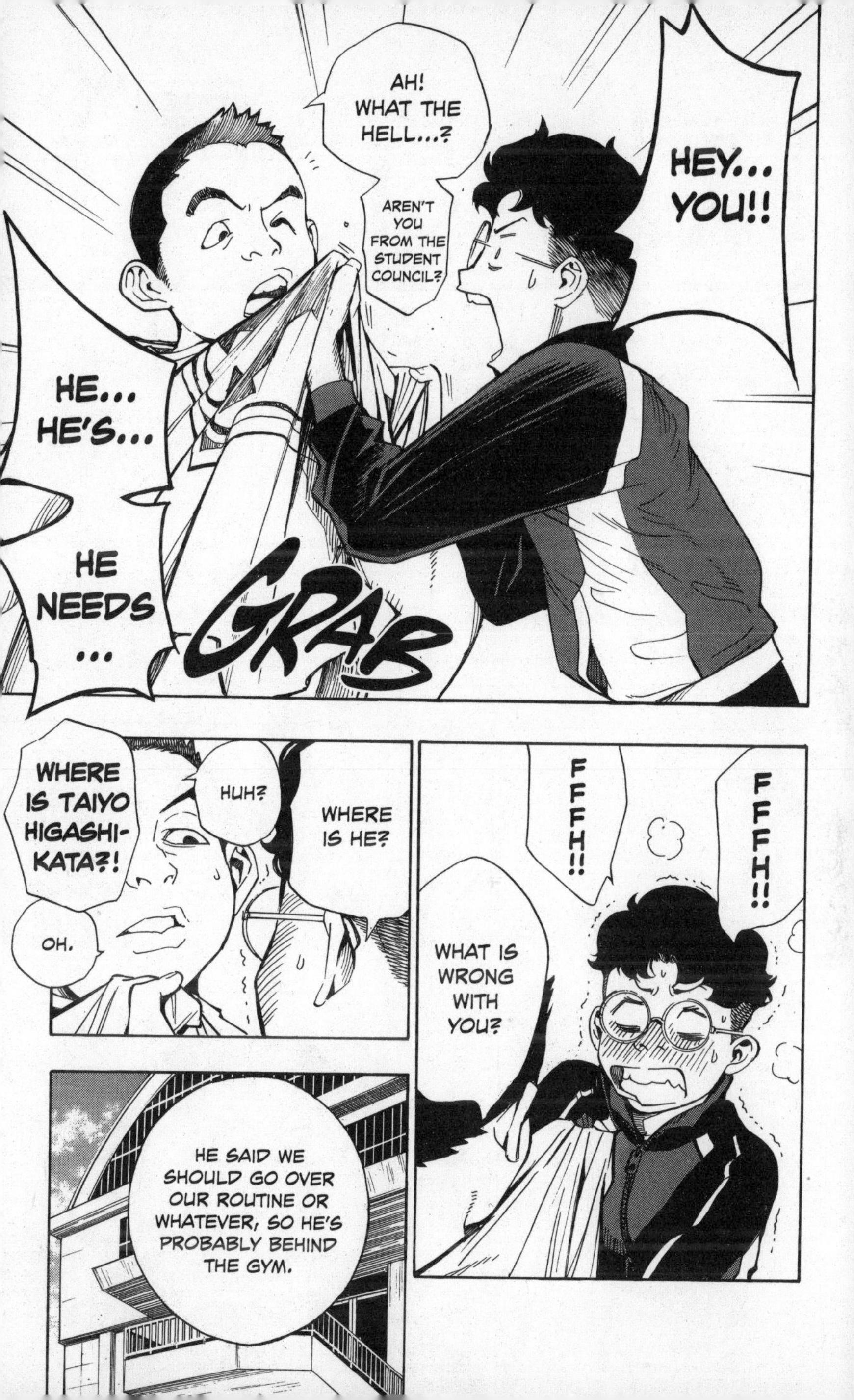
HEY... YOU!!
AH! WHAT THE HELL...?
AREN'T YOU FROM THE STUDENT COUNCIL?
HE... HE'S...
HE NEEDS ...
GRAB
FFFH!!
FFFH!!
WHAT IS WRONG WITH YOU?
WHERE IS HE?
HUH?
WHERE IS TAIYO HIGASHI-KATA?!
OH.
HE SAID WE SHOULD GO OVER OUR ROUTINE OR WHATEVER, SO HE'S PROBABLY BEHIND THE GYM.

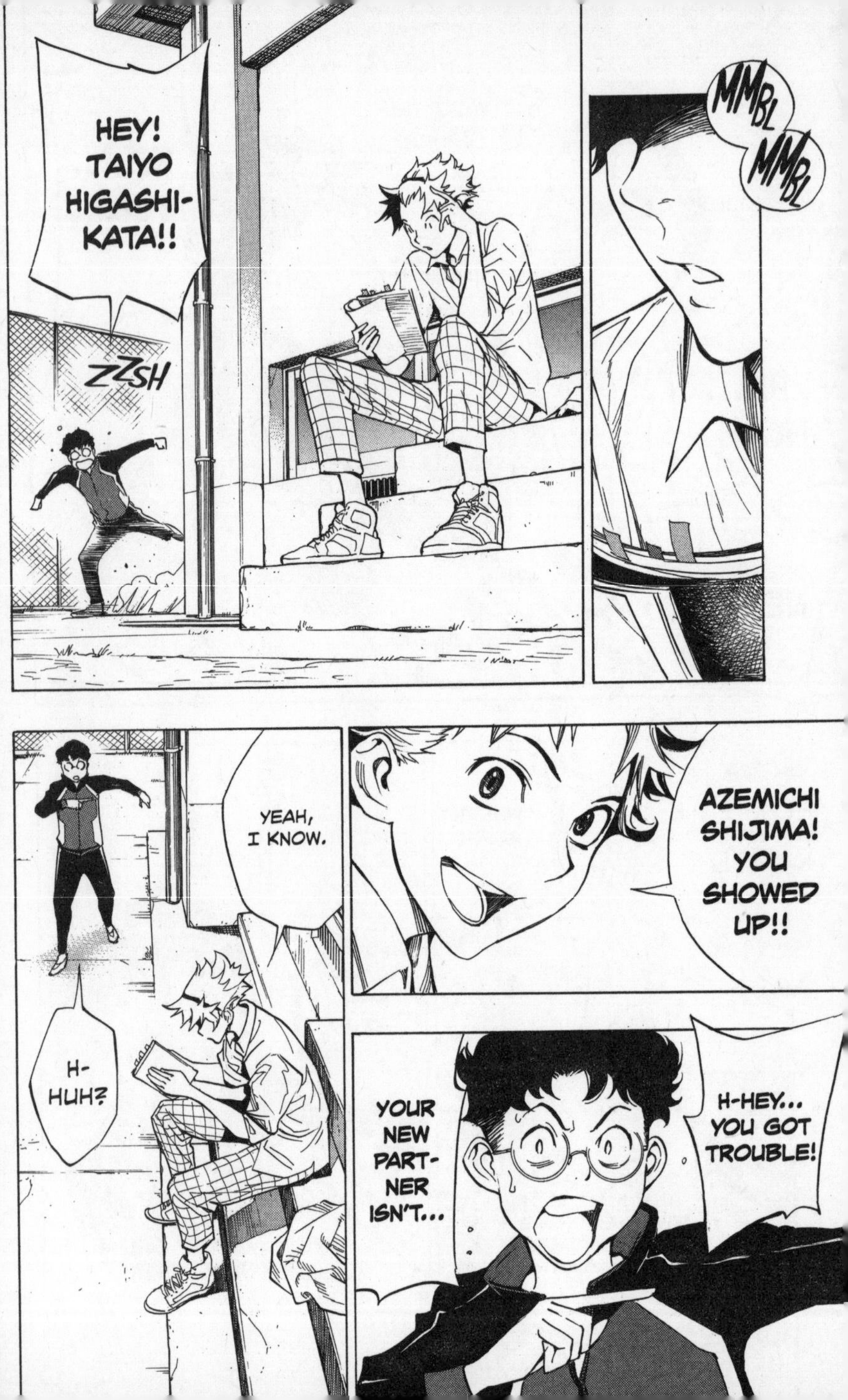
MMBL
MMBL
HEY! TAIYO HIGASHI-KATA!!
ZZSH
AZEMICHI SHIJIMA! YOU SHOWED UP!!
H-HEY... YOU GOT TROUBLE!
YOUR NEW PART-NER ISN'T...
YEAH, I KNOW.
H-HUH?

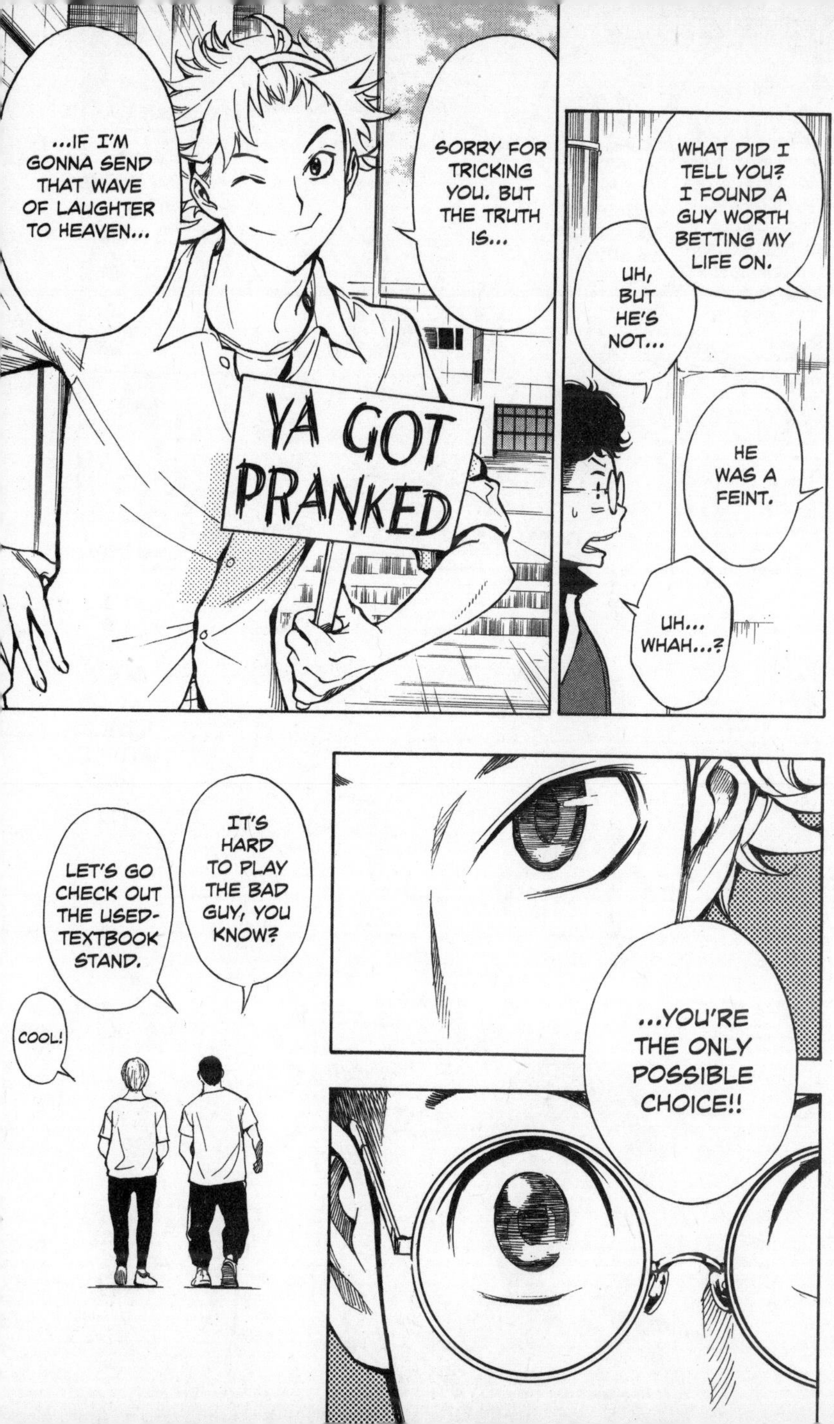
WHAT DID I TELL YOU? I FOUND A GUY WORTH BETTING MY LIFE ON.
UH, BUT HE'S NOT...
HE WAS A FEINT.
UH... WHAH...?
SORRY FOR TRICKING YOU. BUT THE TRUTH IS...
...IF I'M GONNA SEND THAT WAVE OF LAUGHTER TO HEAVEN...
YA GOT PRANKED
...YOU'RE THE ONLY POSSIBLE CHOICE!!
IT'S HARD TO PLAY THE BAD GUY, YOU KNOW?
LET'S GO CHECK OUT THE USED-TEXTBOOK STAND.
COOL!

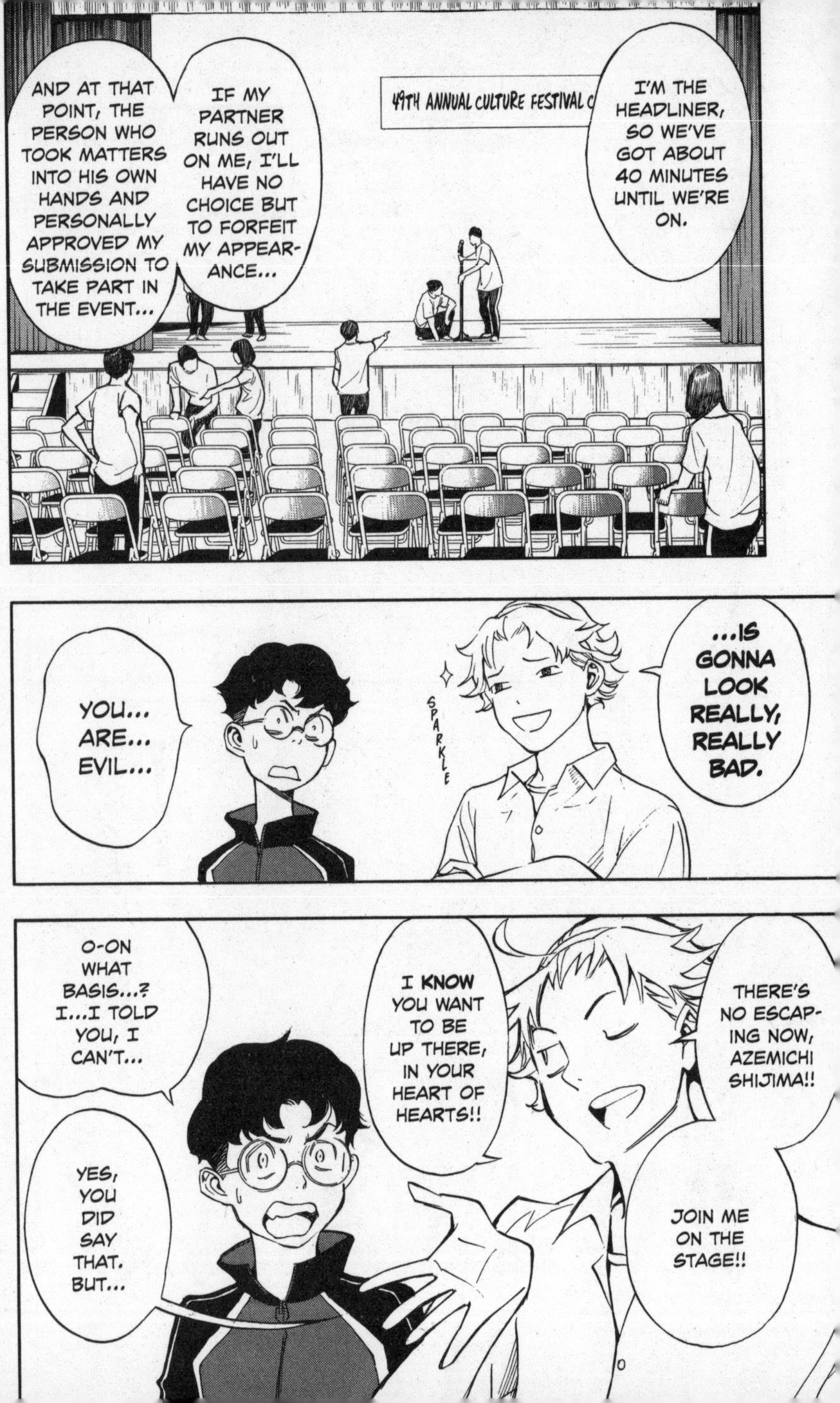
I'M THE HEADLINER, SO WE'VE GOT ABOUT 40 MINUTES UNTIL WE'RE ON.
49TH ANNUAL CULTURE FESTIVAL
IF MY PARTNER RUNS OUT ON ME, I'LL HAVE NO CHOICE BUT TO FORFEIT MY APPEARANCE...
AND AT THAT POINT, THE PERSON WHO TOOK MATTERS INTO HIS OWN HANDS AND PERSONALLY APPROVED MY SUBMISSION TO TAKE PART IN THE EVENT...
...IS GONNA LOOK REALLY, REALLY BAD.
SPARKLE
YOU... ARE... EVIL...
THERE'S NO ESCAPING NOW, AZEMICHI SHIJIMA!!
I KNOW YOU WANT TO BE UP THERE, IN YOUR HEART OF HEARTS!!
O-ON WHAT BASIS...? I...I TOLD YOU, I CAN'T...
JOIN ME ON THE STAGE!!
YES, YOU DID SAY THAT. BUT...

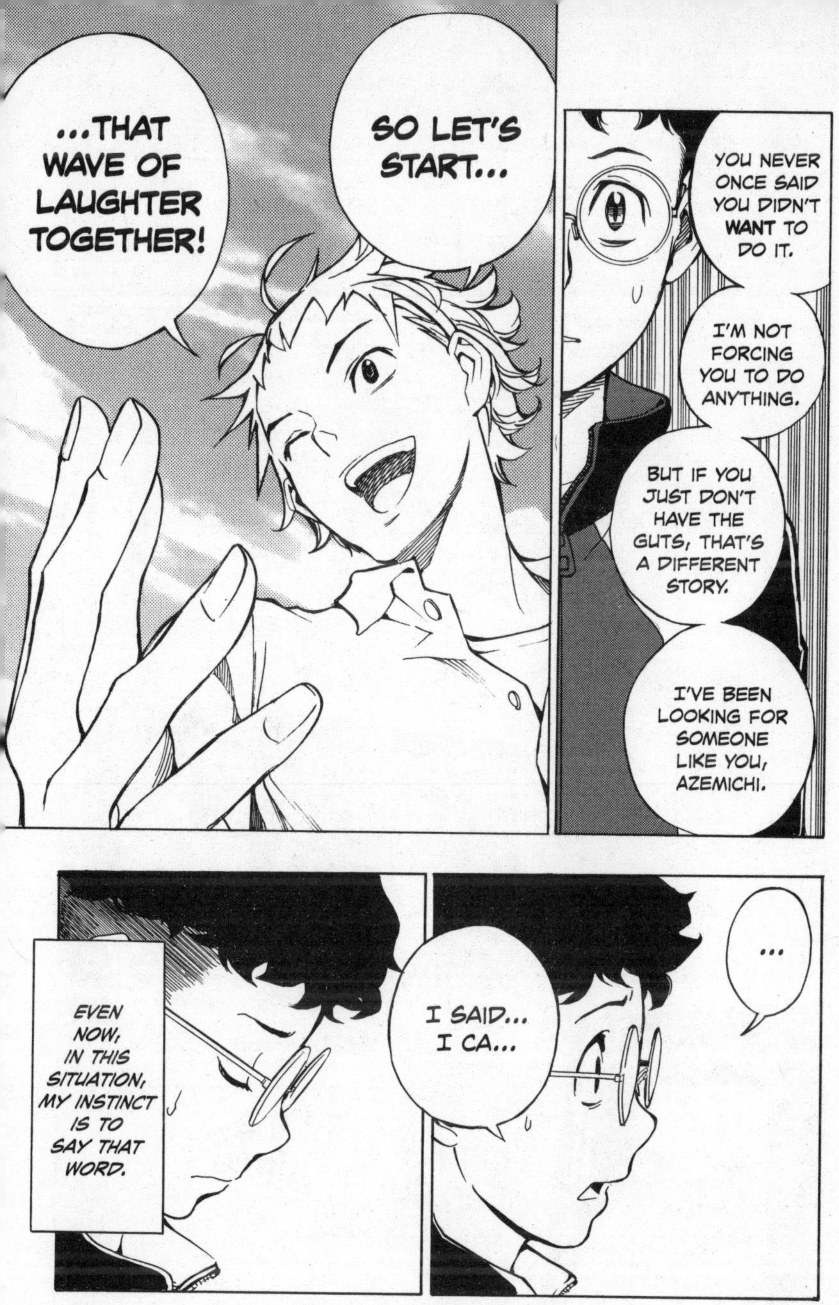

YOU NEVER ONCE SAID YOU DIDN'T WANT TO DO IT.
I'M NOT FORCING YOU TO DO ANYTHING.
BUT IF YOU JUST DON'T HAVE THE GUTS, THAT'S A DIFFERENT STORY.
I'VE BEEN LOOKING FOR SOMEONE LIKE YOU, AZEMICHI.
SO LET'S START...
...THAT WAVE OF LAUGHTER TOGETHER!
...
I SAID... I CA...
EVEN NOW, IN THIS SITUATION, MY INSTINCT IS TO SAY THAT WORD.

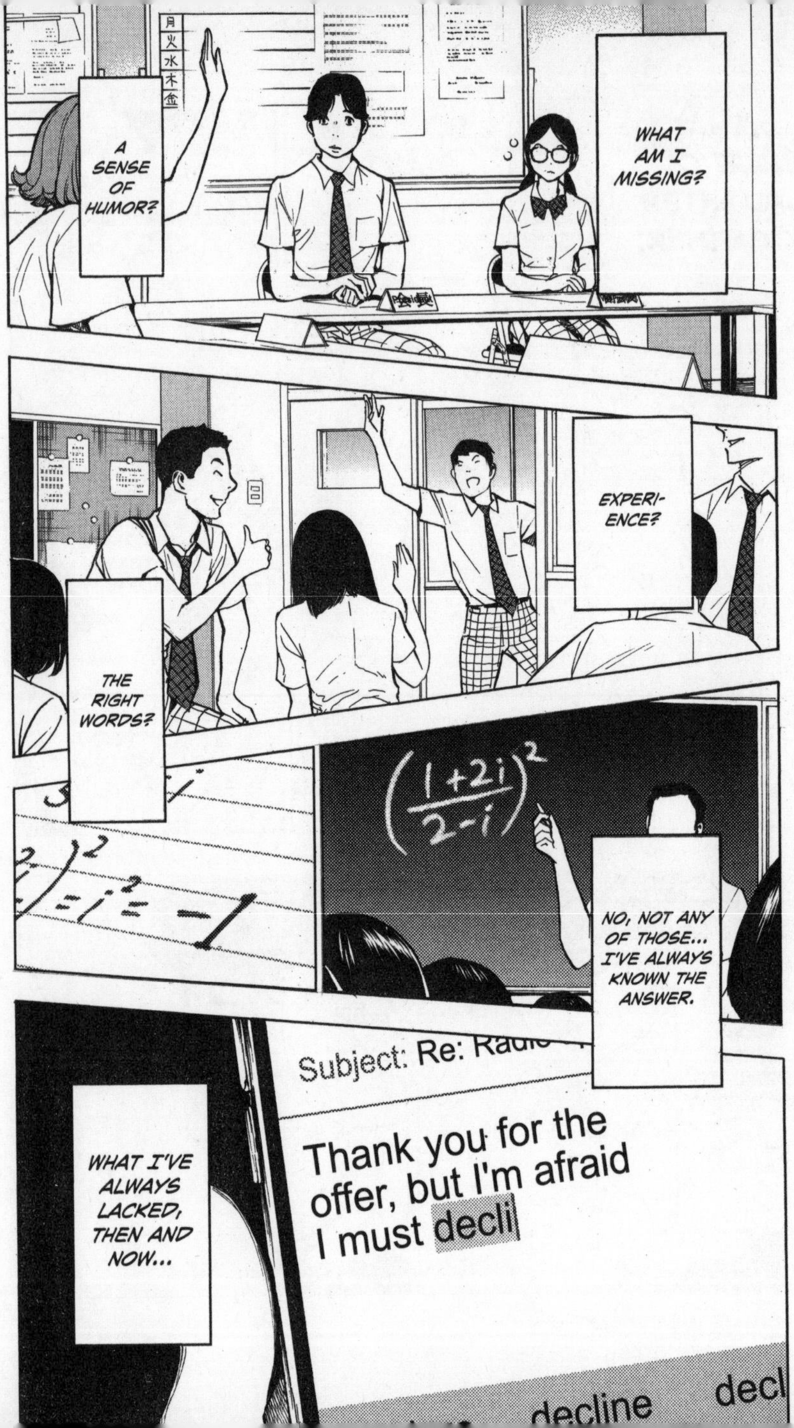
WHAT AM I MISSING?
A SENSE OF HUMOR?
EXPERIENCE?
THE RIGHT WORDS?
NO, NOT ANY OF THOSE... I'VE ALWAYS KNOWN THE ANSWER.
(1+2i / 2-i)²
= i² = -1
Subject: Re: Radi
Thank you for the offer, but I'm afraid I must decli
decline
decl
WHAT I'VE ALWAYS LACKED, THEN AND NOW...

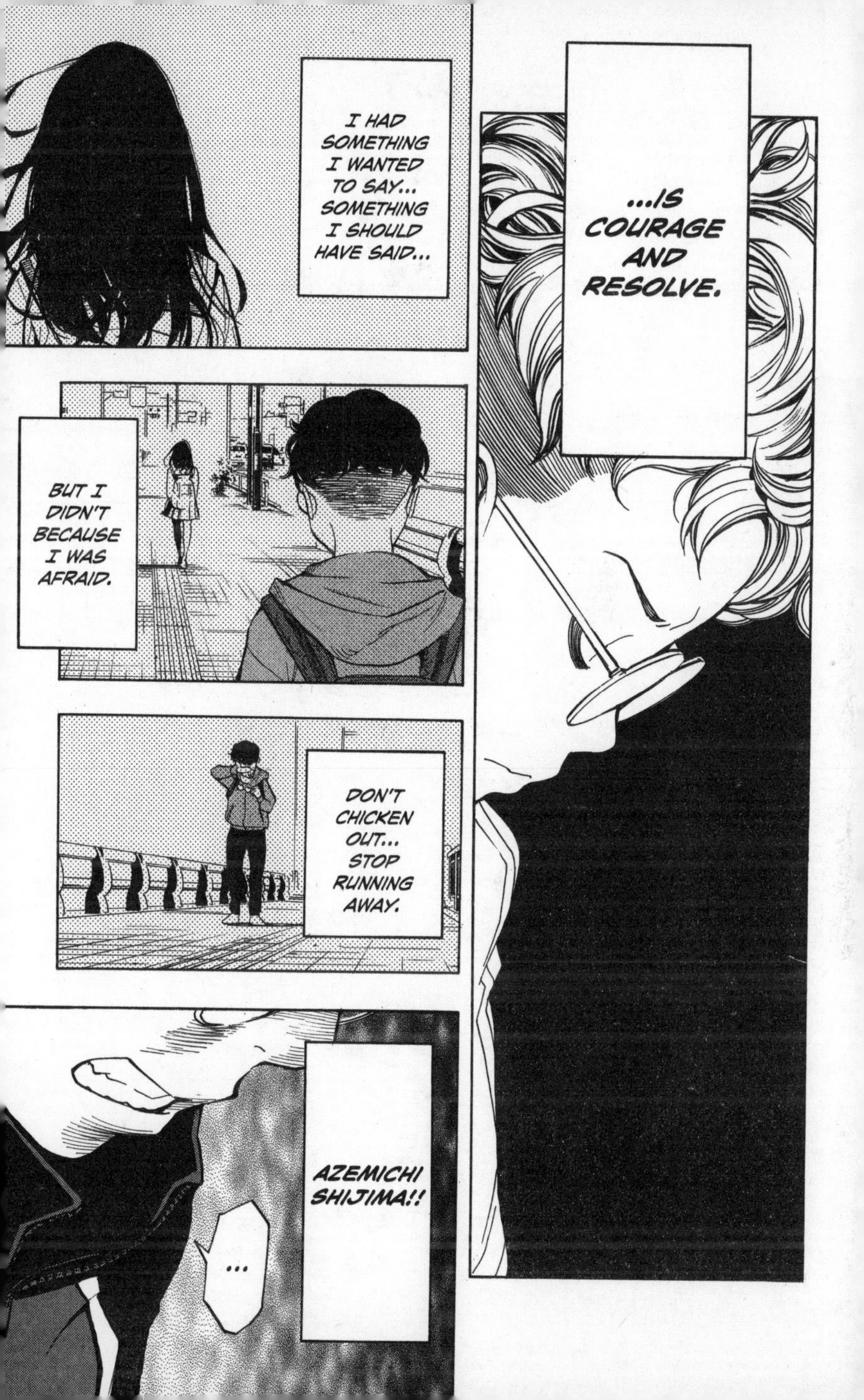
...IS COURAGE AND RESOLVE.
I HAD SOMETHING I WANTED TO SAY... SOMETHING I SHOULD HAVE SAID...
BUT I DIDN'T BECAUSE I WAS AFRAID.
DON'T CHICKEN OUT... STOP RUNNING AWAY.
AZEMICHI SHIJIMA!!
...

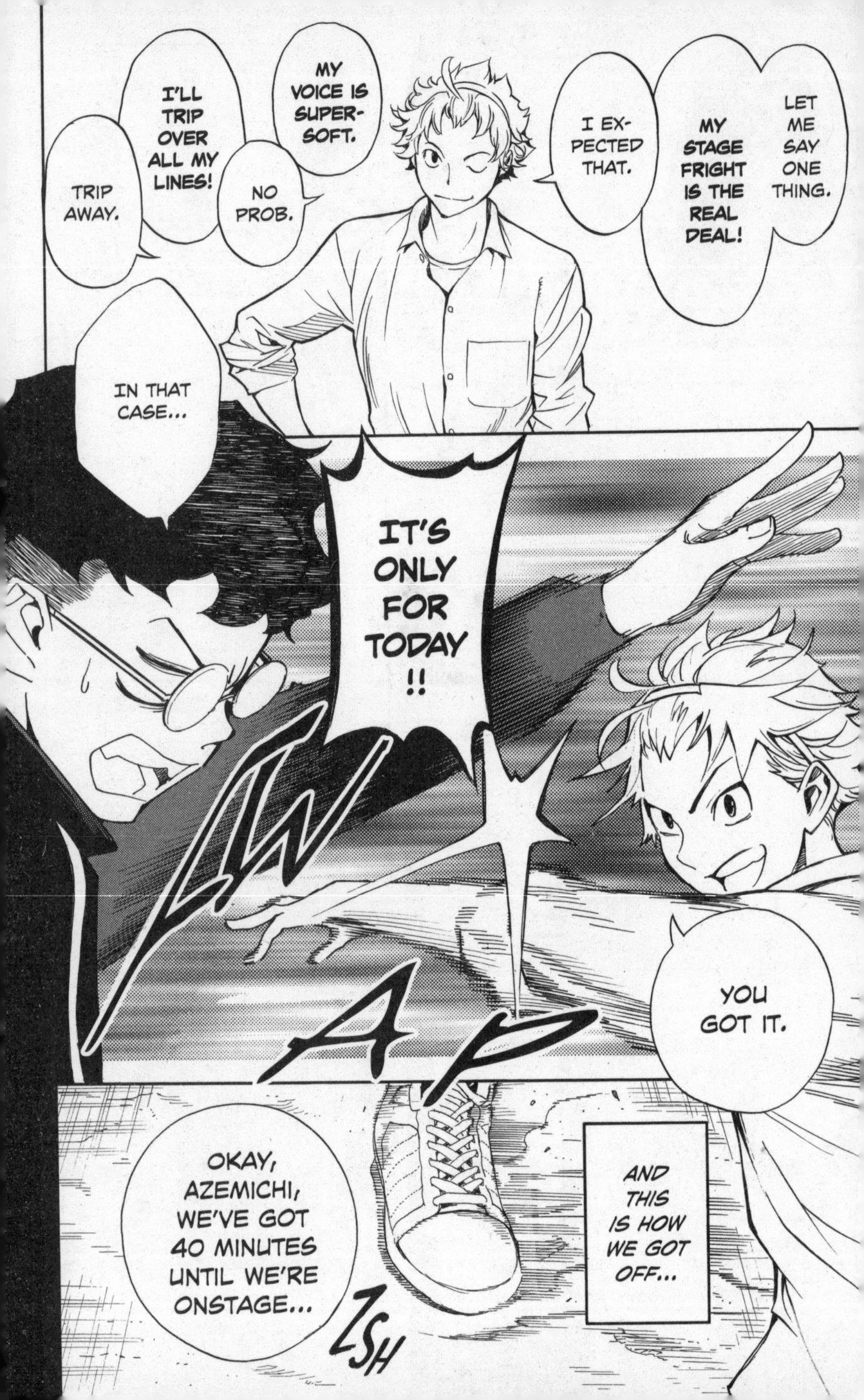
LET ME SAY ONE THING.
MY STAGE FRIGHT IS THE REAL DEAL!
I EXPECTED THAT.
MY VOICE IS SUPER-SOFT.
NO PROB.
I'LL TRIP OVER ALL MY LINES!
TRIP AWAY.
IN THAT CASE...
IT'S ONLY FOR TODAY!!
YOU GOT IT.
AP
AND THIS IS HOW WE GOT OFF...
OKAY, AZEMICHI, WE'VE GOT 40 MINUTES UNTIL WE'RE ONSTAGE...
ZSH

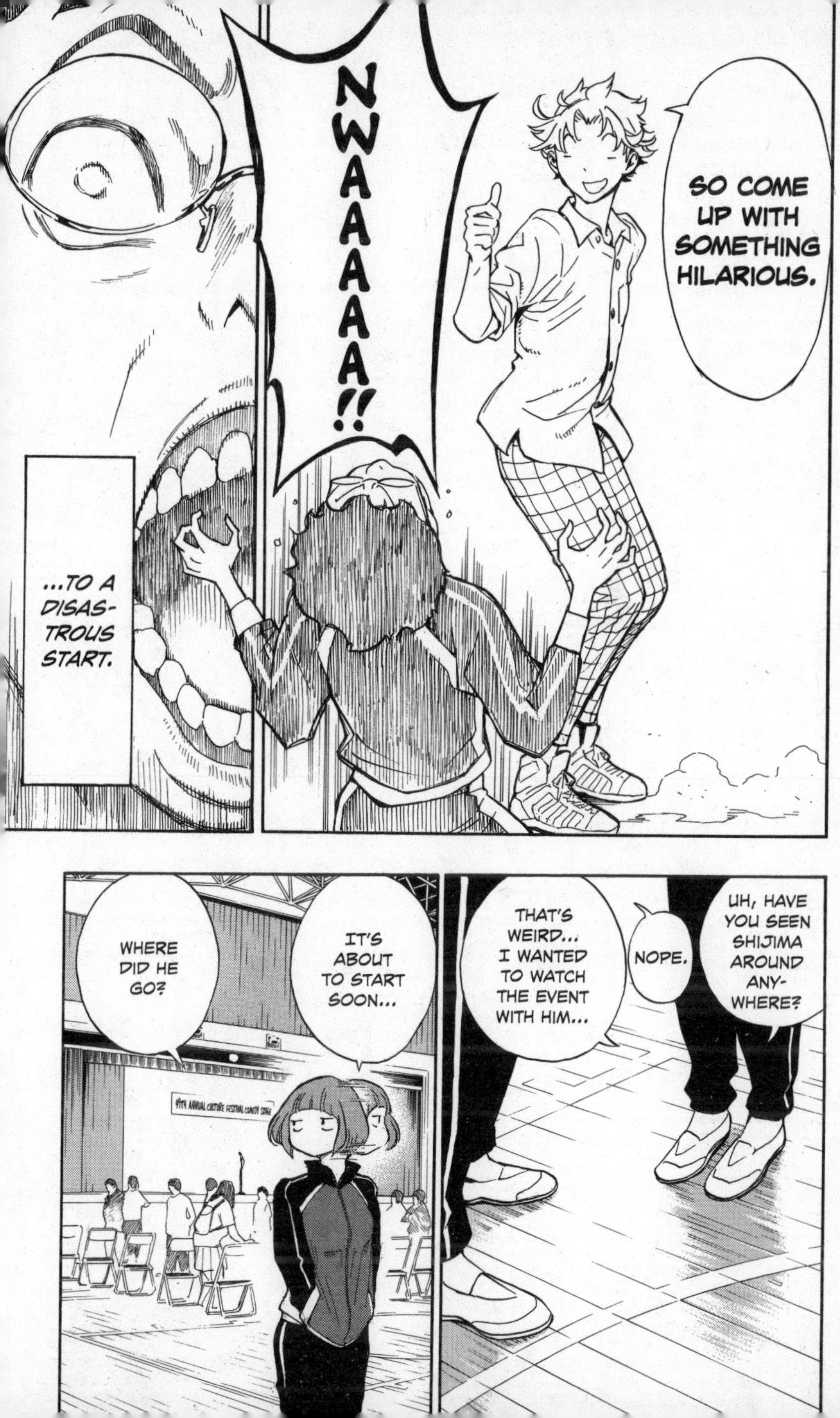
SO COME UP WITH SOMETHING HILARIOUS.
NWAAAAAA!!
...TO A DISASTROUS START.
UH, HAVE YOU SEEN SHIJIMA AROUND ANYWHERE?
NOPE.
THAT'S WEIRD... I WANTED TO WATCH THE EVENT WITH HIM...
IT'S ABOUT TO START SOON...
WHERE DID HE GO?

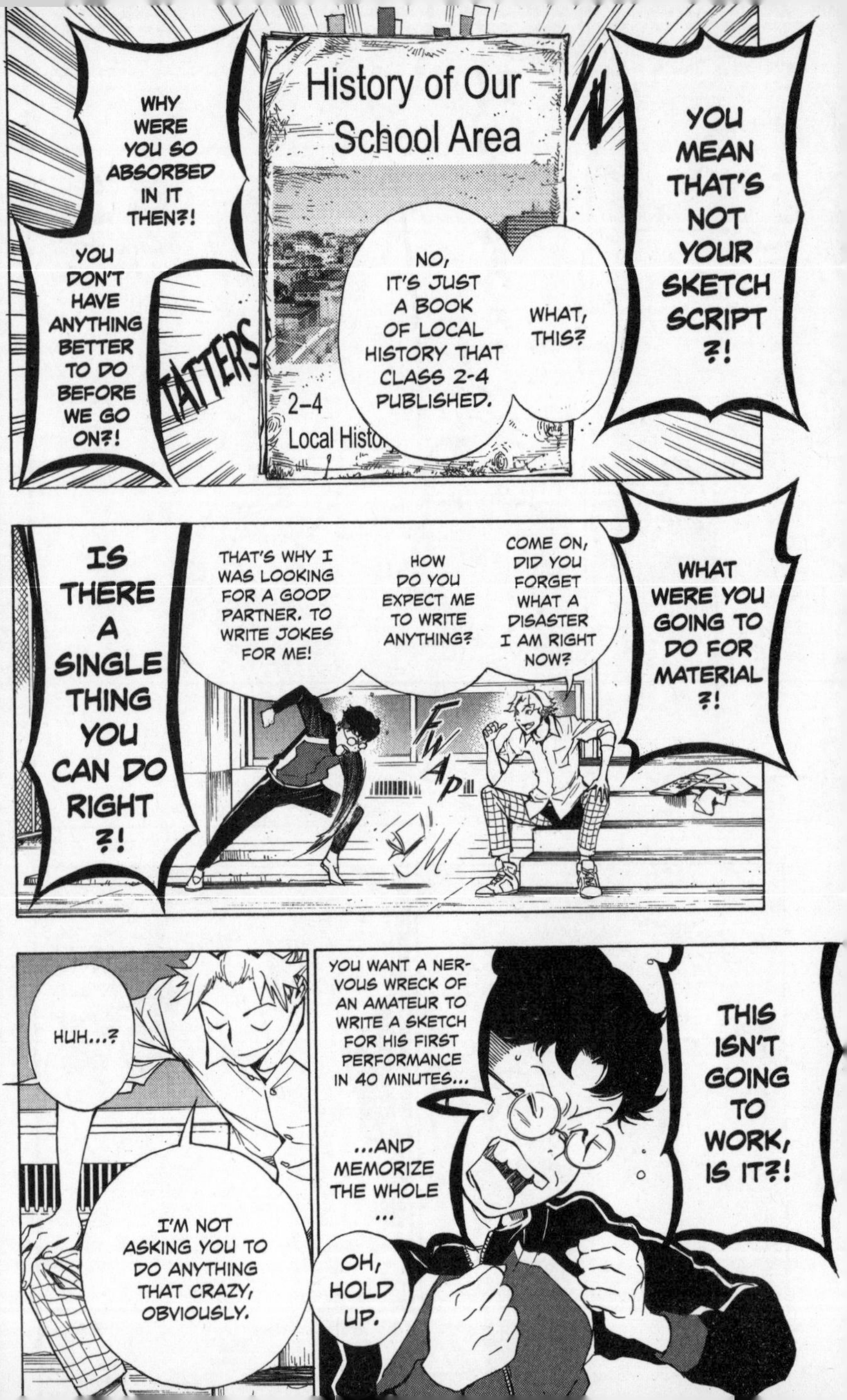
YOU MEAN THAT'S NOT YOUR SKETCH SCRIPT?!
WHAT, THIS?
NO, IT'S JUST A BOOK OF LOCAL HISTORY THAT CLASS 2-4 PUBLISHED.
History of Our School Area
2-4
Local Histor
TATTERS
WHY WERE YOU SO ABSORBED IN IT THEN?!
YOU DON'T HAVE ANYTHING BETTER TO DO BEFORE WE GO ON?!
WHAT WERE YOU GOING TO DO FOR MATERIAL?!
COME ON, DID YOU FORGET WHAT A DISASTER I AM RIGHT NOW?
HOW DO YOU EXPECT ME TO WRITE ANYTHING?
THAT'S WHY I WAS LOOKING FOR A GOOD PARTNER. TO WRITE JOKES FOR ME!
IS THERE A SINGLE THING YOU CAN DO RIGHT?!
FWAP
THIS ISN'T GOING TO WORK, IS IT?!
YOU WANT A NER-VOUS WRECK OF AN AMATEUR TO WRITE A SKETCH FOR HIS FIRST PERFORMANCE IN 40 MINUTES...
...AND MEMORIZE THE WHOLE ...
OH, HOLD UP.
HUH...?
I'M NOT ASKING YOU TO DO ANYTHING THAT CRAZY, OBVIOUSLY.

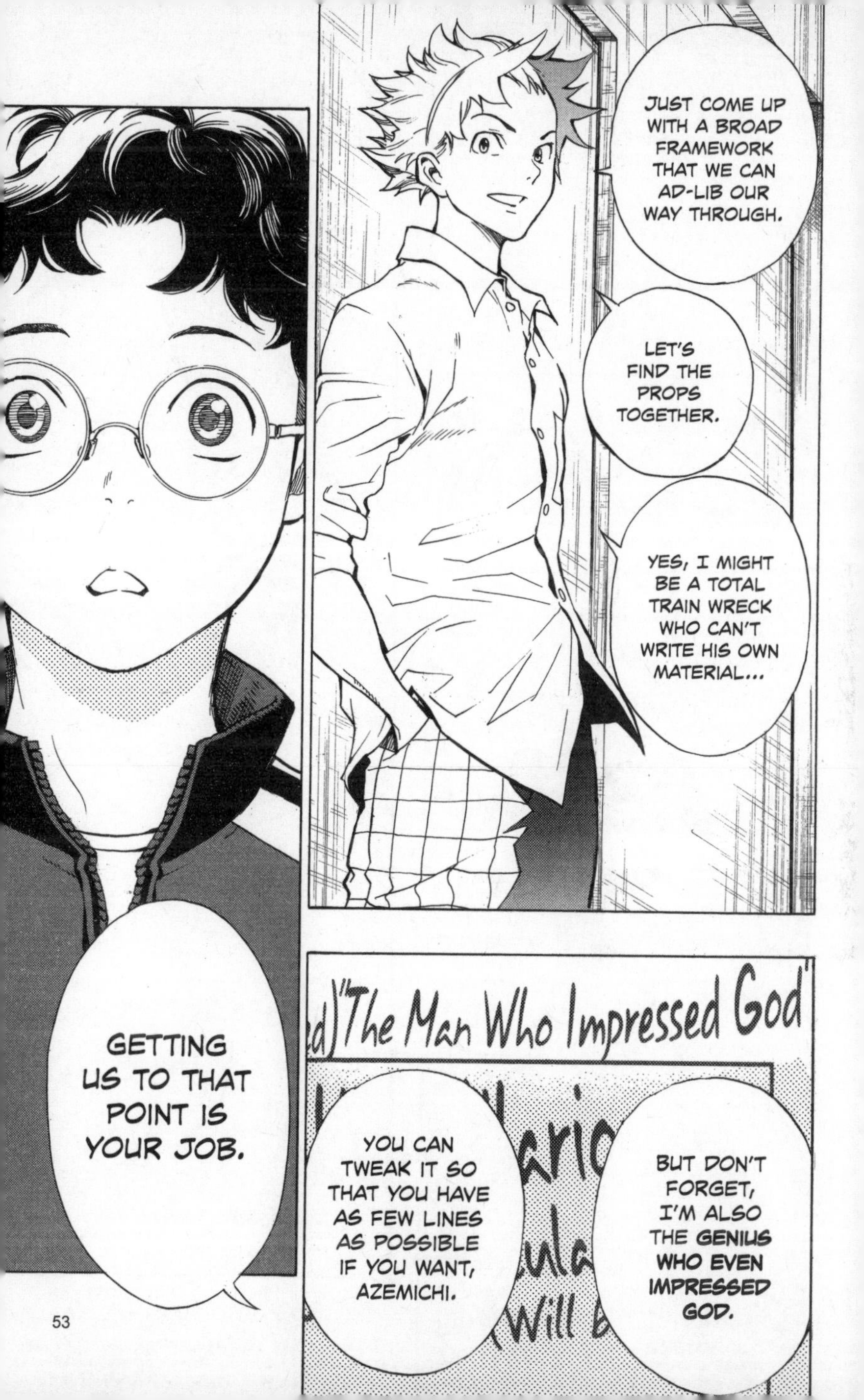
JUST COME UP WITH A BROAD FRAMEWORK THAT WE CAN AD-LIB OUR WAY THROUGH.
LET'S FIND THE PROPS TOGETHER.
YES, I MIGHT BE A TOTAL TRAIN WRECK WHO CAN'T WRITE HIS OWN MATERIAL...
"The Man Who Impressed God"
BUT DON'T FORGET, I'M ALSO THE GENIUS WHO EVEN IMPRESSED GOD.
YOU CAN TWEAK IT SO THAT YOU HAVE AS FEW LINES AS POSSIBLE IF YOU WANT, AZEMICHI.
GETTING US TO THAT POINT IS YOUR JOB.

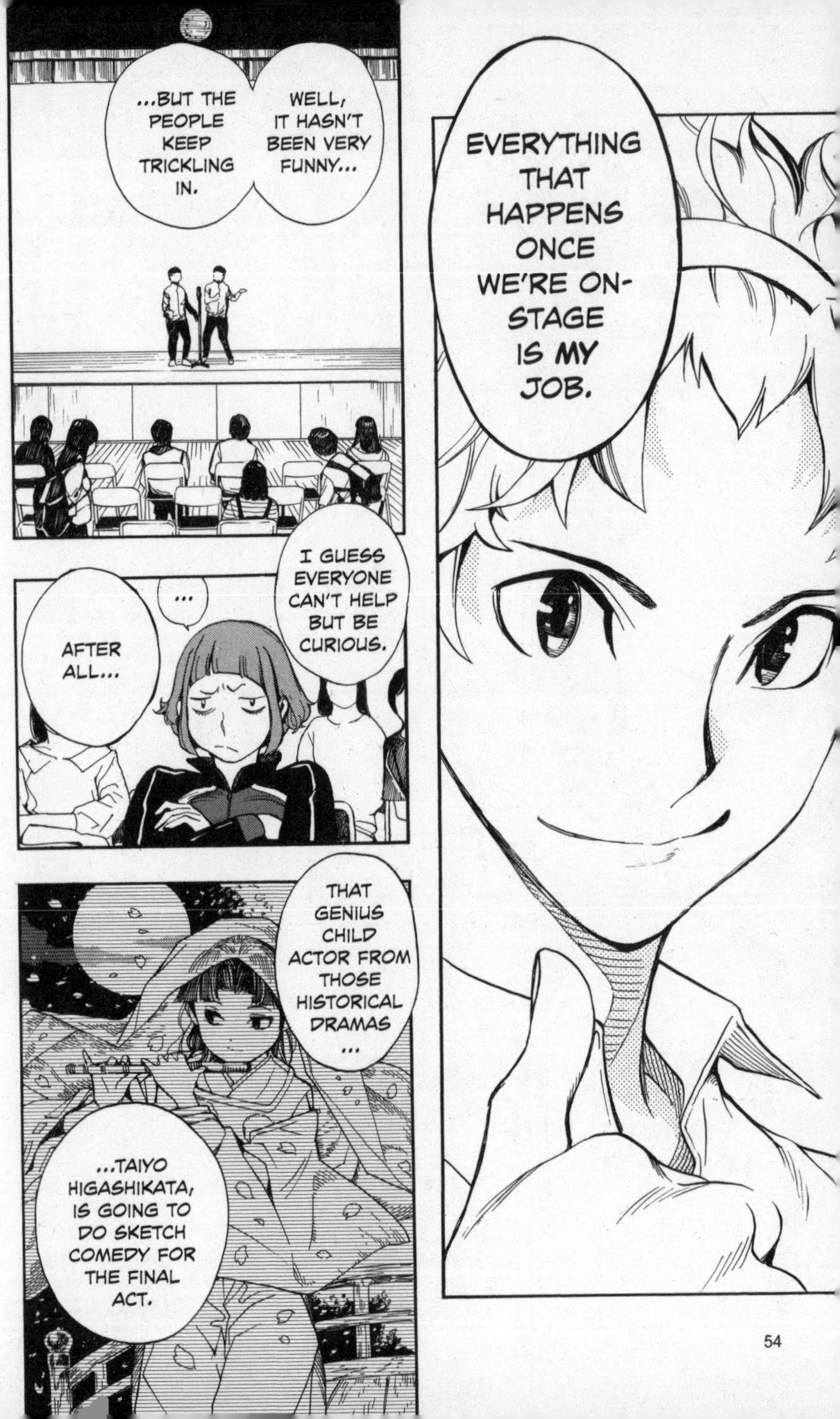
EVERYTHING THAT HAPPENS ONCE WE'RE ON-STAGE IS MY JOB.
WELL, IT HASN'T BEEN VERY FUNNY...
...BUT THE PEOPLE KEEP TRICKLING IN.
I GUESS EVERYONE CAN'T HELP BUT BE CURIOUS.
...
AFTER ALL...
THAT GENIUS CHILD ACTOR FROM THOSE HISTORICAL DRAMAS ...
...TAIYO HIGASHIKATA, IS GOING TO DO SKETCH COMEDY FOR THE FINAL ACT.

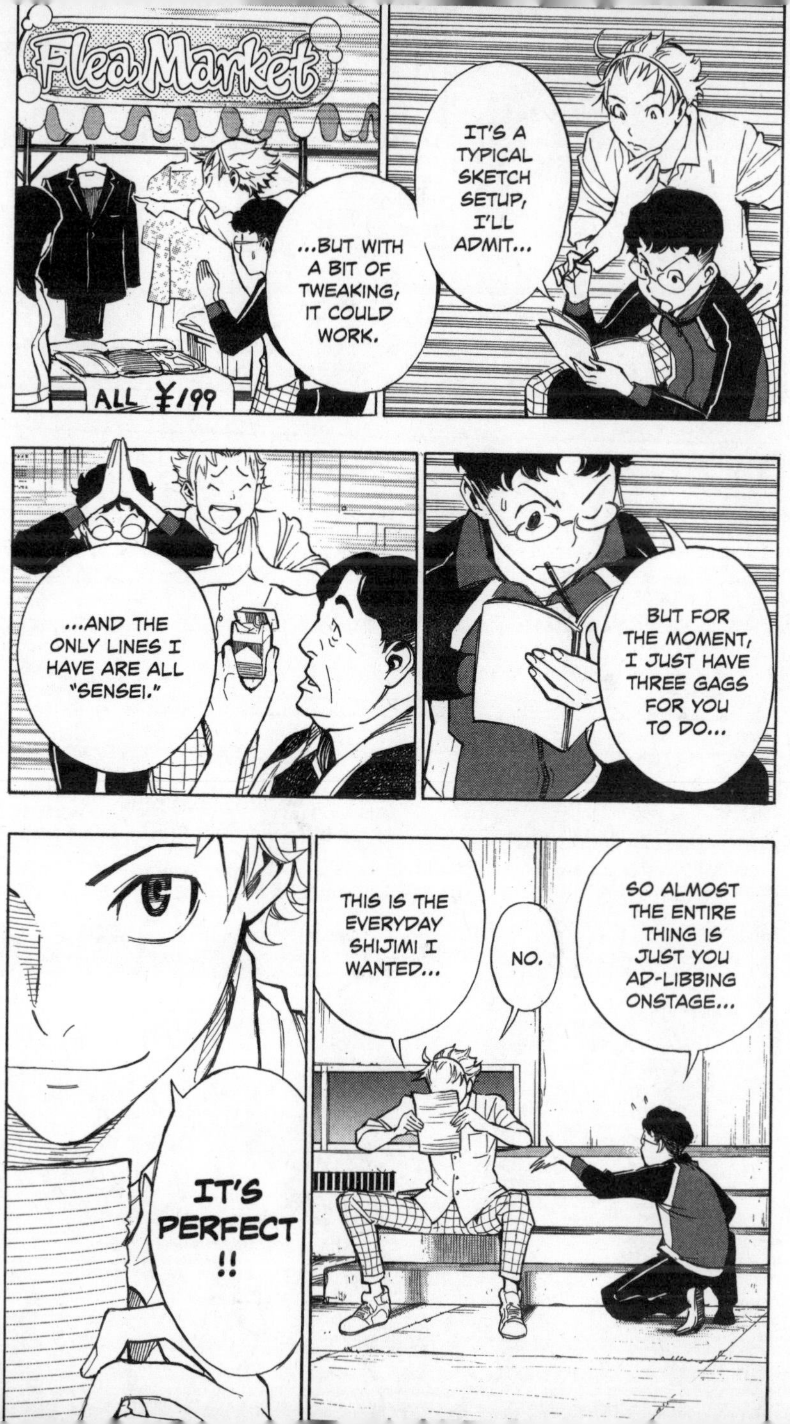
IT'S A TYPICAL SKETCH SETUP, I'LL ADMIT...
Flea Market
...BUT WITH A BIT OF TWEAKING, IT COULD WORK.
ALL ¥199
BUT FOR THE MOMENT, I JUST HAVE THREE GAGS FOR YOU TO DO...
...AND THE ONLY LINES I HAVE ARE ALL "SENSEI."
SO ALMOST THE ENTIRE THING IS JUST YOU AD-LIBBING ONSTAGE...
NO.
THIS IS THE EVERYDAY SHIJIMI I WANTED...
IT'S PERFECT!!

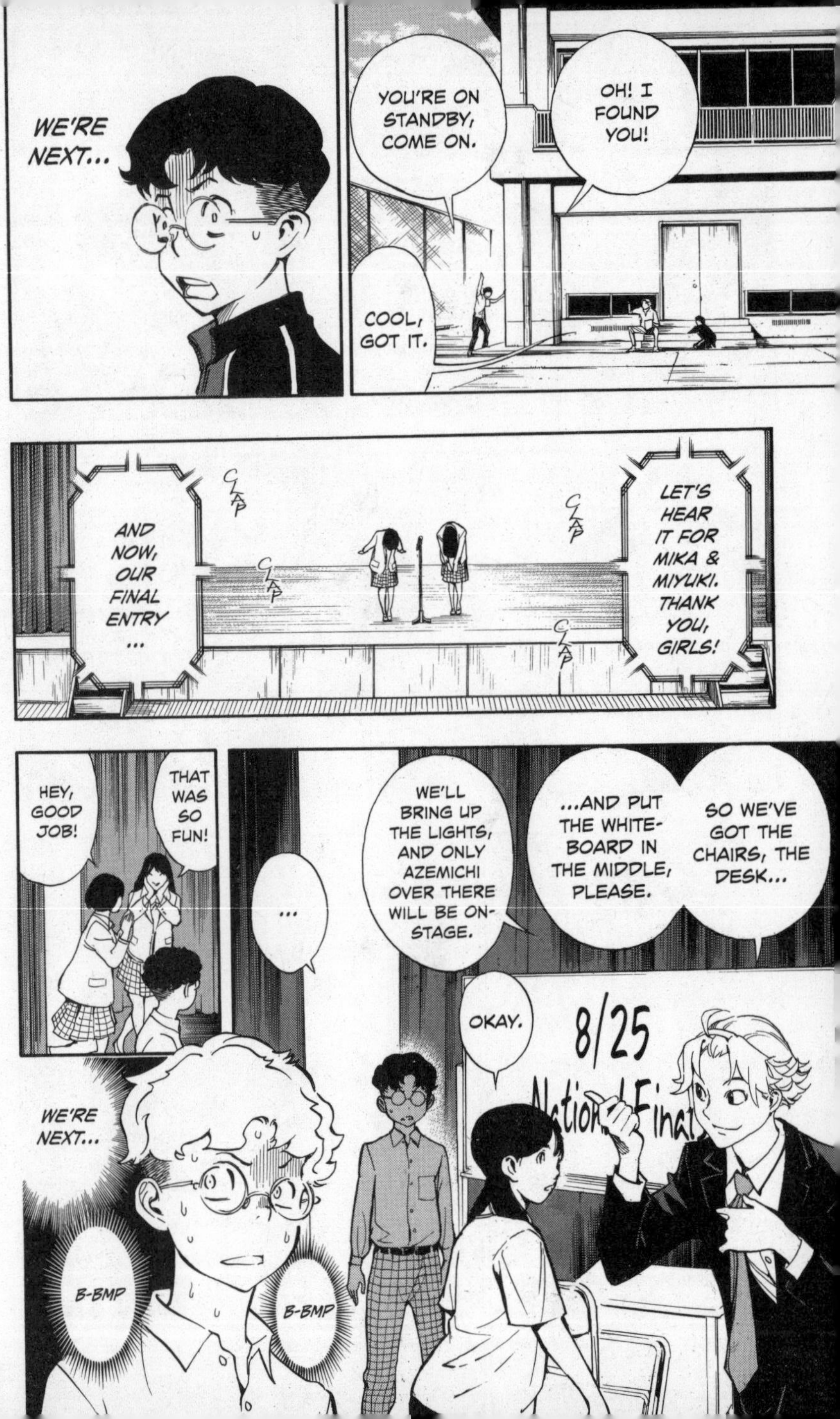
OH! I FOUND YOU!
YOU'RE ON STANDBY, COME ON.
COOL, GOT IT.
WE'RE NEXT...
LET'S HEAR IT FOR MIKA & MIYUKI. THANK YOU, GIRLS!
CLAP
CLAP
CLAP
CLAP
AND NOW, OUR FINAL ENTRY ...
SO WE'VE GOT THE CHAIRS, THE DESK...
...AND PUT THE WHITE-BOARD IN THE MIDDLE, PLEASE.
WE'LL BRING UP THE LIGHTS, AND ONLY AZEMICHI OVER THERE WILL BE ON-STAGE.
...
OKAY.
8/25
THAT WAS SO FUN!
HEY, GOOD JOB!
WE'RE NEXT...
B-BMP
B-BMP

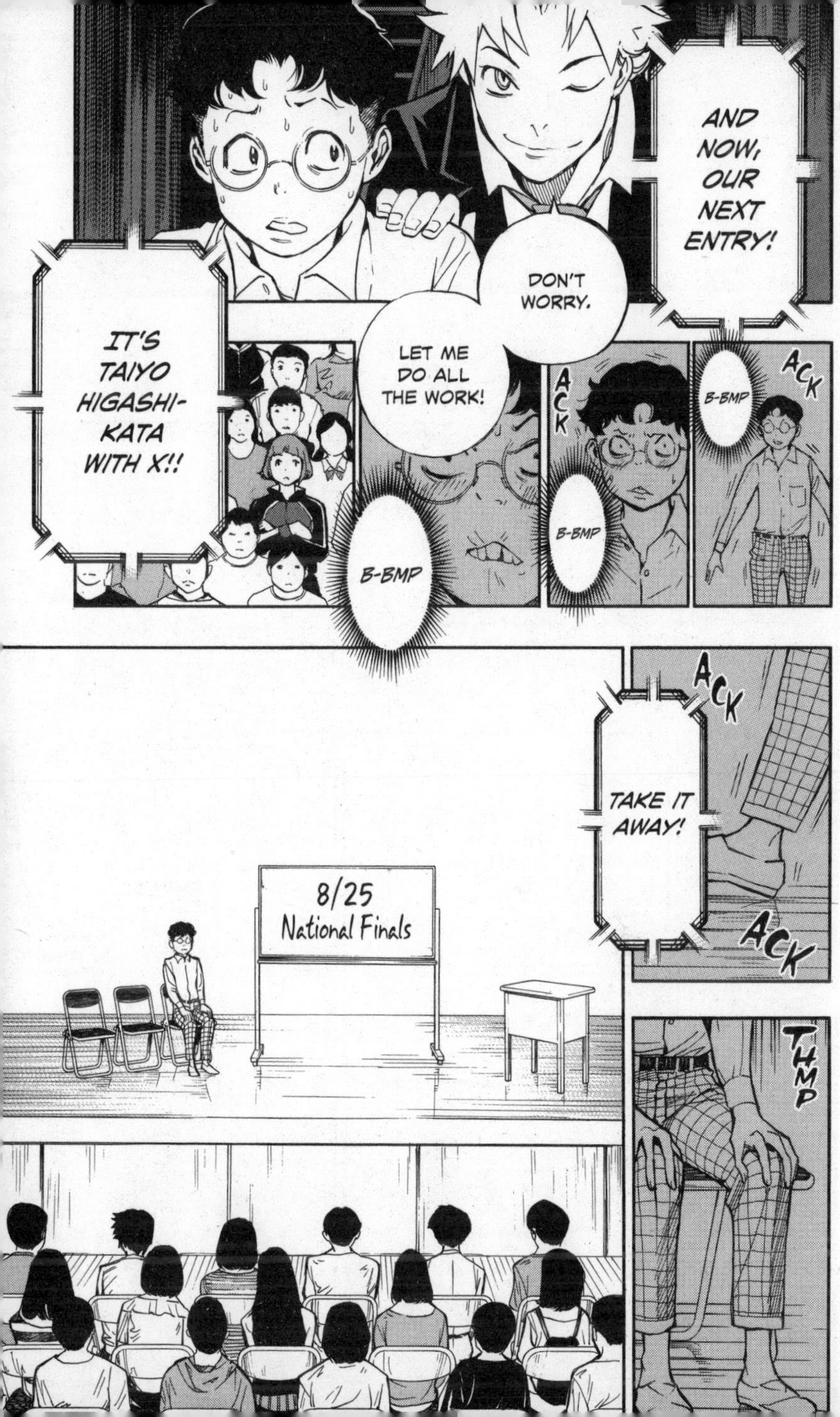
AND NOW, OUR NEXT ENTRY!
DON'T WORRY.
LET ME DO ALL THE WORK!
IT'S TAIYO HIGASHI-KATA WITH X!!
ACK
B-BMP
ACK
B-BMP
B-BMP
ACK
TAKE IT AWAY!
ACK
THMP
8/25
National Finals

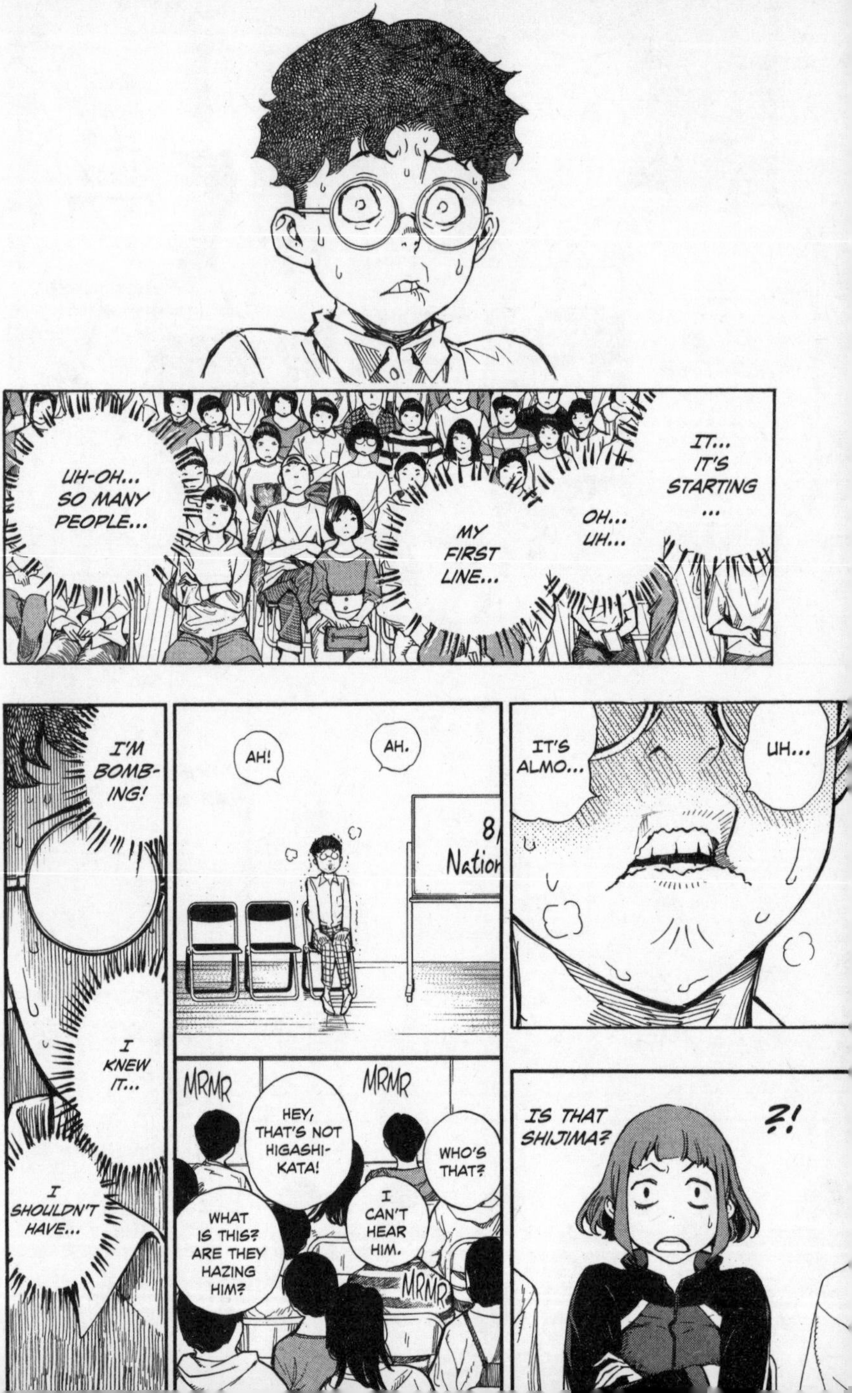
IT... IT'S STARTING ...
OH... UH...
MY FIRST LINE...
UH-OH... SO MANY PEOPLE...
UH...
IT'S ALMO...
AH.
AH!
8/ Nation
?!
IS THAT SHIJIMA?
MRMR
WHO'S THAT?
HEY, THAT'S NOT HIGASHI-KATA!
MRMR
I CAN'T HEAR HIM.
WHAT IS THIS? ARE THEY HAZING HIM?
MRMR
I'M BOMB-ING!
I KNEW IT...
I SHOULDN'T HAVE...

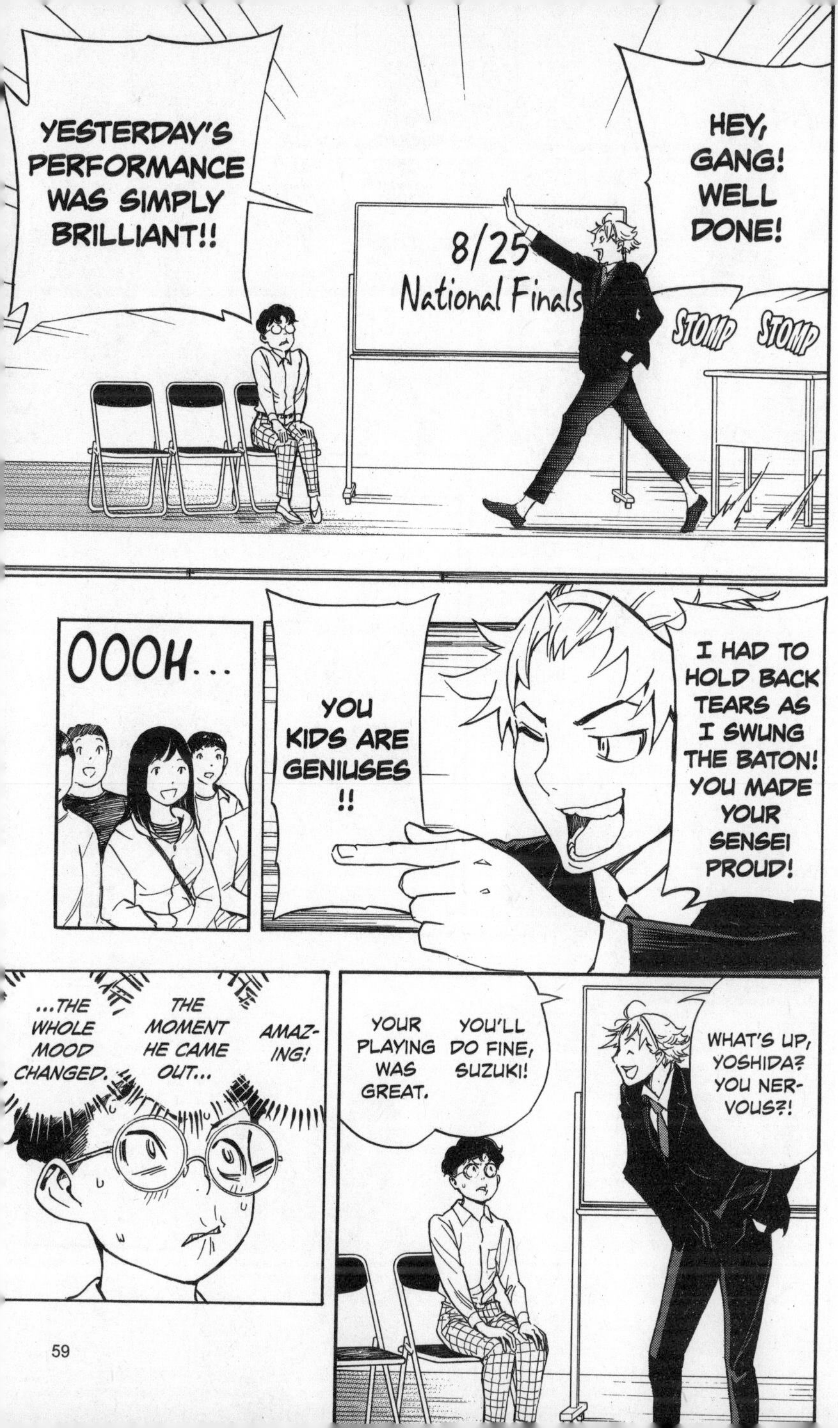
HEY, GANG! WELL DONE!
YESTERDAY'S PERFORMANCE WAS SIMPLY BRILLIANT!!
8/25 National Finals
STOMP STOMP
I HAD TO HOLD BACK TEARS AS I SWUNG THE BATON! YOU MADE YOUR SENSEI PROUD!
YOU KIDS ARE GENIUSES!!
OOOH...
WHAT'S UP, YOSHIDA? YOU NERVOUS?!
YOU'LL DO FINE, SUZUKI!
YOUR PLAYING WAS GREAT.
AMAZING!
THE MOMENT HE CAME OUT...
...THE WHOLE MOOD CHANGED.

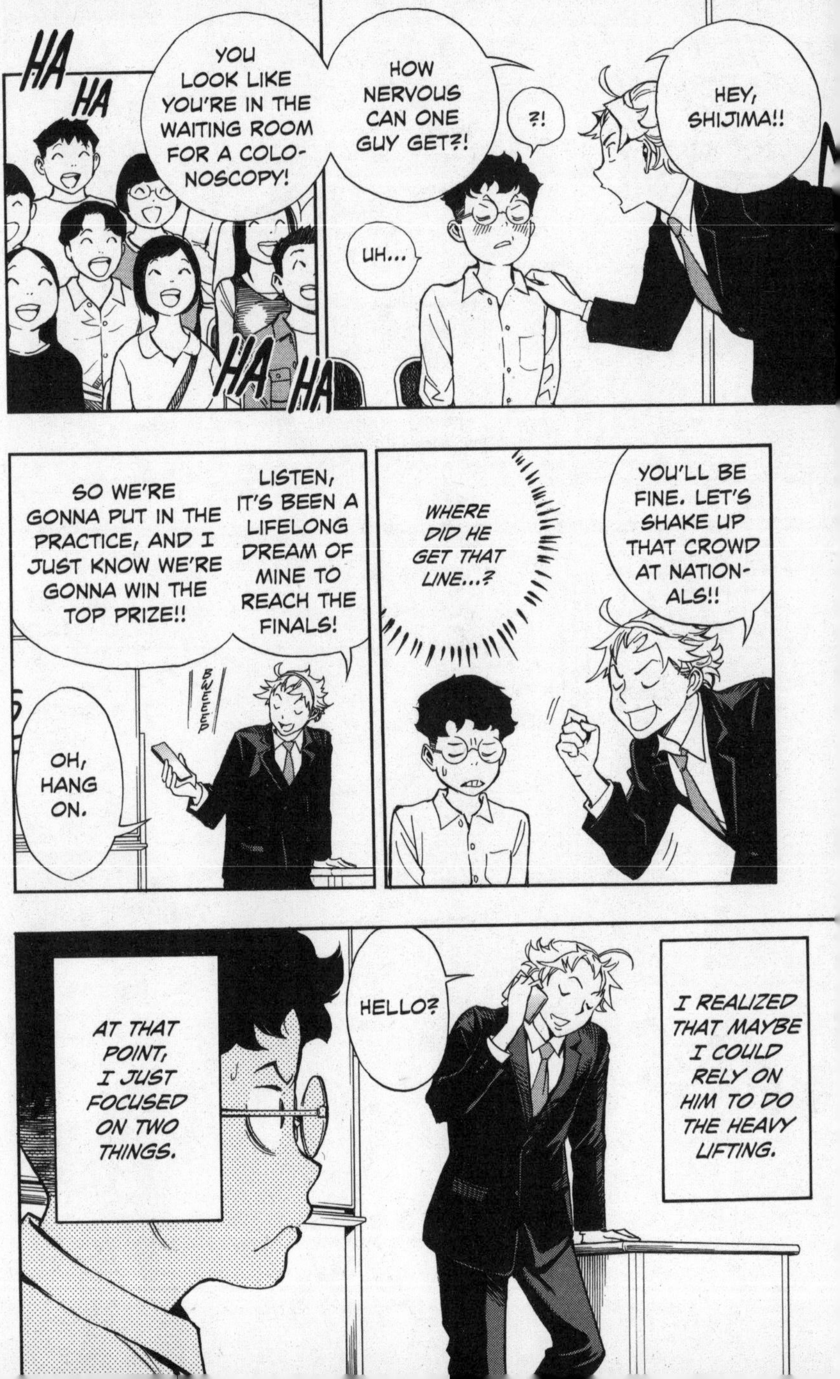
HEY, SHIJIMA!!
?!
HOW NERVOUS CAN ONE GUY GET?!
UH...
YOU LOOK LIKE YOU'RE IN THE WAITING ROOM FOR A COLO-NOSCOPY!
HA HA
HA HA
YOU'LL BE FINE. LET'S SHAKE UP THAT CROWD AT NATION-ALS!!
WHERE DID HE GET THAT LINE...?
LISTEN, IT'S BEEN A LIFELONG DREAM OF MINE TO REACH THE FINALS!
SO WE'RE GONNA PUT IN THE PRACTICE, AND I JUST KNOW WE'RE GONNA WIN THE TOP PRIZE!!
BWEEEP
OH, HANG ON.
I REALIZED THAT MAYBE I COULD RELY ON HIM TO DO THE HEAVY LIFTING.
HELLO?
AT THAT POINT, I JUST FOCUSED ON TWO THINGS.

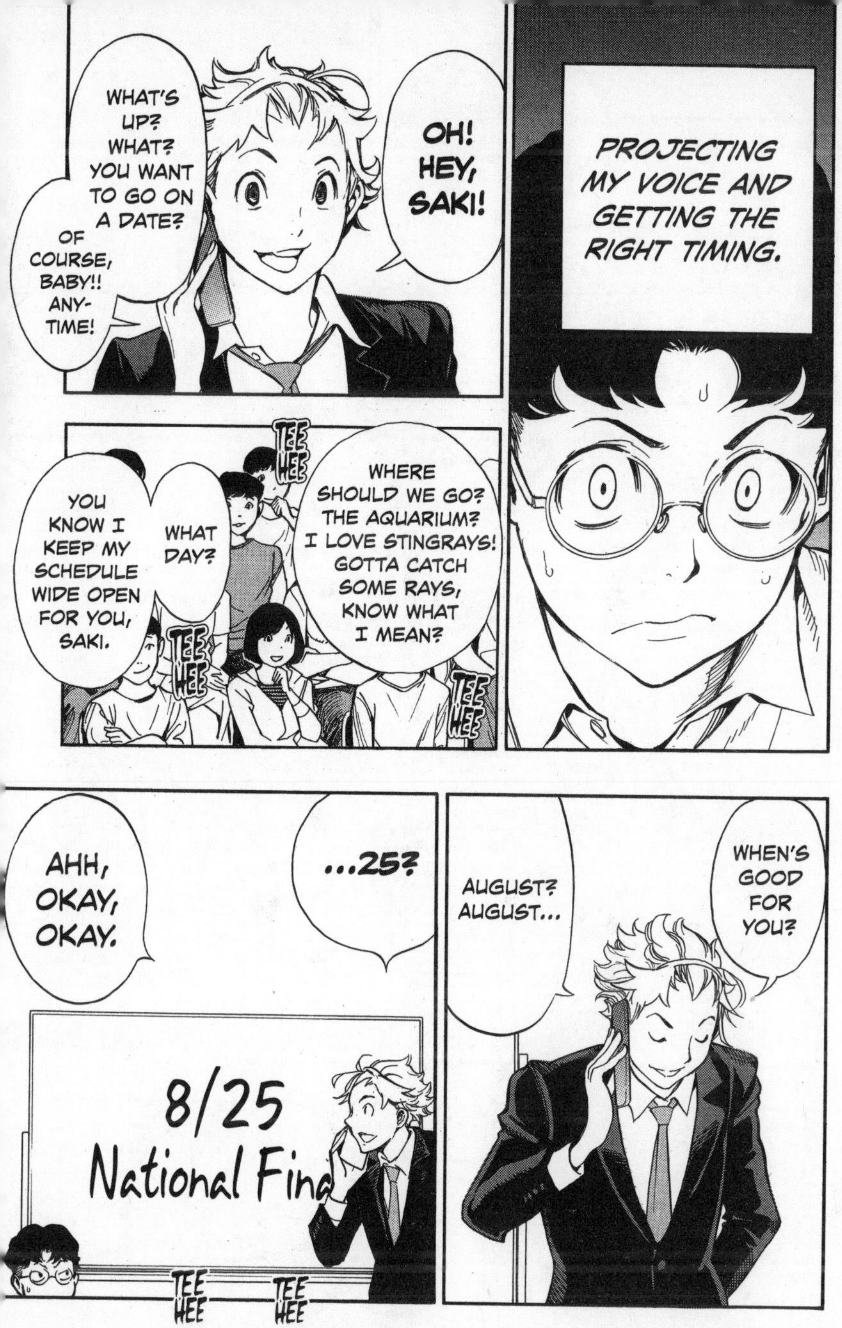
PROJECTING MY VOICE AND GETTING THE RIGHT TIMING.
OH! HEY, SAKI!
WHAT'S UP? WHAT? YOU WANT TO GO ON A DATE?
OF COURSE, BABY!! ANY-TIME!
TEE HEE
WHERE SHOULD WE GO? THE AQUARIUM? I LOVE STINGRAYS! GOTTA CATCH SOME RAYS, KNOW WHAT I MEAN?
WHAT DAY?
YOU KNOW I KEEP MY SCHEDULE WIDE OPEN FOR YOU, SAKI.
TEE HEE
TEE HEE
WHEN'S GOOD FOR YOU?
AUGUST? AUGUST...
...25?
AHH, OKAY, OKAY.
8/25
National Fina
TEE HEE
TEE HEE

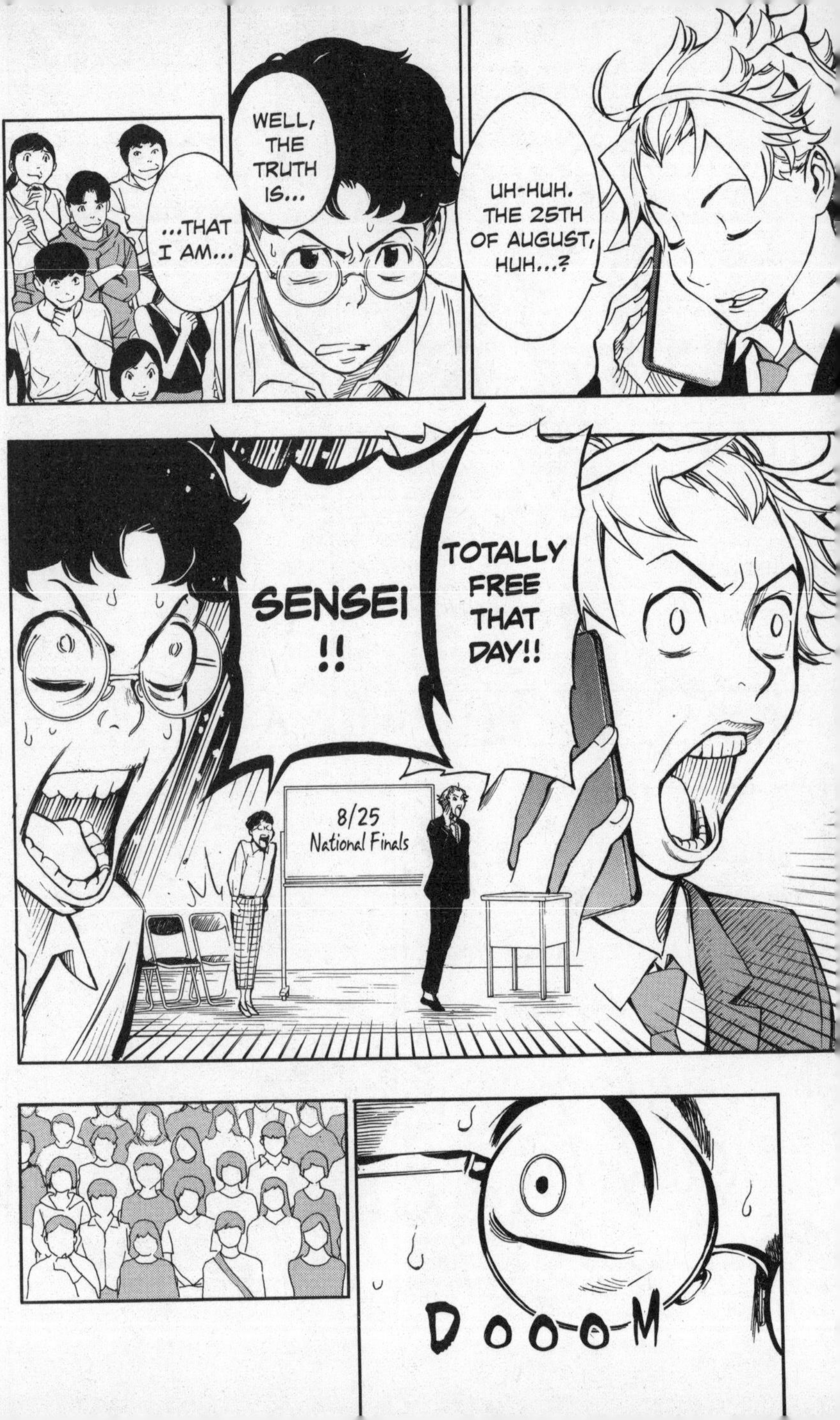
UH-HUH. THE 25TH OF AUGUST, HUH...?
WELL, THE TRUTH IS...
...THAT I AM...
TOTALLY FREE THAT DAY!!
SENSEI!!
8/25 National Finals
DOOOM

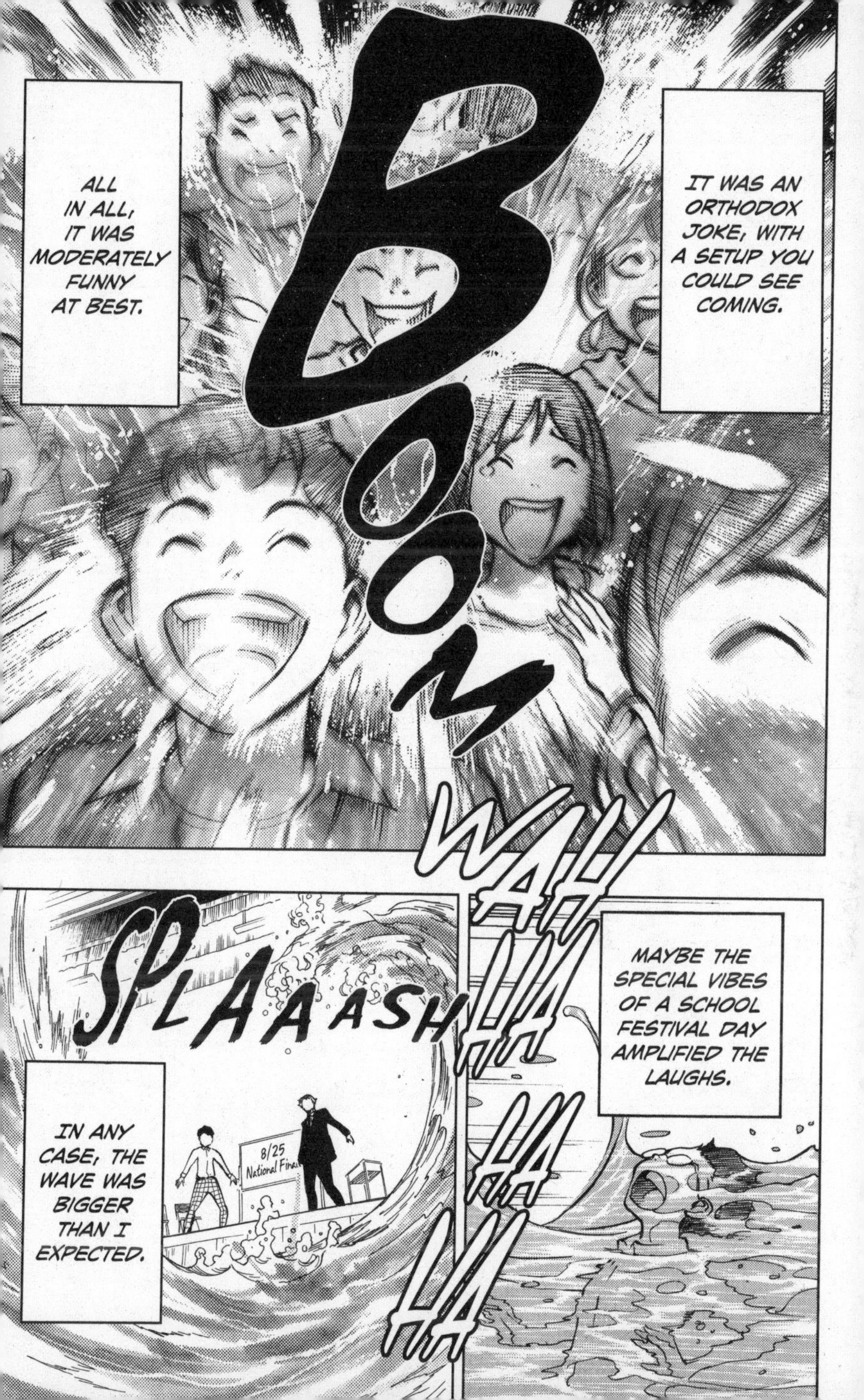
IT WAS AN ORTHODOX JOKE, WITH A SETUP YOU COULD SEE COMING.
BOOM
ALL IN ALL, IT WAS MODERATELY FUNNY AT BEST.
WAH HA HA HA HA
MAYBE THE SPECIAL VIBES OF A SCHOOL FESTIVAL DAY AMPLIFIED THE LAUGHS.
SPLAAASH
IN ANY CASE, THE WAVE WAS BIGGER THAN I EXPECTED.
8/25
National Final

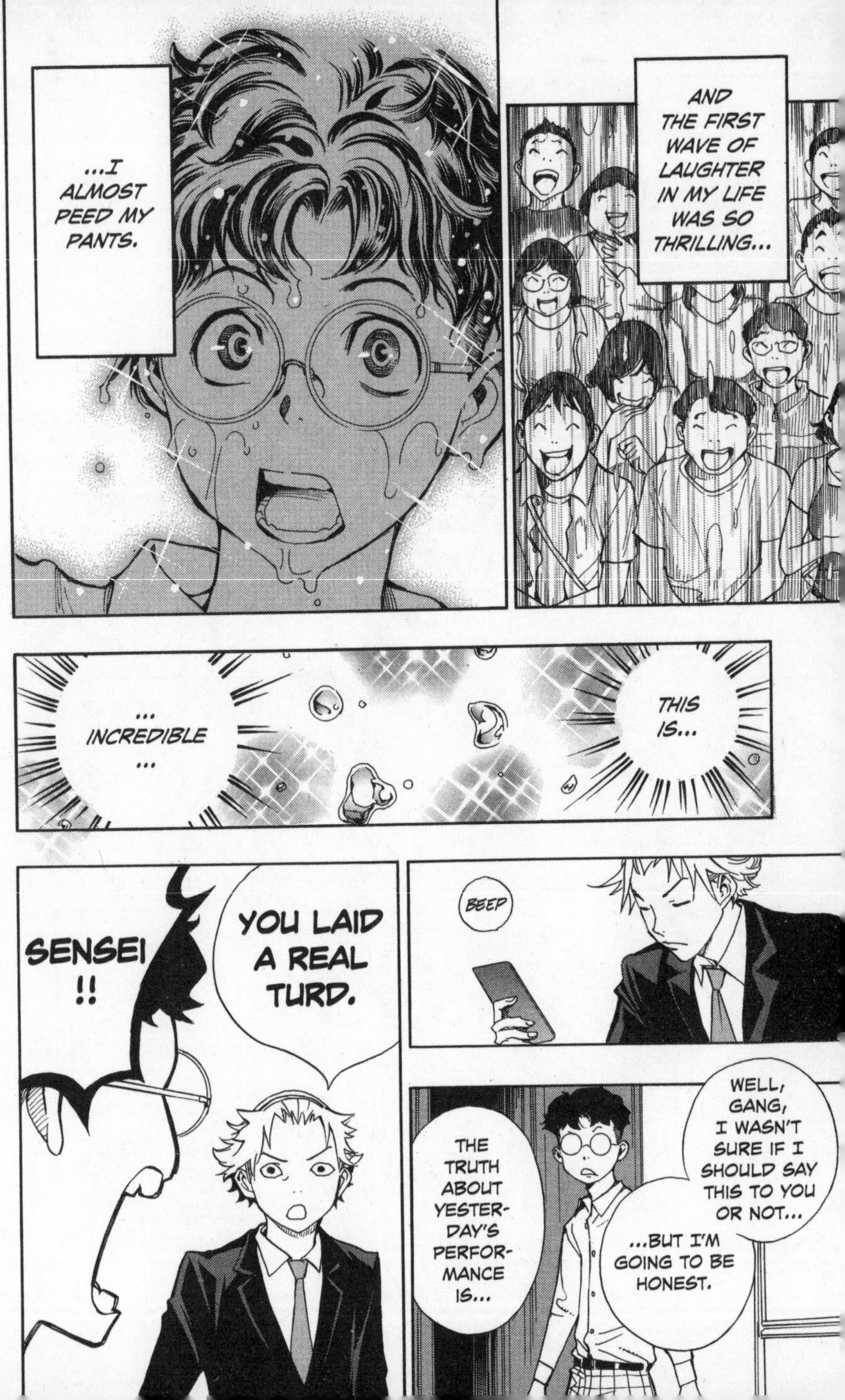
AND THE FIRST WAVE OF LAUGHTER IN MY LIFE WAS SO THRILLING...
...I ALMOST PEED MY PANTS.
THIS IS...
...INCREDIBLE...
BEEP
WELL, GANG, I WASN'T SURE IF I SHOULD SAY THIS TO YOU OR NOT...
...BUT I'M GOING TO BE HONEST.
THE TRUTH ABOUT YESTER-DAY'S PERFOR-MANCE IS...
YOU LAID A REAL TURD.
SENSEI!!

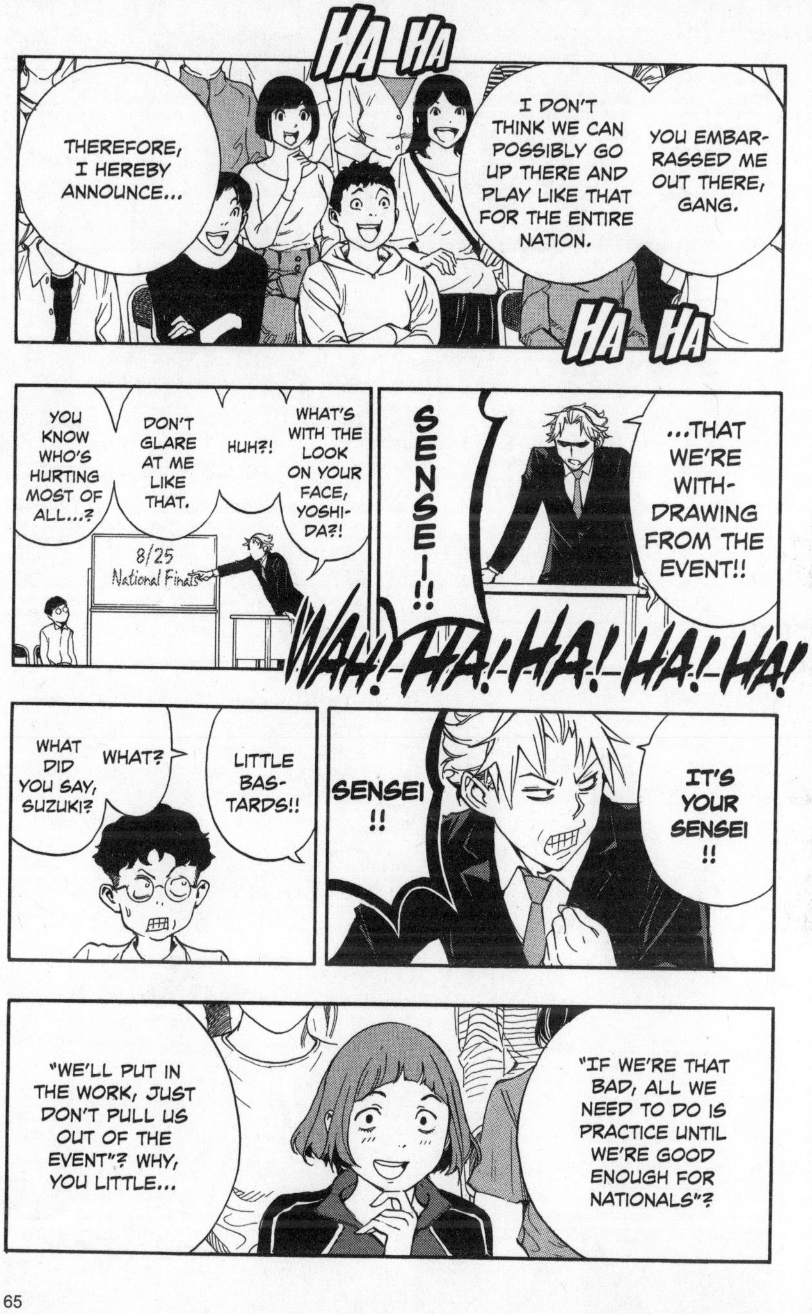
HA HA
YOU EMBARRASSED ME OUT THERE, GANG.
I DON'T THINK WE CAN POSSIBLY GO UP THERE AND PLAY LIKE THAT FOR THE ENTIRE NATION.
THEREFORE, I HEREBY ANNOUNCE...
HA HA
...THAT WE'RE WITHDRAWING FROM THE EVENT!!
SENSEI!!
WAH! HA! HA! HA! HA!
WHAT'S WITH THE LOOK ON YOUR FACE, YOSHIDA?!
HUH?!
DON'T GLARE AT ME LIKE THAT.
YOU KNOW WHO'S HURTING MOST OF ALL...?
8/25 National Finals
IT'S YOUR SENSEI!!
SENSEI!!
LITTLE BASTARDS!!
WHAT?
WHAT DID YOU SAY, SUZUKI?
"IF WE'RE THAT BAD, ALL WE NEED TO DO IS PRACTICE UNTIL WE'RE GOOD ENOUGH FOR NATIONALS"?
"WE'LL PUT IN THE WORK, JUST DON'T PULL US OUT OF THE EVENT"? WHY, YOU LITTLE...

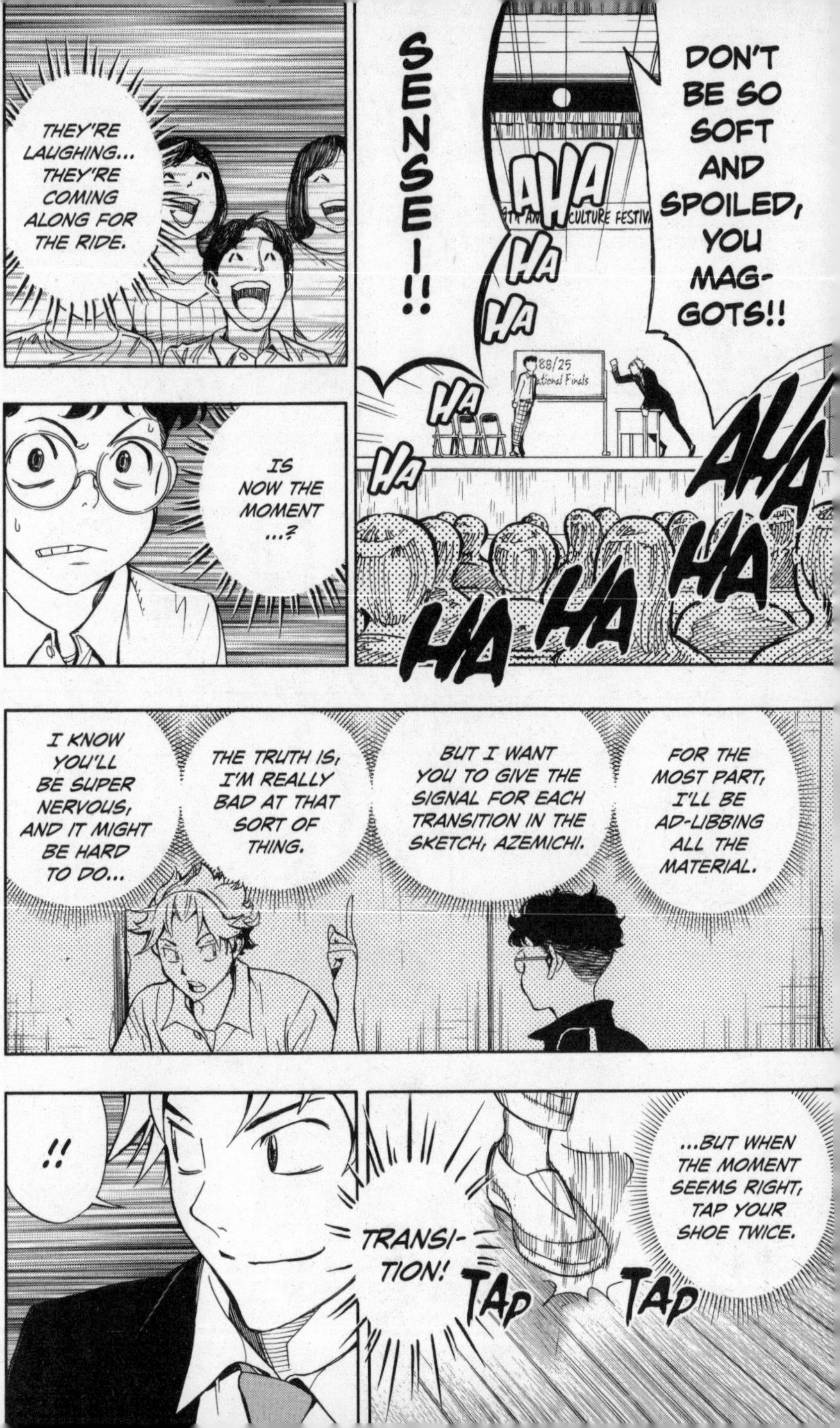
DON'T BE SO SOFT AND SPOILED, YOU MAG-GOTS!!
SENSEI!!
AHA HA HA
HA
HA
AHA HA HA HA HA
THEY'RE LAUGHING... THEY'RE COMING ALONG FOR THE RIDE.
IS NOW THE MOMENT ...?
FOR THE MOST PART, I'LL BE AD-LIBBING ALL THE MATERIAL.
BUT I WANT YOU TO GIVE THE SIGNAL FOR EACH TRANSITION IN THE SKETCH, AZEMICHI.
THE TRUTH IS, I'M REALLY BAD AT THAT SORT OF THING.
I KNOW YOU'LL BE SUPER NERVOUS, AND IT MIGHT BE HARD TO DO...
...BUT WHEN THE MOMENT SEEMS RIGHT, TAP YOUR SHOE TWICE.
TAP
TAP
TRANSI-TION!
!!

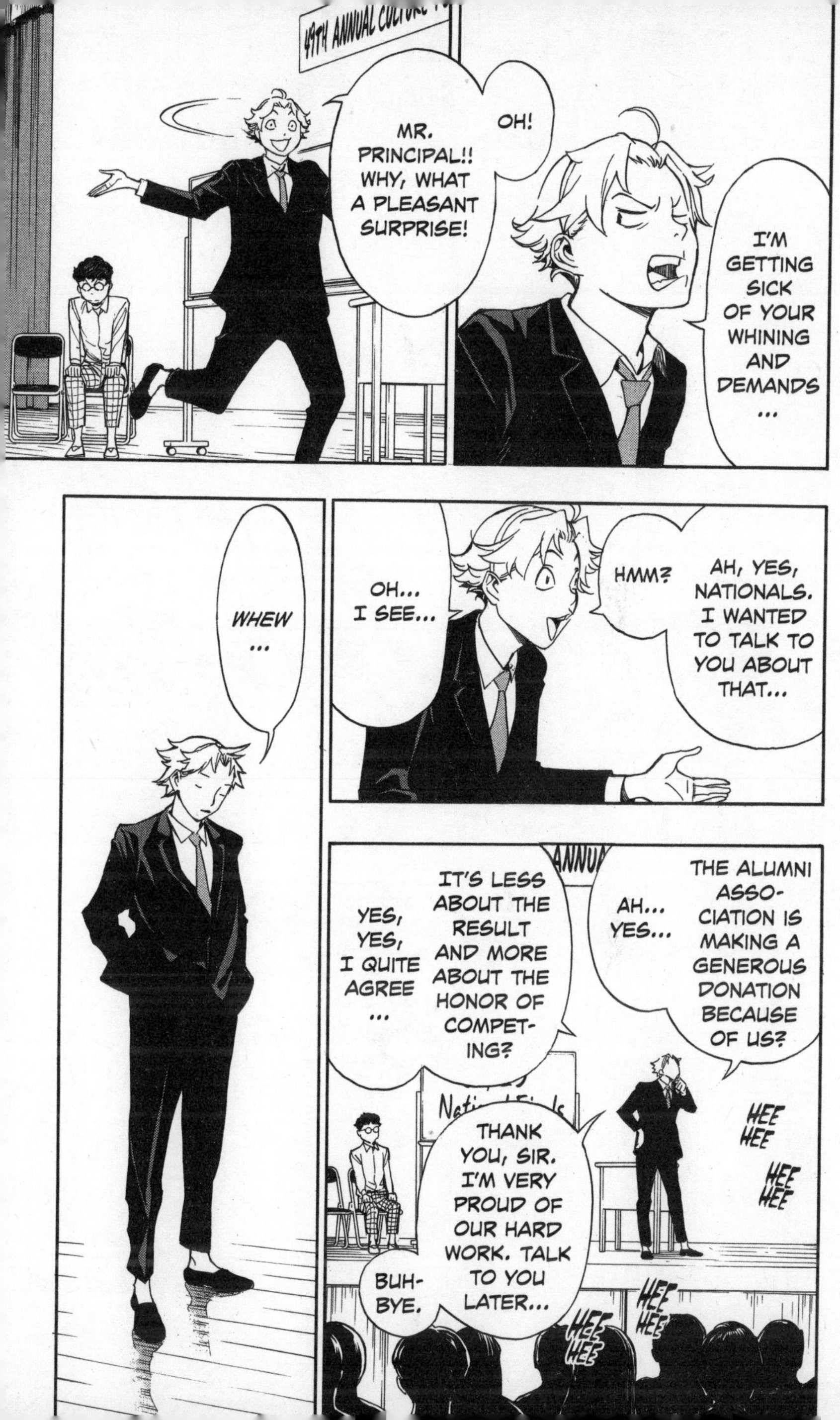
I'M GETTING SICK OF YOUR WHINING AND DEMANDS...
OH!
MR. PRINCIPAL!! WHY, WHAT A PLEASANT SURPRISE!
HMM?
AH, YES, NATIONALS. I WANTED TO TALK TO YOU ABOUT THAT...
OH... I SEE...
THE ALUMNI ASSOCIATION IS MAKING A GENEROUS DONATION BECAUSE OF US?
AH... YES...
IT'S LESS ABOUT THE RESULT AND MORE ABOUT THE HONOR OF COMPETING?
YES, YES, I QUITE AGREE...
HEE HEE
HEE HEE
THANK YOU, SIR. I'M VERY PROUD OF OUR HARD WORK. TALK TO YOU LATER...
BUH-BYE.
HEE HEE
HEE HEE
WHEW...

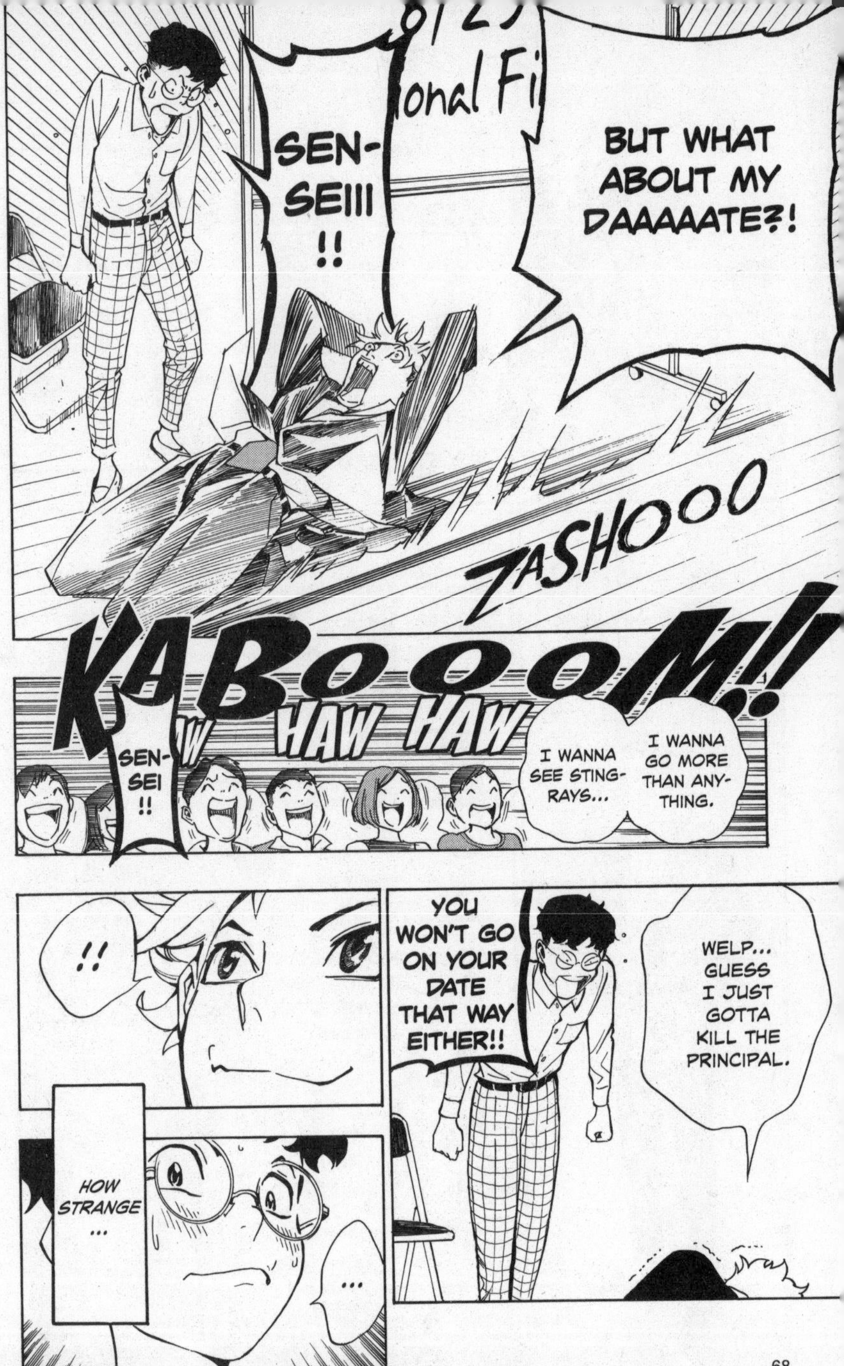
BUT WHAT ABOUT MY DAAAAATE?!
SEN-SEIIII !!
ZASHOOO
KABOOOM!!
I WANNA GO MORE THAN ANY-THING.
I WANNA SEE STING-RAYS...
HAW HAW
SEN-SEI !!
WELP... GUESS I JUST GOTTA KILL THE PRINCIPAL.
YOU WON'T GO ON YOUR DATE THAT WAY EITHER!!
!!
HOW STRANGE ...
...

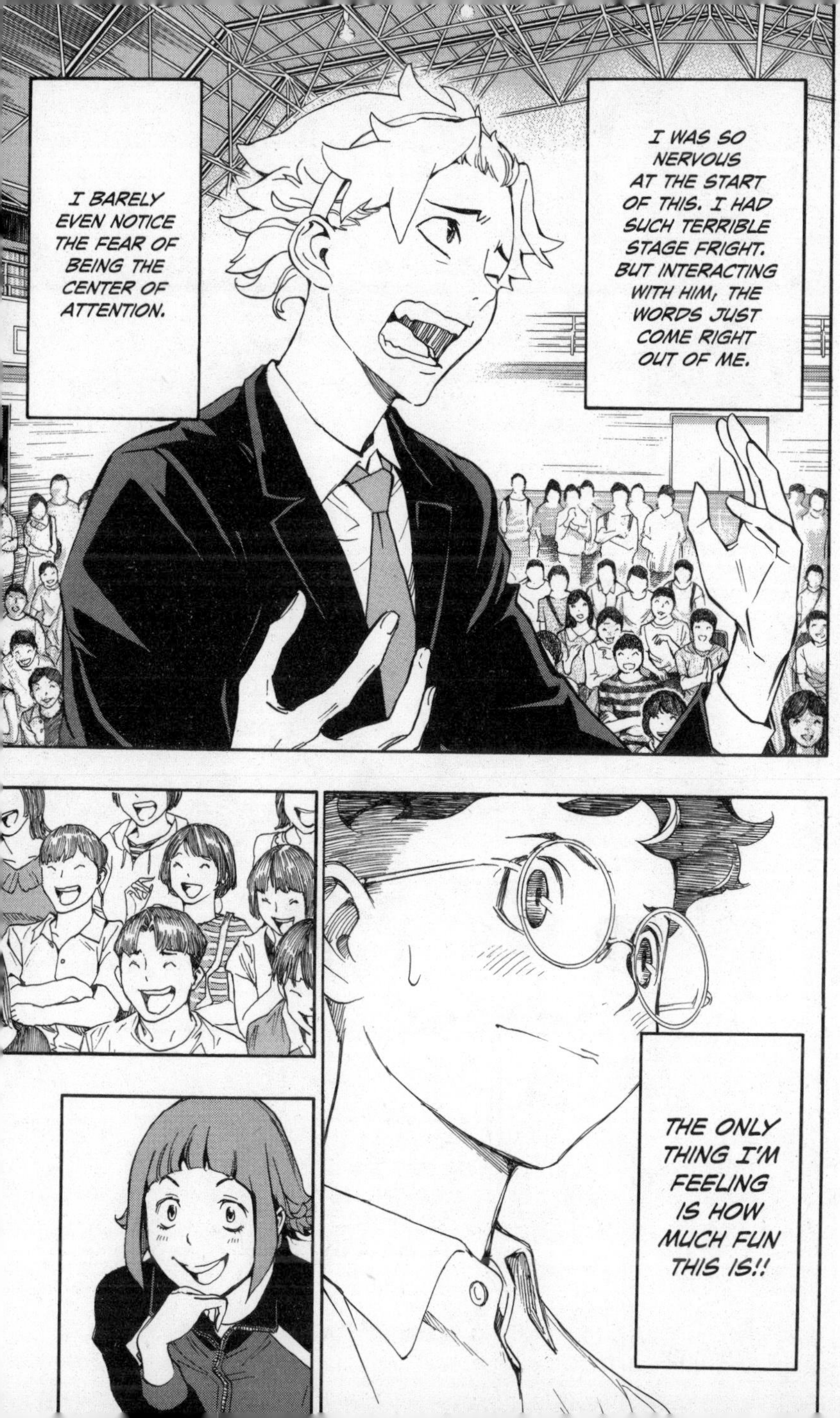
I WAS SO NERVOUS AT THE START OF THIS. I HAD SUCH TERRIBLE STAGE FRIGHT. BUT INTERACTING WITH HIM, THE WORDS JUST COME RIGHT OUT OF ME.
I BARELY EVEN NOTICE THE FEAR OF BEING THE CENTER OF ATTENTION.
THE ONLY THING I'M FEELING IS HOW MUCH FUN THIS IS!!

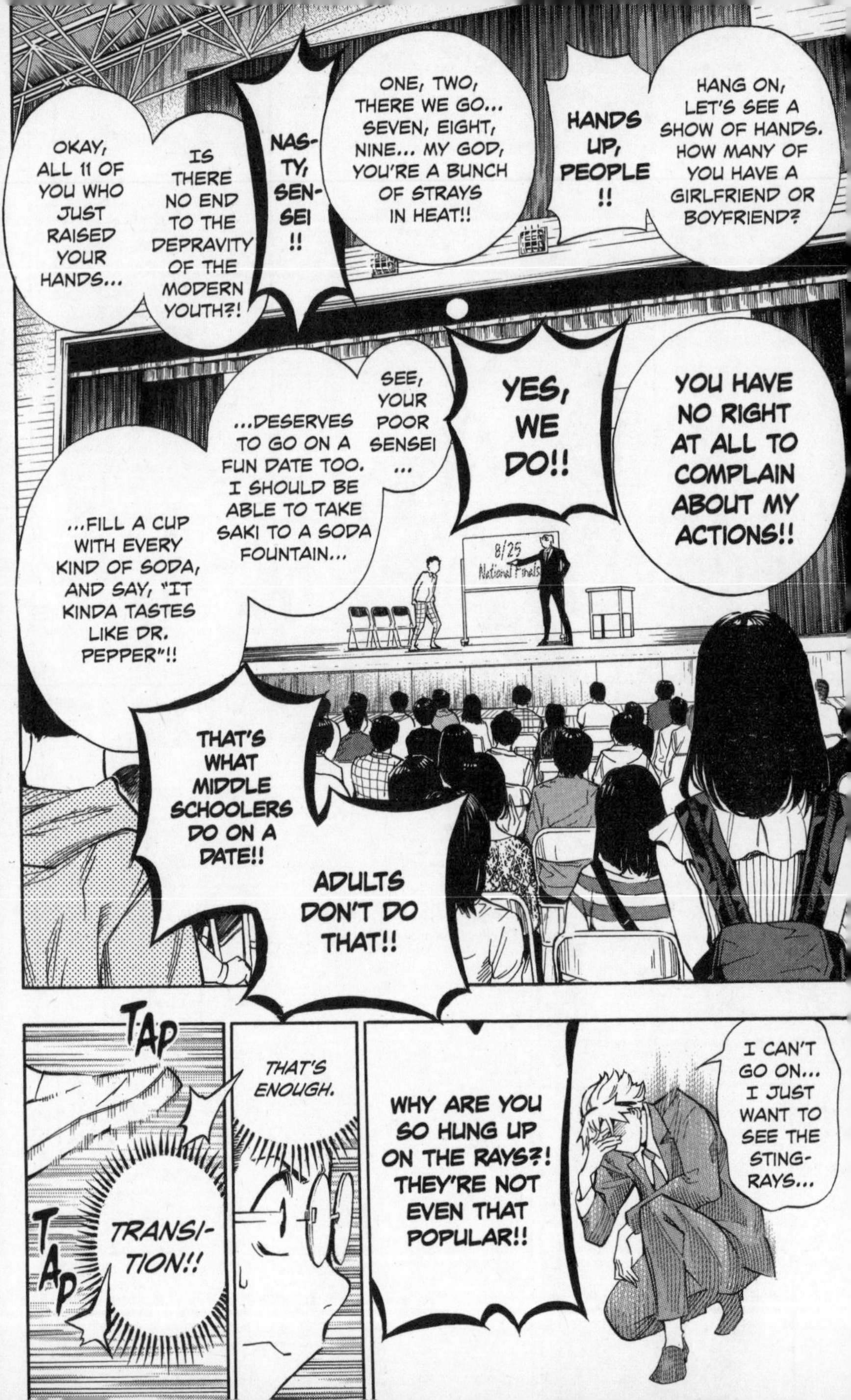
HANG ON, LET'S SEE A SHOW OF HANDS. HOW MANY OF YOU HAVE A GIRLFRIEND OR BOYFRIEND?
HANDS UP, PEOPLE!!
ONE, TWO, THERE WE GO... SEVEN, EIGHT, NINE... MY GOD, YOU'RE A BUNCH OF STRAYS IN HEAT!!
NAS-TY, SEN-SEI!!
IS THERE NO END TO THE DEPRAVITY OF THE MODERN YOUTH?!
OKAY, ALL 11 OF YOU WHO JUST RAISED YOUR HANDS...
YOU HAVE NO RIGHT AT ALL TO COMPLAIN ABOUT MY ACTIONS!!
YES, WE DO!!
SEE, YOUR POOR SENSEI...
...DESERVES TO GO ON A FUN DATE TOO. I SHOULD BE ABLE TO TAKE SAKI TO A SODA FOUNTAIN...
...FILL A CUP WITH EVERY KIND OF SODA, AND SAY, "IT KINDA TASTES LIKE DR. PEPPER"!!
8/25 National Finals
THAT'S WHAT MIDDLE SCHOOLERS DO ON A DATE!!
ADULTS DON'T DO THAT!!
I CAN'T GO ON... I JUST WANT TO SEE THE STING-RAYS...
WHY ARE YOU SO HUNG UP ON THE RAYS?! THEY'RE NOT EVEN THAT POPULAR!!
THAT'S ENOUGH.
TAP
TRANSI-TION!!
TAP
TAP

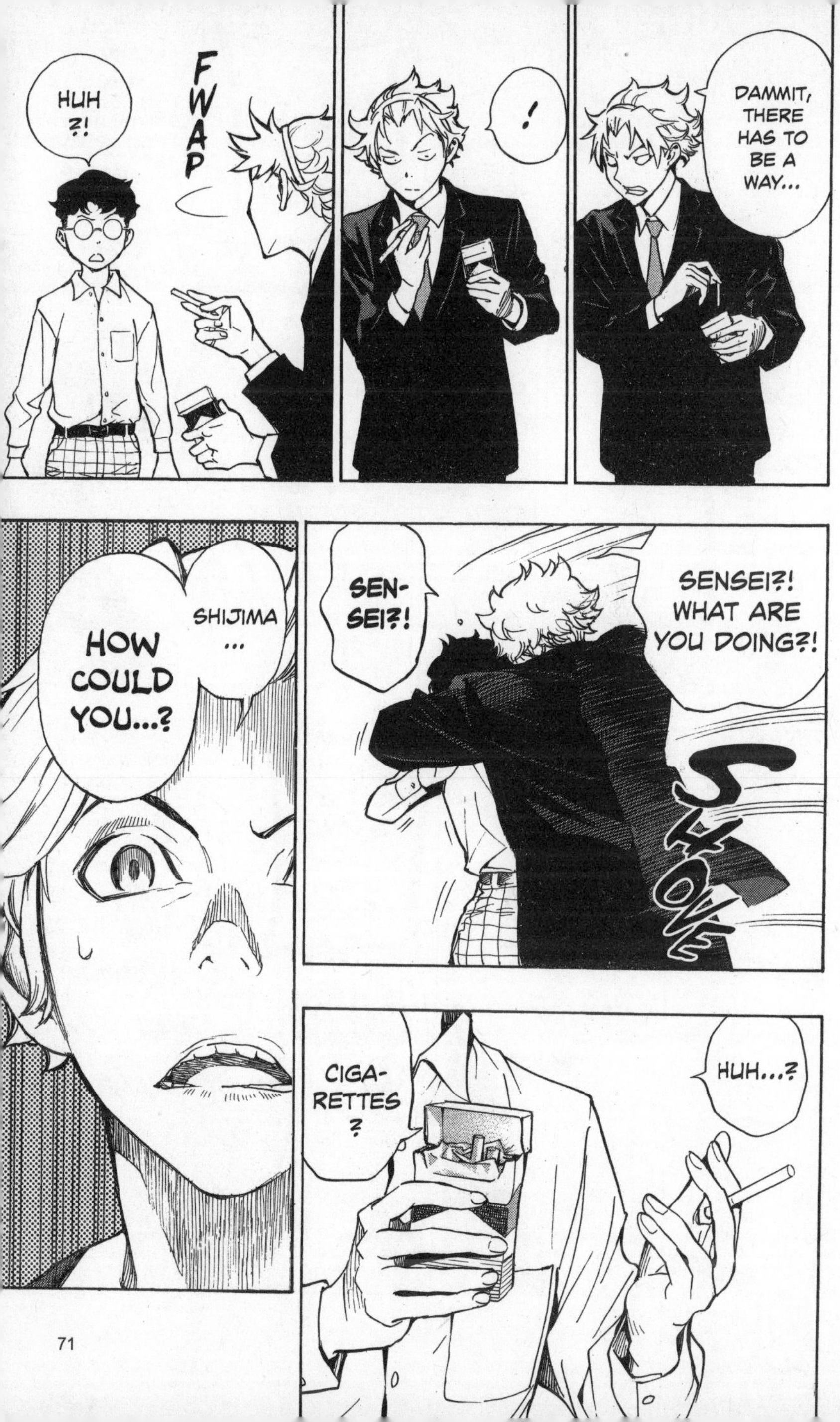
DAMMIT, THERE HAS TO BE A WAY...
!
FWAP
HUH ?!
SENSEI?! WHAT ARE YOU DOING?!
SEN-SEI?!
SHOVE
HUH...?
CIGA-RETTES ?
SHIJIMA ...
HOW COULD YOU...?

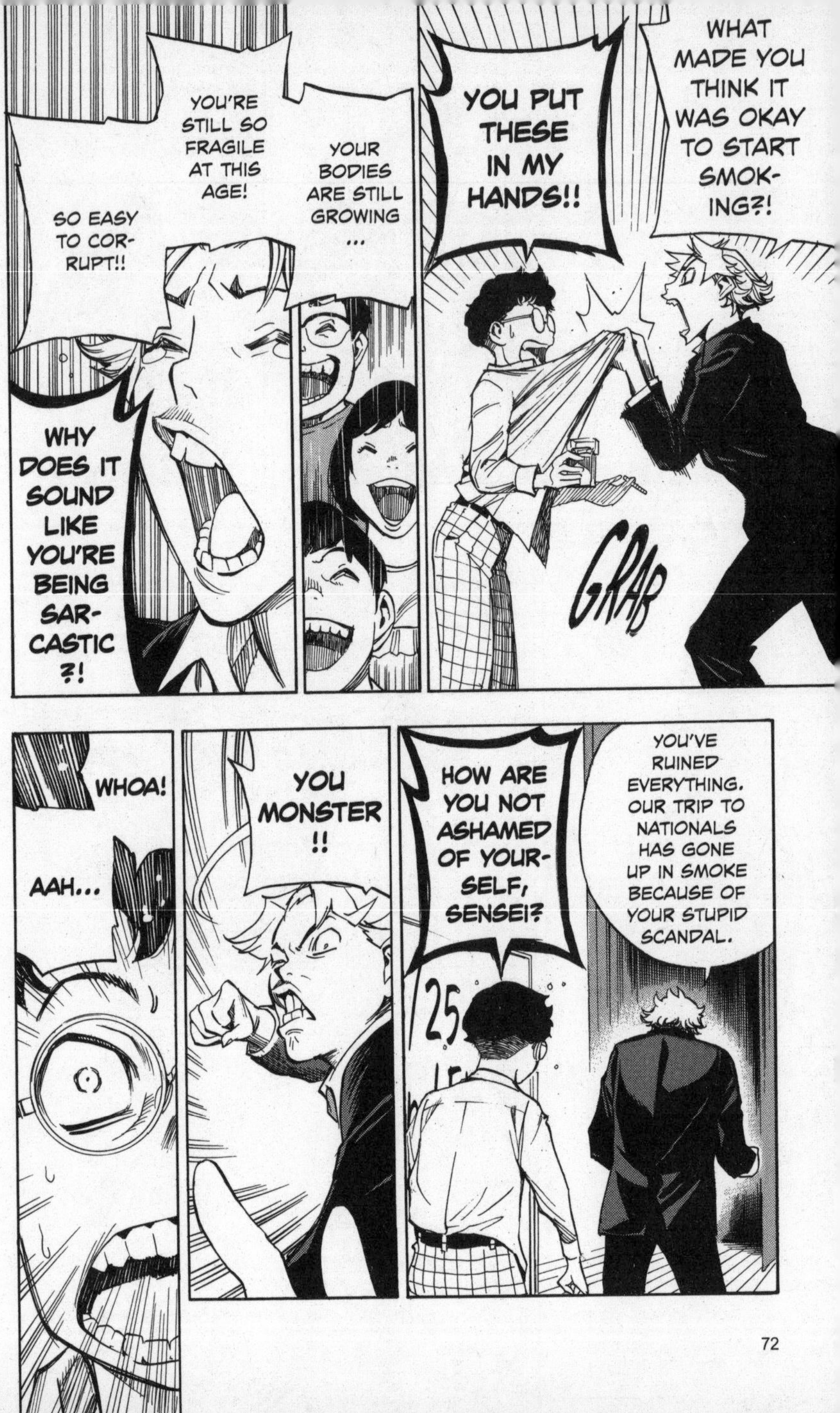
WHAT MADE YOU THINK IT WAS OKAY TO START SMOK-ING?!
YOU PUT THESE IN MY HANDS!!
GRAB
YOUR BODIES ARE STILL GROWING...
YOU'RE STILL SO FRAGILE AT THIS AGE!
SO EASY TO COR-RUPT!!
WHY DOES IT SOUND LIKE YOU'RE BEING SAR-CASTIC?!
YOU'VE RUINED EVERYTHING. OUR TRIP TO NATIONALS HAS GONE UP IN SMOKE BECAUSE OF YOUR STUPID SCANDAL.
HOW ARE YOU NOT ASHAMED OF YOUR-SELF, SENSEI?
25
YOU MONSTER!!
WHOA!
AAH...

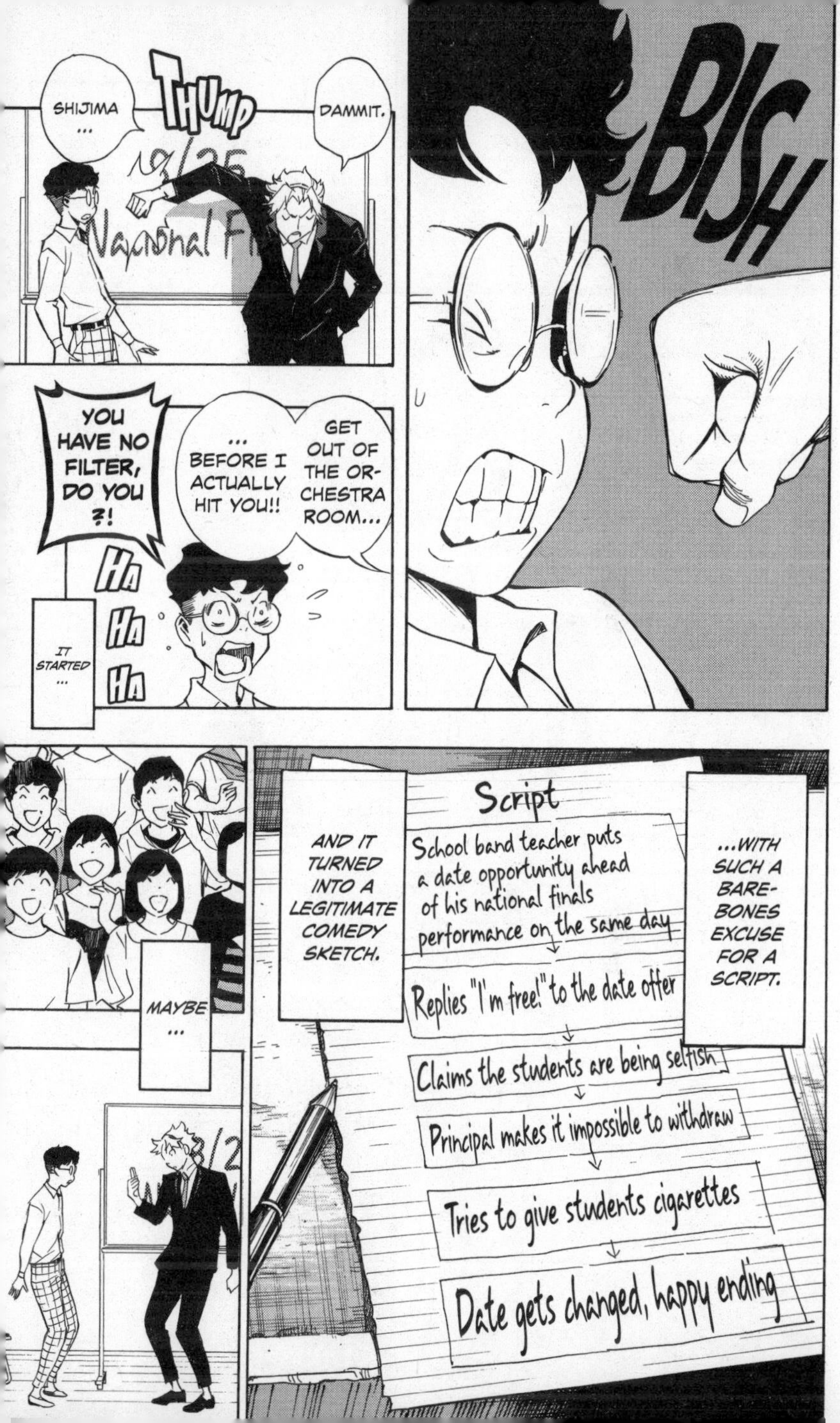
BISH
DAMMIT.
THUMP
SHIJIMA ...
GET OUT OF THE OR-CHESTRA ROOM...
... BEFORE I ACTUALLY HIT YOU!!
YOU HAVE NO FILTER, DO YOU ?!
HA HA HA
IT STARTED ...
...WITH SUCH A BARE-BONES EXCUSE FOR A SCRIPT.
Script
School band teacher puts a date opportunity ahead of his national finals performance on the same day
Replies "I'm free!" to the date offer
Claims the students are being selfish
Principal makes it impossible to withdraw
Tries to give students cigarettes
Date gets changed, happy ending
AND IT TURNED INTO A LEGITIMATE COMEDY SKETCH.
MAYBE ...

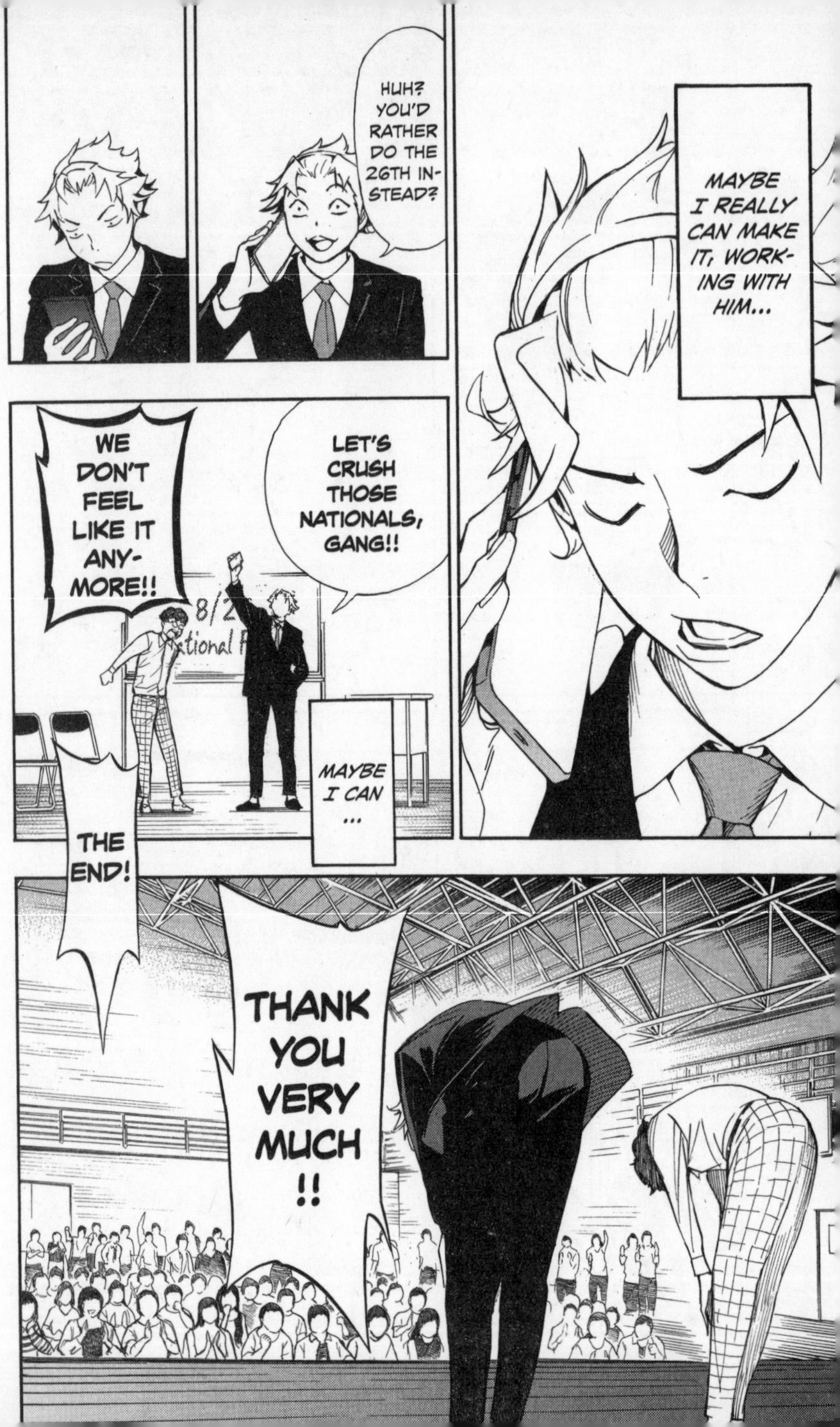
MAYBE I REALLY CAN MAKE IT, WORKING WITH HIM...
HUH? YOU'D RATHER DO THE 26TH IN-STEAD?
LET'S CRUSH THOSE NATIONALS, GANG!!
WE DON'T FEEL LIKE IT ANY-MORE!!
MAYBE I CAN...
THE END!
THANK YOU VERY MUCH!!

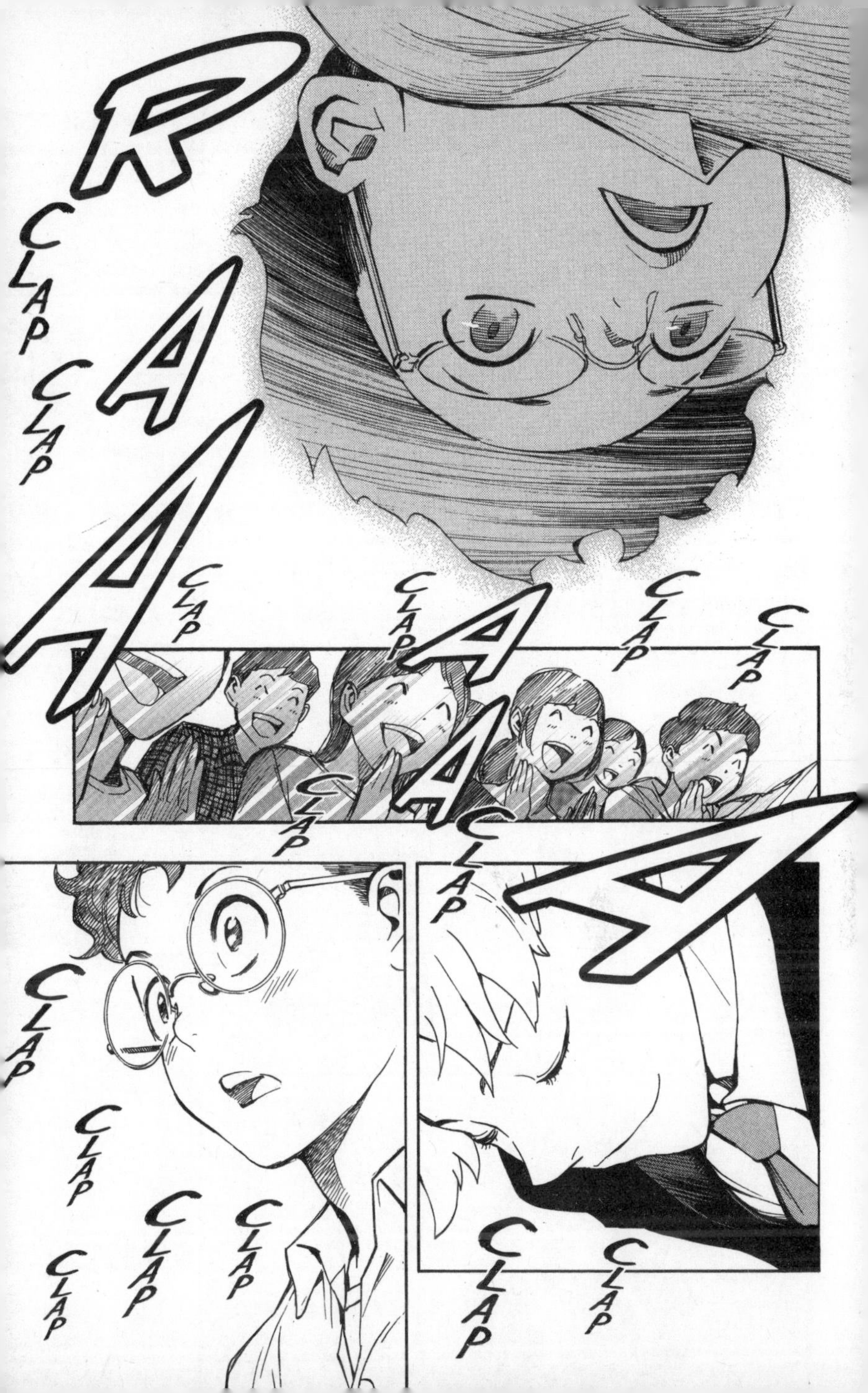
RAAAAA
CLAP CLAP
CLAP CLAP CLAP CLAP
CLAP
CLAP
CLAP CLAP
CLAP CLAP CLAP CLAP CLAP

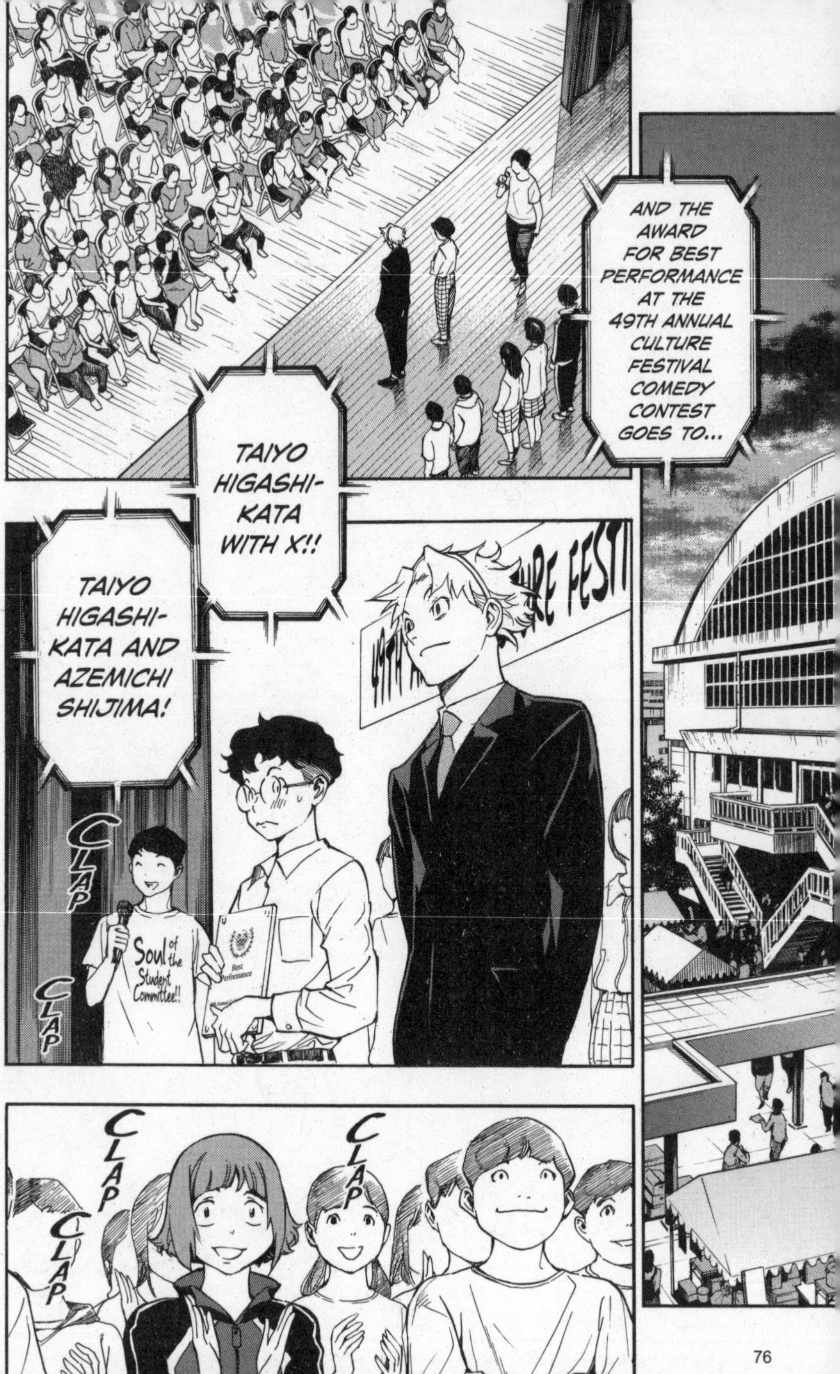
AND THE AWARD FOR BEST PERFORMANCE AT THE 49TH ANNUAL CULTURE FESTIVAL COMEDY CONTEST GOES TO...
TAIYO HIGASHI-KATA WITH X!!
TAIYO HIGASHI-KATA AND AZEMICHI SHIJIMA!
Soul of the Student Committee!!
Best Performance
CLAP
CLAP
CLAP
CLAP
CLAP

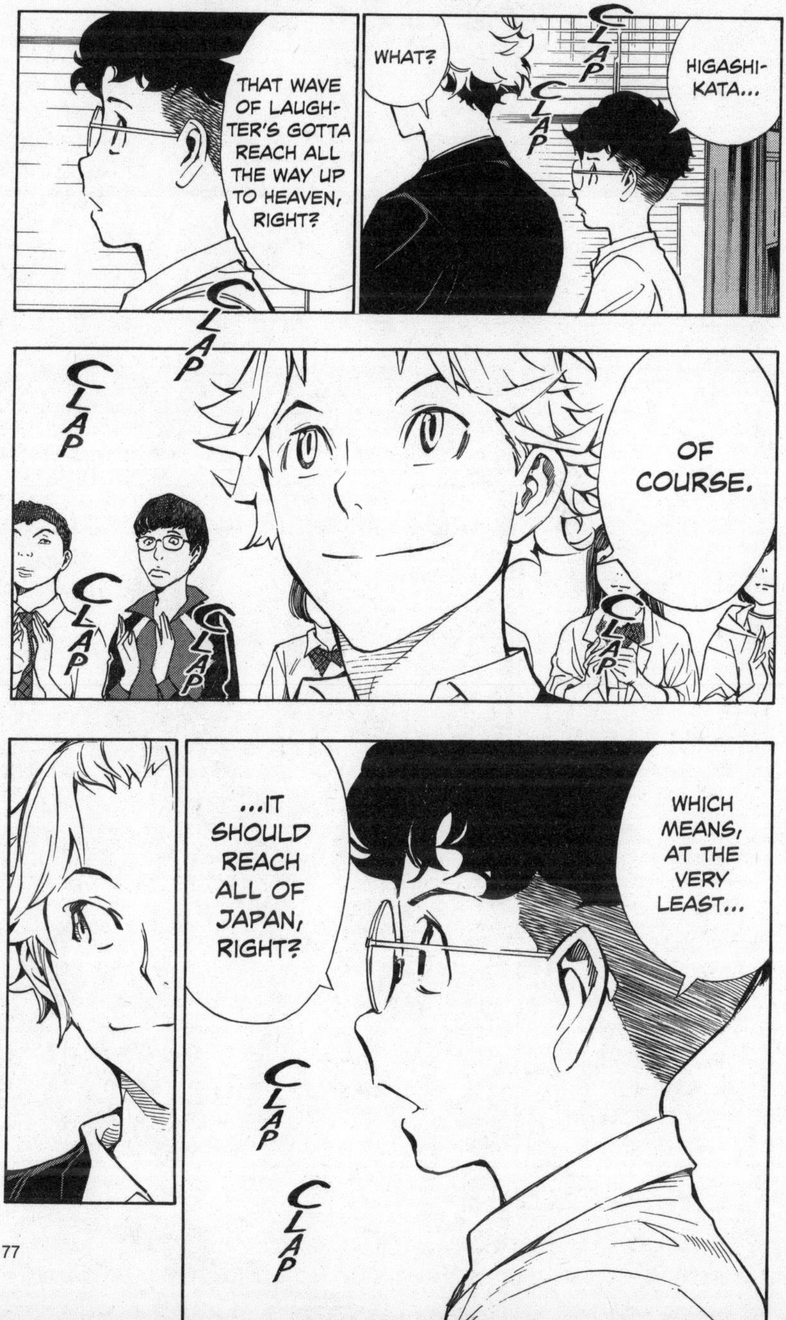
HIGASHI-KATA...
CLAP CLAP
WHAT?
THAT WAVE OF LAUGHTER'S GOTTA REACH ALL THE WAY UP TO HEAVEN, RIGHT?
CLAP
OF COURSE.
CLAP
CLAP
CLAP
CLAP
WHICH MEANS, AT THE VERY LEAST...
...IT SHOULD REACH ALL OF JAPAN, RIGHT?
CLAP
CLAP

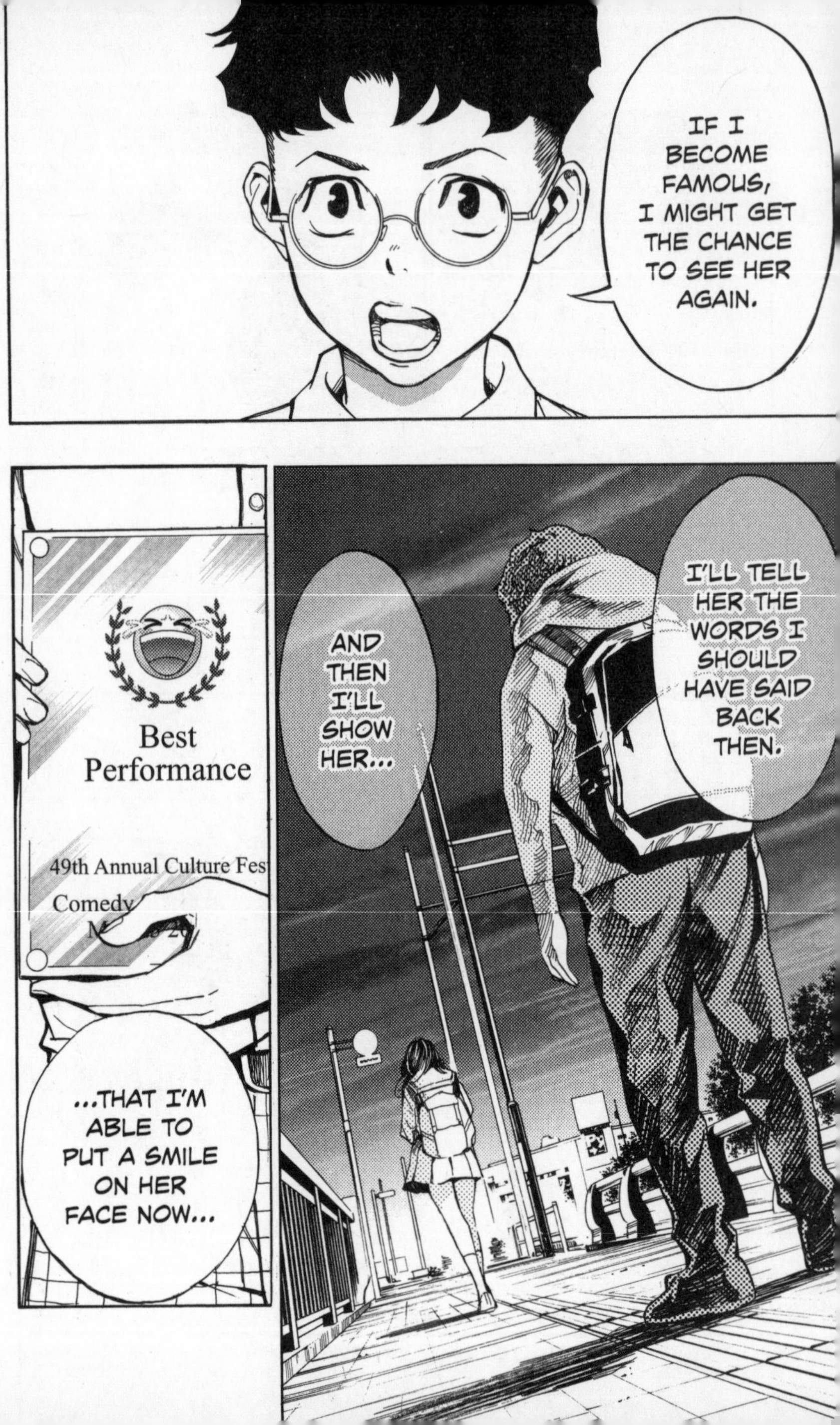
IF I BECOME FAMOUS, I MIGHT GET THE CHANCE TO SEE HER AGAIN.
I'LL TELL HER THE WORDS I SHOULD HAVE SAID BACK THEN.
AND THEN I'LL SHOW HER...
Best Performance
49th Annual Culture Fes
Comedy
...THAT I'M ABLE TO PUT A SMILE ON HER FACE NOW...

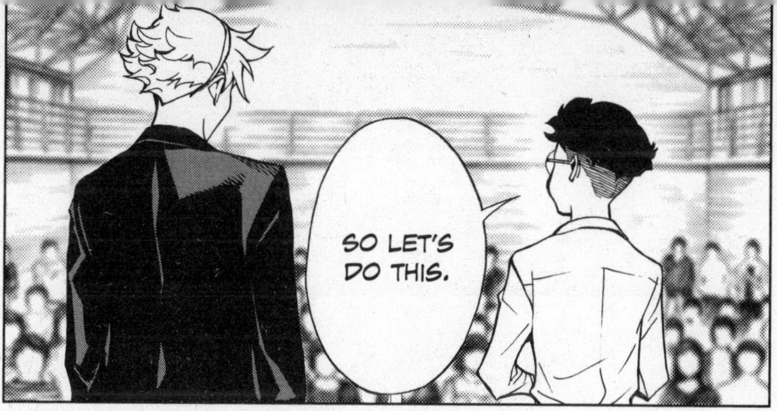
SO LET'S DO THIS.

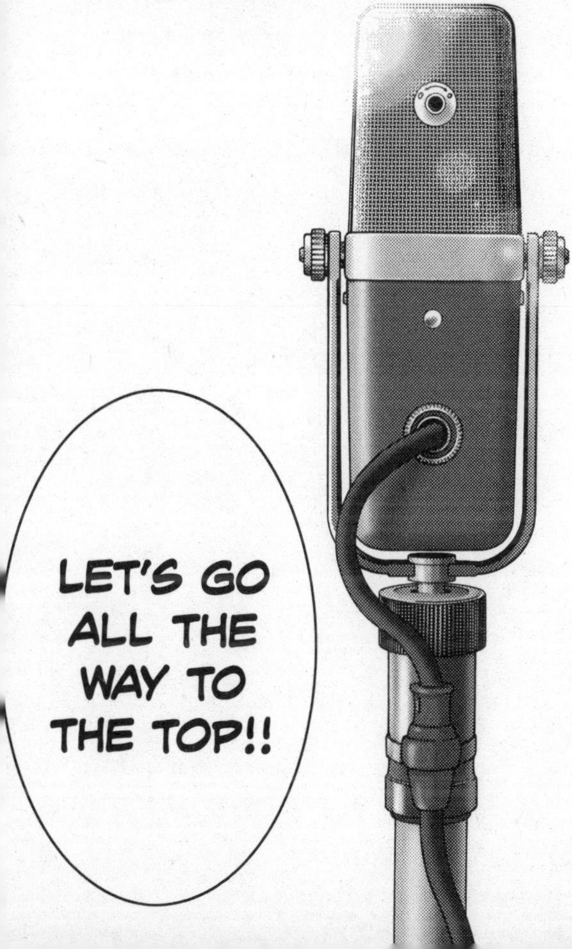
LET'S GO ALL THE WAY TO THE TOP!!

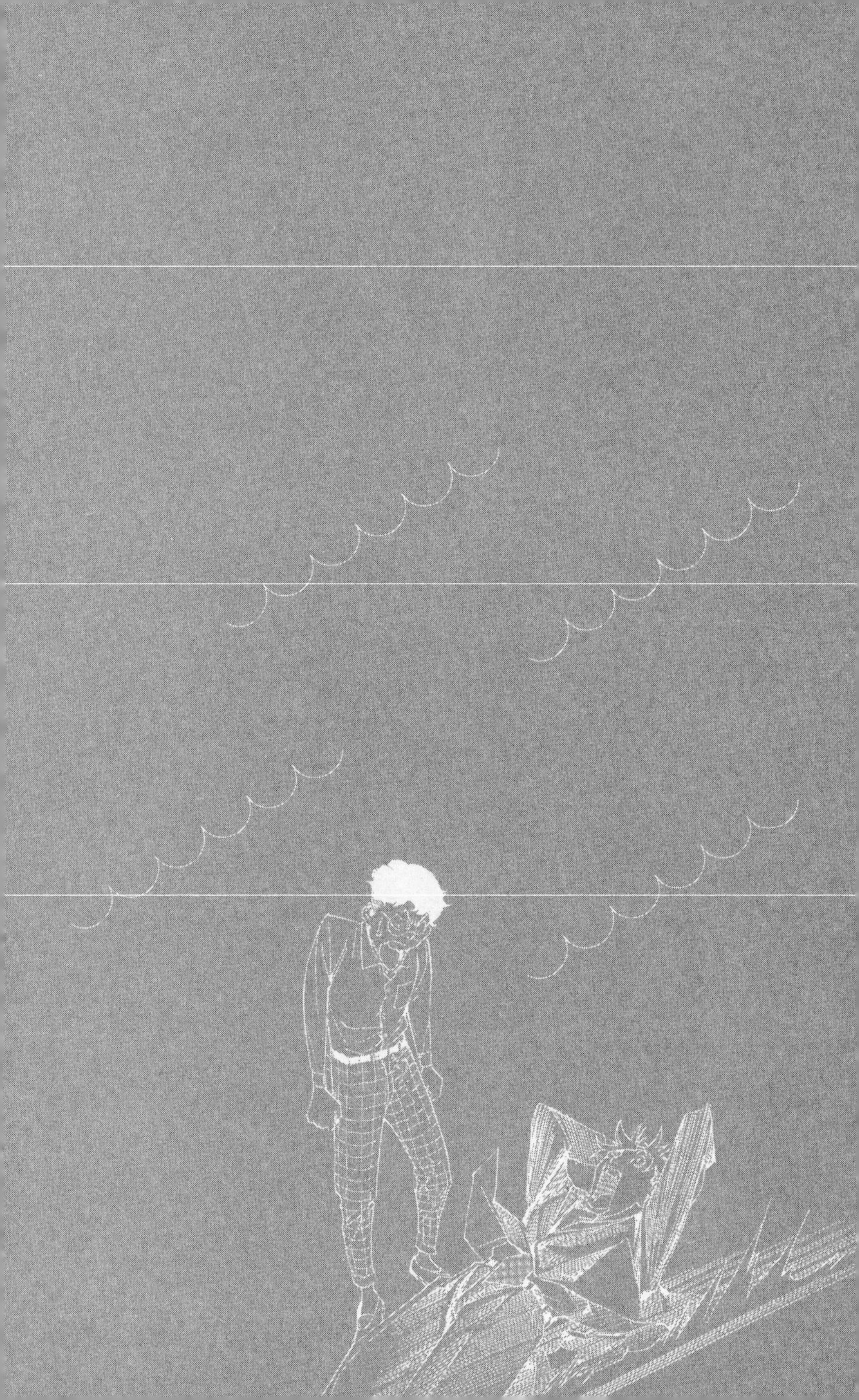

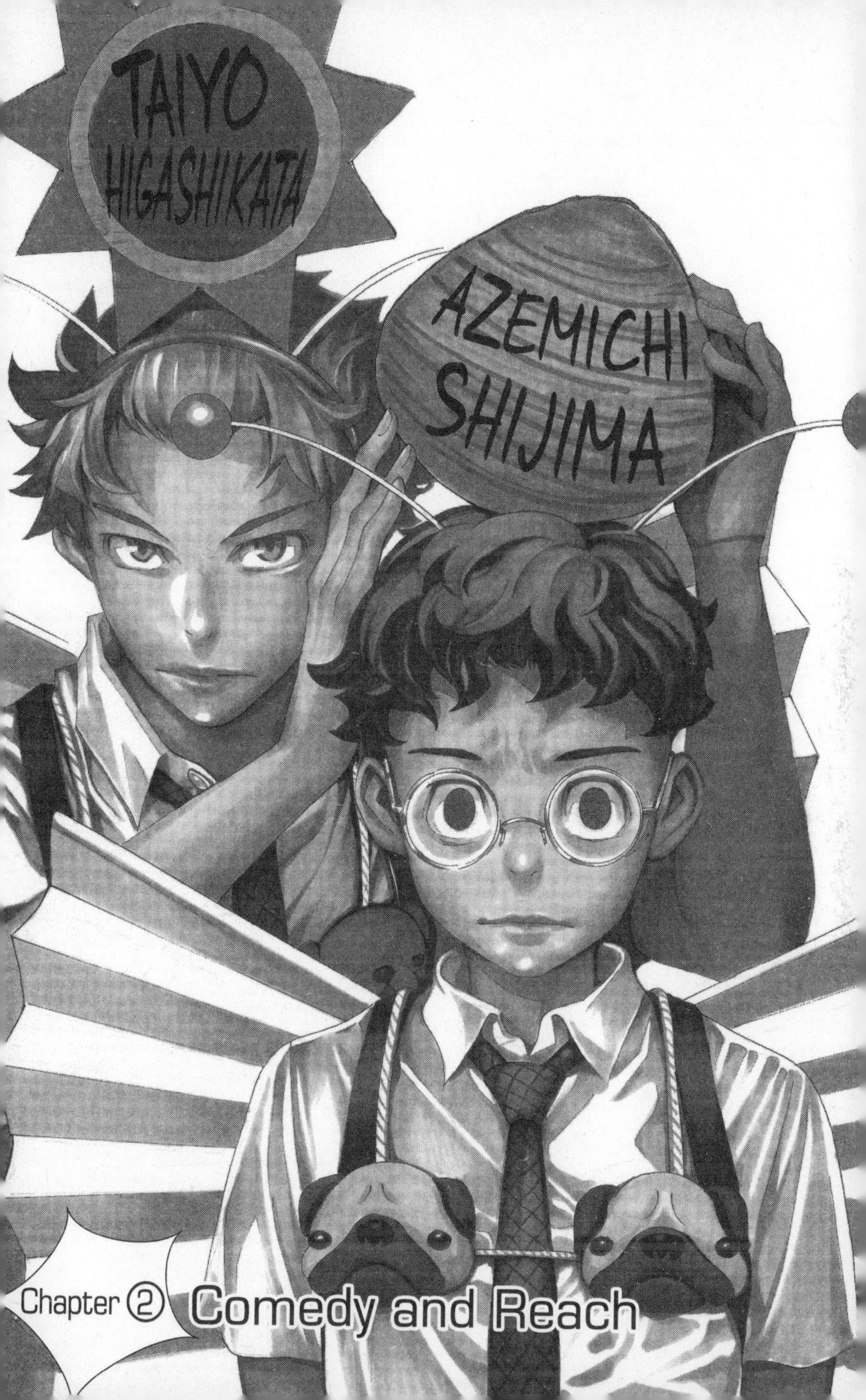
TAIYO HIGASHIKATA
AZEMICHI SHIJIMA
Chapter 2 Comedy and Reach

Show-ha Shoten!

SHOW-HA SHOTEN!

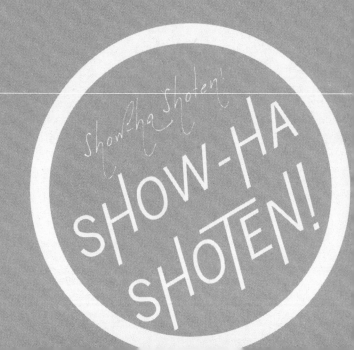

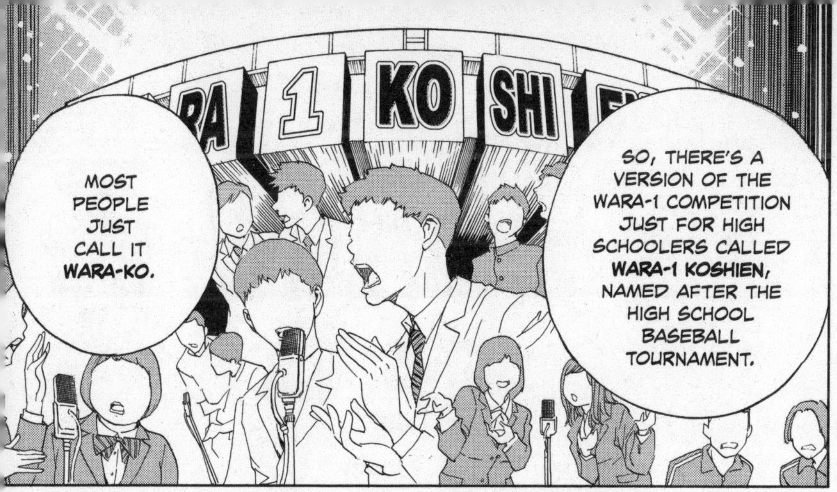
SO, THERE'S A VERSION OF THE WARA-1 COMPETITION JUST FOR HIGH SCHOOLERS CALLED **WARA-1 KOSHIEN,** NAMED AFTER THE HIGH SCHOOL BASEBALL TOURNAMENT.
MOST PEOPLE JUST CALL IT **WARA-KO.**

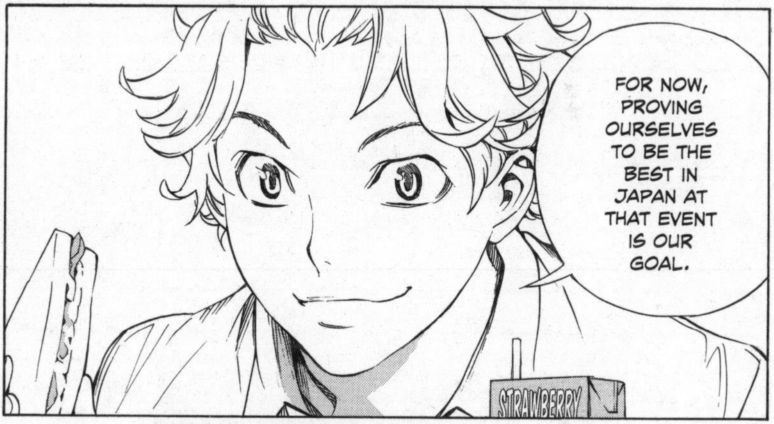
FOR NOW, PROVING OURSELVES TO BE THE BEST IN JAPAN AT THAT EVENT IS OUR GOAL.
STRAWBERRY

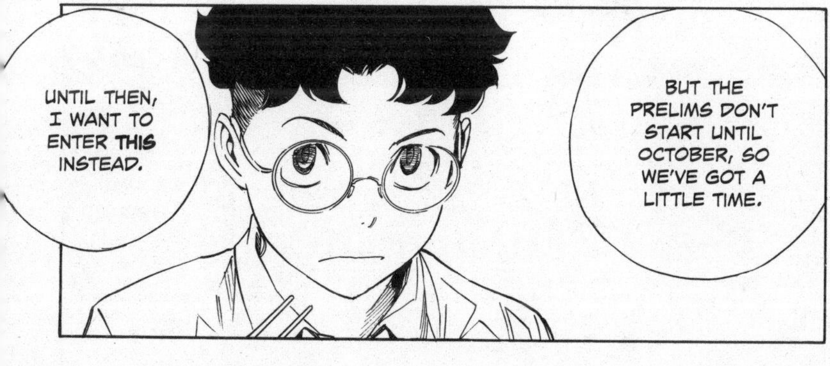
BUT THE PRELIMS DON'T START UNTIL OCTOBER, SO WE'VE GOT A LITTLE TIME.
UNTIL THEN, I WANT TO ENTER **THIS** INSTEAD.

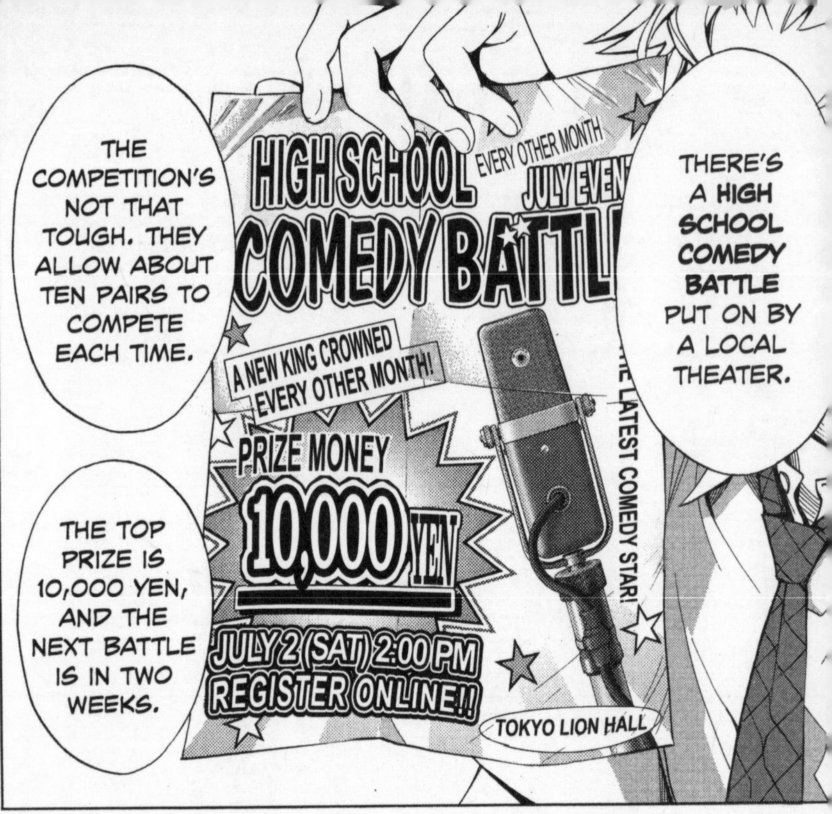
THERE'S A HIGH SCHOOL COMEDY BATTLE PUT ON BY A LOCAL THEATER.
HIGH SCHOOL COMEDY BATTL
EVERY OTHER MONTH
JULY EVEN
HE LATEST COMEDY STAR!
A NEW KING CROWNED EVERY OTHER MONTH!
PRIZE MONEY 10,000 YEN
JULY 2 (SAT) 2:00 PM
REGISTER ONLINE!!
TOKYO LION HALL
THE COMPETITION'S NOT THAT TOUGH. THEY ALLOW ABOUT TEN PAIRS TO COMPETE EACH TIME.
THE TOP PRIZE IS 10,000 YEN, AND THE NEXT BATTLE IS IN TWO WEEKS.
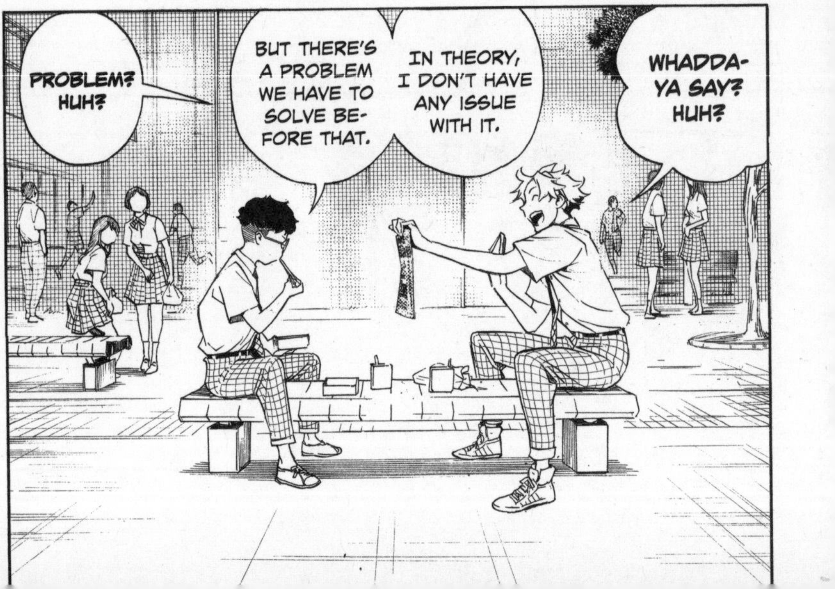
WHADDA-YA SAY? HUH?
IN THEORY, I DON'T HAVE ANY ISSUE WITH IT.
BUT THERE'S A PROBLEM WE HAVE TO SOLVE BE-FORE THAT.
PROBLEM? HUH?

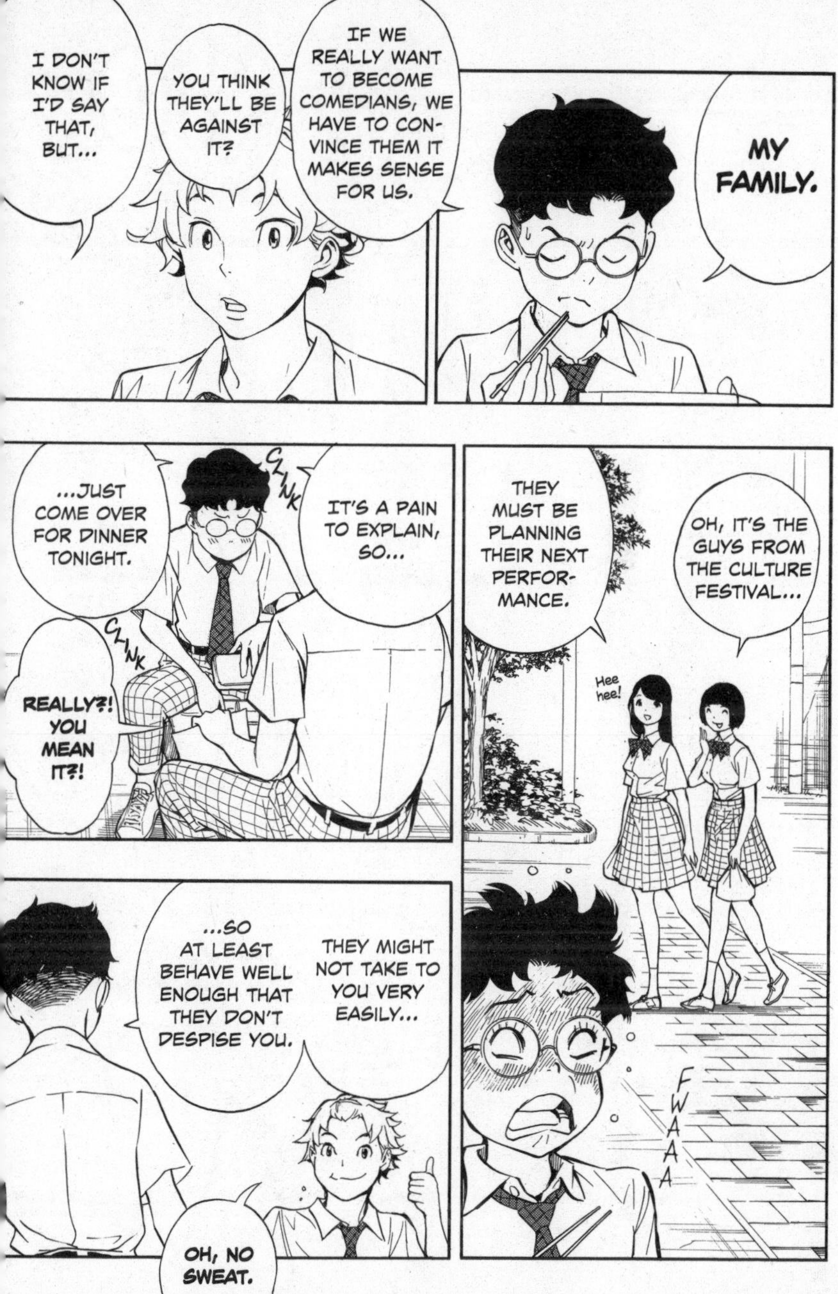
MY FAMILY.
IF WE REALLY WANT TO BECOME COMEDIANS, WE HAVE TO CONVINCE THEM IT MAKES SENSE FOR US.
YOU THINK THEY'LL BE AGAINST IT?
I DON'T KNOW IF I'D SAY THAT, BUT...
OH, IT'S THE GUYS FROM THE CULTURE FESTIVAL...
THEY MUST BE PLANNING THEIR NEXT PERFORMANCE.
Hee hee!
FWAAA
IT'S A PAIN TO EXPLAIN, SO...
CLINK
...JUST COME OVER FOR DINNER TONIGHT.
CLINK
REALLY?! YOU MEAN IT?!
THEY MIGHT NOT TAKE TO YOU VERY EASILY...
...SO AT LEAST BEHAVE WELL ENOUGH THAT THEY DON'T DESPISE YOU.
OH, NO SWEAT.

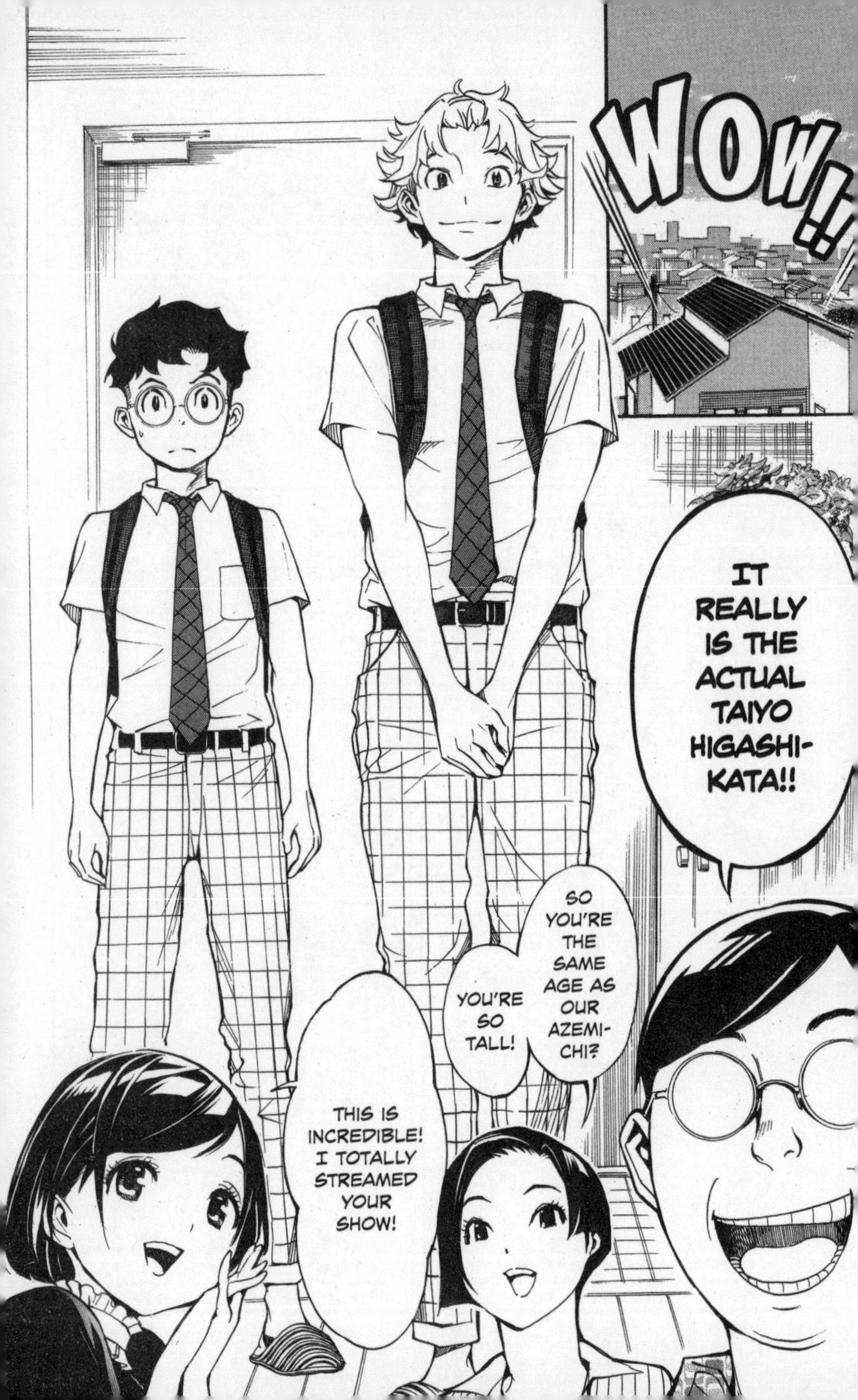
WOW!!
IT REALLY IS THE ACTUAL TAIYO HIGASHI-KATA!!
SO YOU'RE THE SAME AGE AS OUR AZEMI-CHI?
YOU'RE SO TALL!
THIS IS INCREDIBLE! I TOTALLY STREAMED YOUR SHOW!

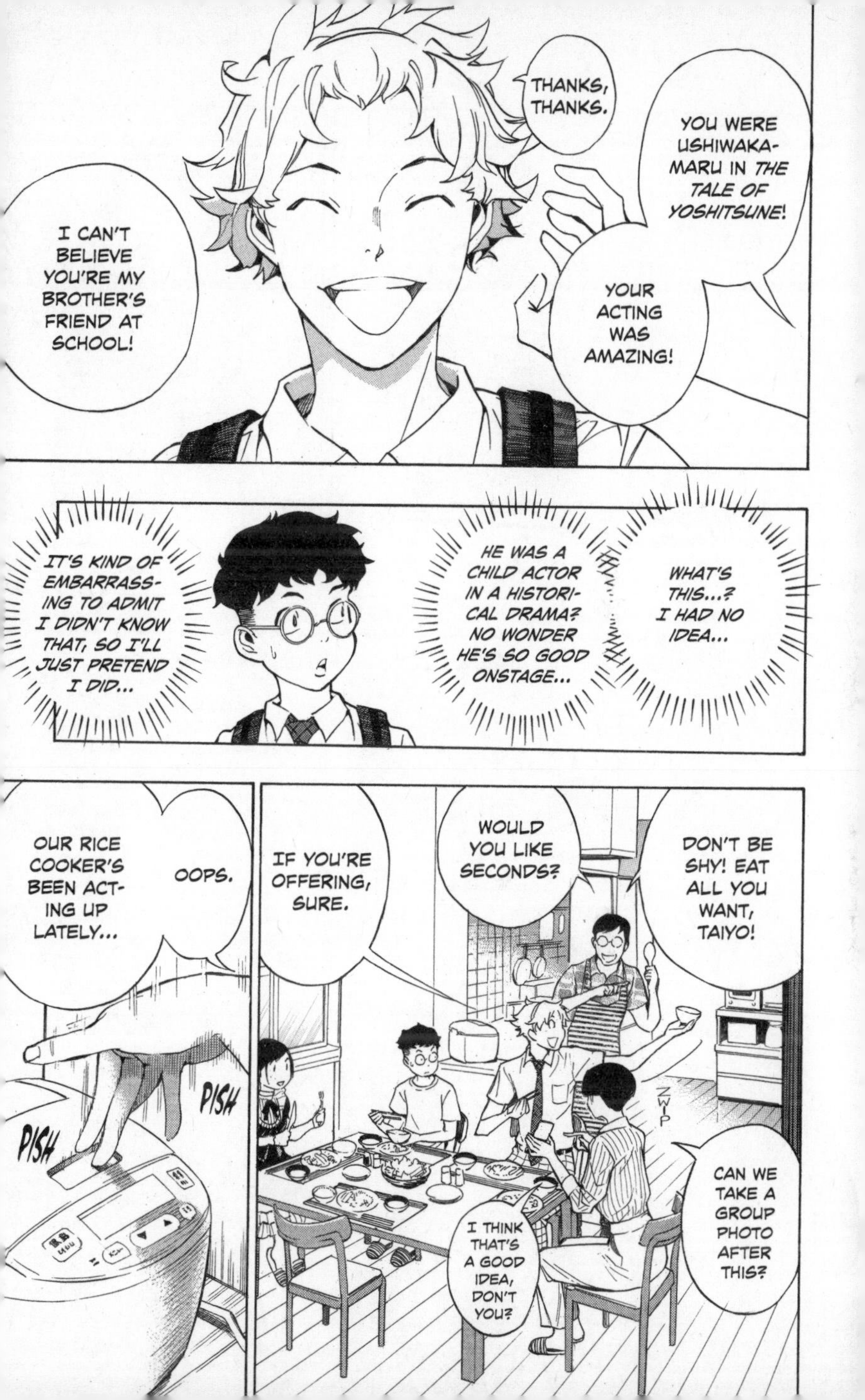
YOU WERE USHIWAKAMARU IN THE TALE OF YOSHITSUNE!
THANKS, THANKS.
YOUR ACTING WAS AMAZING!
I CAN'T BELIEVE YOU'RE MY BROTHER'S FRIEND AT SCHOOL!
WHAT'S THIS...? I HAD NO IDEA...
HE WAS A CHILD ACTOR IN A HISTORICAL DRAMA? NO WONDER HE'S SO GOOD ONSTAGE...
IT'S KIND OF EMBARRASSING TO ADMIT I DIDN'T KNOW THAT, SO I'LL JUST PRETEND I DID...
DON'T BE SHY! EAT ALL YOU WANT, TAIYO!
WOULD YOU LIKE SECONDS?
IF YOU'RE OFFERING, SURE.
ZWIP
CAN WE TAKE A GROUP PHOTO AFTER THIS?
I THINK THAT'S A GOOD IDEA, DON'T YOU?
OOPS.
OUR RICE COOKER'S BEEN ACTING UP LATELY...
PISH
PISH

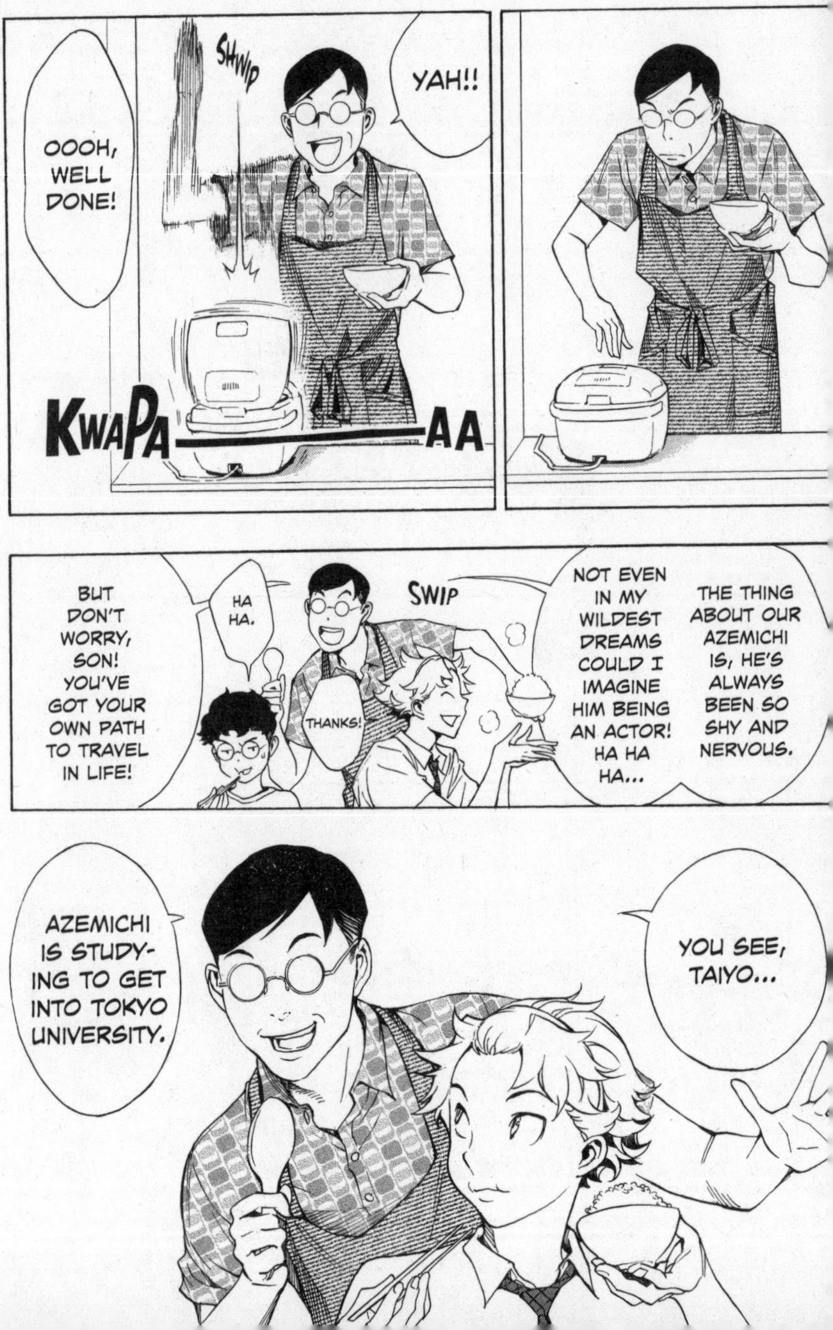
YAH!!
SHWIP
OOOH, WELL DONE!
KWAPA—AA
THE THING ABOUT OUR AZEMICHI IS, HE'S ALWAYS BEEN SO SHY AND NERVOUS.
NOT EVEN IN MY WILDEST DREAMS COULD I IMAGINE HIM BEING AN ACTOR! HA HA HA...
SWIP
HA HA.
THANKS!
BUT DON'T WORRY, SON! YOU'VE GOT YOUR OWN PATH TO TRAVEL IN LIFE!
YOU SEE, TAIYO...
AZEMICHI IS STUDY-ING TO GET INTO TOKYO UNIVERSITY.

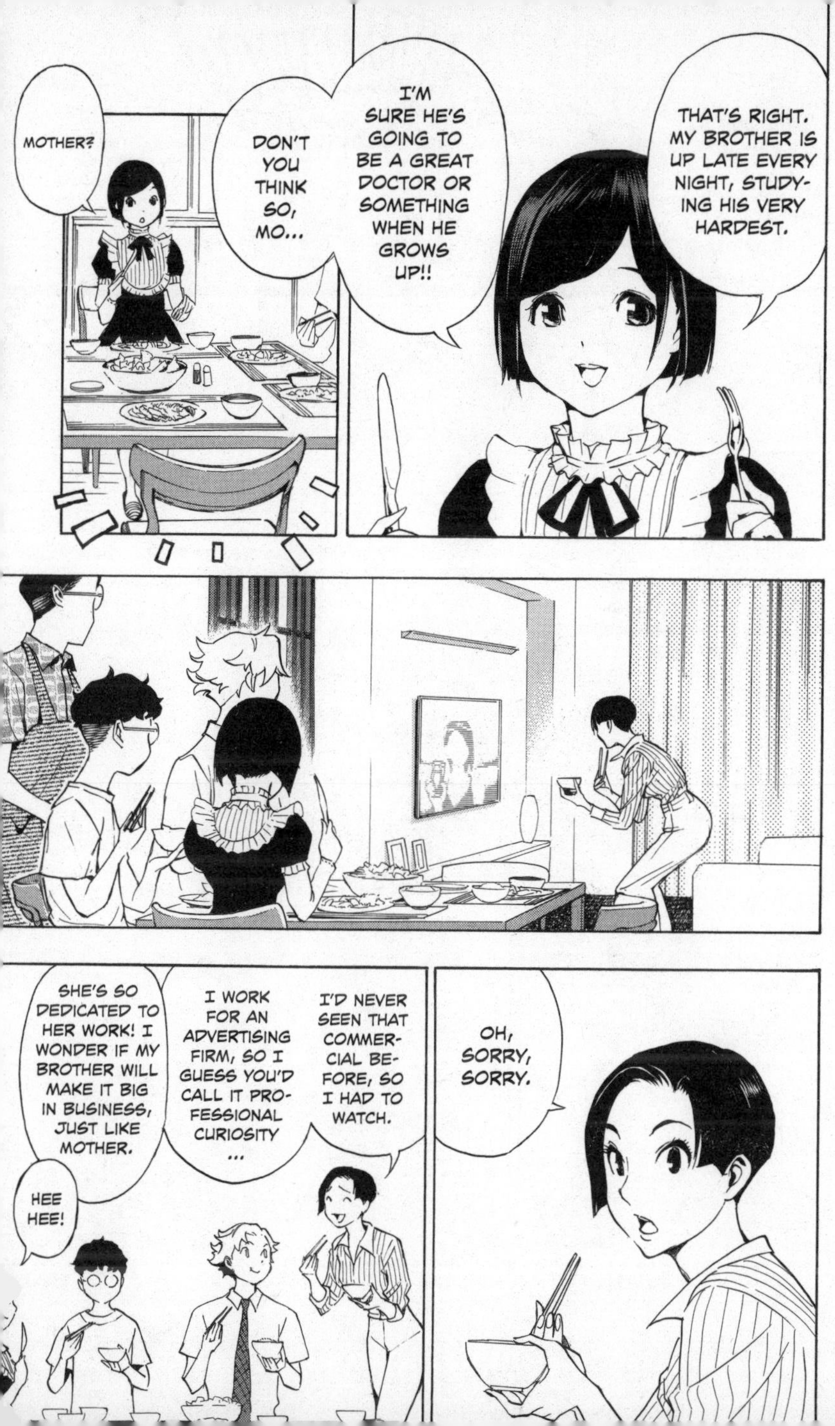
THAT'S RIGHT. MY BROTHER IS UP LATE EVERY NIGHT, STUDYING HIS VERY HARDEST.
I'M SURE HE'S GOING TO BE A GREAT DOCTOR OR SOMETHING WHEN HE GROWS UP!!
DON'T YOU THINK SO, MO...
MOTHER?
OH, SORRY, SORRY.
I'D NEVER SEEN THAT COMMERCIAL BEFORE, SO I HAD TO WATCH.
I WORK FOR AN ADVERTISING FIRM, SO I GUESS YOU'D CALL IT PROFESSIONAL CURIOSITY ...
SHE'S SO DEDICATED TO HER WORK! I WONDER IF MY BROTHER WILL MAKE IT BIG IN BUSINESS, JUST LIKE MOTHER.
HEE HEE!

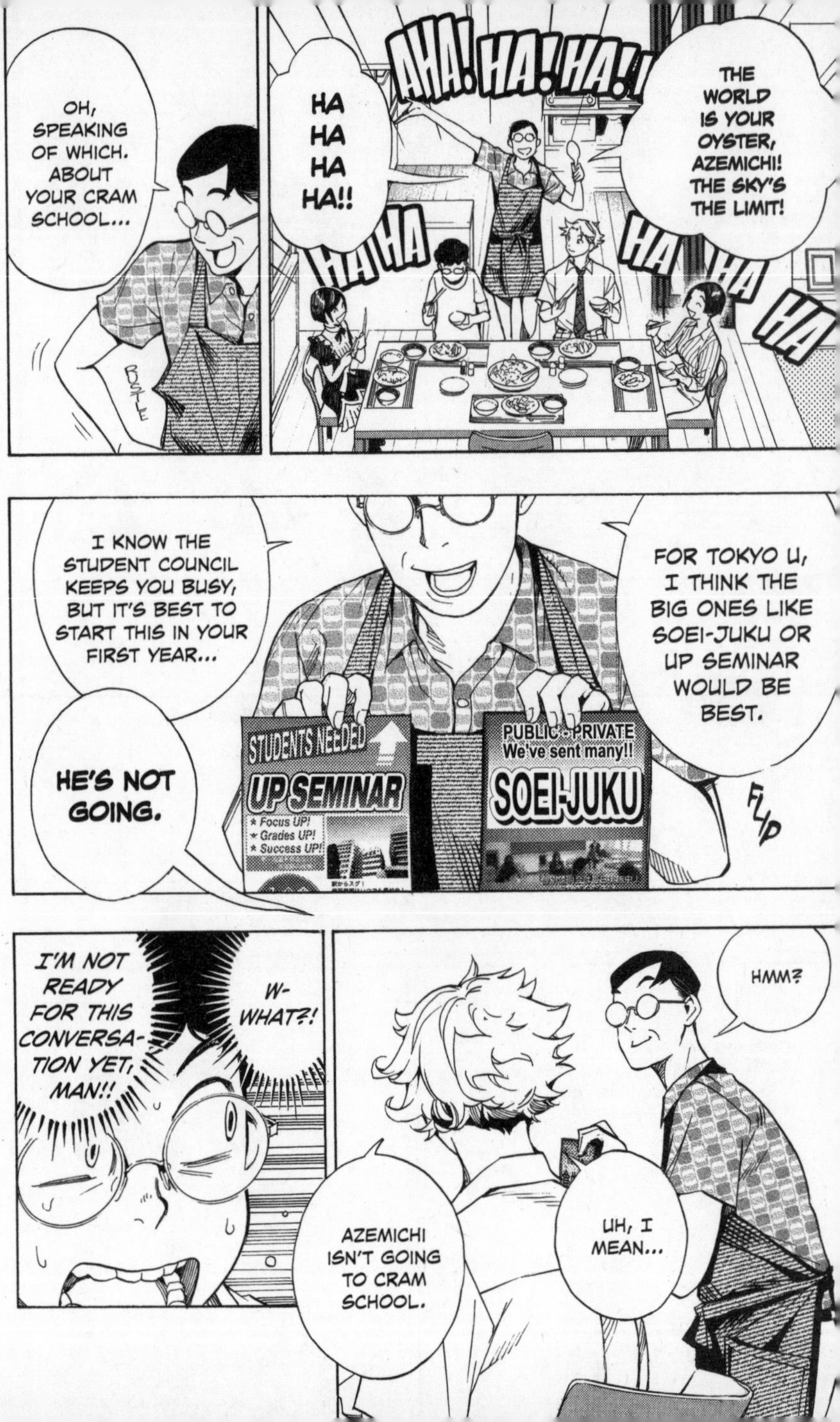

AHA! HA! HA!!
THE WORLD IS YOUR OYSTER, AZEMICHI! THE SKY'S THE LIMIT!
HA HA HA HA!!
HA HA
HA HA HA
OH, SPEAKING OF WHICH. ABOUT YOUR CRAM SCHOOL...
RUSTLE
FOR TOKYO U, I THINK THE BIG ONES LIKE SOEI-JUKU OR UP SEMINAR WOULD BE BEST.
FLIP
PUBLIC • PRIVATE We've sent many!!
SOEI-JUKU
STUDENTS NEEDED
UP SEMINAR
* Focus UP! * Grades UP! * Success UP!
I KNOW THE STUDENT COUNCIL KEEPS YOU BUSY, BUT IT'S BEST TO START THIS IN YOUR FIRST YEAR...
HE'S NOT GOING.
HMM?
UH, I MEAN...
AZEMICHI ISN'T GOING TO CRAM SCHOOL.
W-WHAT?!
I'M NOT READY FOR THIS CONVERSATION YET, MAN!!

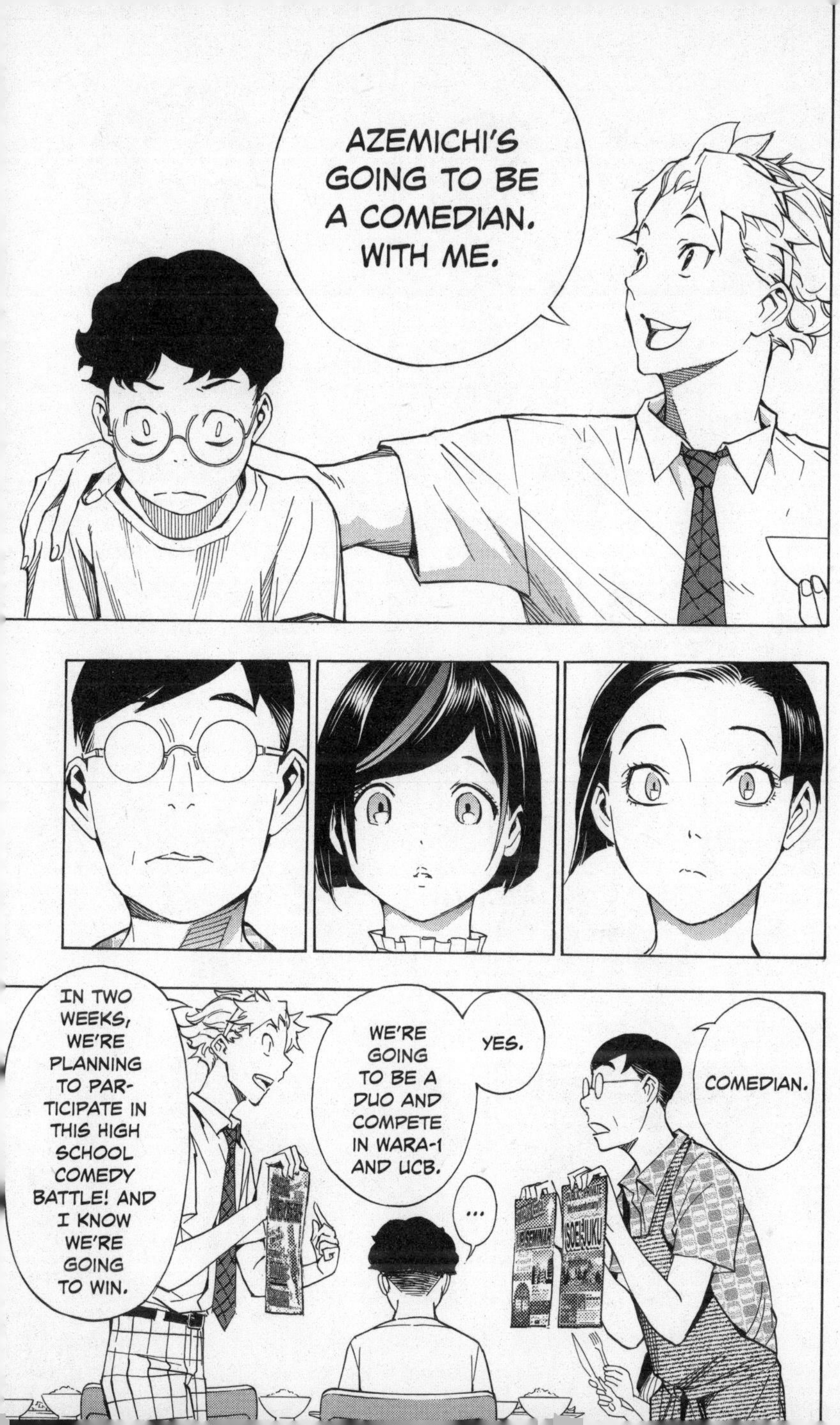
AZEMICHI'S GOING TO BE A COMEDIAN. WITH ME.
COMEDIAN.
YES.
WE'RE GOING TO BE A DUO AND COMPETE IN WARA-1 AND UCB.
IN TWO WEEKS, WE'RE PLANNING TO PARTICIPATE IN THIS HIGH SCHOOL COMEDY BATTLE! AND I KNOW WE'RE GOING TO WIN.
...

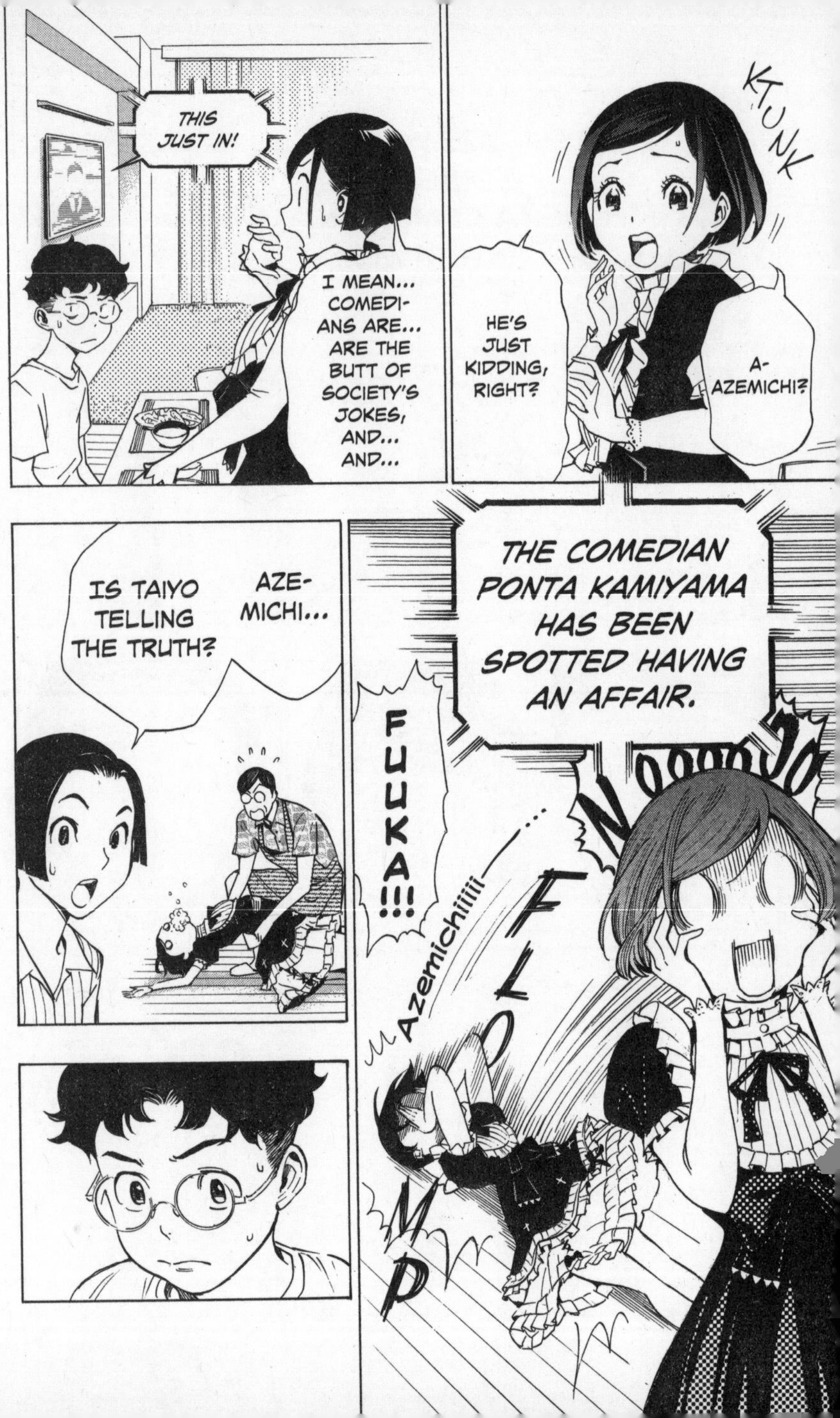
KTUNK
A-AZEMICHI?
HE'S JUST KIDDING, RIGHT?
I MEAN... COMEDIANS ARE... ARE THE BUTT OF SOCIETY'S JOKES, AND... AND...
THIS JUST IN!
THE COMEDIAN PONTA KAMIYAMA HAS BEEN SPOTTED HAVING AN AFFAIR.
Nooooooo
FLOMP
Azemichiiiiii...
FUUKA!!!
AZE-MICHI...
IS TAIYO TELLING THE TRUTH?

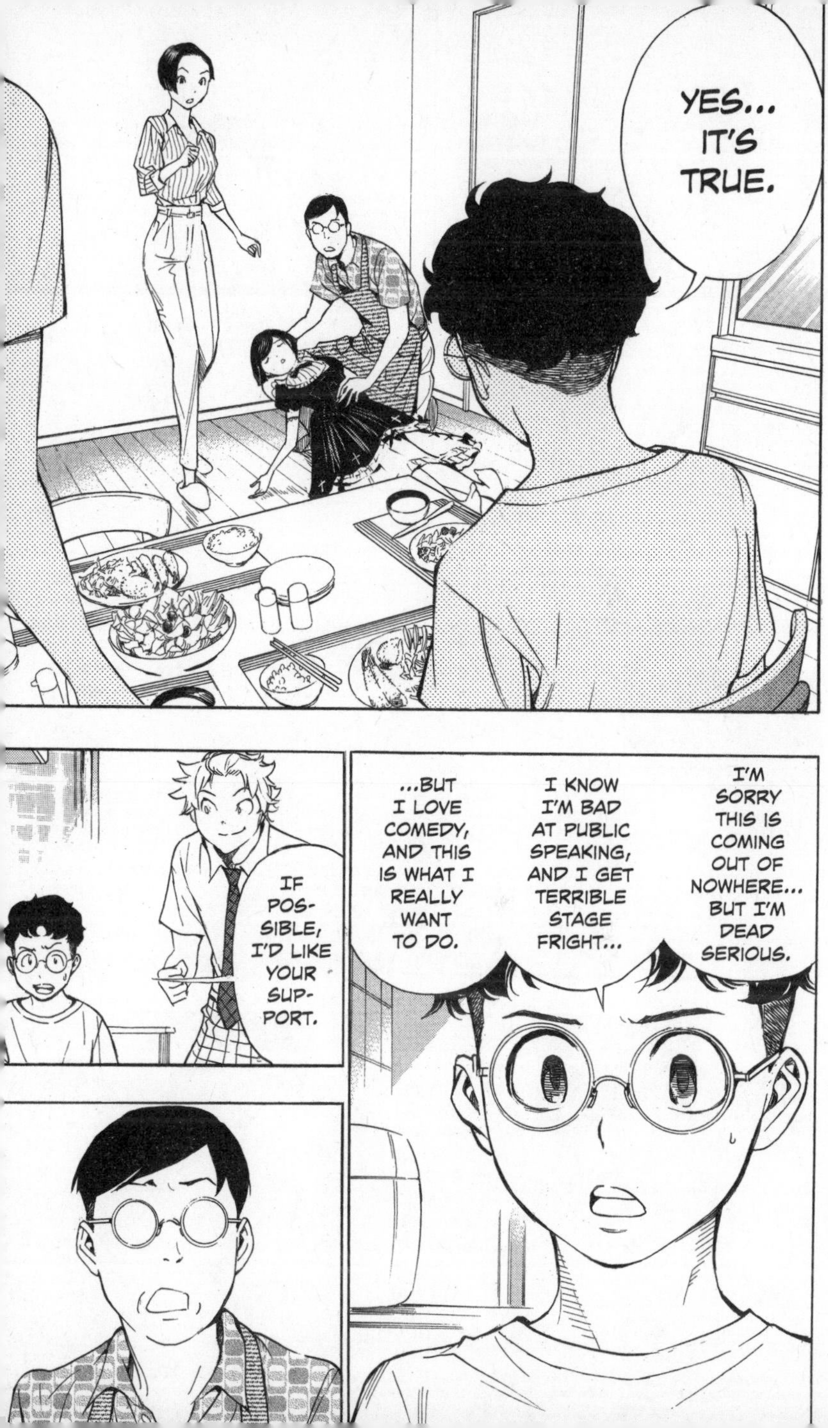
YES... IT'S TRUE.
I'M SORRY THIS IS COMING OUT OF NOWHERE... BUT I'M DEAD SERIOUS.
I KNOW I'M BAD AT PUBLIC SPEAKING, AND I GET TERRIBLE STAGE FRIGHT...
...BUT I LOVE COMEDY, AND THIS IS WHAT I REALLY WANT TO DO.
IF POS-SIBLE, I'D LIKE YOUR SUP-PORT.

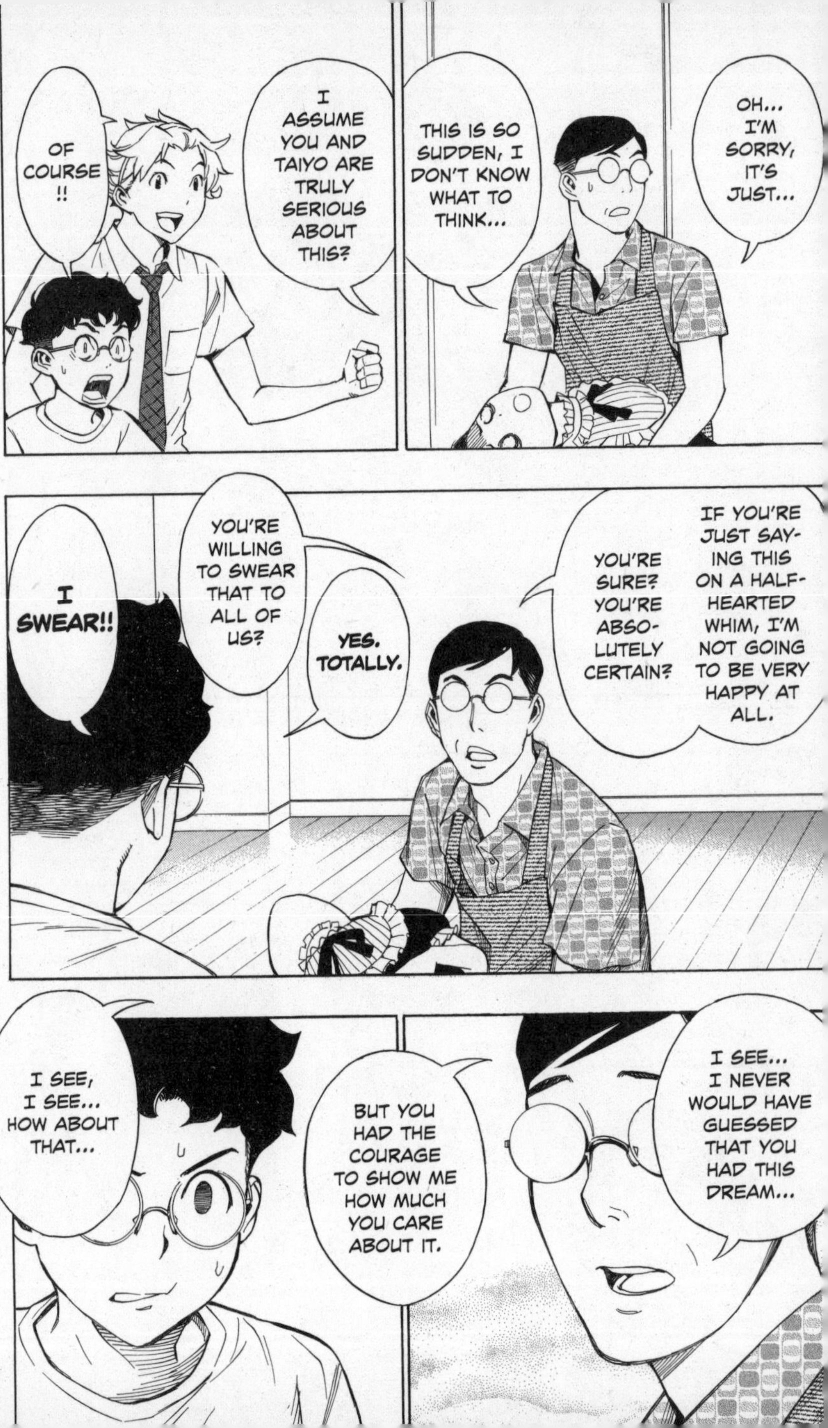
OH... I'M SORRY, IT'S JUST...
THIS IS SO SUDDEN, I DON'T KNOW WHAT TO THINK...
I ASSUME YOU AND TAIYO ARE TRULY SERIOUS ABOUT THIS?
OF COURSE !!
IF YOU'RE JUST SAYING THIS ON A HALF-HEARTED WHIM, I'M NOT GOING TO BE VERY HAPPY AT ALL.
YOU'RE SURE? YOU'RE ABSOLUTELY CERTAIN?
YES. TOTALLY.
YOU'RE WILLING TO SWEAR THAT TO ALL OF US?
I SWEAR!!
I SEE... I NEVER WOULD HAVE GUESSED THAT YOU HAD THIS DREAM...
BUT YOU HAD THE COURAGE TO SHOW ME HOW MUCH YOU CARE ABOUT IT.
I SEE, I SEE... HOW ABOUT THAT...

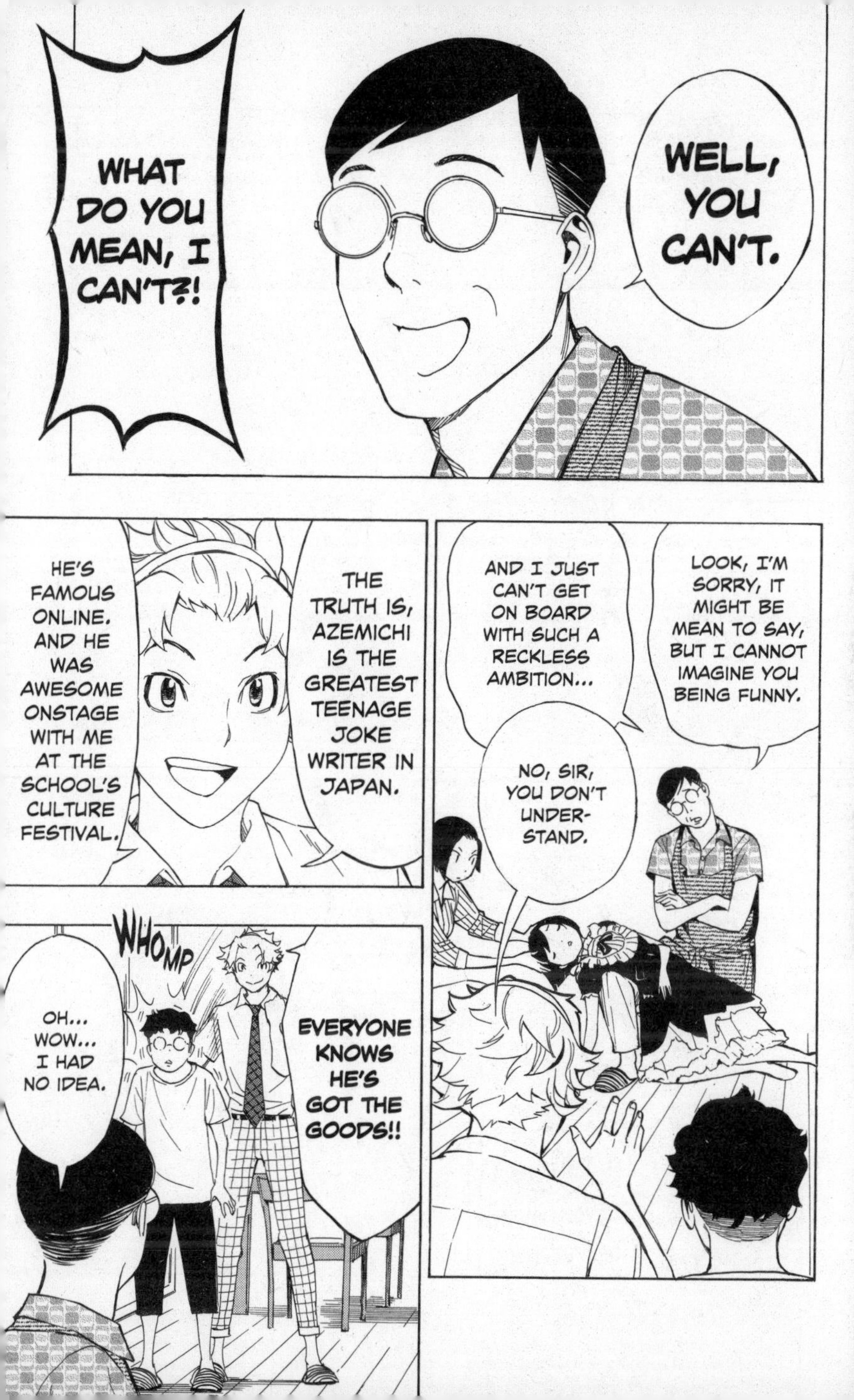
WELL, YOU CAN'T.
WHAT DO YOU MEAN, I CAN'T?!
LOOK, I'M SORRY, IT MIGHT BE MEAN TO SAY, BUT I CANNOT IMAGINE YOU BEING FUNNY.
AND I JUST CAN'T GET ON BOARD WITH SUCH A RECKLESS AMBITION...
NO, SIR, YOU DON'T UNDER-STAND.
THE TRUTH IS, AZEMICHI IS THE GREATEST TEENAGE JOKE WRITER IN JAPAN.
HE'S FAMOUS ONLINE. AND HE WAS AWESOME ONSTAGE WITH ME AT THE SCHOOL'S CULTURE FESTIVAL.
WHOMP
EVERYONE KNOWS HE'S GOT THE GOODS!!
OH... WOW... I HAD NO IDEA.

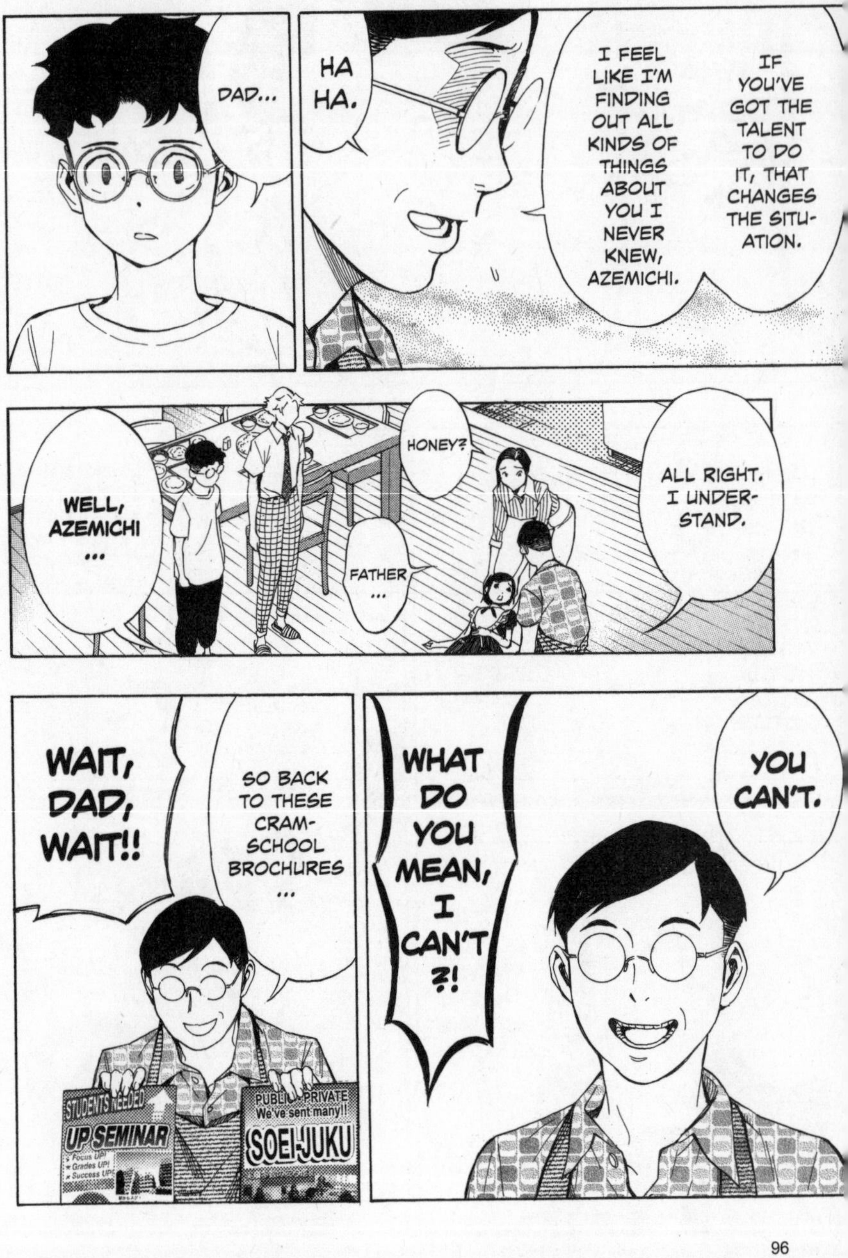
IF YOU'VE GOT THE TALENT TO DO IT, THAT CHANGES THE SITUATION.
I FEEL LIKE I'M FINDING OUT ALL KINDS OF THINGS ABOUT YOU I NEVER KNEW, AZEMICHI.
HA HA.
DAD...
ALL RIGHT. I UNDERSTAND.
HONEY?
FATHER...
WELL, AZEMICHI...
YOU CAN'T.
WHAT DO YOU MEAN, I CAN'T?!
SO BACK TO THESE CRAM-SCHOOL BROCHURES...
WAIT, DAD, WAIT!!
PUBLIC PRIVATE We've sent many!!
SOEI-JUKU
STUDENTS NEEDED
UP SEMINAR
Focus UP!
Grades UP!
Success UP!

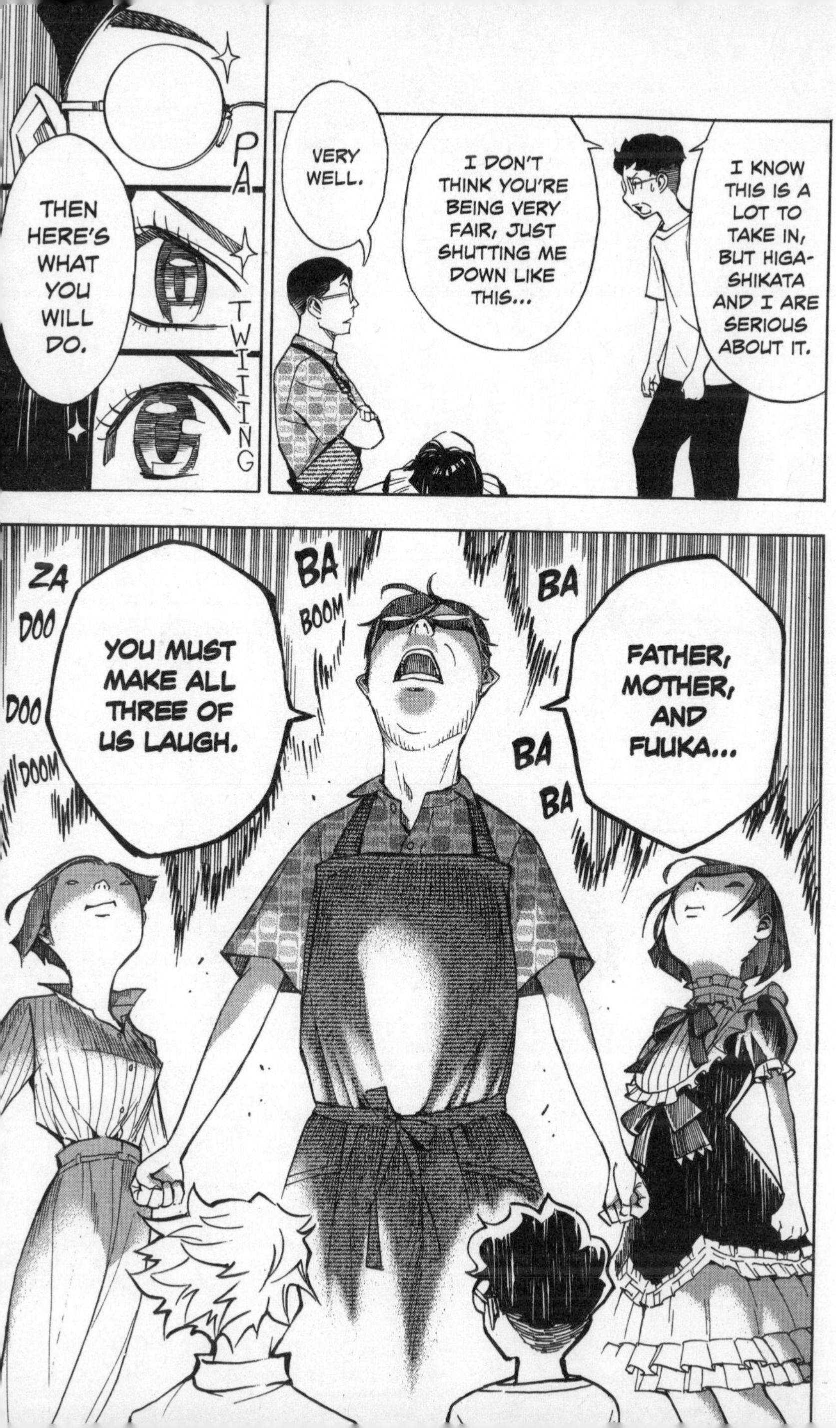
I KNOW THIS IS A LOT TO TAKE IN, BUT HIGA-SHIKATA AND I ARE SERIOUS ABOUT IT.
I DON'T THINK YOU'RE BEING VERY FAIR, JUST SHUTTING ME DOWN LIKE THIS...
VERY WELL.
PA
THEN HERE'S WHAT YOU WILL DO.
TWIIIING
BA
FATHER, MOTHER, AND FUUKA...
BA BA BA
BA BOOM
YOU MUST MAKE ALL THREE OF US LAUGH.
ZA DOO DOO DOOM

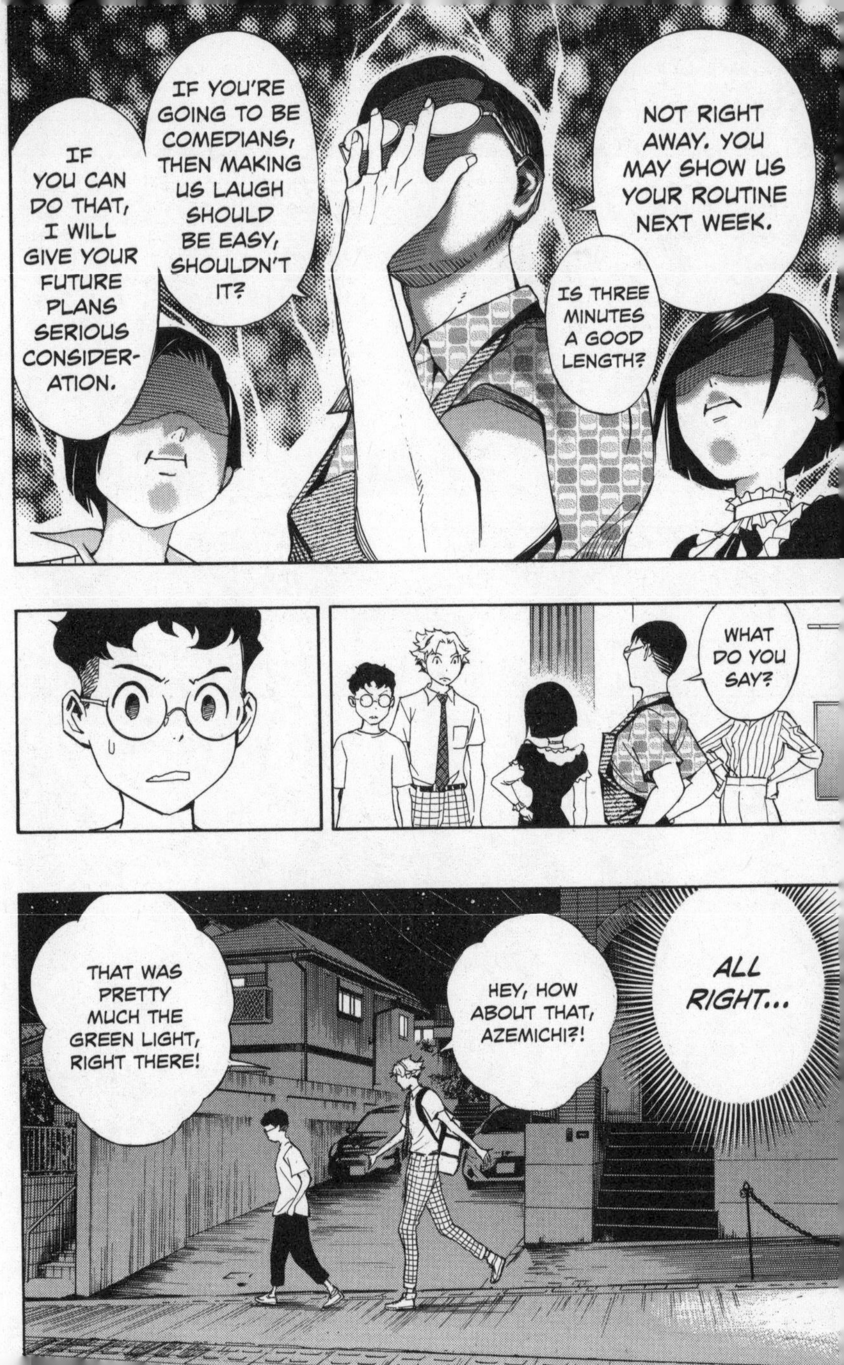
NOT RIGHT AWAY. YOU MAY SHOW US YOUR ROUTINE NEXT WEEK.
IS THREE MINUTES A GOOD LENGTH?
IF YOU'RE GOING TO BE COMEDIANS, THEN MAKING US LAUGH SHOULD BE EASY, SHOULDN'T IT?
IF YOU CAN DO THAT, I WILL GIVE YOUR FUTURE PLANS SERIOUS CONSIDERATION.
WHAT DO YOU SAY?
ALL RIGHT...
HEY, HOW ABOUT THAT, AZEMICHI?!
THAT WAS PRETTY MUCH THE GREEN LIGHT, RIGHT THERE!

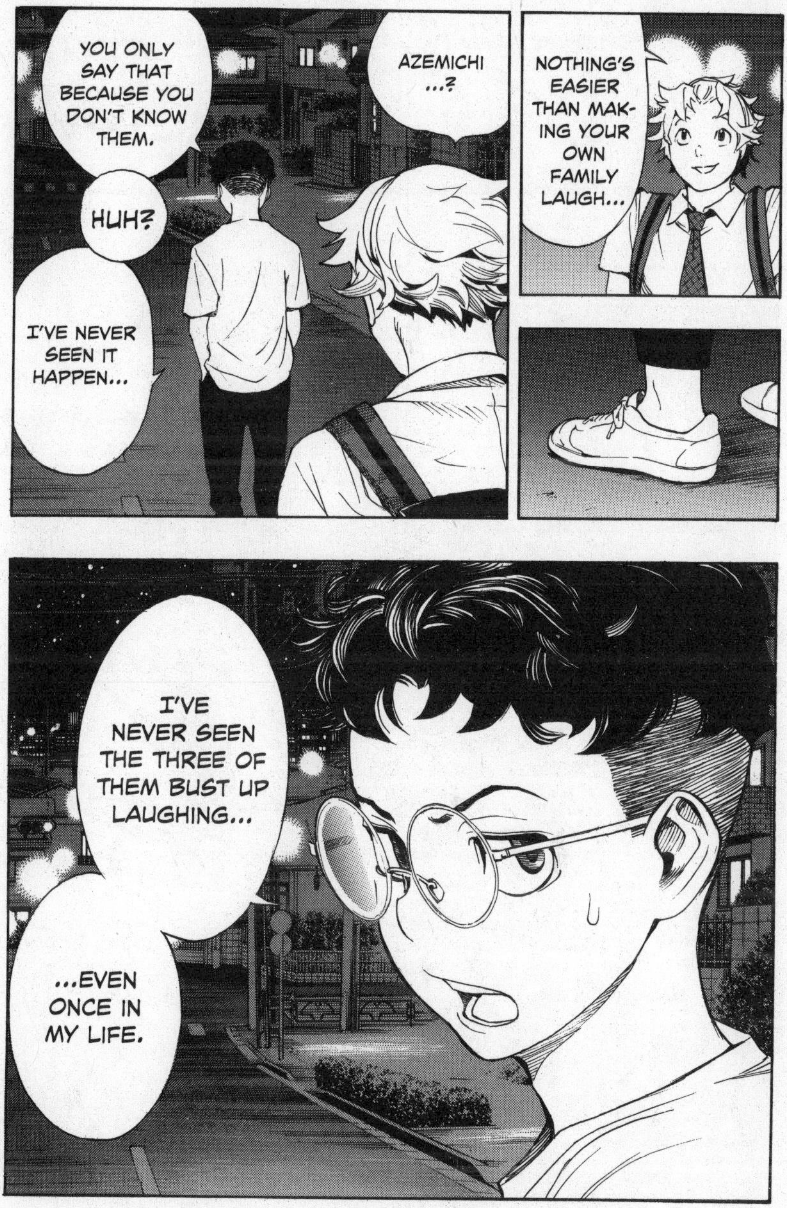
NOTHING'S EASIER THAN MAKING YOUR OWN FAMILY LAUGH...
AZEMICHI ...?
YOU ONLY SAY THAT BECAUSE YOU DON'T KNOW THEM.
HUH?
I'VE NEVER SEEN IT HAPPEN...
I'VE NEVER SEEN THE THREE OF THEM BUST UP LAUGHING...
...EVEN ONCE IN MY LIFE.

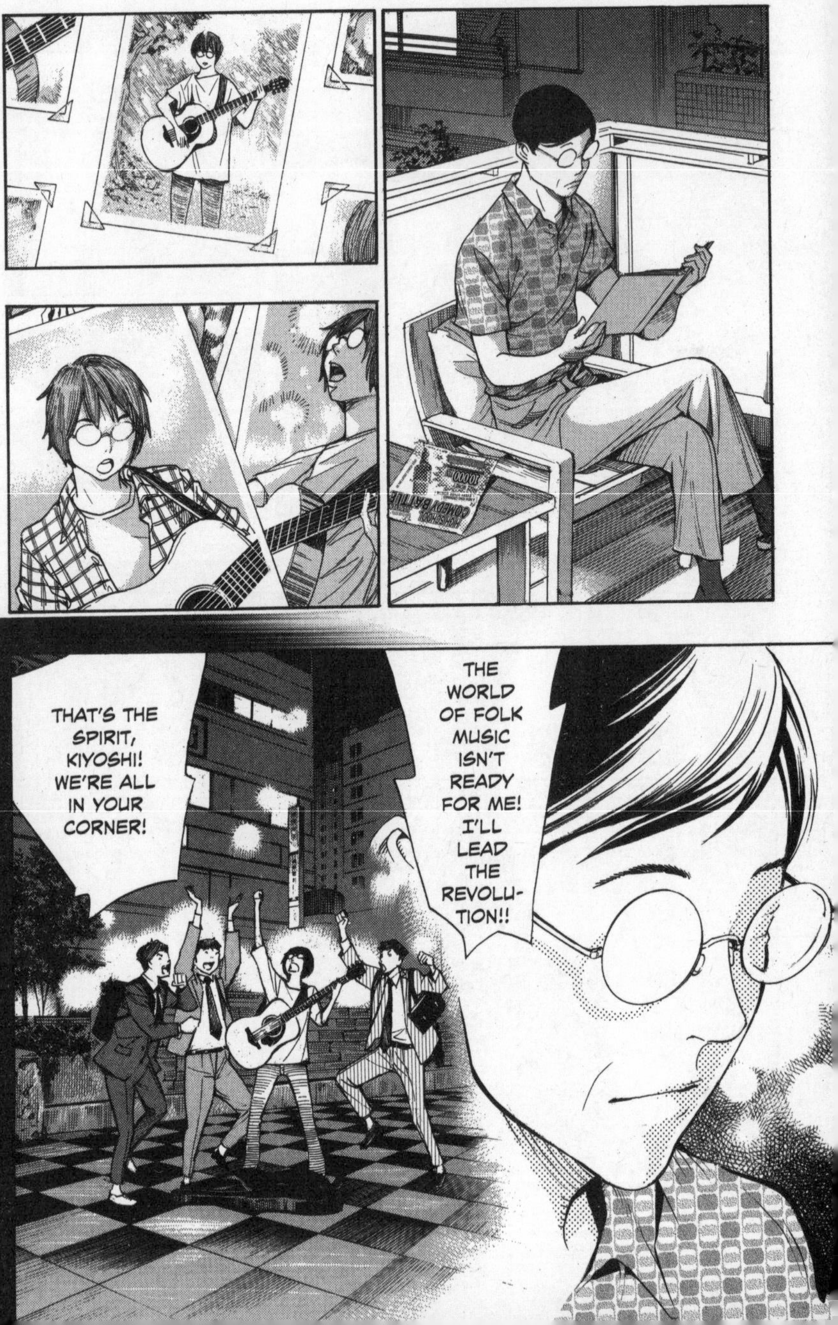
HIGH SCHOOL COMEDY BATTLE
10,000
THE WORLD OF FOLK MUSIC ISN'T READY FOR ME! I'LL LEAD THE REVOLUTION!!
THAT'S THE SPIRIT, KIYOSHI! WE'RE ALL IN YOUR CORNER!

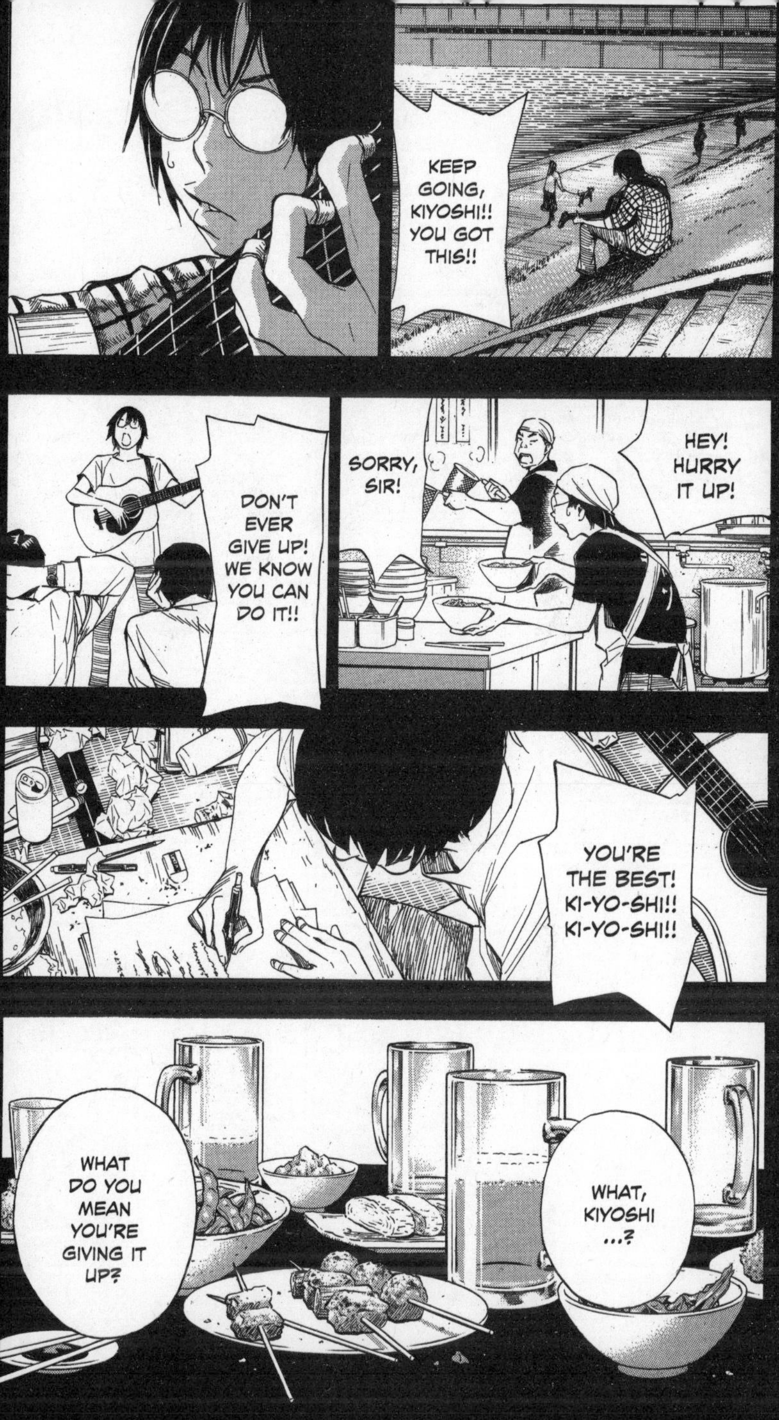
KEEP GOING, KIYOSHI!! YOU GOT THIS!!
HEY! HURRY IT UP!
SORRY, SIR!
DON'T EVER GIVE UP! WE KNOW YOU CAN DO IT!!
YOU'RE THE BEST! KI-YO-SHI!! KI-YO-SHI!!
WHAT, KIYOSHI ...?
WHAT DO YOU MEAN YOU'RE GIVING IT UP?

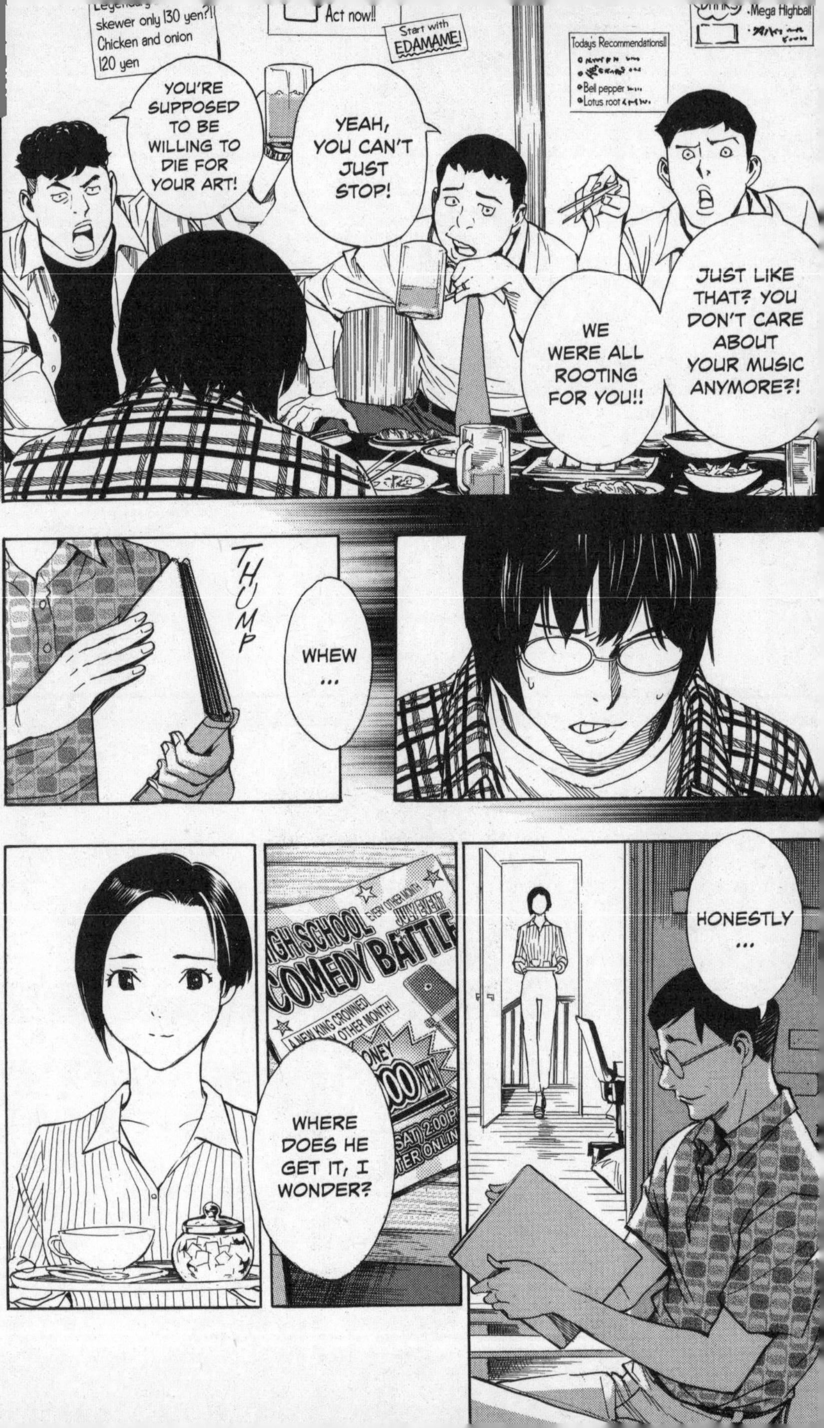

.Mega Highball
Today's Recommendations!!
Bell pepper
Lotus root
Start with EDAMAME!
Act now!!
skewer only 130 yen?! Chicken and onion 120 yen
JUST LIKE THAT? YOU DON'T CARE ABOUT YOUR MUSIC ANYMORE?!
WE WERE ALL ROOTING FOR YOU!!
YEAH, YOU CAN'T JUST STOP!
YOU'RE SUPPOSED TO BE WILLING TO DIE FOR YOUR ART!
WHEW ...
THUMP
HONESTLY ...
EVERY OTHER MONTH JULY EVENT
COMEDY BATTLE
WHERE DOES HE GET IT, I WONDER?

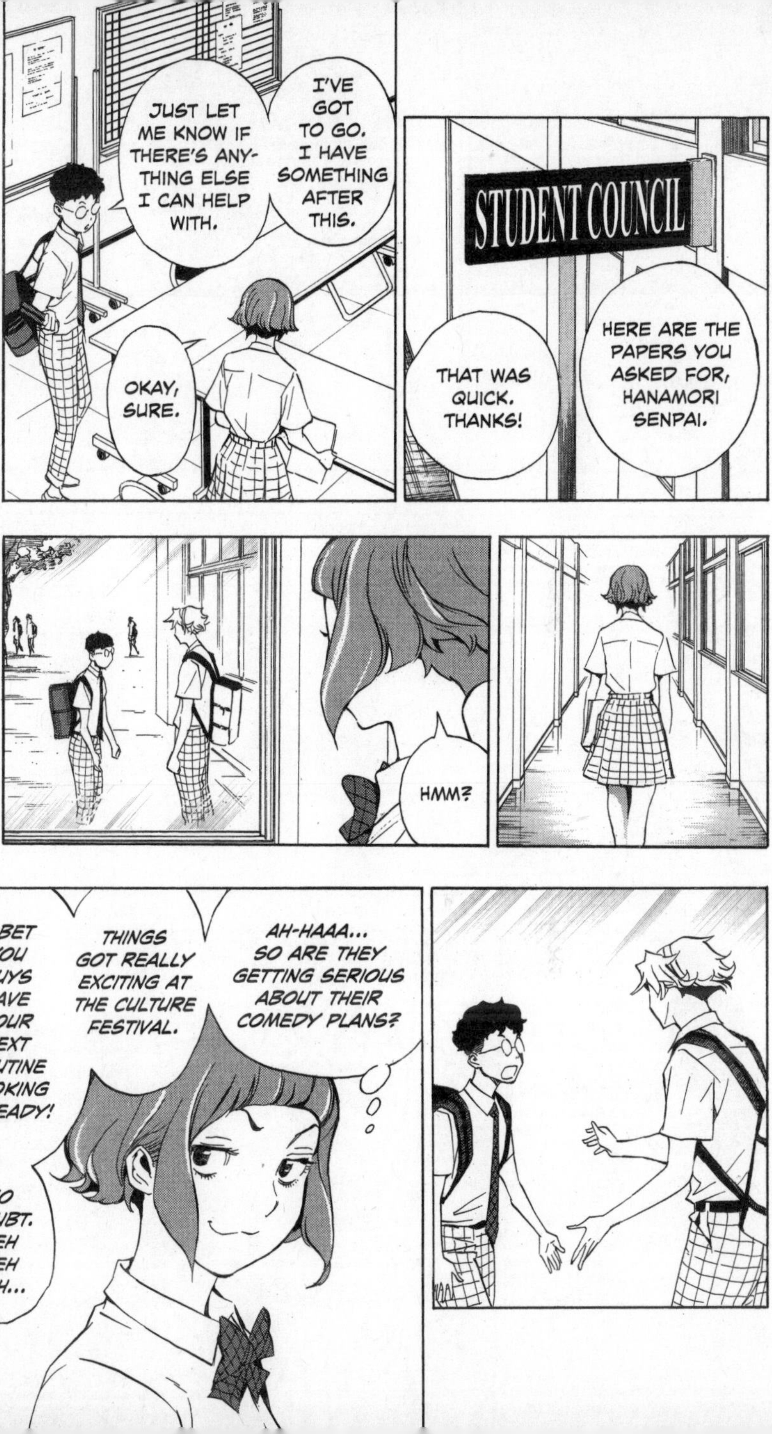
STUDENT COUNCIL
HERE ARE THE PAPERS YOU ASKED FOR, HANAMORI SENPAI.
THAT WAS QUICK. THANKS!
I'VE GOT TO GO. I HAVE SOMETHING AFTER THIS.
JUST LET ME KNOW IF THERE'S ANY-THING ELSE I CAN HELP WITH.
OKAY, SURE.
HMM?
AH-HAAA... SO ARE THEY GETTING SERIOUS ABOUT THEIR COMEDY PLANS?
THINGS GOT REALLY EXCITING AT THE CULTURE FESTIVAL.
I BET YOU GUYS HAVE YOUR NEXT ROUTINE COOKING ALREADY!
NO DOUBT. HEH HEH HEH...

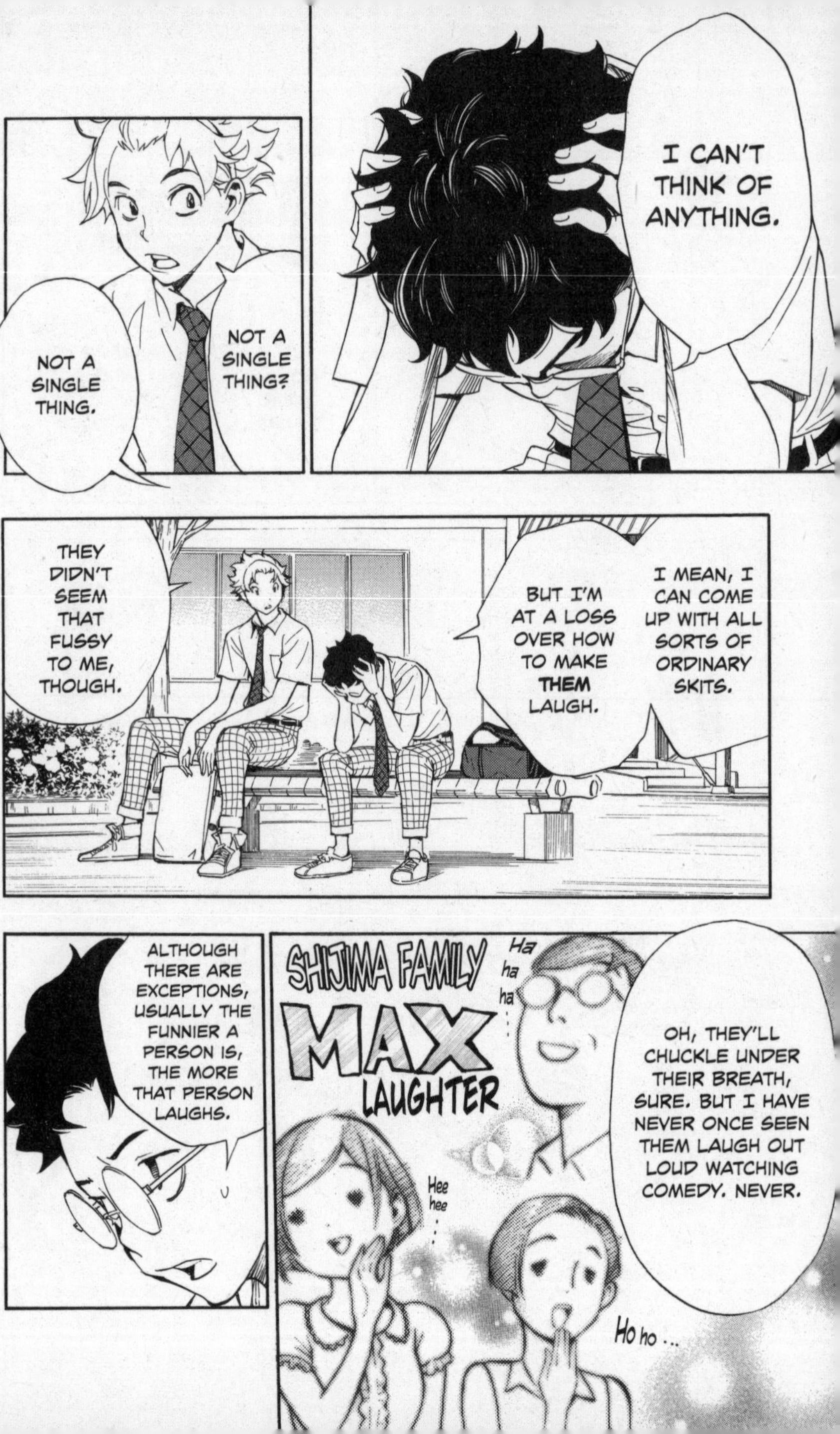
I CAN'T THINK OF ANYTHING.
NOT A SINGLE THING?
NOT A SINGLE THING.
I MEAN, I CAN COME UP WITH ALL SORTS OF ORDINARY SKITS.
BUT I'M AT A LOSS OVER HOW TO MAKE **THEM** LAUGH.
THEY DIDN'T SEEM THAT FUSSY TO ME, THOUGH.
OH, THEY'LL CHUCKLE UNDER THEIR BREATH, SURE. BUT I HAVE NEVER ONCE SEEN THEM LAUGH OUT LOUD WATCHING COMEDY. NEVER.
Ha ha ha
SHIJIMA FAMILY MAX LAUGHTER
Hee hee
Ho ho ...
ALTHOUGH THERE ARE EXCEPTIONS, USUALLY THE FUNNIER A PERSON IS, THE MORE THAT PERSON LAUGHS.

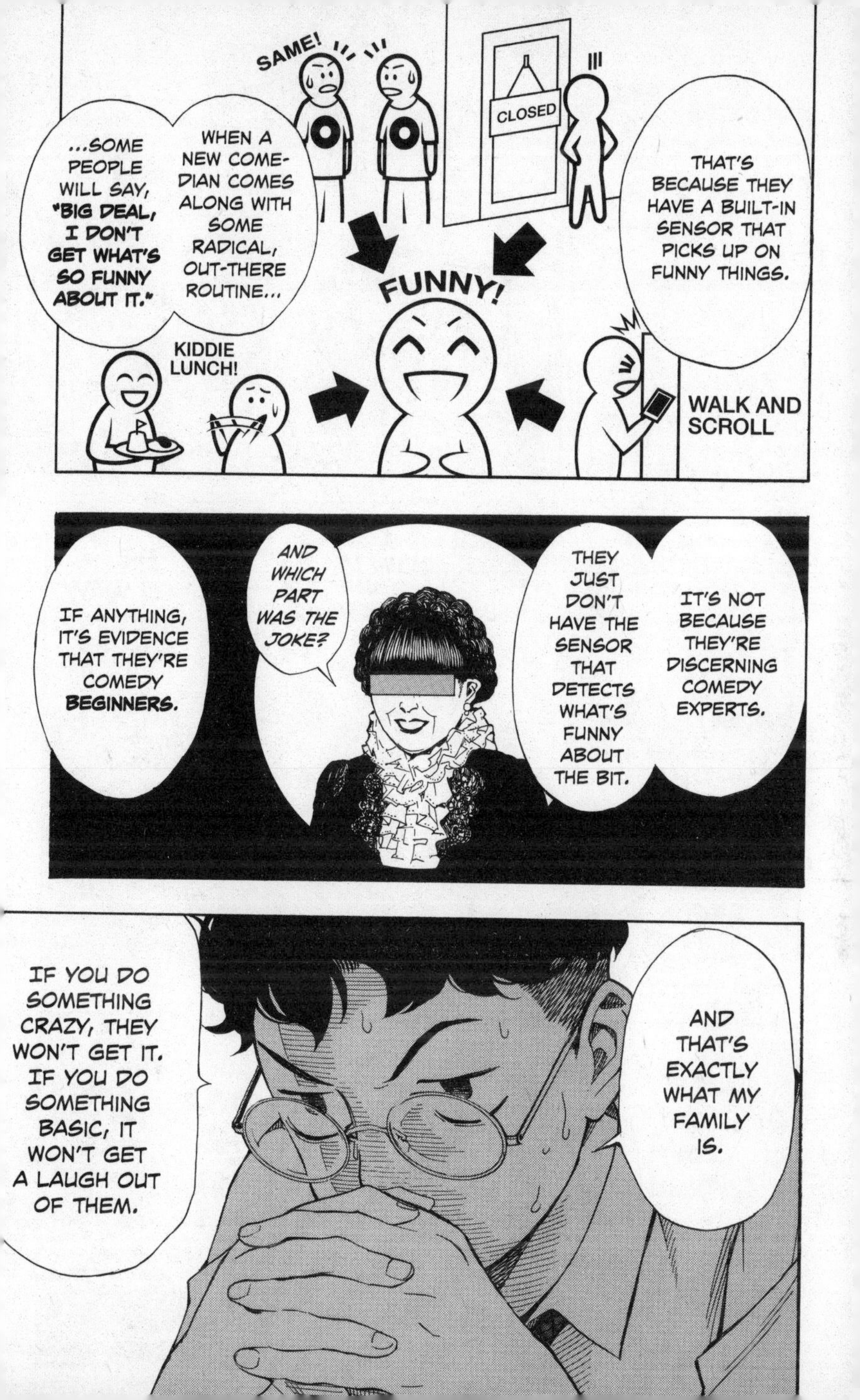
THAT'S BECAUSE THEY HAVE A BUILT-IN SENSOR THAT PICKS UP ON FUNNY THINGS.
CLOSED
SAME!
WHEN A NEW COMEDIAN COMES ALONG WITH SOME RADICAL, OUT-THERE ROUTINE...
...SOME PEOPLE WILL SAY, "BIG DEAL, I DON'T GET WHAT'S SO FUNNY ABOUT IT."
FUNNY!
WALK AND SCROLL
KIDDIE LUNCH!
IT'S NOT BECAUSE THEY'RE DISCERNING COMEDY EXPERTS.
THEY JUST DON'T HAVE THE SENSOR THAT DETECTS WHAT'S FUNNY ABOUT THE BIT.
AND WHICH PART WAS THE JOKE?
IF ANYTHING, IT'S EVIDENCE THAT THEY'RE COMEDY BEGINNERS.
AND THAT'S EXACTLY WHAT MY FAMILY IS.
IF YOU DO SOMETHING CRAZY, THEY WON'T GET IT. IF YOU DO SOMETHING BASIC, IT WON'T GET A LAUGH OUT OF THEM.

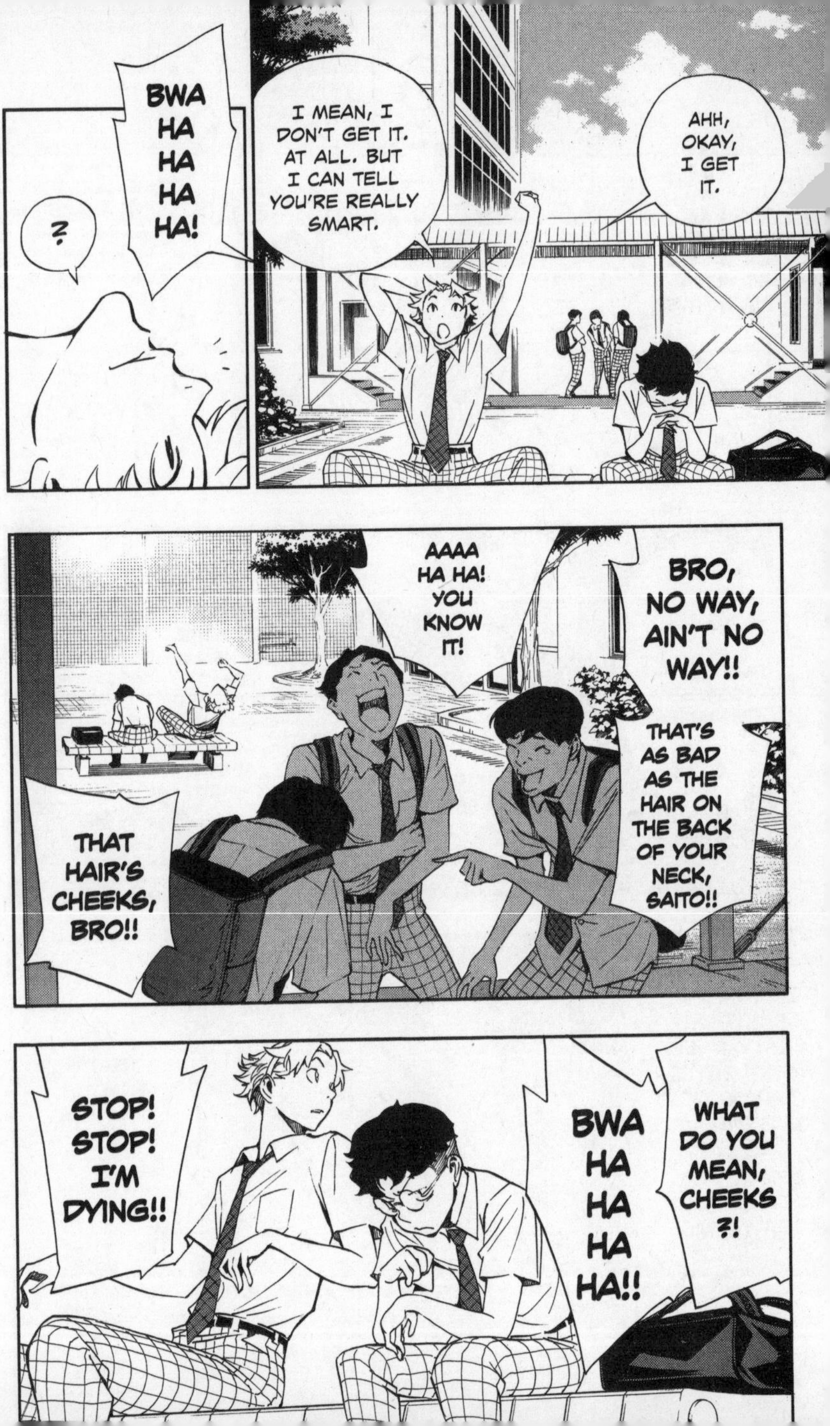
AHH, OKAY, I GET IT.
I MEAN, I DON'T GET IT. AT ALL. BUT I CAN TELL YOU'RE REALLY SMART.
BWA HA HA HA HA!
?
BRO, NO WAY, AIN'T NO WAY!!
AAAA HA HA! YOU KNOW IT!
THAT'S AS BAD AS THE HAIR ON THE BACK OF YOUR NECK, SAITO!!
THAT HAIR'S CHEEKS, BRO!!
WHAT DO YOU MEAN, CHEEKS?!
BWA HA HA HA HA!!
STOP! STOP! I'M DYING!!

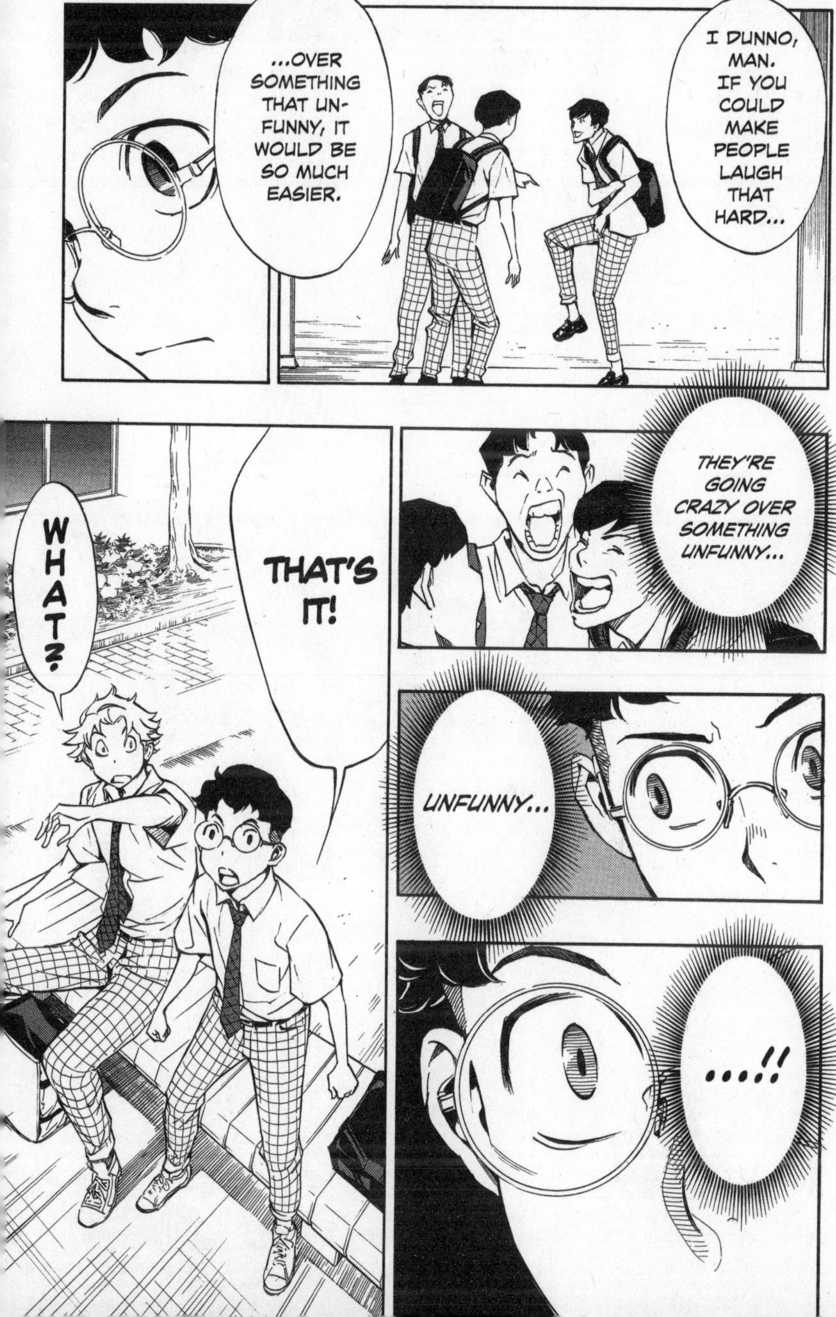
I DUNNO, MAN. IF YOU COULD MAKE PEOPLE LAUGH THAT HARD...
...OVER SOMETHING THAT UN-FUNNY, IT WOULD BE SO MUCH EASIER.
THEY'RE GOING CRAZY OVER SOMETHING UNFUNNY...
UNFUNNY...
....!!
THAT'S IT!
WHAT?

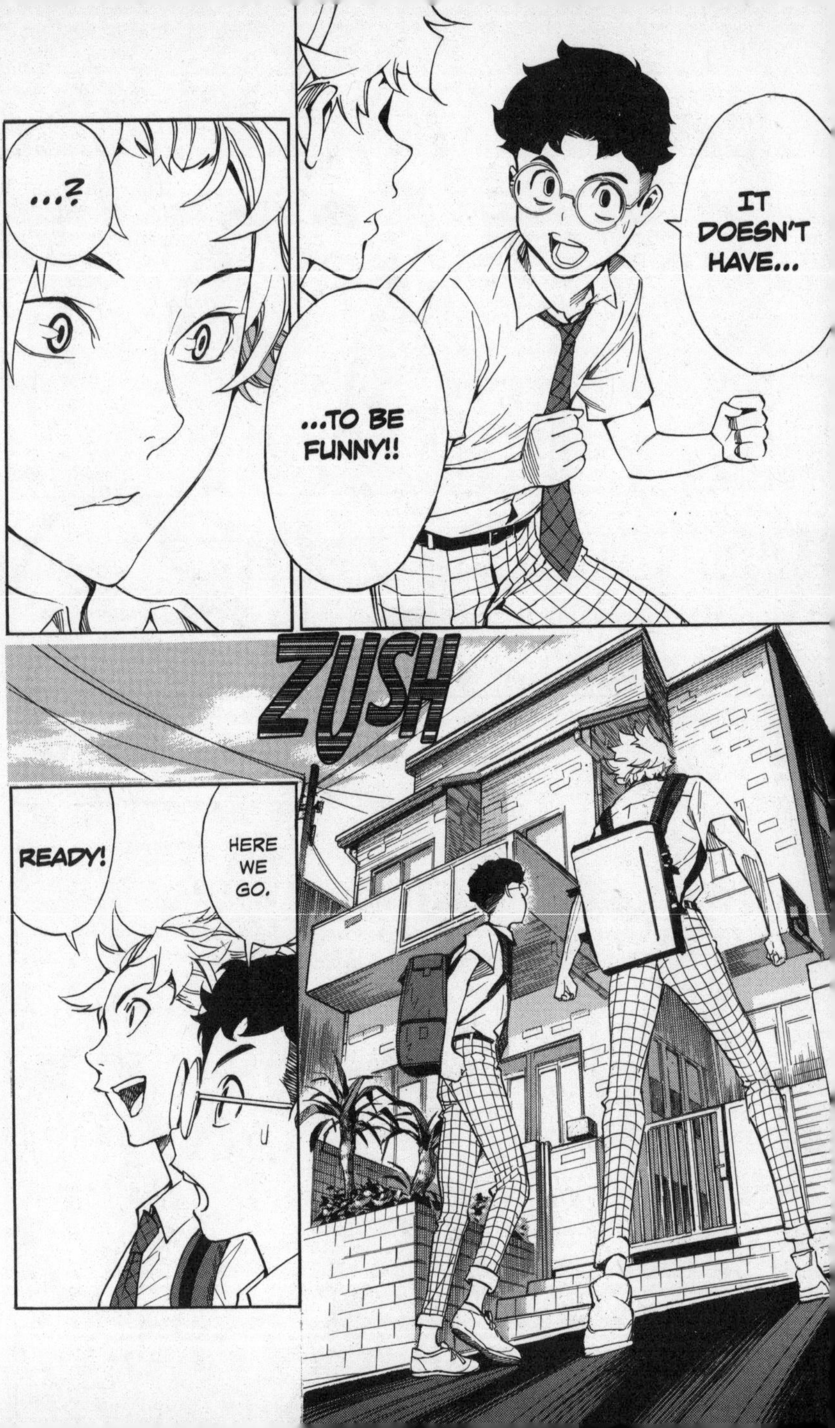
IT DOESN'T HAVE...
...TO BE FUNNY!!
...?
ZUSH
HERE WE GO.
READY!

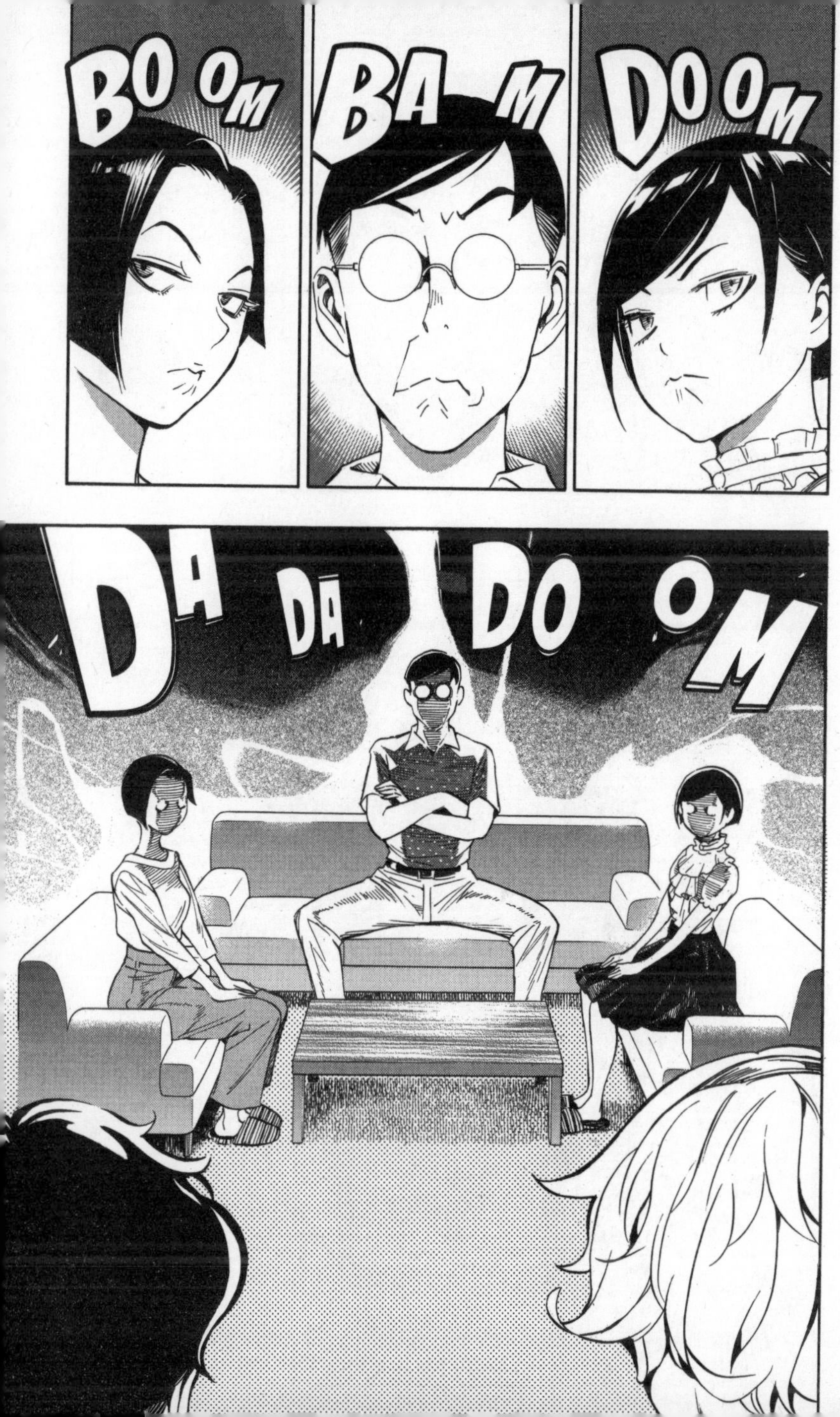
DOOM
BAM
BOOM
DA DA DOOM

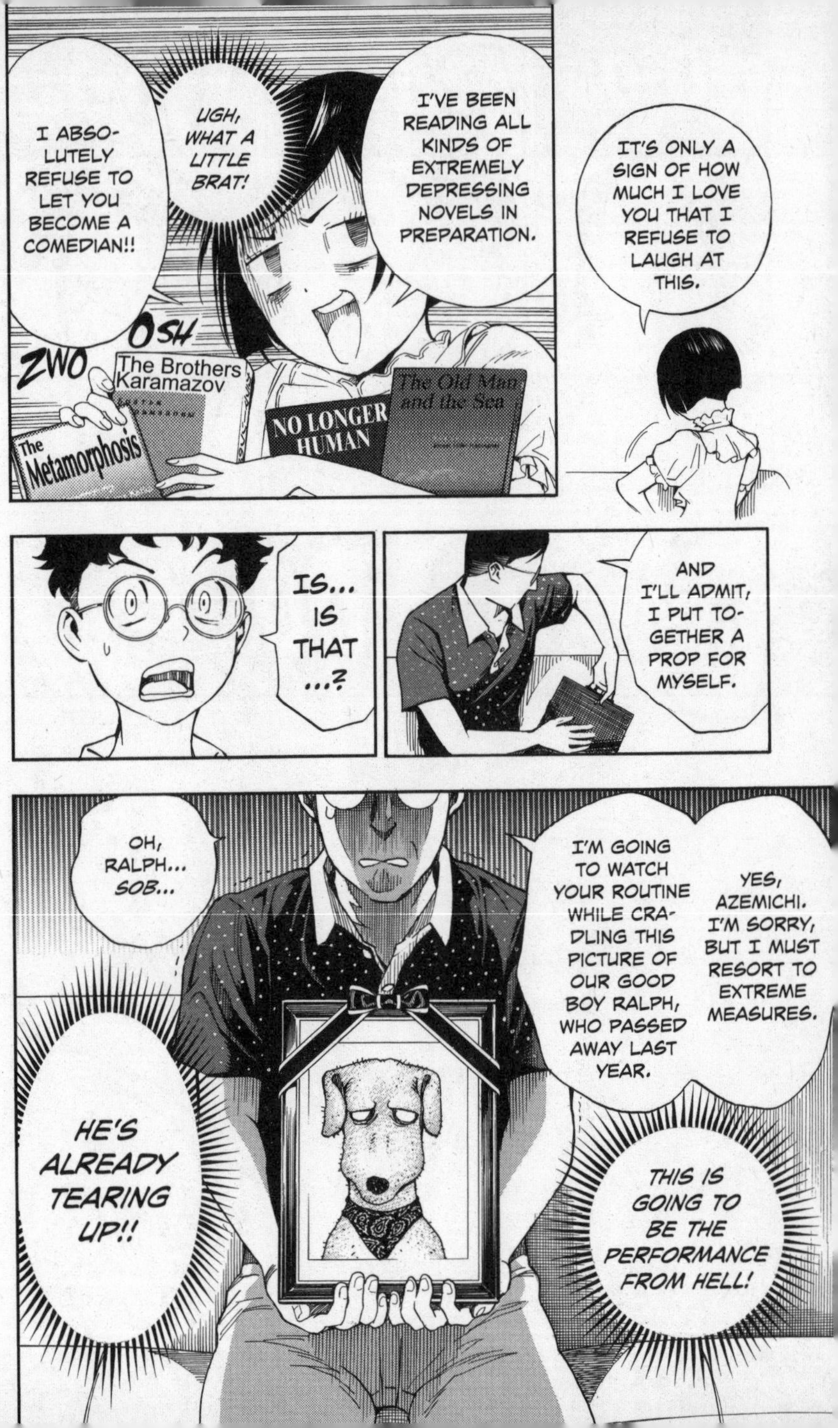

IT'S ONLY A SIGN OF HOW MUCH I LOVE YOU THAT I REFUSE TO LAUGH AT THIS.
I'VE BEEN READING ALL KINDS OF EXTREMELY DEPRESSING NOVELS IN PREPARATION.
UGH, WHAT A LITTLE BRAT!
I ABSOLUTELY REFUSE TO LET YOU BECOME A COMEDIAN!!
ZWOOSH
The Old Man and the Sea
NO LONGER HUMAN
The Brothers Karamazov
The Metamorphosis
AND I'LL ADMIT, I PUT TOGETHER A PROP FOR MYSELF.
IS... IS THAT...?
YES, AZEMICHI. I'M SORRY, BUT I MUST RESORT TO EXTREME MEASURES.
I'M GOING TO WATCH YOUR ROUTINE WHILE CRADLING THIS PICTURE OF OUR GOOD BOY RALPH, WHO PASSED AWAY LAST YEAR.
OH, RALPH... SOB...
THIS IS GOING TO BE THE PERFORMANCE FROM HELL!
HE'S ALREADY TEARING UP!!

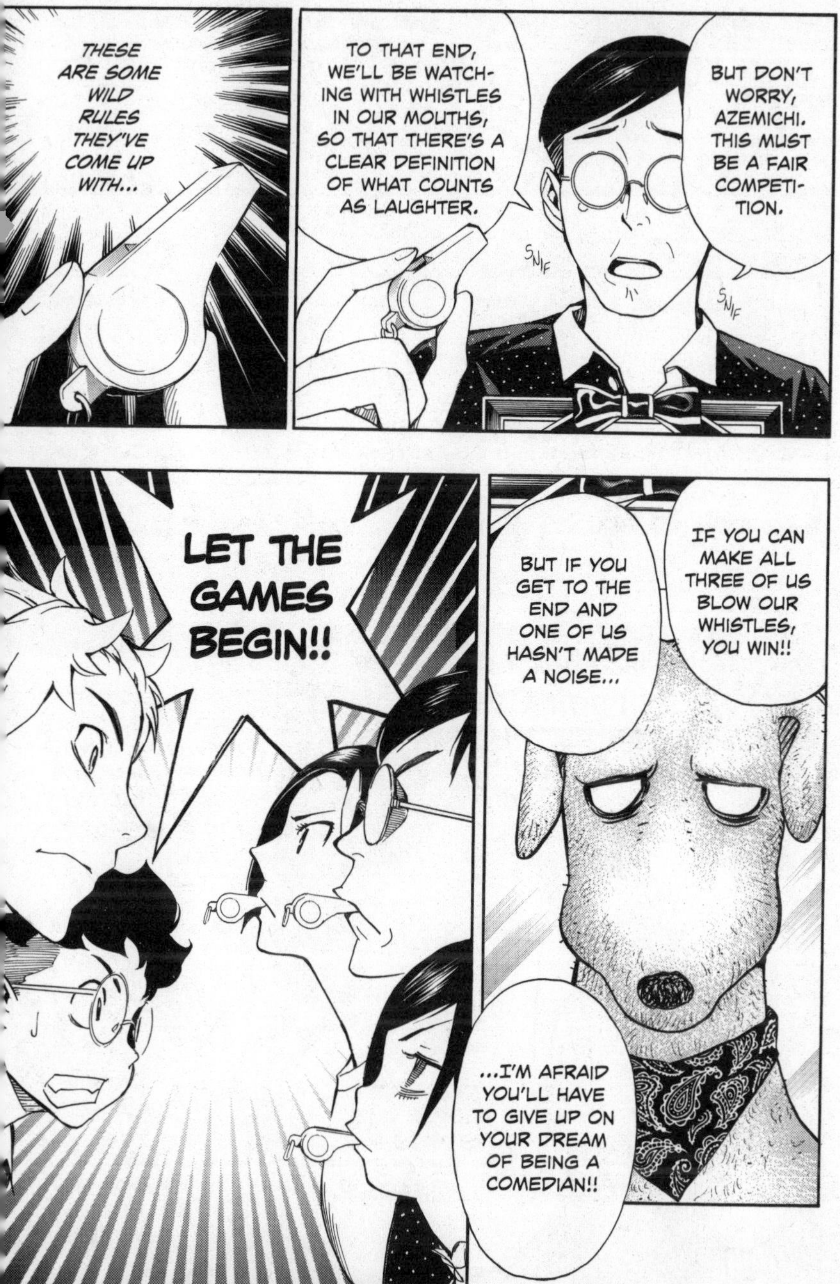
BUT DON'T WORRY, AZEMICHI. THIS MUST BE A FAIR COMPETITION.
SNIF
SNIF
TO THAT END, WE'LL BE WATCHING WITH WHISTLES IN OUR MOUTHS, SO THAT THERE'S A CLEAR DEFINITION OF WHAT COUNTS AS LAUGHTER.
THESE ARE SOME WILD RULES THEY'VE COME UP WITH...
IF YOU CAN MAKE ALL THREE OF US BLOW OUR WHISTLES, YOU WIN!!
BUT IF YOU GET TO THE END AND ONE OF US HASN'T MADE A NOISE...
...I'M AFRAID YOU'LL HAVE TO GIVE UP ON YOUR DREAM OF BEING A COMEDIAN!!
LET THE GAMES BEGIN!!

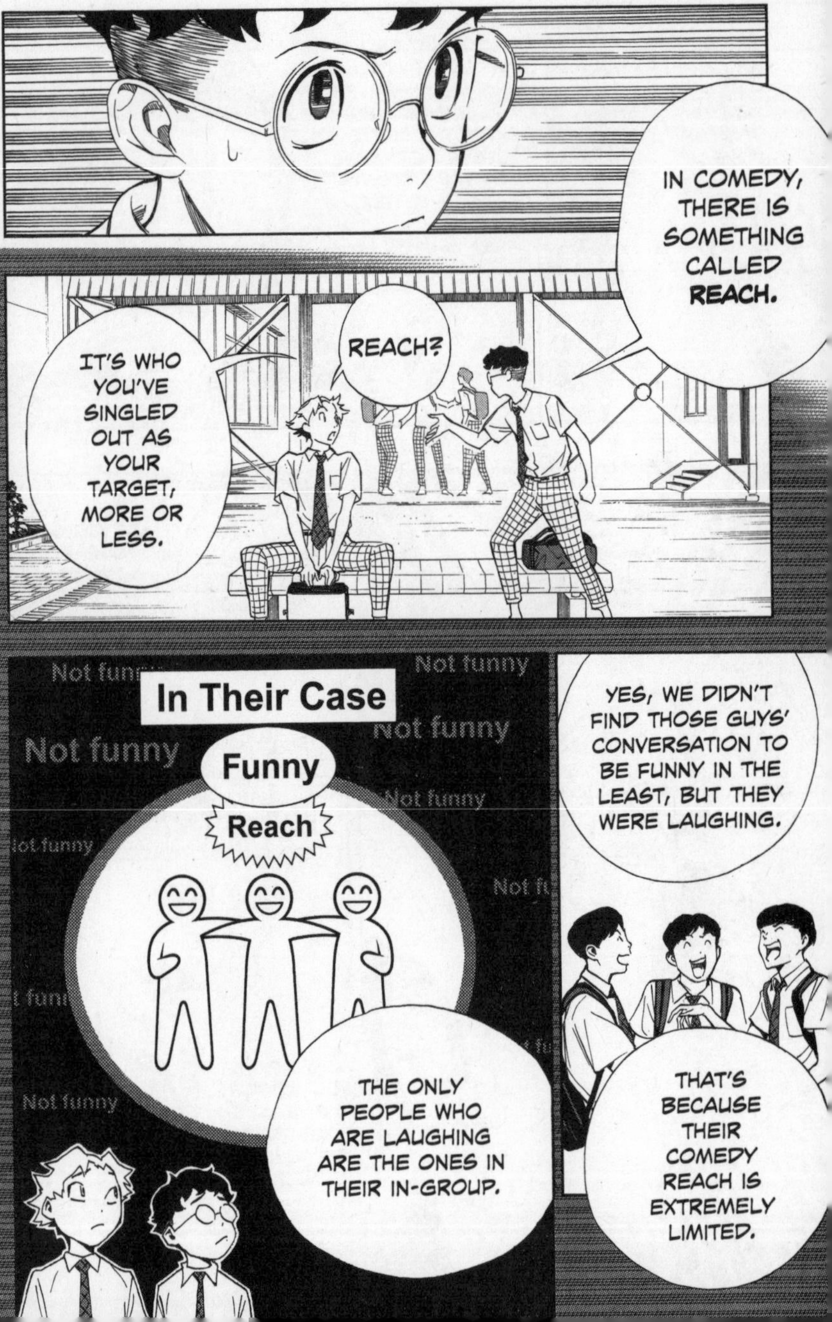
IN COMEDY, THERE IS SOMETHING CALLED REACH.
REACH?
IT'S WHO YOU'VE SINGLED OUT AS YOUR TARGET, MORE OR LESS.
YES, WE DIDN'T FIND THOSE GUYS' CONVERSATION TO BE FUNNY IN THE LEAST, BUT THEY WERE LAUGHING.
THAT'S BECAUSE THEIR COMEDY REACH IS EXTREMELY LIMITED.
Not funny
In Their Case
Not funny
Not funny
Funny
Not funny
Reach
Not funny
THE ONLY PEOPLE WHO ARE LAUGHING ARE THE ONES IN THEIR IN-GROUP.

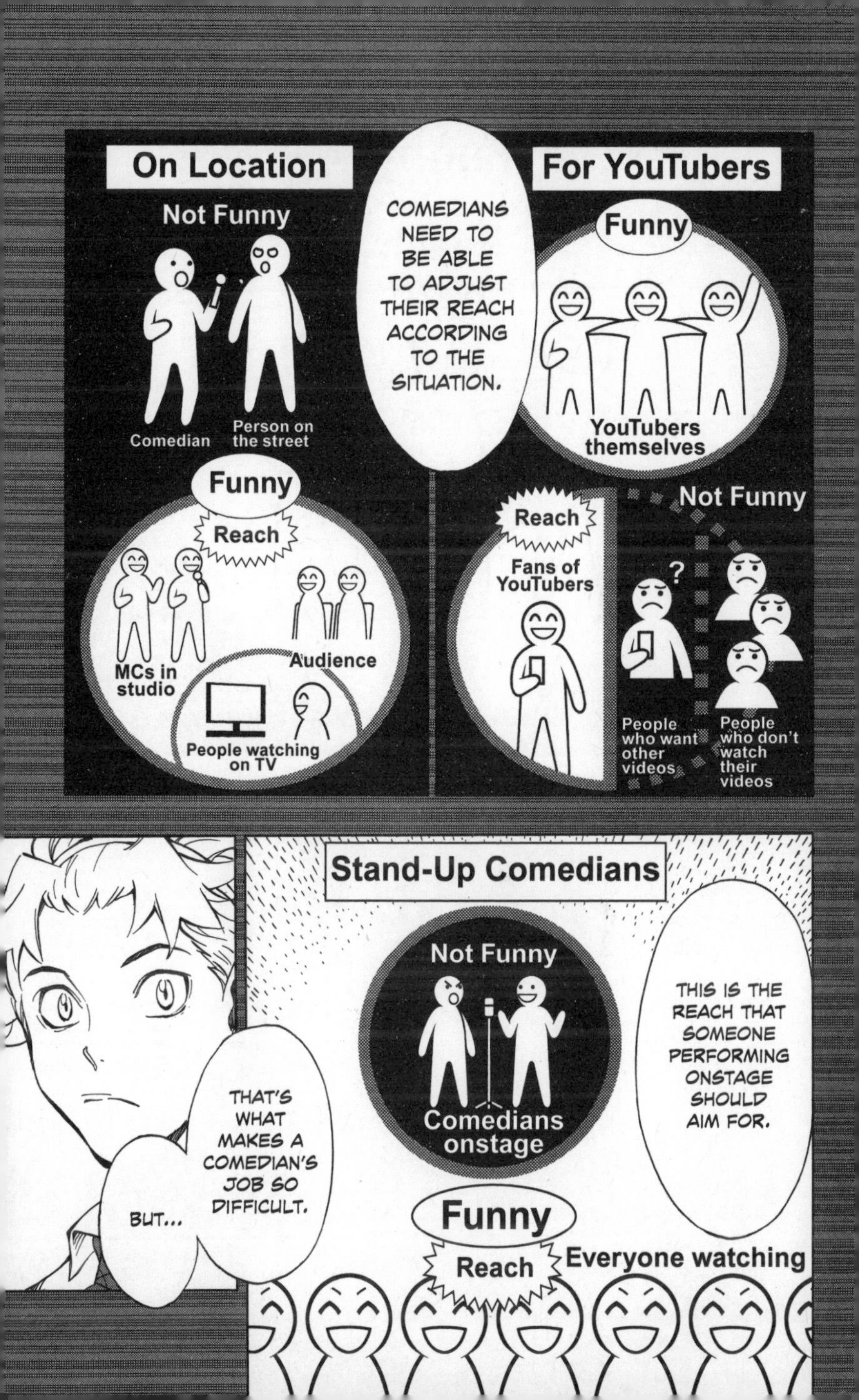
For YouTubers
Funny
YouTubers themselves
Reach
Fans of YouTubers
Not Funny
People who want other videos
People who don't watch their videos
COMEDIANS NEED TO BE ABLE TO ADJUST THEIR REACH ACCORDING TO THE SITUATION.
On Location
Not Funny
Comedian
Person on the street
Funny
Reach
MCs in studio
Audience
People watching on TV
Stand-Up Comedians
Not Funny
Comedians onstage
THIS IS THE REACH THAT SOMEONE PERFORMING ONSTAGE SHOULD AIM FOR.
Funny
Reach
Everyone watching
THAT'S WHAT MAKES A COMEDIAN'S JOB SO DIFFICULT.
BUT...

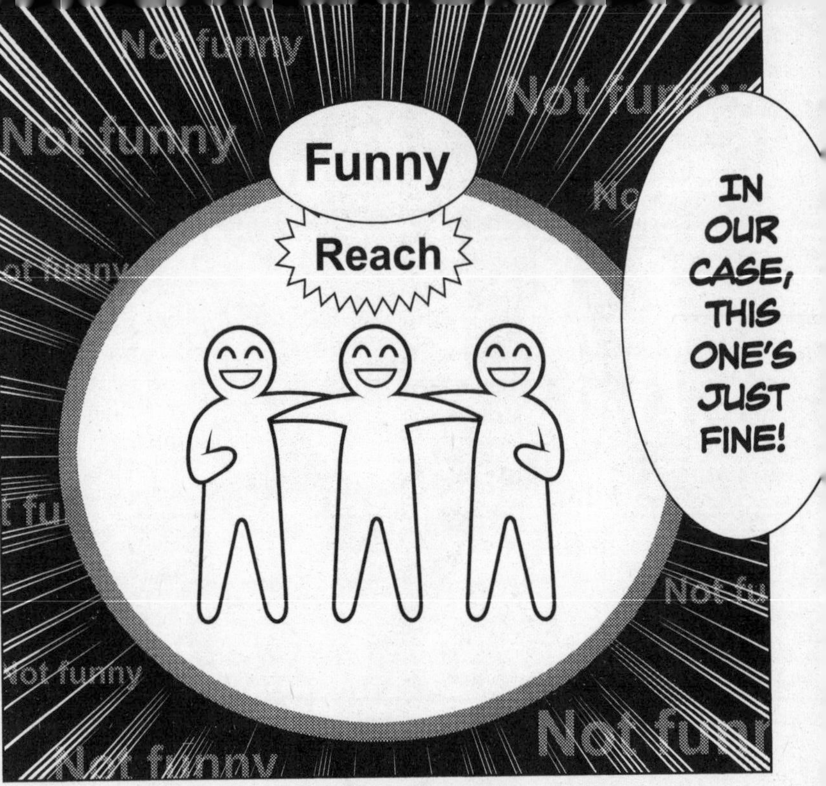
IN OUR CASE, THIS ONE'S JUST FINE!
Not funny
Not funny
Funny
Reach
Not funny

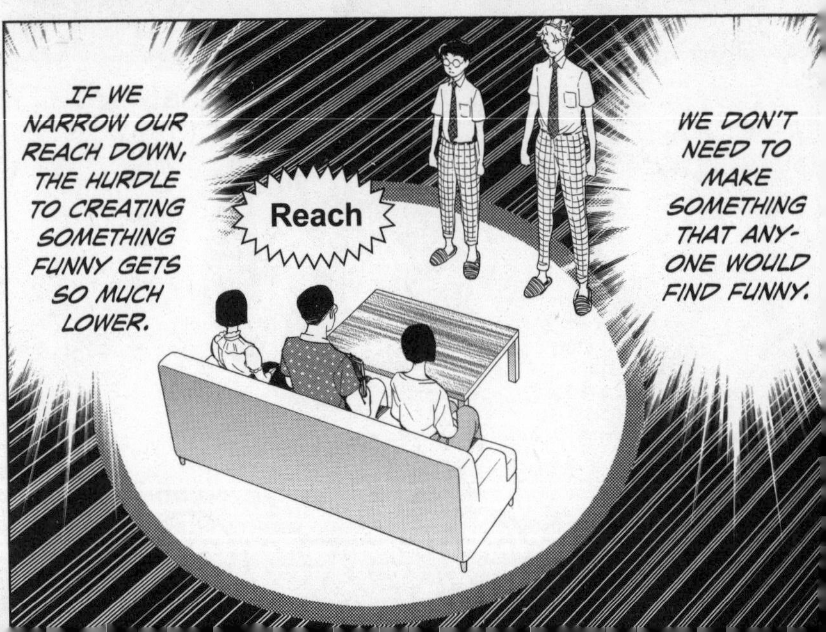
WE DON'T NEED TO MAKE SOMETHING THAT ANY-ONE WOULD FIND FUNNY.
Reach
IF WE NARROW OUR REACH DOWN, THE HURDLE TO CREATING SOMETHING FUNNY GETS SO MUCH LOWER.

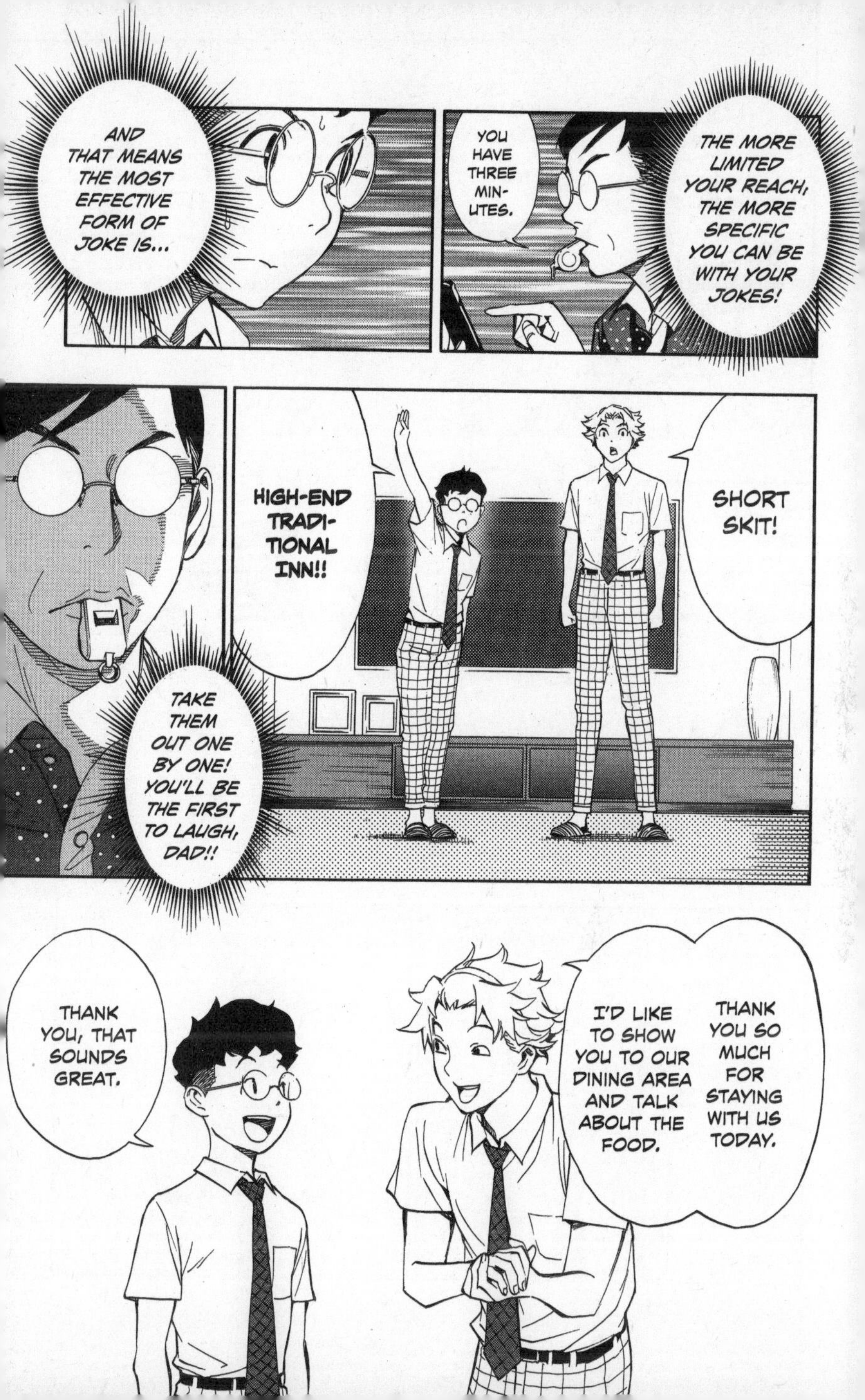
THE MORE LIMITED YOUR REACH, THE MORE SPECIFIC YOU CAN BE WITH YOUR JOKES!
YOU HAVE THREE MIN-UTES.
AND THAT MEANS THE MOST EFFECTIVE FORM OF JOKE IS...
SHORT SKIT!
HIGH-END TRADI-TIONAL INN!!
TAKE THEM OUT ONE BY ONE! YOU'LL BE THE FIRST TO LAUGH, DAD!!
THANK YOU SO MUCH FOR STAYING WITH US TODAY.
I'D LIKE TO SHOW YOU TO OUR DINING AREA AND TALK ABOUT THE FOOD.
THANK YOU, THAT SOUNDS GREAT.

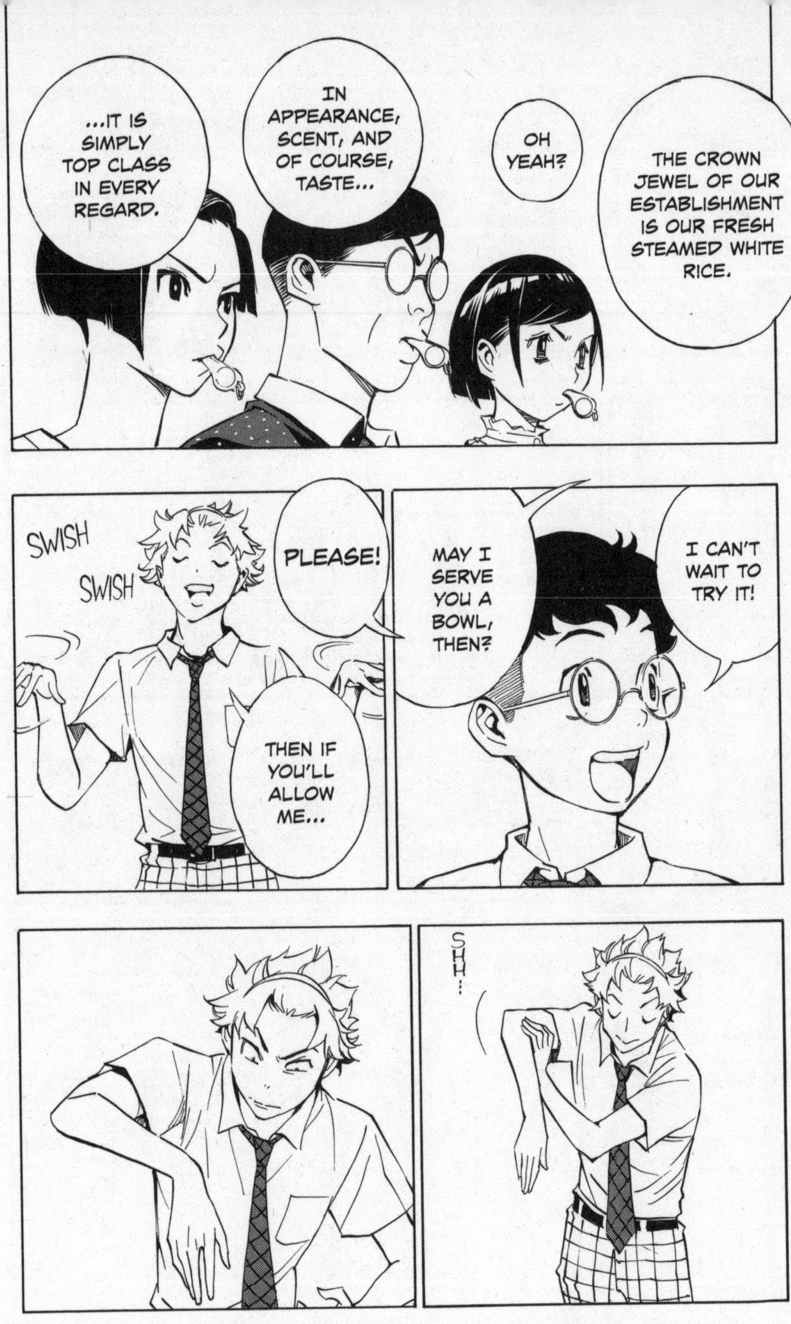
THE CROWN JEWEL OF OUR ESTABLISHMENT IS OUR FRESH STEAMED WHITE RICE.
OH YEAH?
IN APPEARANCE, SCENT, AND OF COURSE, TASTE...
...IT IS SIMPLY TOP CLASS IN EVERY REGARD.
I CAN'T WAIT TO TRY IT!
MAY I SERVE YOU A BOWL, THEN?
PLEASE!
SWISH
SWISH
THEN IF YOU'LL ALLOW ME...
SHH...

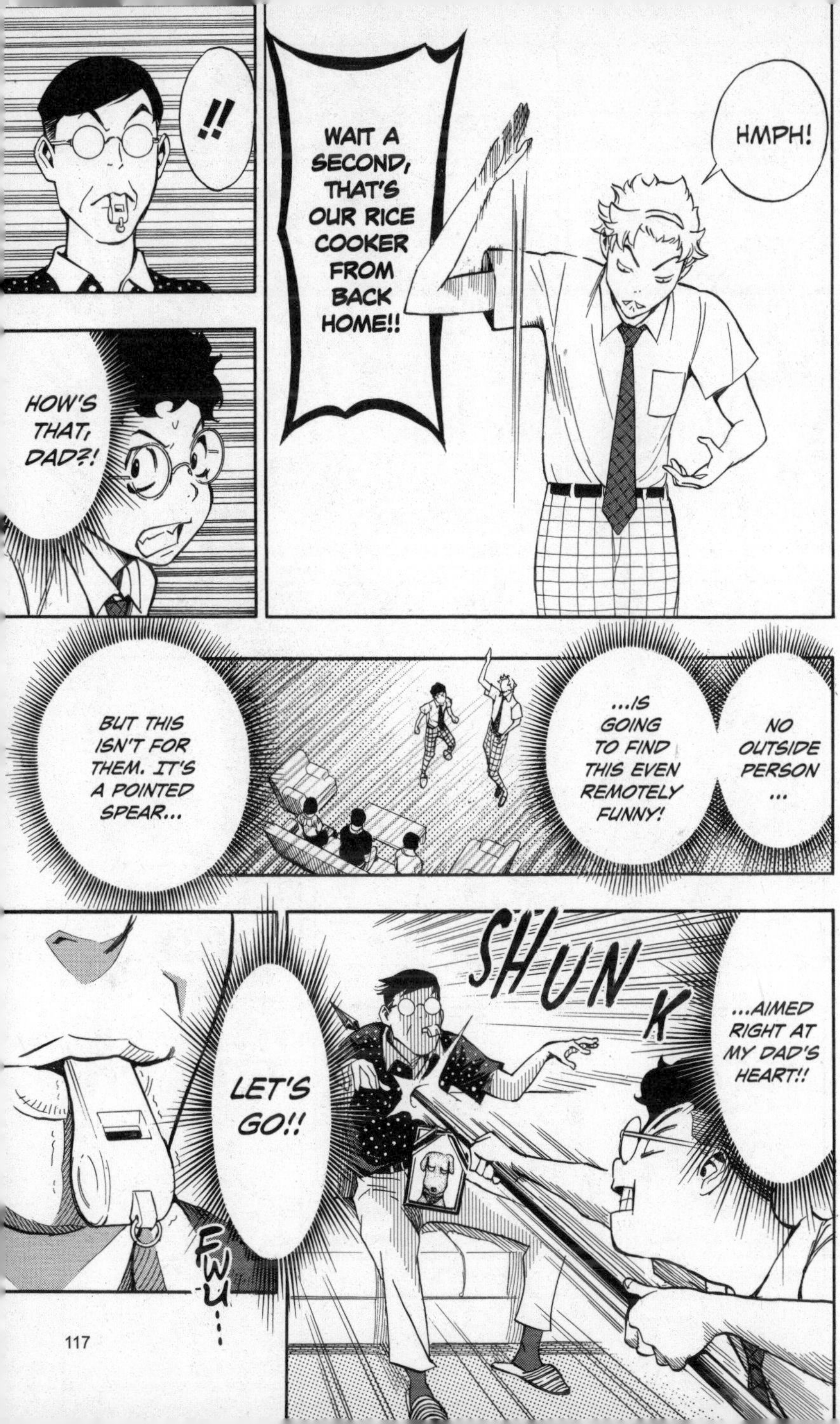
HMPH!
WAIT A SECOND, THAT'S OUR RICE COOKER FROM BACK HOME!!
!!
HOW'S THAT, DAD?!
NO OUTSIDE PERSON ...
...IS GOING TO FIND THIS EVEN REMOTELY FUNNY!
BUT THIS ISN'T FOR THEM. IT'S A POINTED SPEAR...
...AIMED RIGHT AT MY DAD'S HEART!!
SHUNK
LET'S GO!!
FWU...

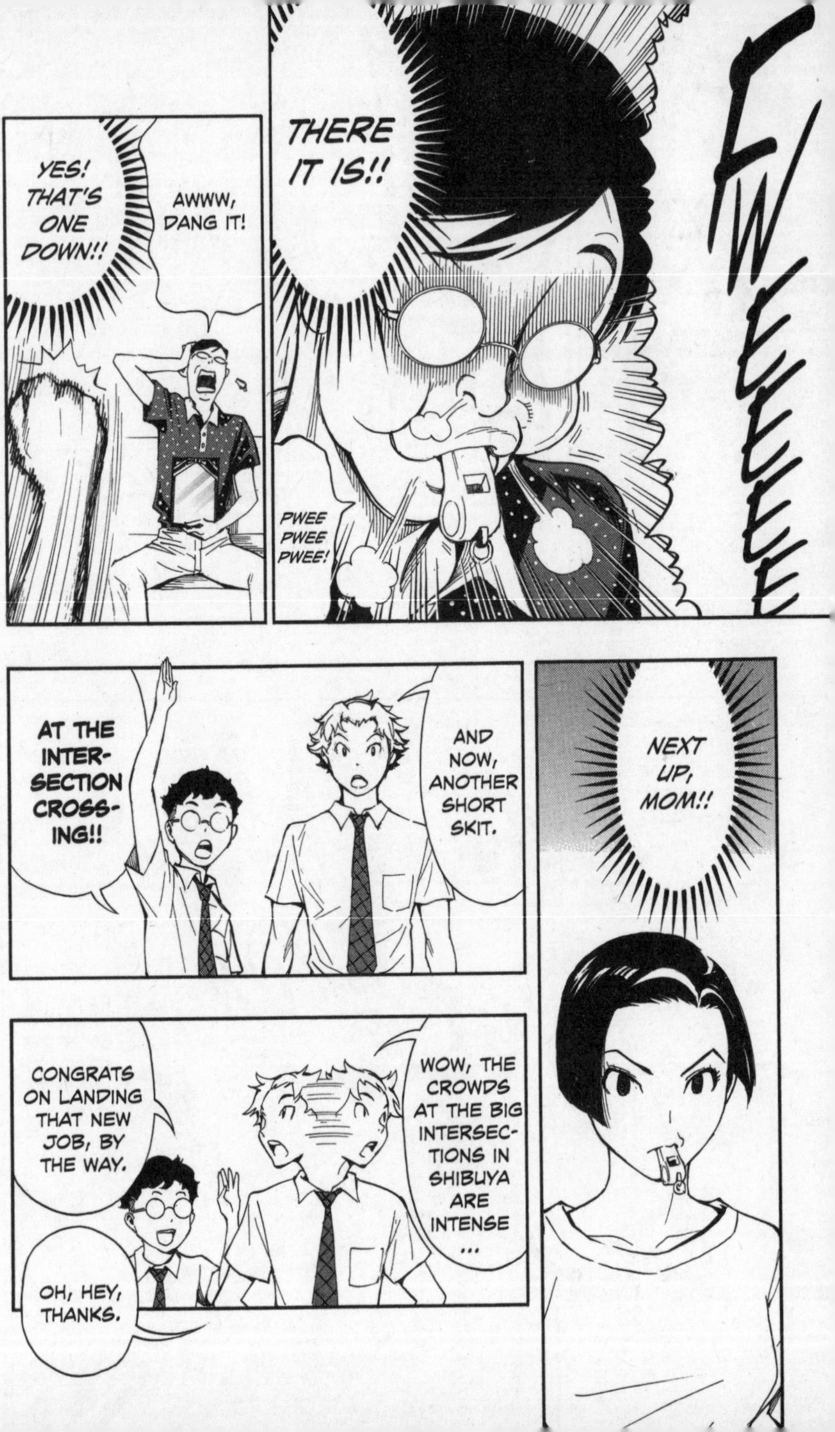
FWEEEEEE
THERE IT IS!!
PWEE PWEE PWEE!
AWWW, DANG IT!
YES! THAT'S ONE DOWN!!
NEXT UP, MOM!!
AND NOW, ANOTHER SHORT SKIT.
AT THE INTER-SECTION CROSS-ING!!
WOW, THE CROWDS AT THE BIG INTERSEC-TIONS IN SHIBUYA ARE INTENSE...
CONGRATS ON LANDING THAT NEW JOB, BY THE WAY.
OH, HEY, THANKS.

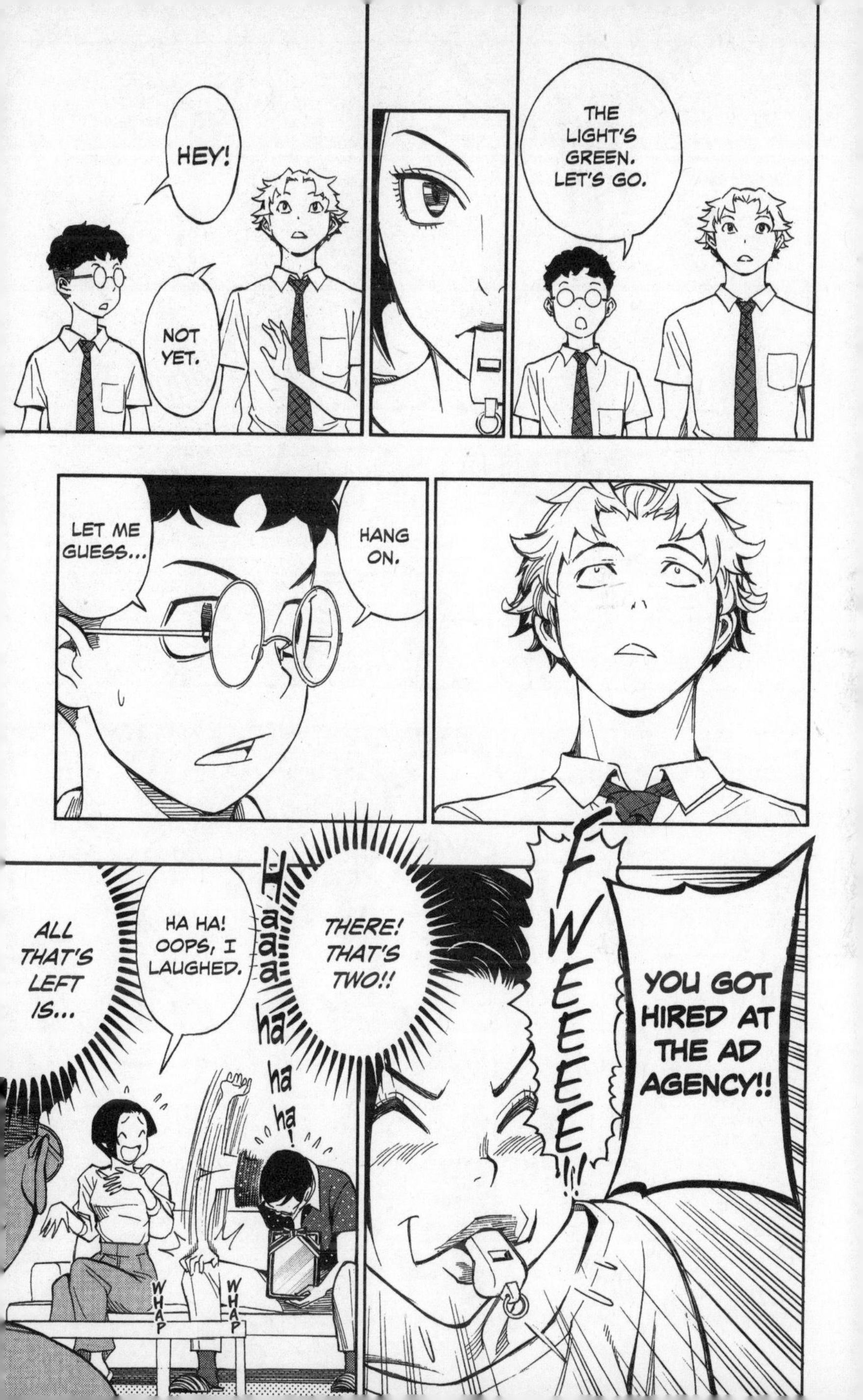
THE LIGHT'S GREEN. LET'S GO.
HEY!
NOT YET.
HANG ON.
LET ME GUESS...
FWEEEEE!!
YOU GOT HIRED AT THE AD AGENCY!!
THERE! THAT'S TWO!!
Haaaa ha ha ha!
HA HA! OOPS, I LAUGHED.
ALL THAT'S LEFT IS...
WHAP
WHAP

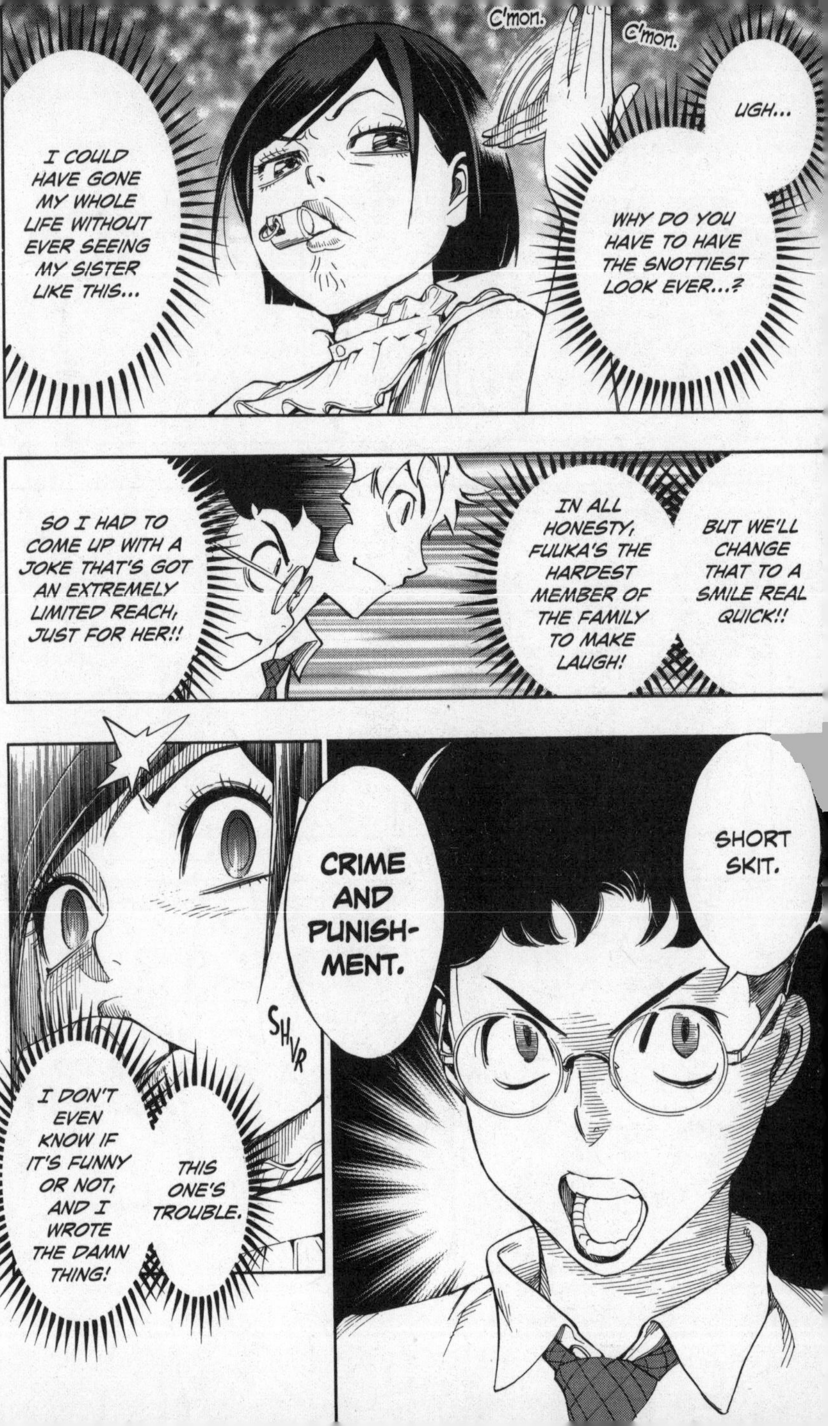
C'mon.
C'mon.
UGH...
WHY DO YOU HAVE TO HAVE THE SNOTTIEST LOOK EVER...?
I COULD HAVE GONE MY WHOLE LIFE WITHOUT EVER SEEING MY SISTER LIKE THIS...
IN ALL HONESTY, FUUKA'S THE HARDEST MEMBER OF THE FAMILY TO MAKE LAUGH!
BUT WE'LL CHANGE THAT TO A SMILE REAL QUICK!!
SO I HAD TO COME UP WITH A JOKE THAT'S GOT AN EXTREMELY LIMITED REACH, JUST FOR HER!!
SHORT SKIT.
CRIME AND PUNISH-MENT.
SHVR
THIS ONE'S TROUBLE.
I DON'T EVEN KNOW IF IT'S FUNNY OR NOT, AND I WROTE THE DAMN THING!

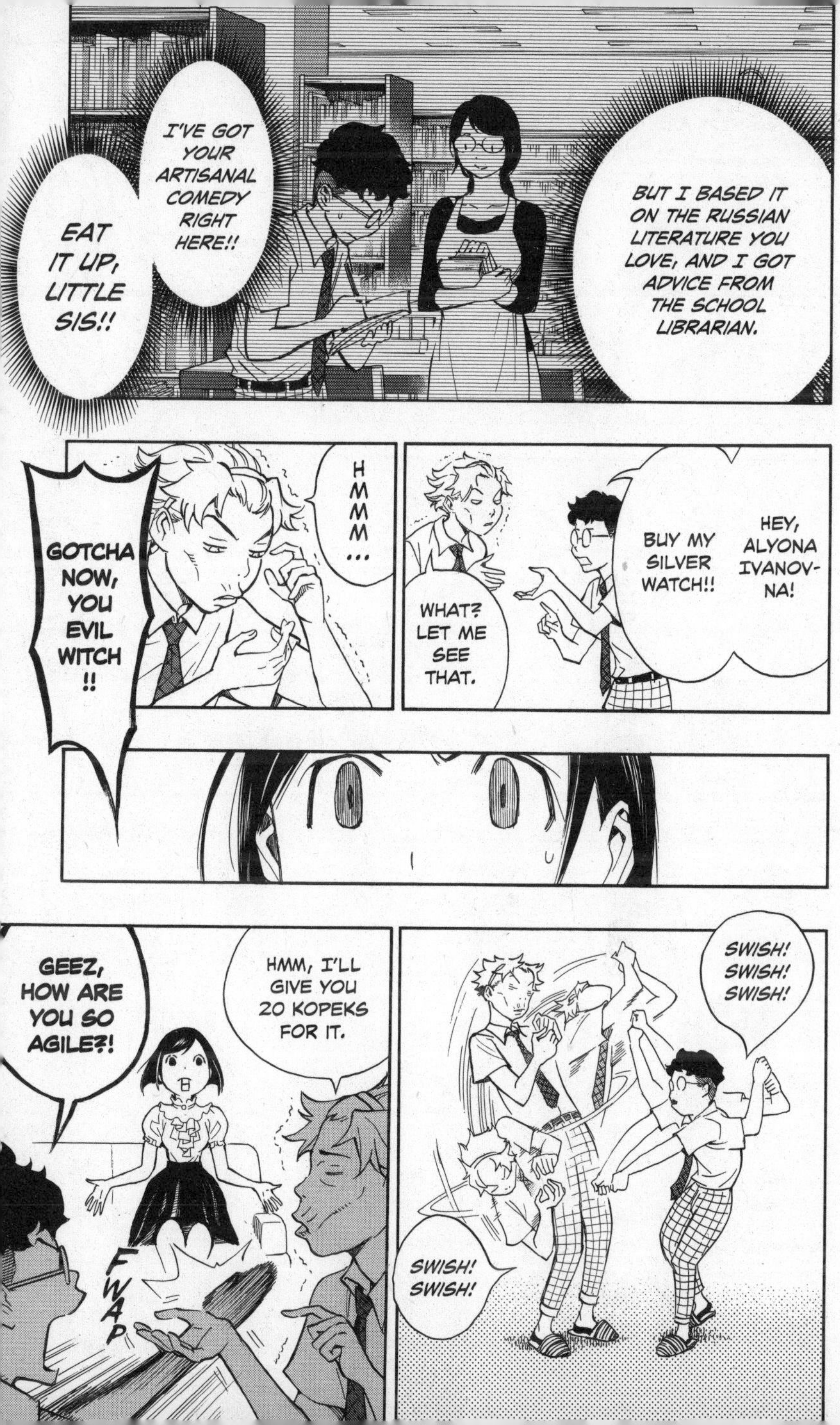
BUT I BASED IT ON THE RUSSIAN LITERATURE YOU LOVE, AND I GOT ADVICE FROM THE SCHOOL LIBRARIAN.
I'VE GOT YOUR ARTISANAL COMEDY RIGHT HERE!!
EAT IT UP, LITTLE SIS!!
HEY, ALYONA IVANOV-NA!
BUY MY SILVER WATCH!!
WHAT? LET ME SEE THAT.
HMMM...
GOTCHA NOW, YOU EVIL WITCH!!
SWISH! SWISH! SWISH!
SWISH! SWISH!
HMM, I'LL GIVE YOU 20 KOPEKS FOR IT.
GEEZ, HOW ARE YOU SO AGILE?!
FWAP

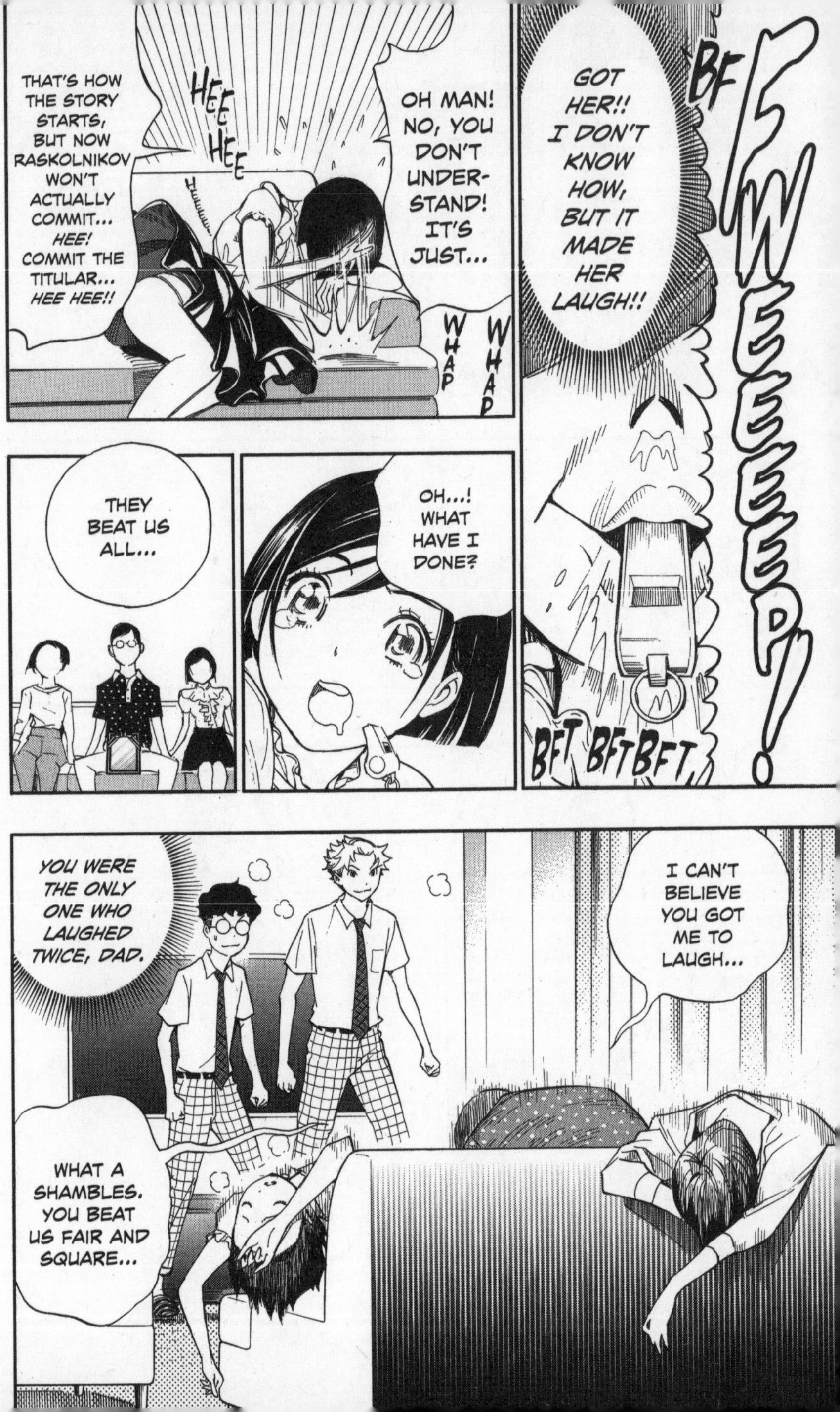
GOT HER!! I DON'T KNOW HOW, BUT IT MADE HER LAUGH!!
BFWEEEEEEP!
BFT BFT BFT
OH MAN! NO, YOU DON'T UNDER-STAND! IT'S JUST...
HEE HEE
THAT'S HOW THE STORY STARTS, BUT NOW RASKOLNIKOV WON'T ACTUALLY COMMIT... HEE! COMMIT THE TITULAR... HEE HEE!!
WHAP WHAP
OH...! WHAT HAVE I DONE?
THEY BEAT US ALL...
I CAN'T BELIEVE YOU GOT ME TO LAUGH...
YOU WERE THE ONLY ONE WHO LAUGHED TWICE, DAD.
WHAT A SHAMBLES. YOU BEAT US FAIR AND SQUARE...

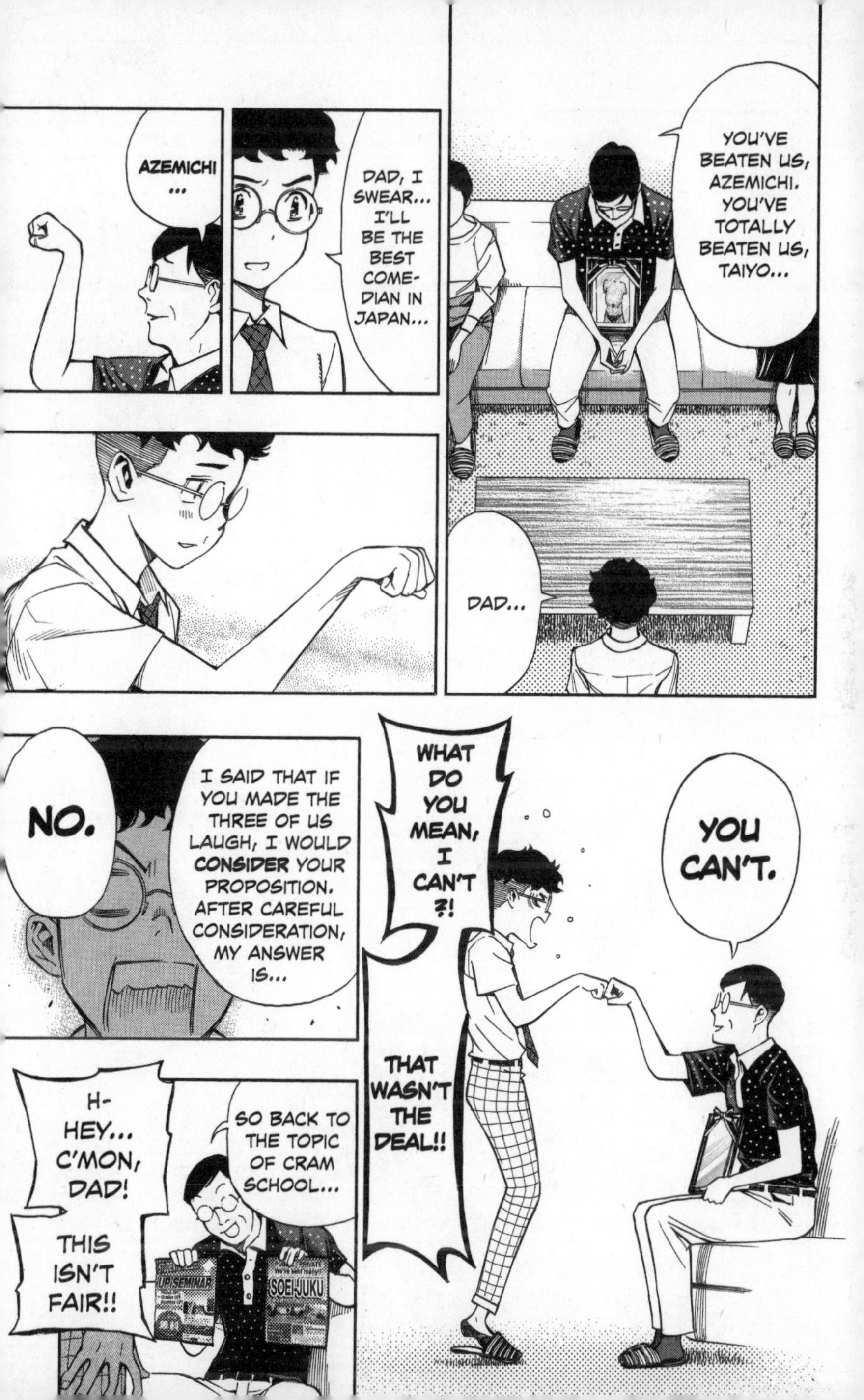

YOU'VE BEATEN US, AZEMICHI. YOU'VE TOTALLY BEATEN US, TAIYO...
DAD...
DAD, I SWEAR... I'LL BE THE BEST COMEDIAN IN JAPAN...
AZEMICHI...
YOU CAN'T.
WHAT DO YOU MEAN, I CAN'T?!
THAT WASN'T THE DEAL!!
I SAID THAT IF YOU MADE THE THREE OF US LAUGH, I WOULD **CONSIDER** YOUR PROPOSITION. AFTER CAREFUL CONSIDERATION, MY ANSWER IS...
NO.
SO BACK TO THE TOPIC OF CRAM SCHOOL...
UP SEMINAR
SOEI-JUKU
H-HEY... C'MON, DAD!
THIS ISN'T FAIR!!

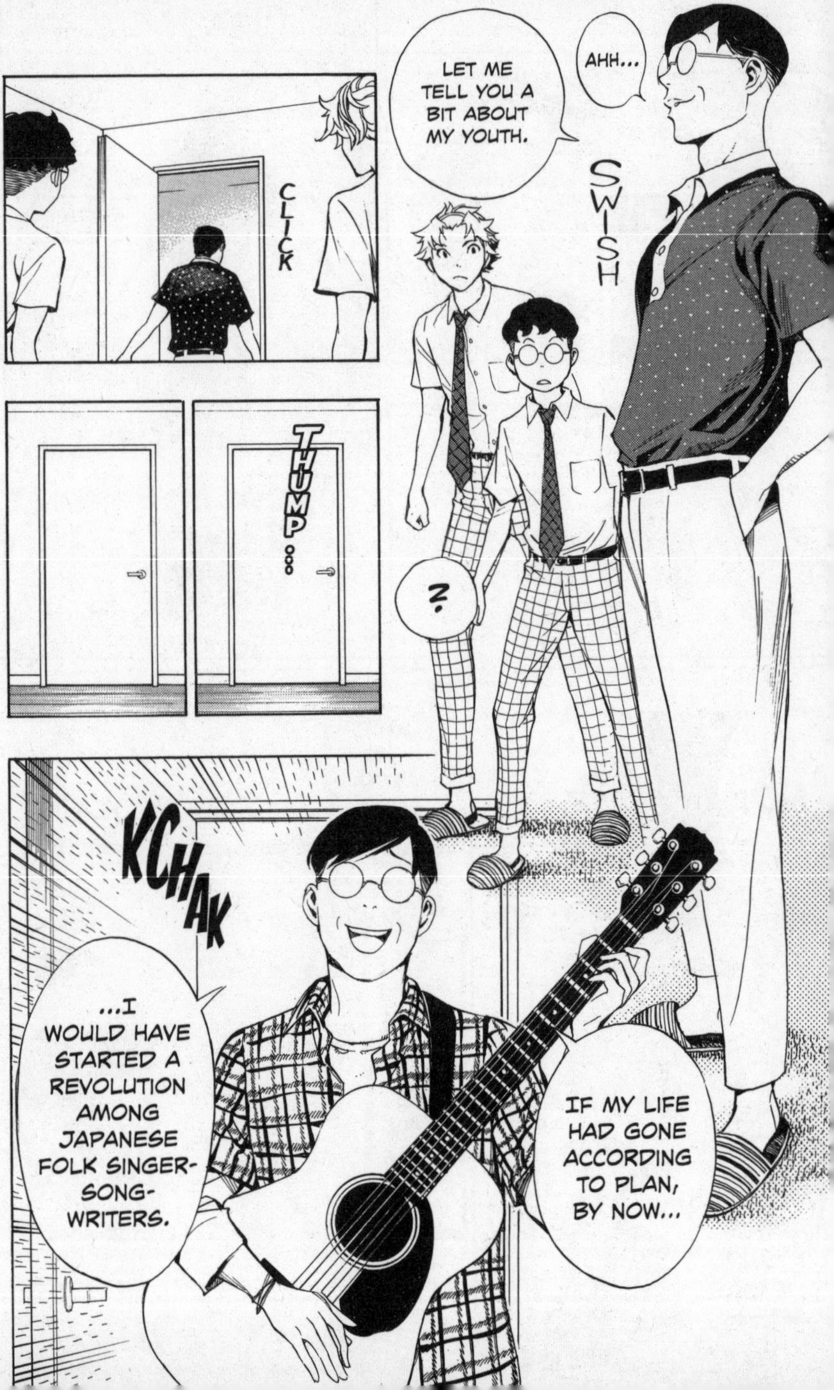
AHH...
LET ME TELL YOU A BIT ABOUT MY YOUTH.
SWISH
?
CLICK
THUMP...
KCHAK
IF MY LIFE HAD GONE ACCORDING TO PLAN, BY NOW...
...I WOULD HAVE STARTED A REVOLUTION AMONG JAPANESE FOLK SINGER-SONG-WRITERS.

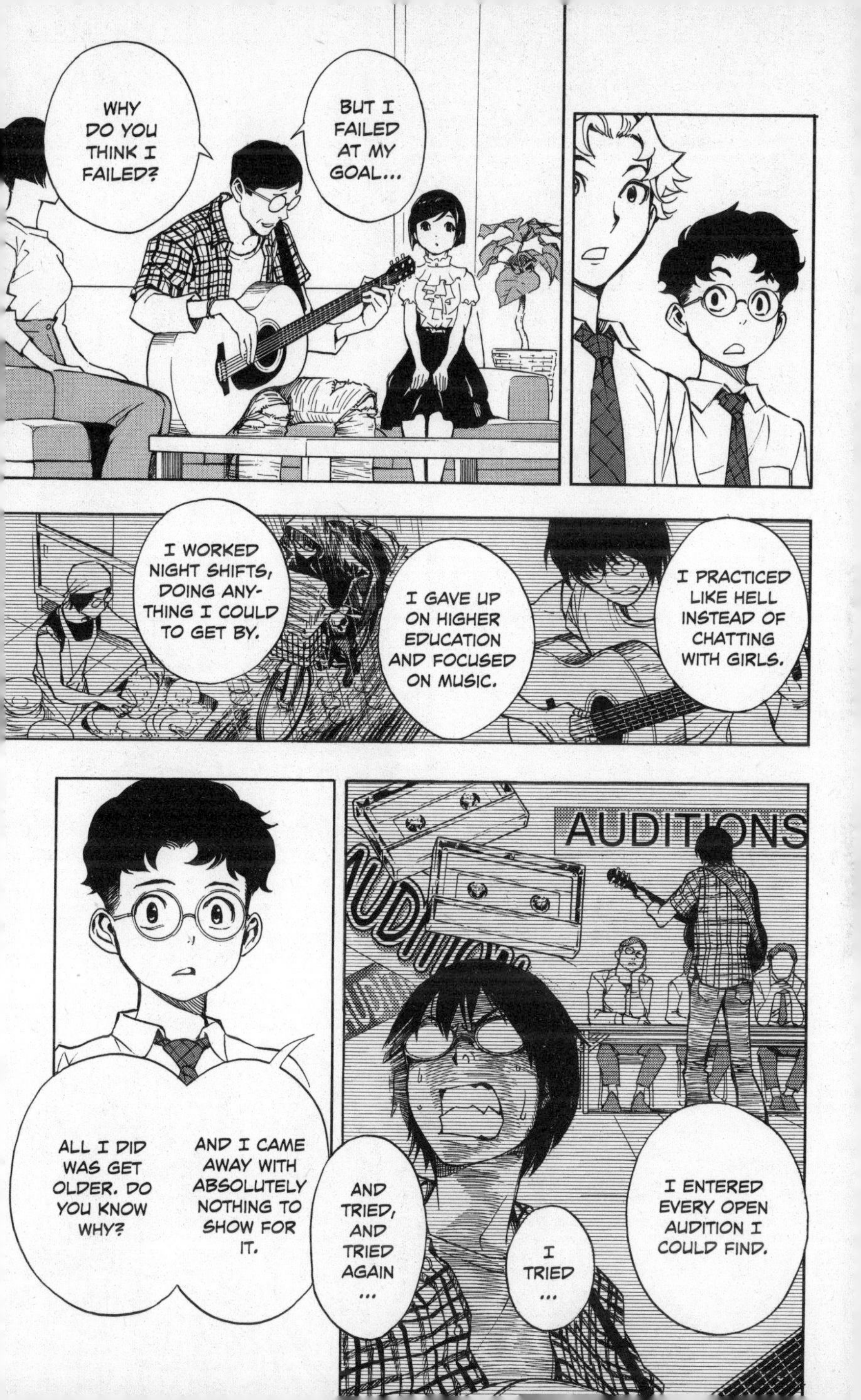
BUT I FAILED AT MY GOAL...
WHY DO YOU THINK I FAILED?
I PRACTICED LIKE HELL INSTEAD OF CHATTING WITH GIRLS.
I GAVE UP ON HIGHER EDUCATION AND FOCUSED ON MUSIC.
I WORKED NIGHT SHIFTS, DOING ANYTHING I COULD TO GET BY.
AUDITIONS
I ENTERED EVERY OPEN AUDITION I COULD FIND.
I TRIED...
AND TRIED, AND TRIED AGAIN...
AND I CAME AWAY WITH ABSOLUTELY NOTHING TO SHOW FOR IT.
ALL I DID WAS GET OLDER. DO YOU KNOW WHY?

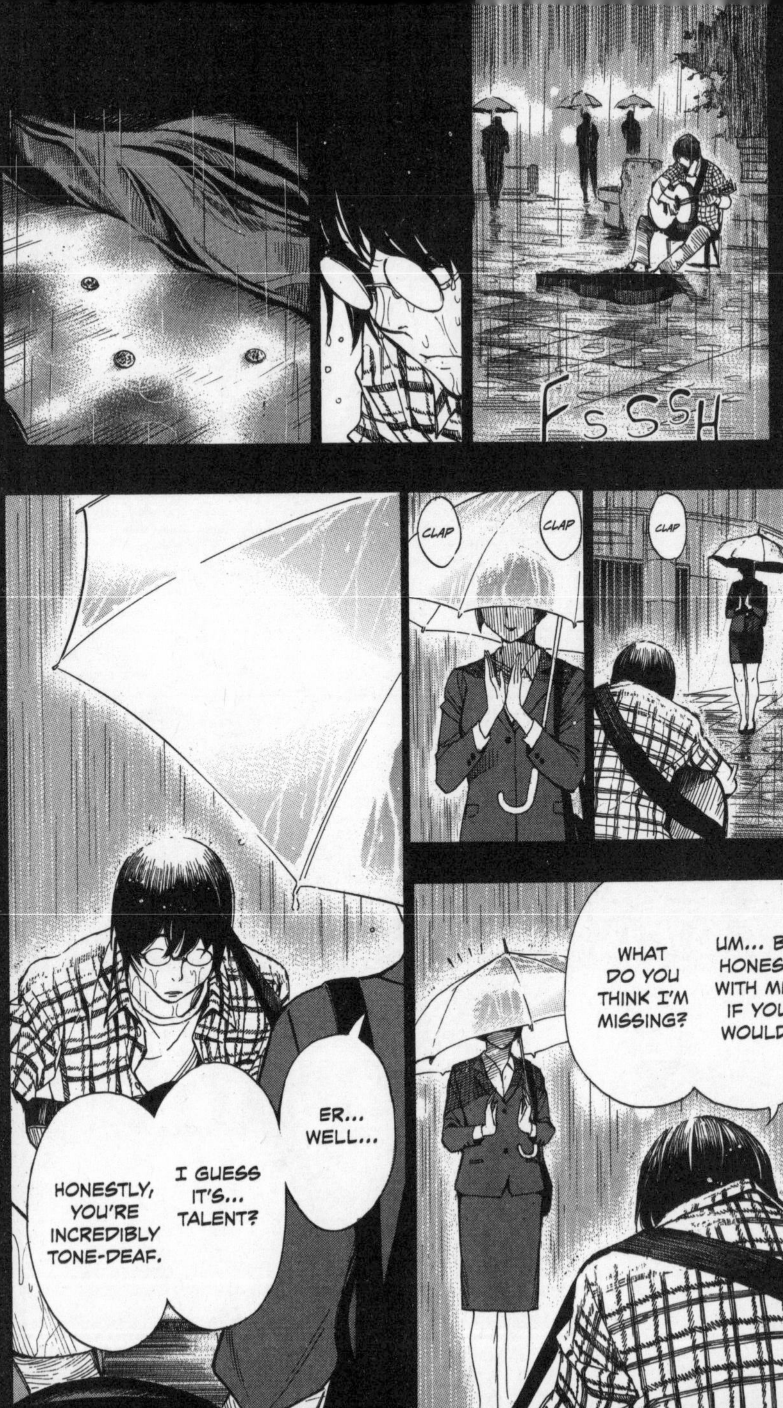
FSSSH
CLAP
CLAP
CLAP
CLAP
UM... BE HONEST WITH ME, IF YOU WOULD.
WHAT DO YOU THINK I'M MISSING?
ER... WELL...
I GUESS IT'S... TALENT?
HONESTLY, YOU'RE INCREDIBLY TONE-DEAF.

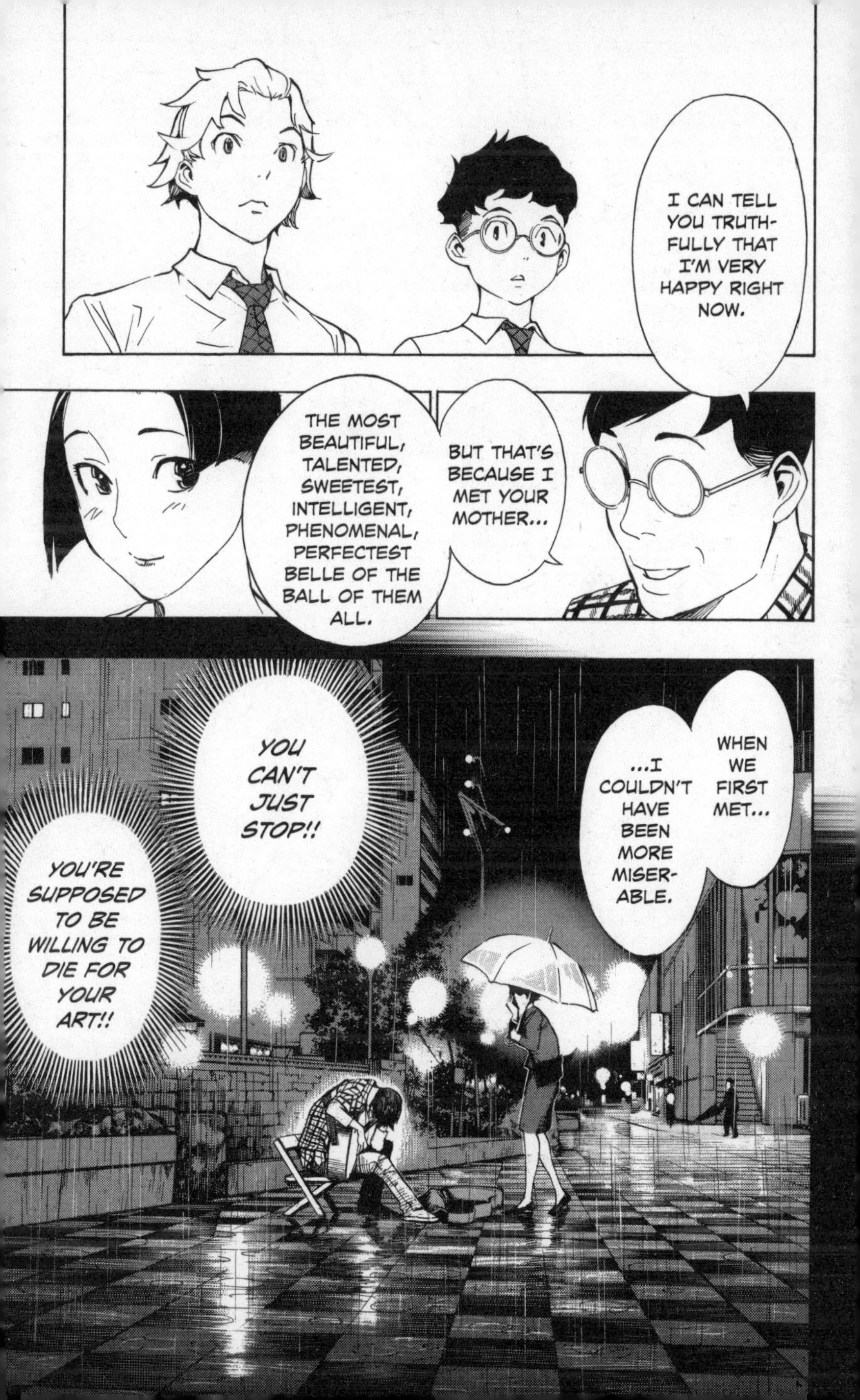
I CAN TELL YOU TRUTH-FULLY THAT I'M VERY HAPPY RIGHT NOW.
BUT THAT'S BECAUSE I MET YOUR MOTHER...
THE MOST BEAUTIFUL, TALENTED, SWEETEST, INTELLIGENT, PHENOMENAL, PERFECTEST BELLE OF THE BALL OF THEM ALL.
WHEN WE FIRST MET...
...I COULDN'T HAVE BEEN MORE MISER-ABLE.
YOU CAN'T JUST STOP!!
YOU'RE SUPPOSED TO BE WILLING TO DIE FOR YOUR ART!!

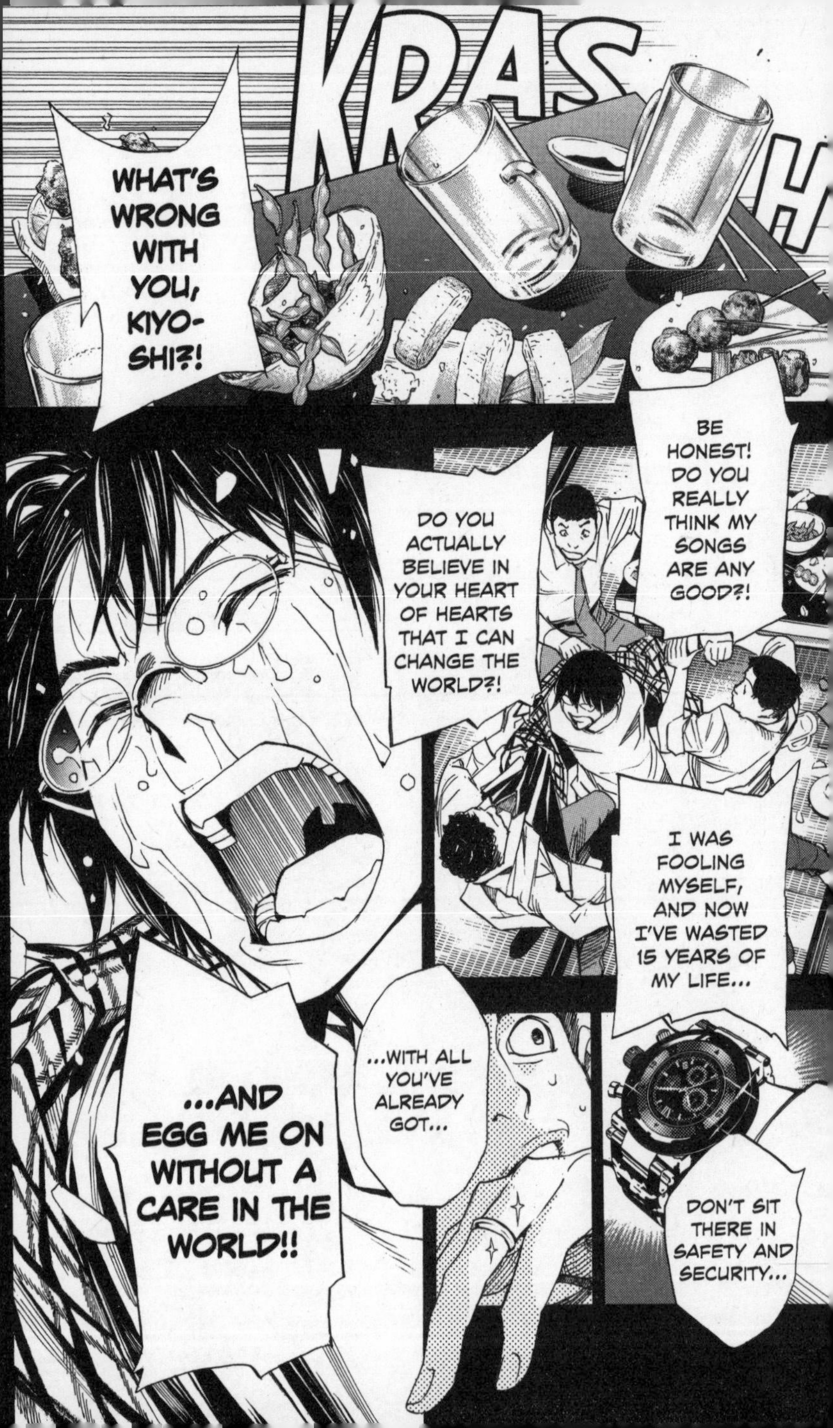
KRASH
WHAT'S WRONG WITH YOU, KIYOSHI?!
BE HONEST! DO YOU REALLY THINK MY SONGS ARE ANY GOOD?!
DO YOU ACTUALLY BELIEVE IN YOUR HEART OF HEARTS THAT I CAN CHANGE THE WORLD?!
I WAS FOOLING MYSELF, AND NOW I'VE WASTED 15 YEARS OF MY LIFE...
DON'T SIT THERE IN SAFETY AND SECURITY...
...WITH ALL YOU'VE ALREADY GOT...
...AND EGG ME ON WITHOUT A CARE IN THE WORLD!!

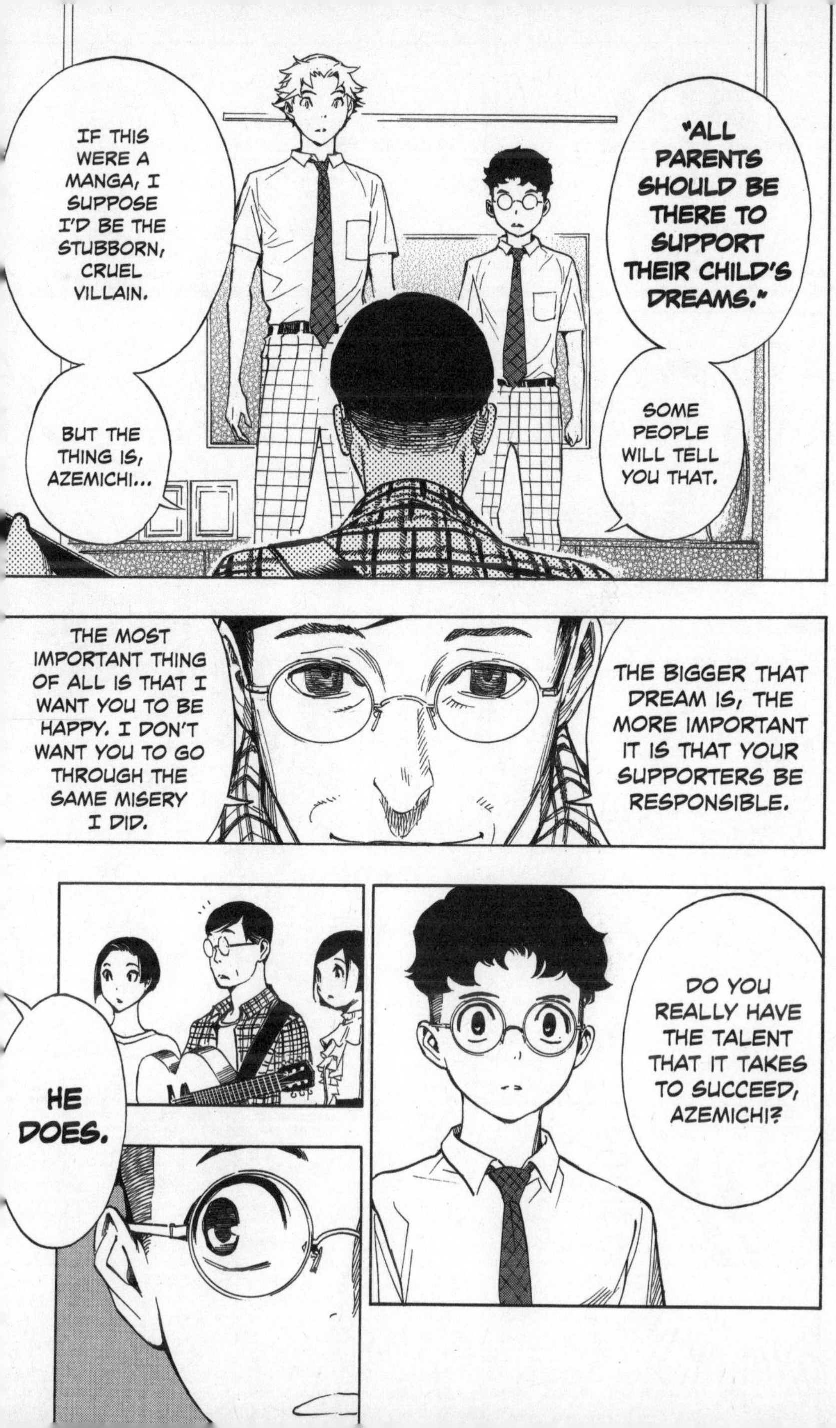
"ALL PARENTS SHOULD BE THERE TO SUPPORT THEIR CHILD'S DREAMS."
SOME PEOPLE WILL TELL YOU THAT.
IF THIS WERE A MANGA, I SUPPOSE I'D BE THE STUBBORN, CRUEL VILLAIN.
BUT THE THING IS, AZEMICHI...
THE BIGGER THAT DREAM IS, THE MORE IMPORTANT IT IS THAT YOUR SUPPORTERS BE RESPONSIBLE.
THE MOST IMPORTANT THING OF ALL IS THAT I WANT YOU TO BE HAPPY. I DON'T WANT YOU TO GO THROUGH THE SAME MISERY I DID.
DO YOU REALLY HAVE THE TALENT THAT IT TAKES TO SUCCEED, AZEMICHI?
HE DOES.

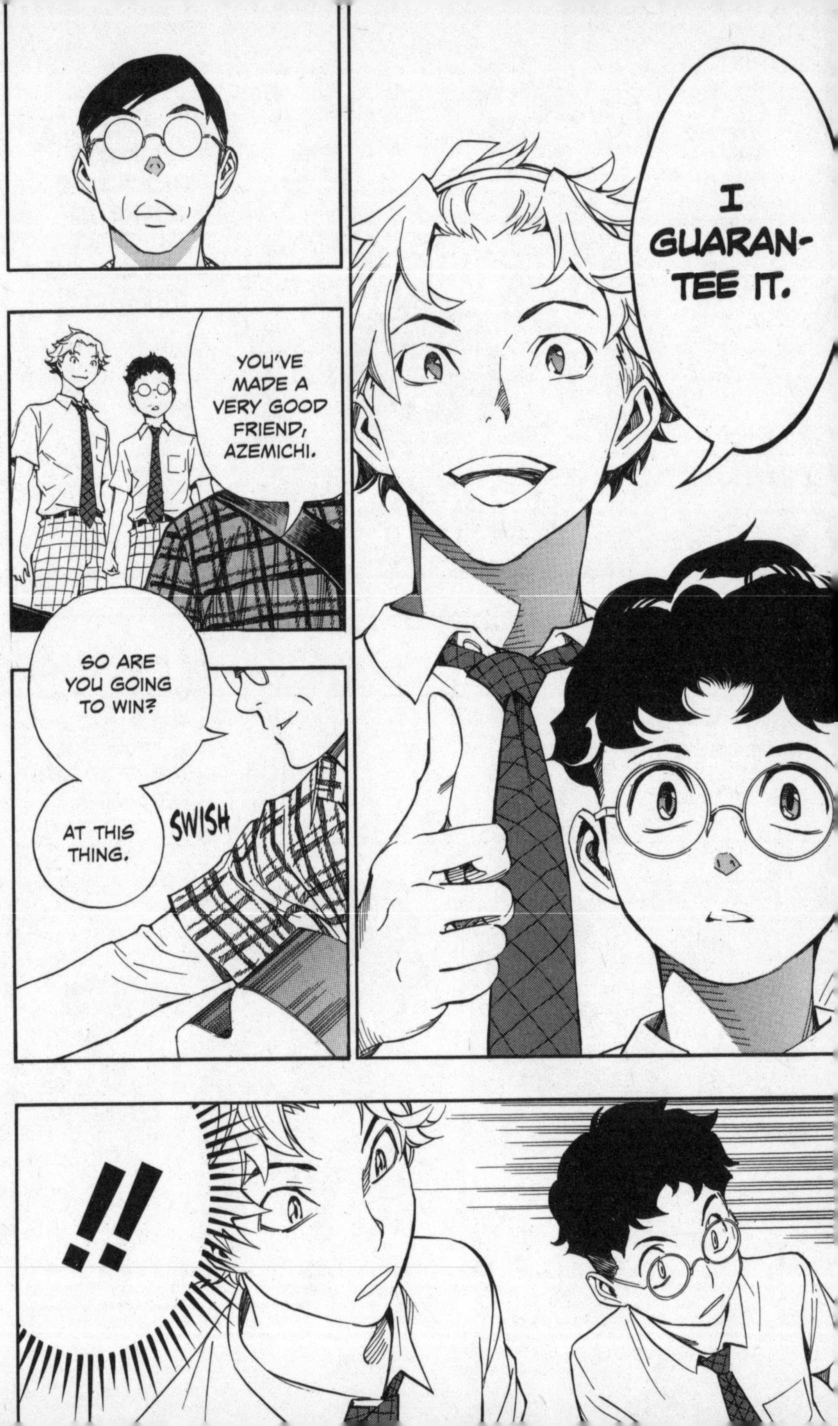
I GUARANTEE IT.
YOU'VE MADE A VERY GOOD FRIEND, AZEMICHI.
SO ARE YOU GOING TO WIN?
AT THIS THING.
SWISH
!!

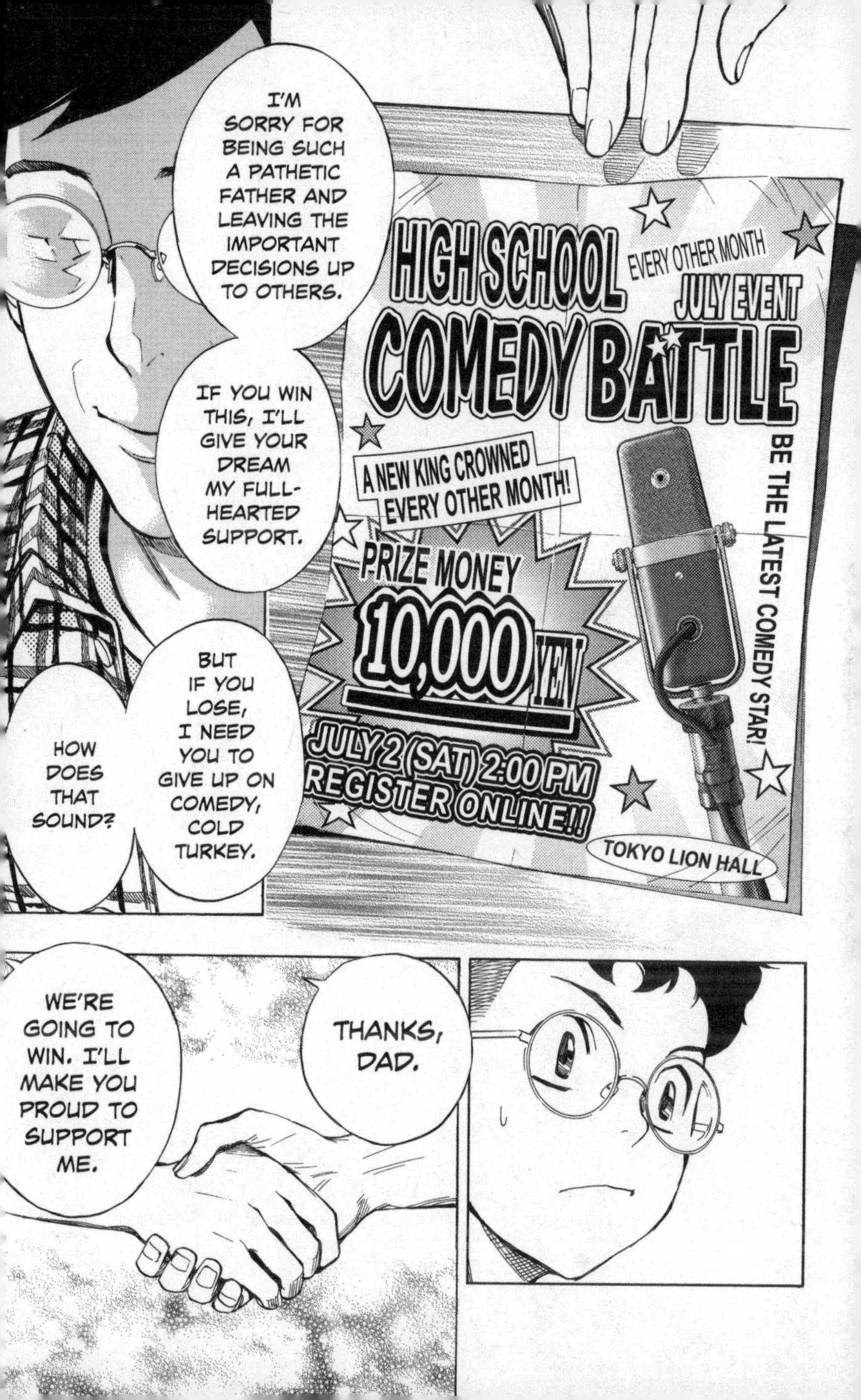
HIGH SCHOOL COMEDY BATTLE
EVERY OTHER MONTH
JULY EVENT
A NEW KING CROWNED EVERY OTHER MONTH!
PRIZE MONEY 10,000 YEN
JULY 2 (SAT) 2:00 PM
REGISTER ONLINE!!
TOKYO LION HALL
BE THE LATEST COMEDY STAR!
I'M SORRY FOR BEING SUCH A PATHETIC FATHER AND LEAVING THE IMPORTANT DECISIONS UP TO OTHERS.
IF YOU WIN THIS, I'LL GIVE YOUR DREAM MY FULL-HEARTED SUPPORT.
BUT IF YOU LOSE, I NEED YOU TO GIVE UP ON COMEDY, COLD TURKEY.
HOW DOES THAT SOUND?
THANKS, DAD.
WE'RE GOING TO WIN. I'LL MAKE YOU PROUD TO SUPPORT ME.

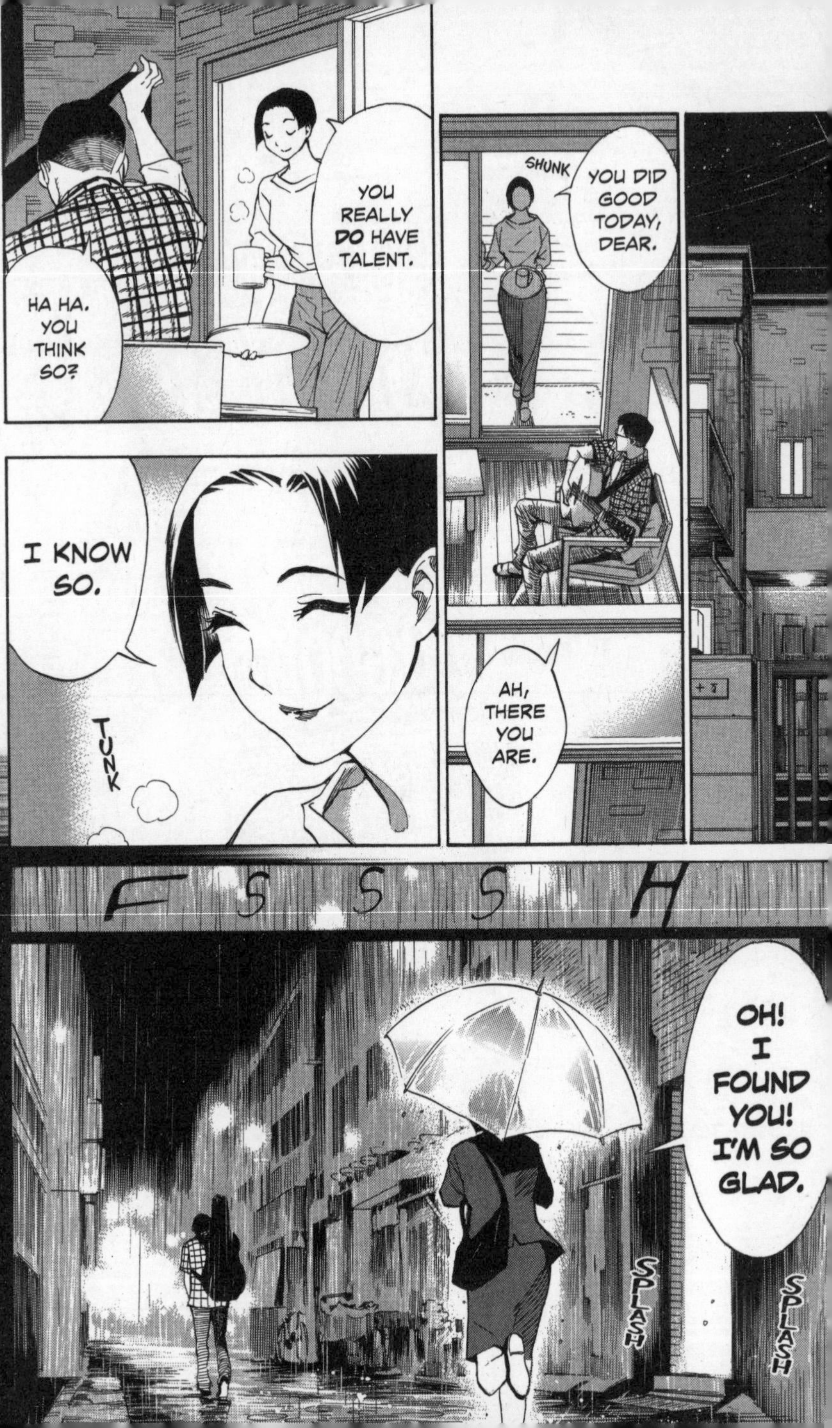
SHUNK
YOU DID GOOD TODAY, DEAR.
AH, THERE YOU ARE.
YOU REALLY DO HAVE TALENT.
HA HA. YOU THINK SO?
I KNOW SO.
TUNK
FSSSH
OH! I FOUND YOU! I'M SO GLAD.
SPLASH
SPLASH

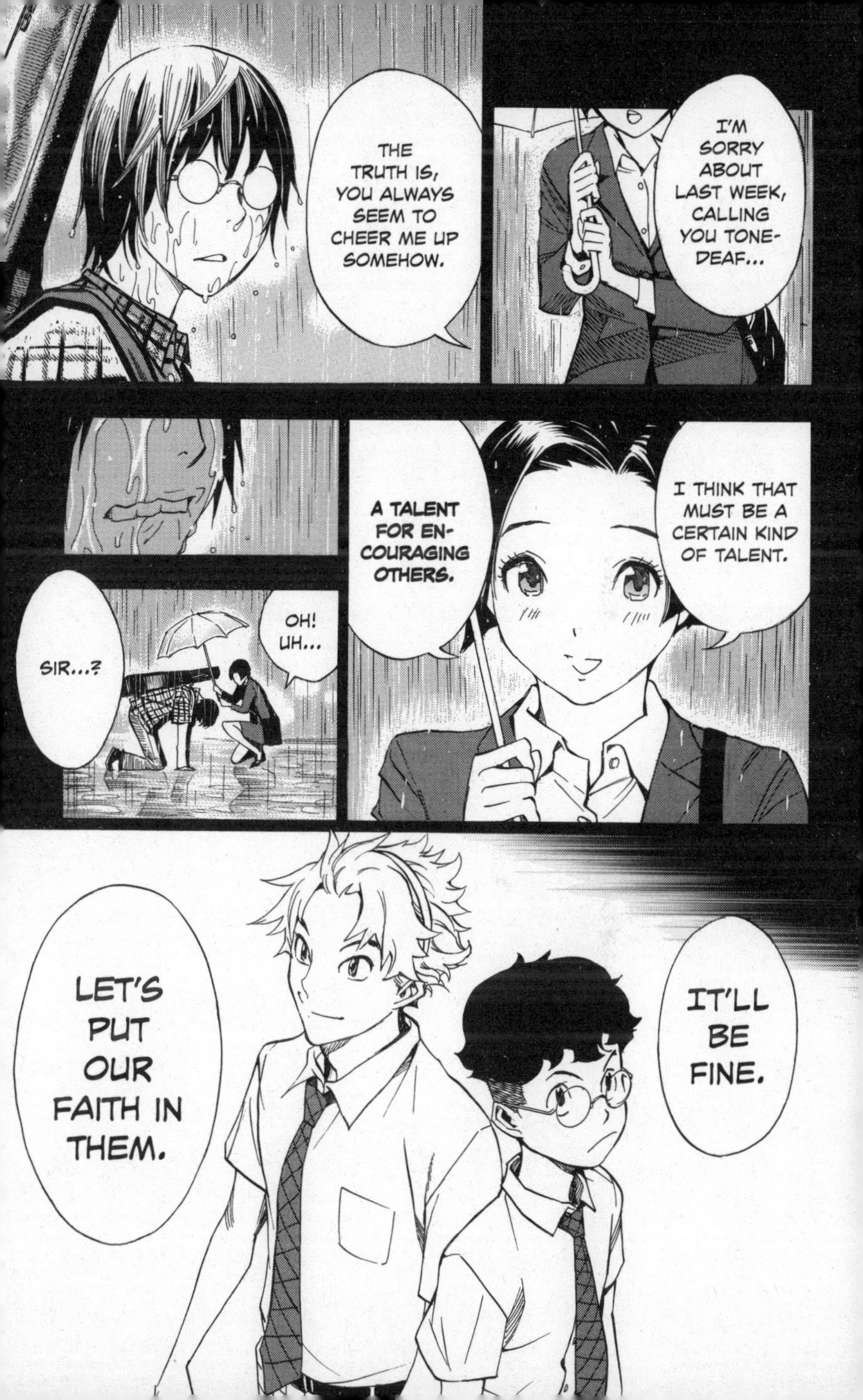
I'M SORRY ABOUT LAST WEEK, CALLING YOU TONE-DEAF...
THE TRUTH IS, YOU ALWAYS SEEM TO CHEER ME UP SOMEHOW.
I THINK THAT MUST BE A CERTAIN KIND OF TALENT.
A TALENT FOR EN-COURAGING OTHERS.
OH! UH...
SIR...?
IT'LL BE FINE.
LET'S PUT OUR FAITH IN THEM.

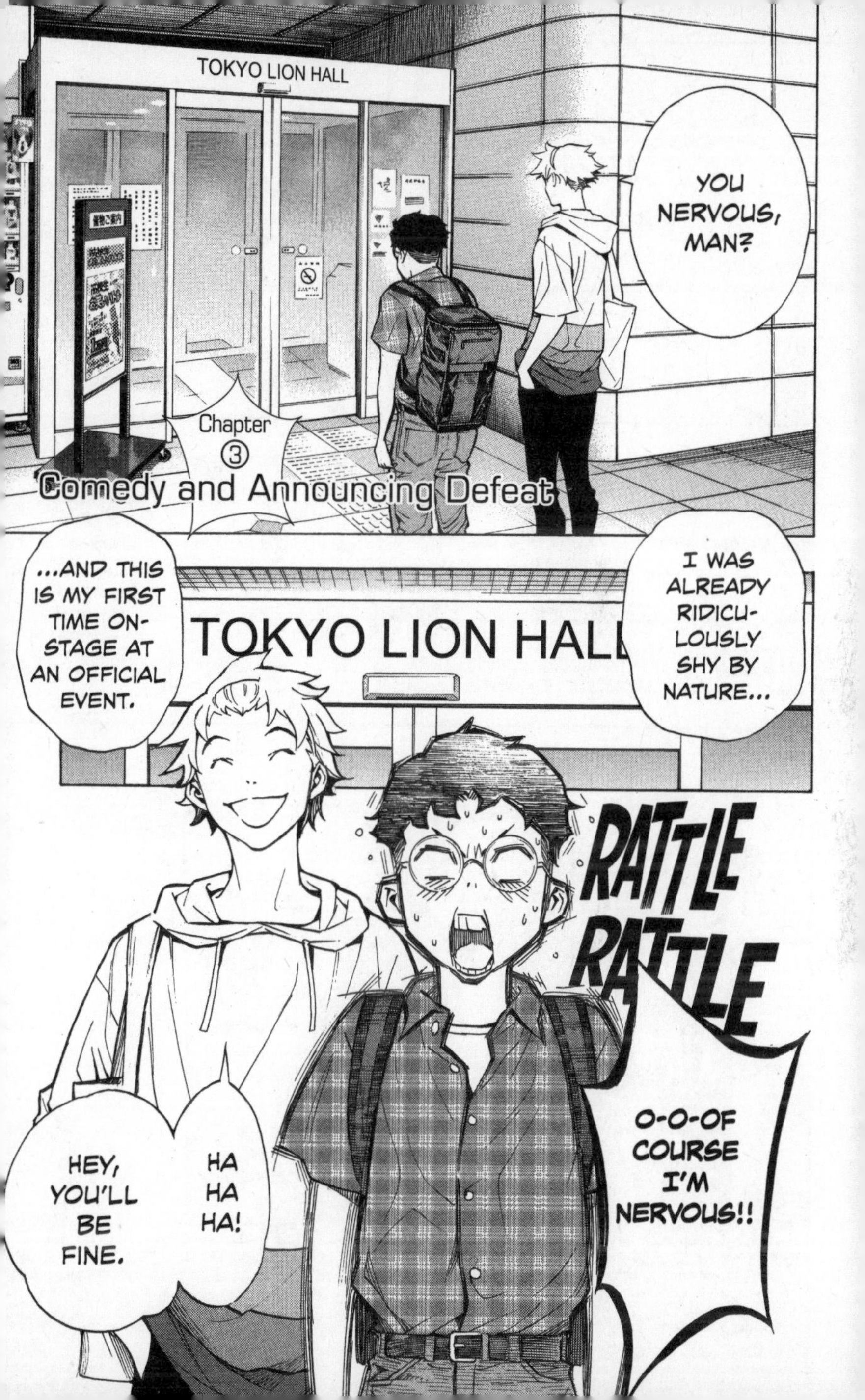
TOKYO LION HALL
YOU NERVOUS, MAN?
Chapter 3
Comedy and Announcing Defeat
I WAS ALREADY RIDICULOUSLY SHY BY NATURE...
...AND THIS IS MY FIRST TIME ON-STAGE AT AN OFFICIAL EVENT.
TOKYO LION HALL
RATTLE RATTLE
O-O-OF COURSE I'M NERVOUS!!
HA HA HA!
HEY, YOU'LL BE FINE.

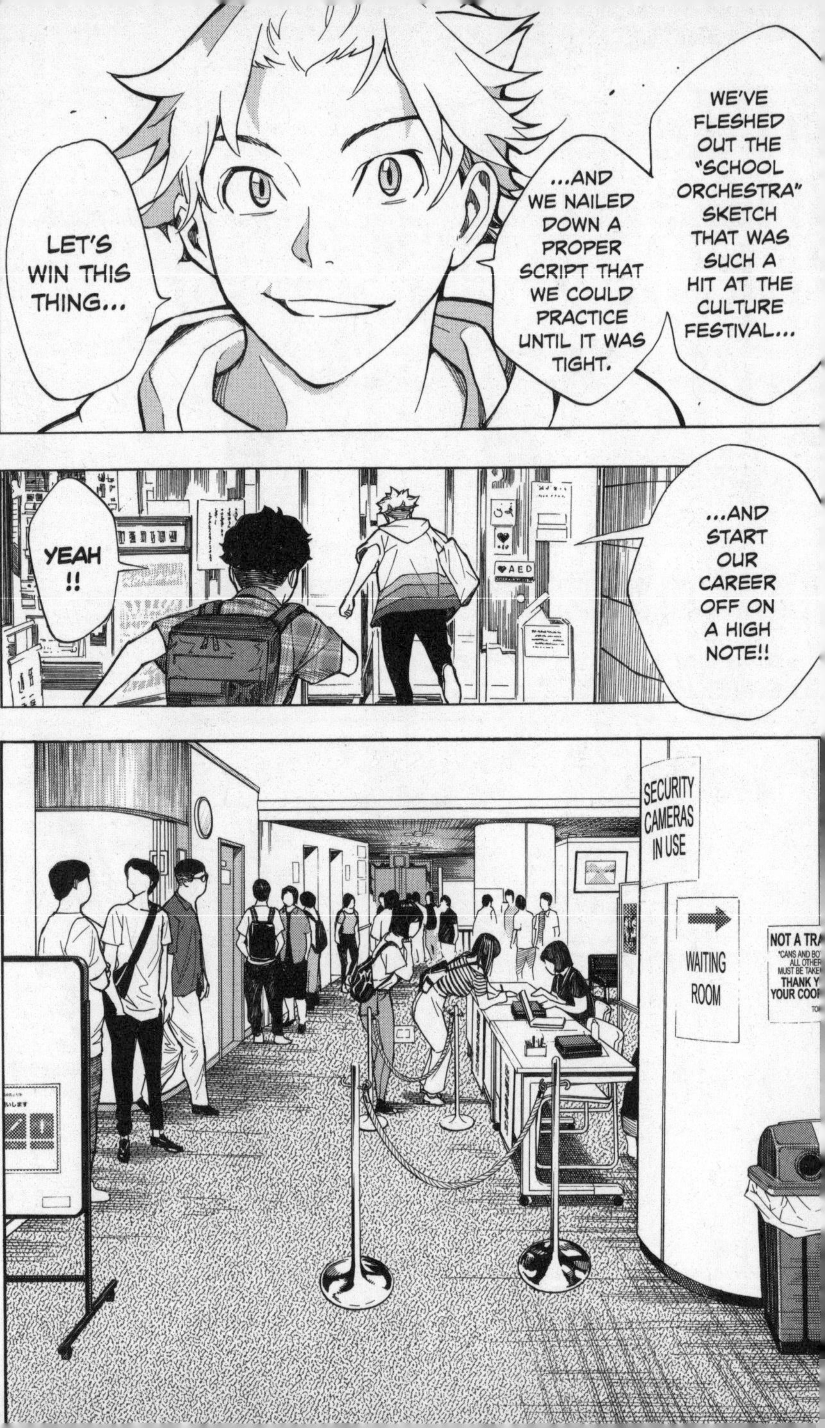
WE'VE FLESHED OUT THE "SCHOOL ORCHESTRA" SKETCH THAT WAS SUCH A HIT AT THE CULTURE FESTIVAL...
...AND WE NAILED DOWN A PROPER SCRIPT THAT WE COULD PRACTICE UNTIL IT WAS TIGHT.
LET'S WIN THIS THING...
...AND START OUR CAREER OFF ON A HIGH NOTE!!
YEAH!!
AED
SECURITY CAMERAS IN USE
WAITING ROOM

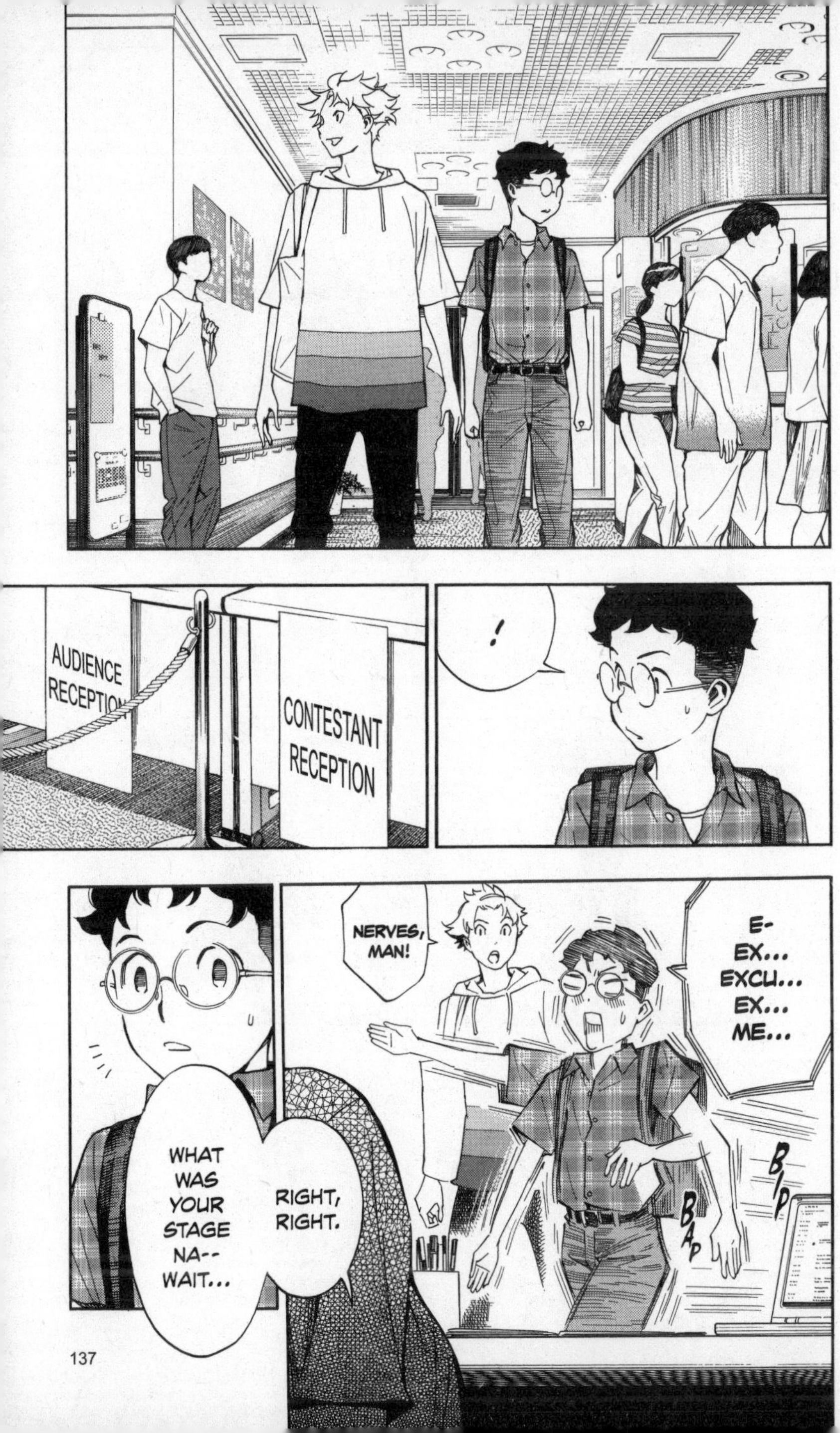
!
AUDIENCE RECEPTION
CONTESTANT RECEPTION
E- EX... EXCU... EX... ME...
NERVES, MAN!
BIP
BAP
RIGHT, RIGHT.
WHAT WAS YOUR STAGE NA-- WAIT...

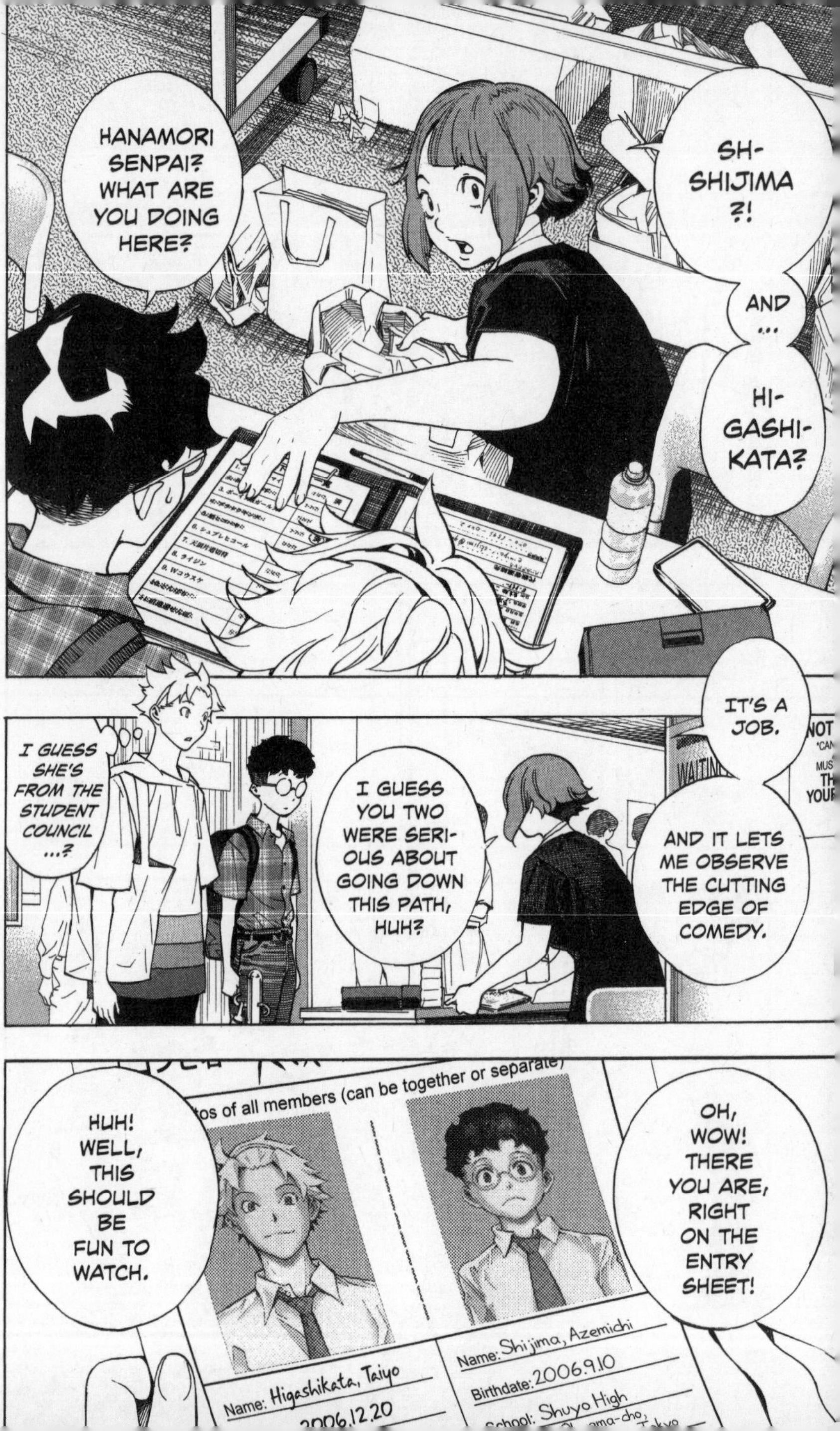
SH-SHIJIMA?!
AND...
HI-GASHI-KATA?
HANAMORI SENPAI? WHAT ARE YOU DOING HERE?
IT'S A JOB.
AND IT LETS ME OBSERVE THE CUTTING EDGE OF COMEDY.
I GUESS YOU TWO WERE SERI-OUS ABOUT GOING DOWN THIS PATH, HUH?
I GUESS SHE'S FROM THE STUDENT COUNCIL...?
OH, WOW! THERE YOU ARE, RIGHT ON THE ENTRY SHEET!
tos of all members (can be together or separate)
Name: Shijima, Azemichi
Birthdate: 2006.9.10
School: Shuyo High
Name: Higashikata, Taiyo
2006.12.20
HUH! WELL, THIS SHOULD BE FUN TO WATCH.

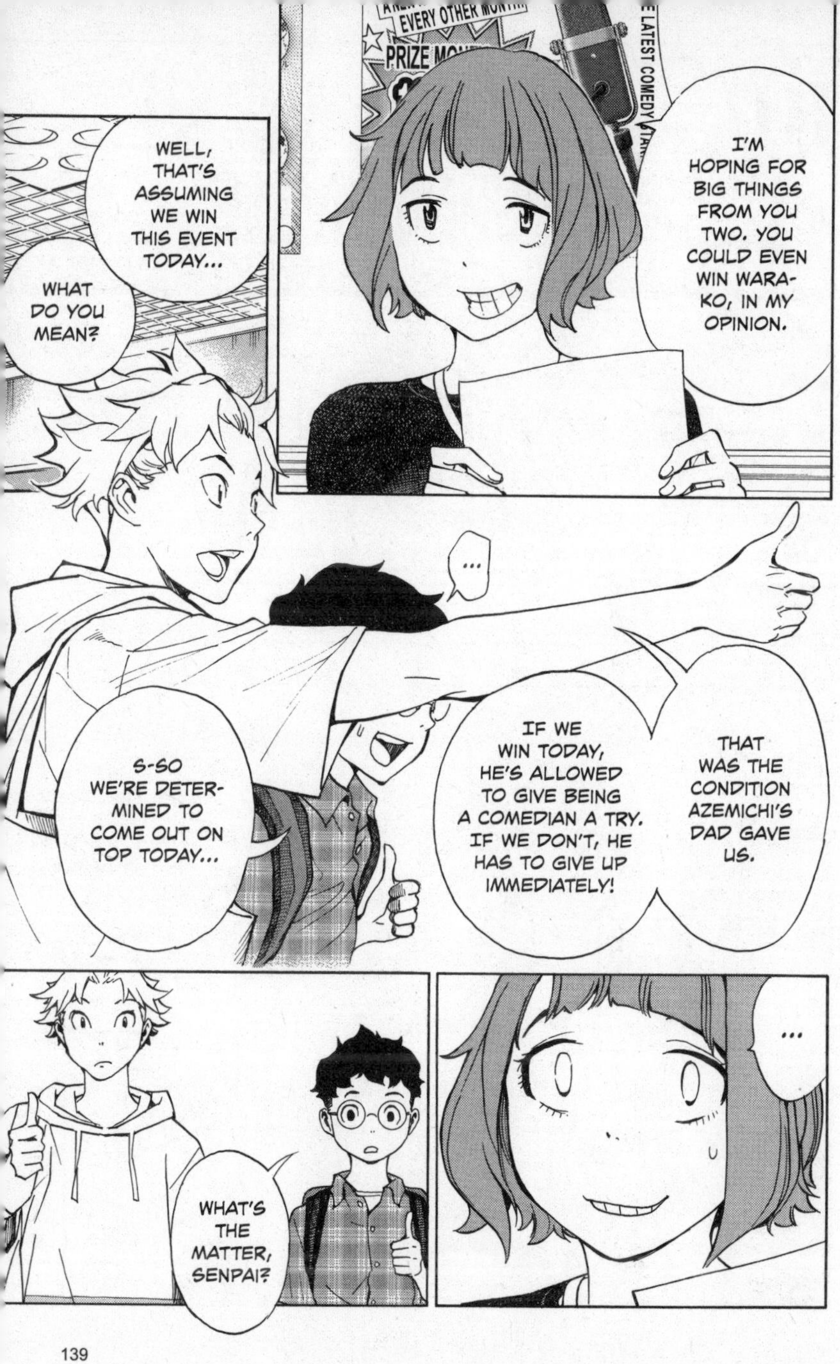
EVERY OTHER MONTH
I'M HOPING FOR BIG THINGS FROM YOU TWO. YOU COULD EVEN WIN WARA-KO, IN MY OPINION.
WELL, THAT'S ASSUMING WE WIN THIS EVENT TODAY...
WHAT DO YOU MEAN?
...
IF WE WIN TODAY, HE'S ALLOWED TO GIVE BEING A COMEDIAN A TRY. IF WE DON'T, HE HAS TO GIVE UP IMMEDIATELY!
THAT WAS THE CONDITION AZEMICHI'S DAD GAVE US.
S-SO WE'RE DETER-MINED TO COME OUT ON TOP TODAY...
...
WHAT'S THE MATTER, SENPAI?

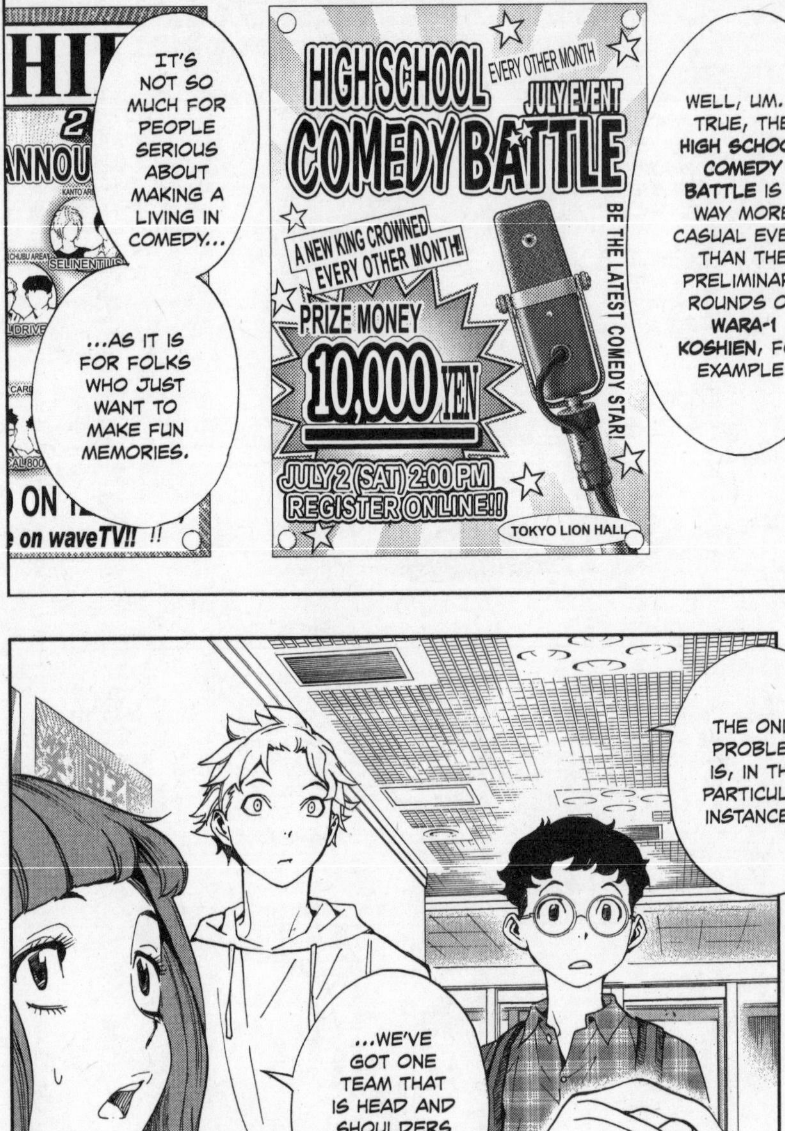
WELL, UM... TRUE, THE HIGH SCHOOL COMEDY BATTLE IS A WAY MORE CASUAL EVENT THAN THE PRELIMINARY ROUNDS OF WARA-1 KOSHIEN, FOR EXAMPLE.
HIGH SCHOOL COMEDY BATTLE
EVERY OTHER MONTH
JULY EVENT
A NEW KING CROWNED EVERY OTHER MONTH!
PRIZE MONEY 10,000 YEN
BE THE LATEST COMEDY STAR!
JULY 2 (SAT) 2:00 PM
REGISTER ONLINE!!
TOKYO LION HALL
IT'S NOT SO MUCH FOR PEOPLE SERIOUS ABOUT MAKING A LIVING IN COMEDY...
...AS IT IS FOR FOLKS WHO JUST WANT TO MAKE FUN MEMORIES.
THE ONLY PROBLEM IS, IN THIS PARTICULAR INSTANCE...
...WE'VE GOT ONE TEAM THAT IS HEAD AND SHOULDERS ABOVE EVERYONE ELSE...

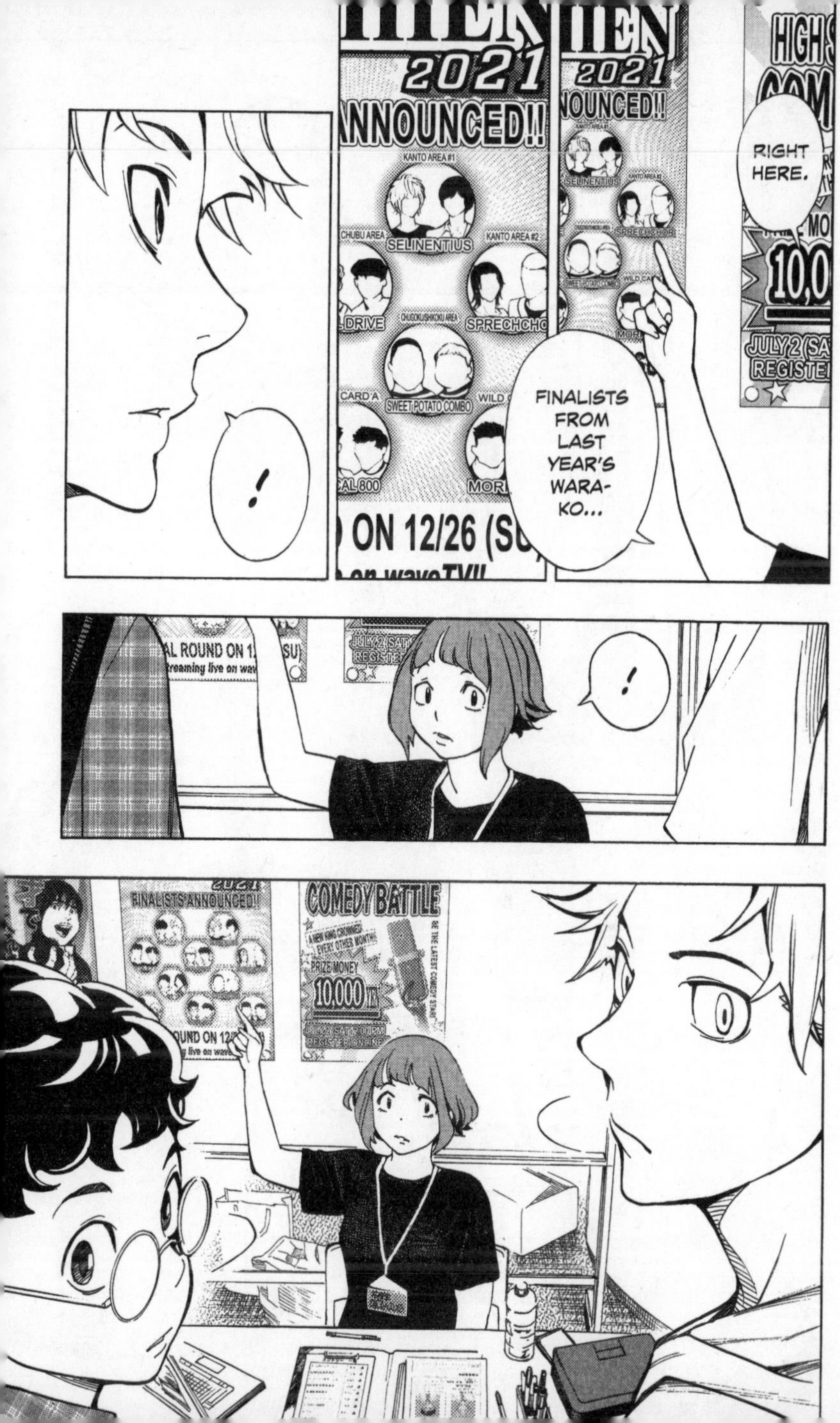
RIGHT HERE.
FINALISTS FROM LAST YEAR'S WARA-KO...
2021
ANNOUNCED!!
KANTO AREA #1
SELINENTIUS
CHUBU AREA
KANTO AREA #2
SPRECHCHOR
SWEET POTATO COMBO
ON 12/26 (SU
10,0
JULY 2 (SA
REGISTE
!
!
AL ROUND ON 1
FINALISTS ANNOUNCED!!
COMEDY BATTLE
A NEW KING CROWNED EVERY OTHER MONTH!
PRIZE MONEY
10,000
BE THE LATEST COMEDY STAR!
JULY 2 (SAT) 2:00 PM
REGISTER ONLINE

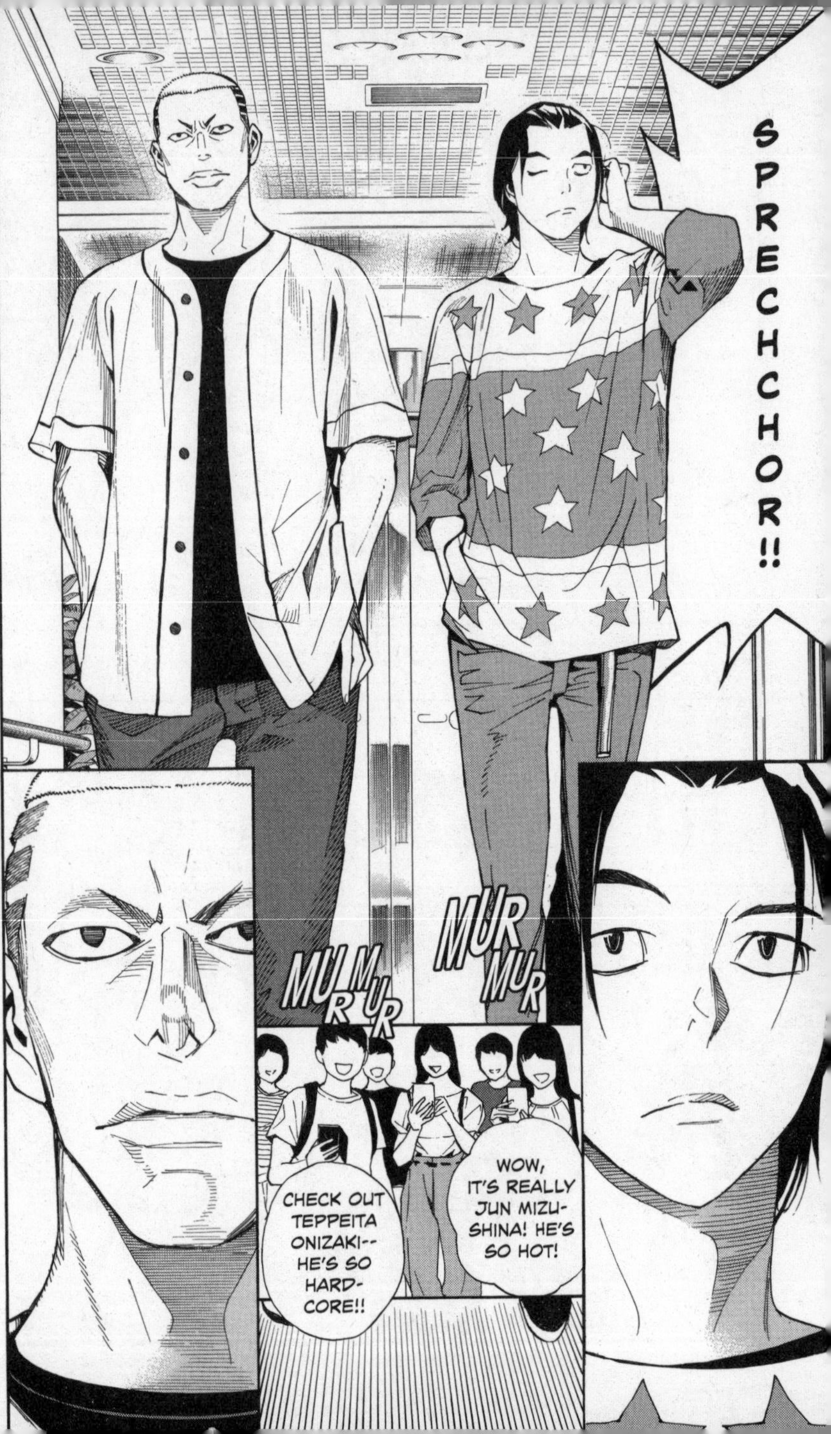
SPRECHCHOR!!
MUR MUR
MUMUR MUR
WOW, IT'S REALLY JUN MIZU-SHINA! HE'S SO HOT!
CHECK OUT TEPPEITA ONIZAKI-- HE'S SO HARD-CORE!!

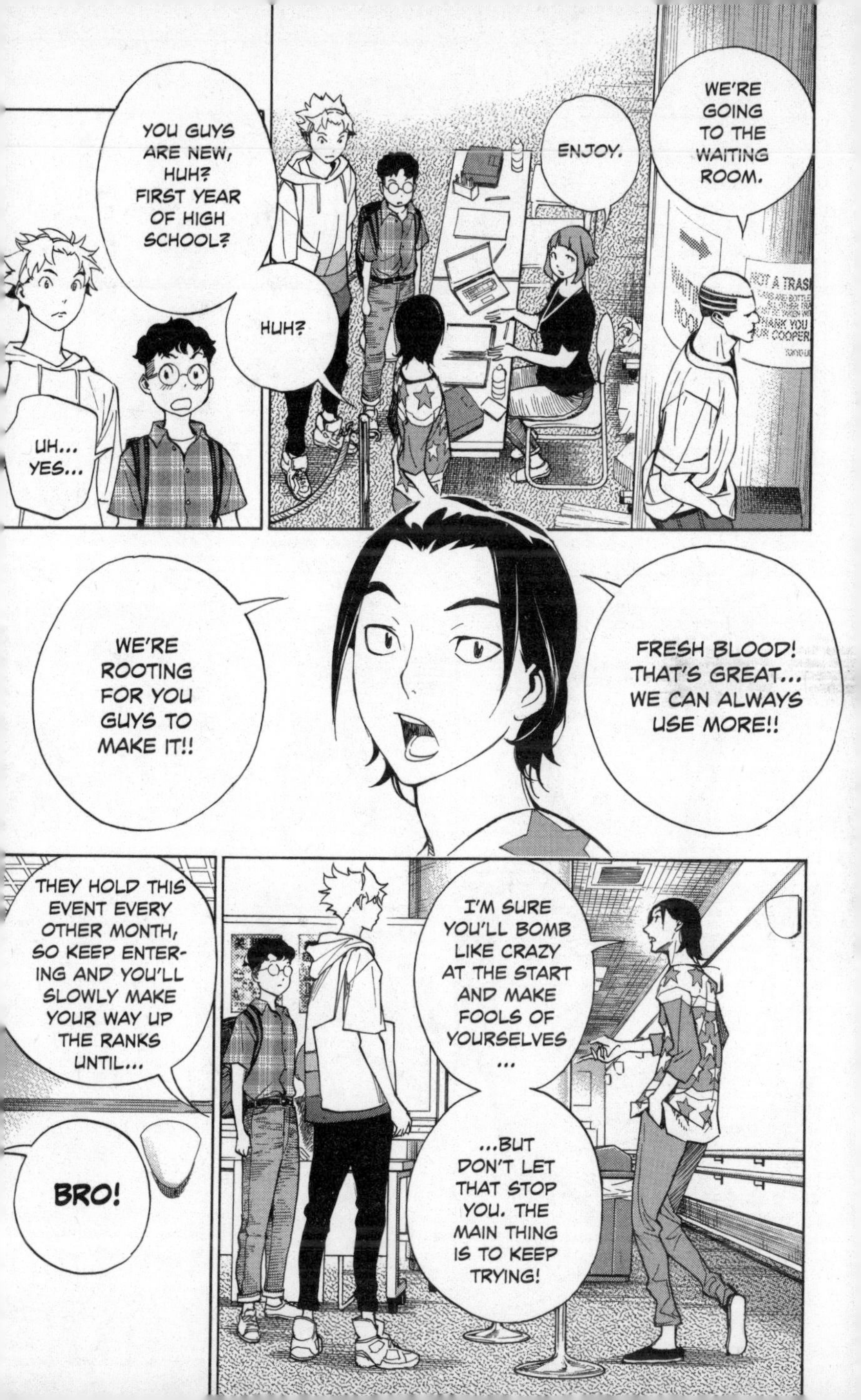
WE'RE GOING TO THE WAITING ROOM.
ENJOY.
YOU GUYS ARE NEW, HUH? FIRST YEAR OF HIGH SCHOOL?
HUH?
UH... YES...
FRESH BLOOD! THAT'S GREAT... WE CAN ALWAYS USE MORE!!
WE'RE ROOTING FOR YOU GUYS TO MAKE IT!!
I'M SURE YOU'LL BOMB LIKE CRAZY AT THE START AND MAKE FOOLS OF YOURSELVES ...
...BUT DON'T LET THAT STOP YOU. THE MAIN THING IS TO KEEP TRYING!
THEY HOLD THIS EVENT EVERY OTHER MONTH, SO KEEP ENTER-ING AND YOU'LL SLOWLY MAKE YOUR WAY UP THE RANKS UNTIL...
BRO!

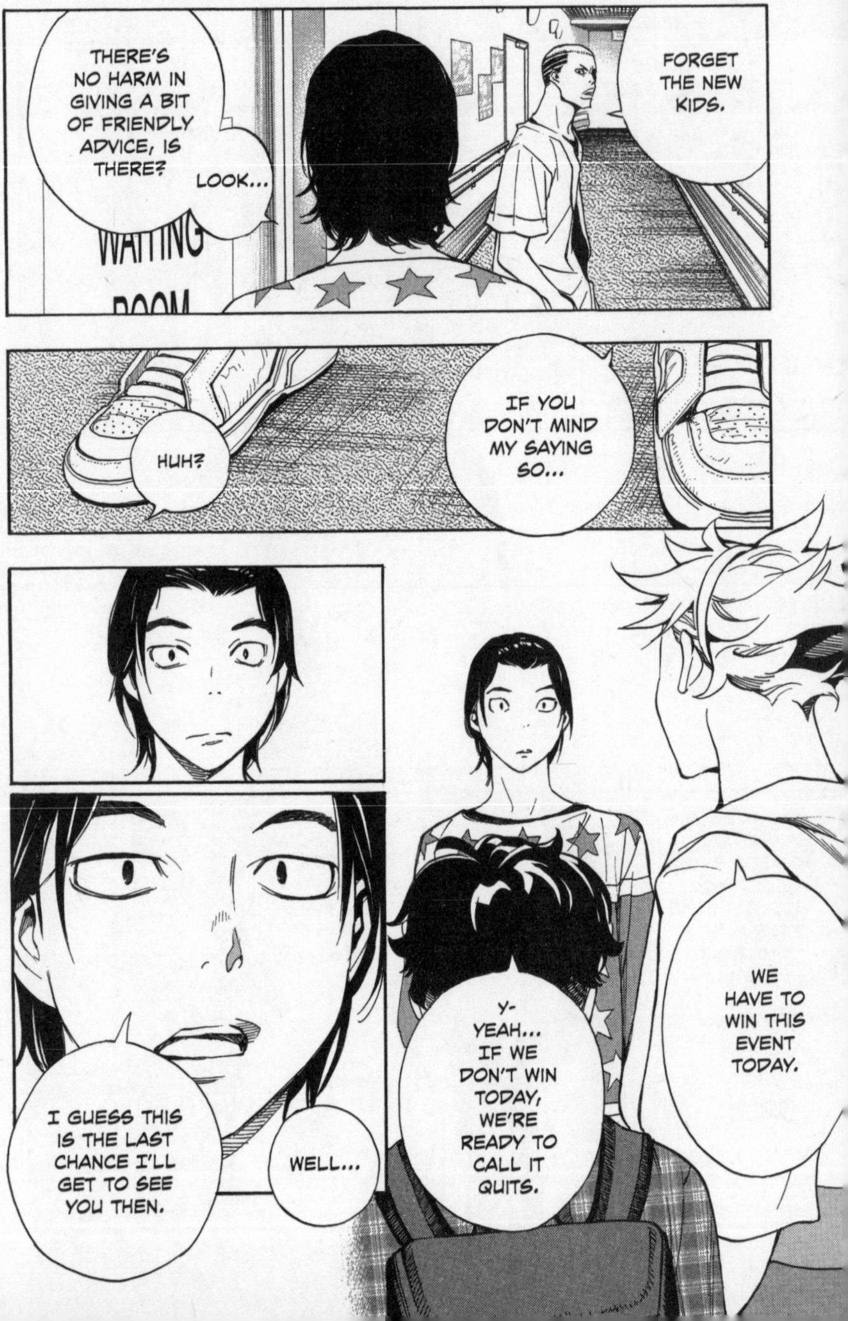
FORGET THE NEW KIDS.
THERE'S NO HARM IN GIVING A BIT OF FRIENDLY ADVICE, IS THERE?
LOOK...
WAITING
IF YOU DON'T MIND MY SAYING SO...
HUH?
WE HAVE TO WIN THIS EVENT TODAY.
Y-YEAH... IF WE DON'T WIN TODAY, WE'RE READY TO CALL IT QUITS.
WELL...
I GUESS THIS IS THE LAST CHANCE I'LL GET TO SEE YOU THEN.

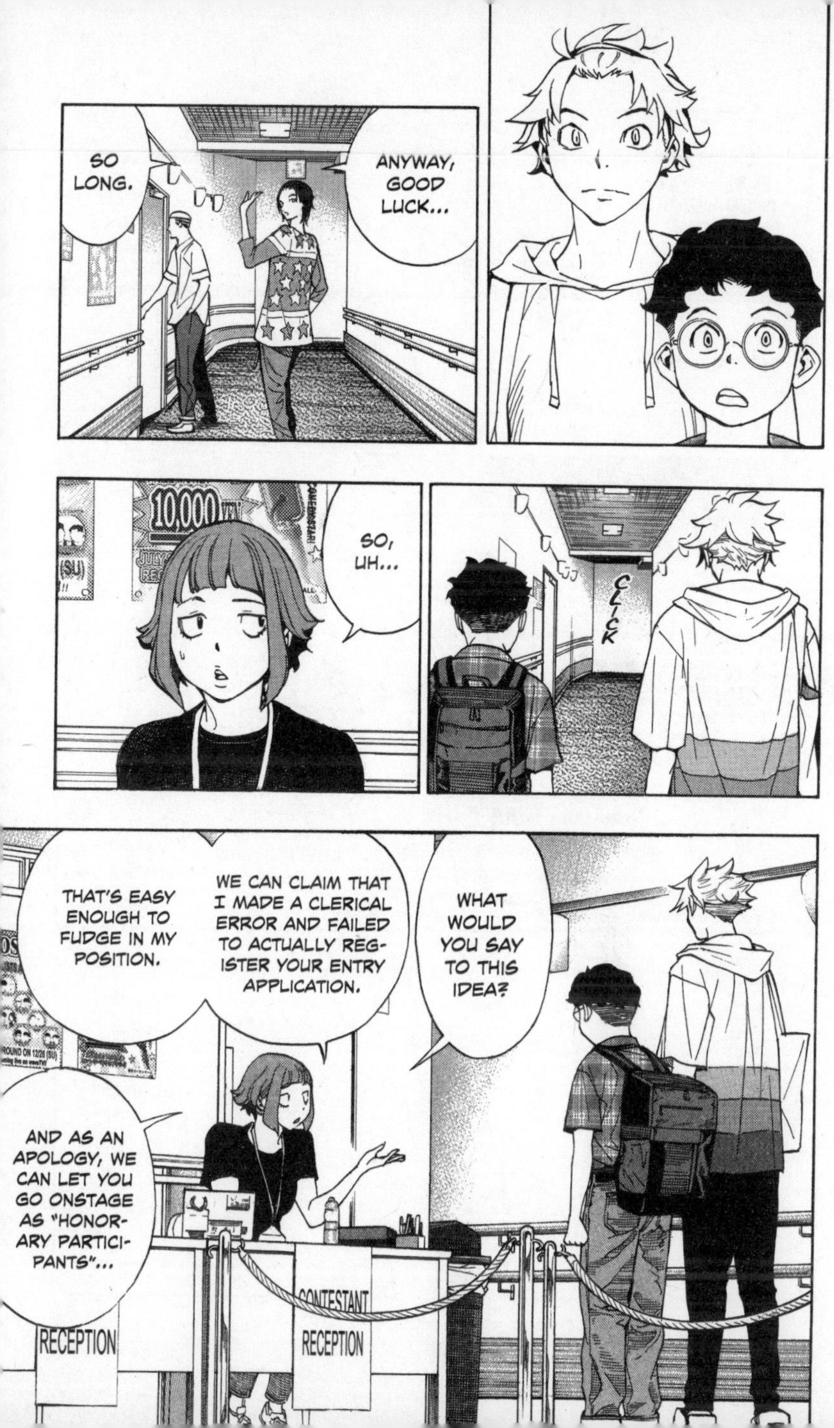
ANYWAY, GOOD LUCK...
SO LONG.
CLICK
SO, UH...
10,000
WHAT WOULD YOU SAY TO THIS IDEA?
WE CAN CLAIM THAT I MADE A CLERICAL ERROR AND FAILED TO ACTUALLY REGISTER YOUR ENTRY APPLICATION.
THAT'S EASY ENOUGH TO FUDGE IN MY POSITION.
AND AS AN APOLOGY, WE CAN LET YOU GO ONSTAGE AS "HONORARY PARTICIPANTS"...
CONTESTANT RECEPTION
RECEPTION

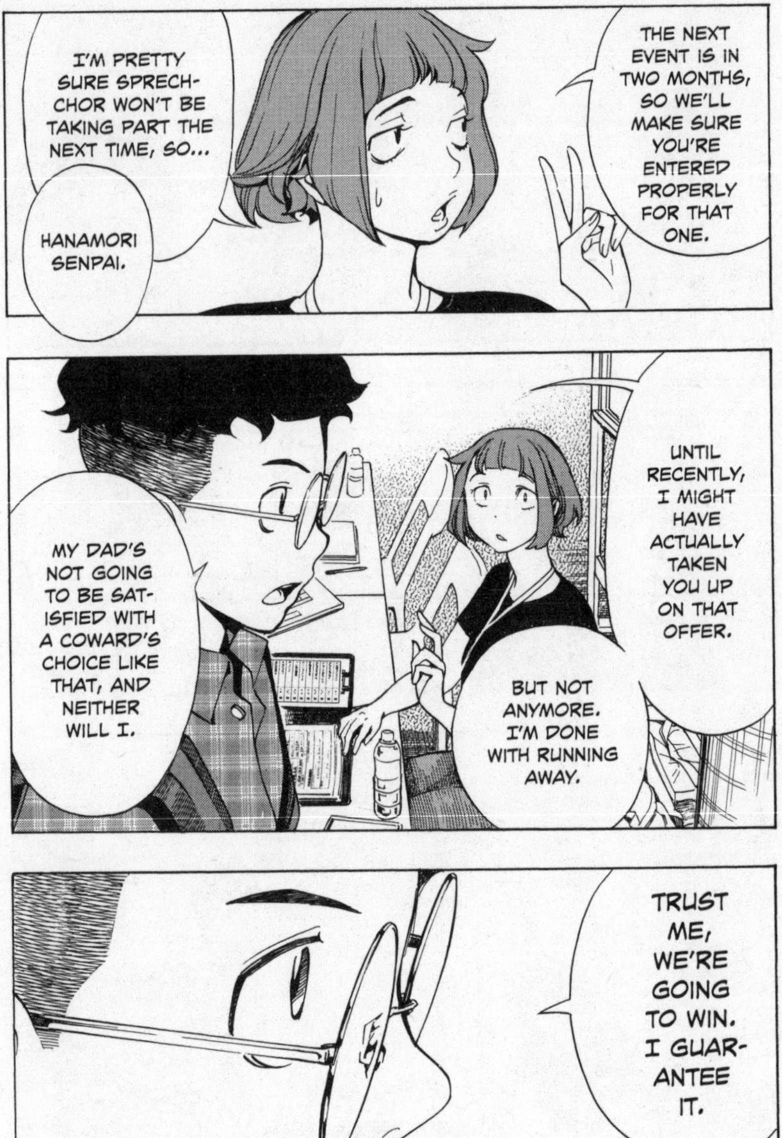
THE NEXT EVENT IS IN TWO MONTHS, SO WE'LL MAKE SURE YOU'RE ENTERED PROPERLY FOR THAT ONE.
I'M PRETTY SURE SPRECHCHOR WON'T BE TAKING PART THE NEXT TIME, SO...
HANAMORI SENPAI.
UNTIL RECENTLY, I MIGHT HAVE ACTUALLY TAKEN YOU UP ON THAT OFFER.
BUT NOT ANYMORE. I'M DONE WITH RUNNING AWAY.
MY DAD'S NOT GOING TO BE SATISFIED WITH A COWARD'S CHOICE LIKE THAT, AND NEITHER WILL I.
TRUST ME, WE'RE GOING TO WIN. I GUARANTEE IT.

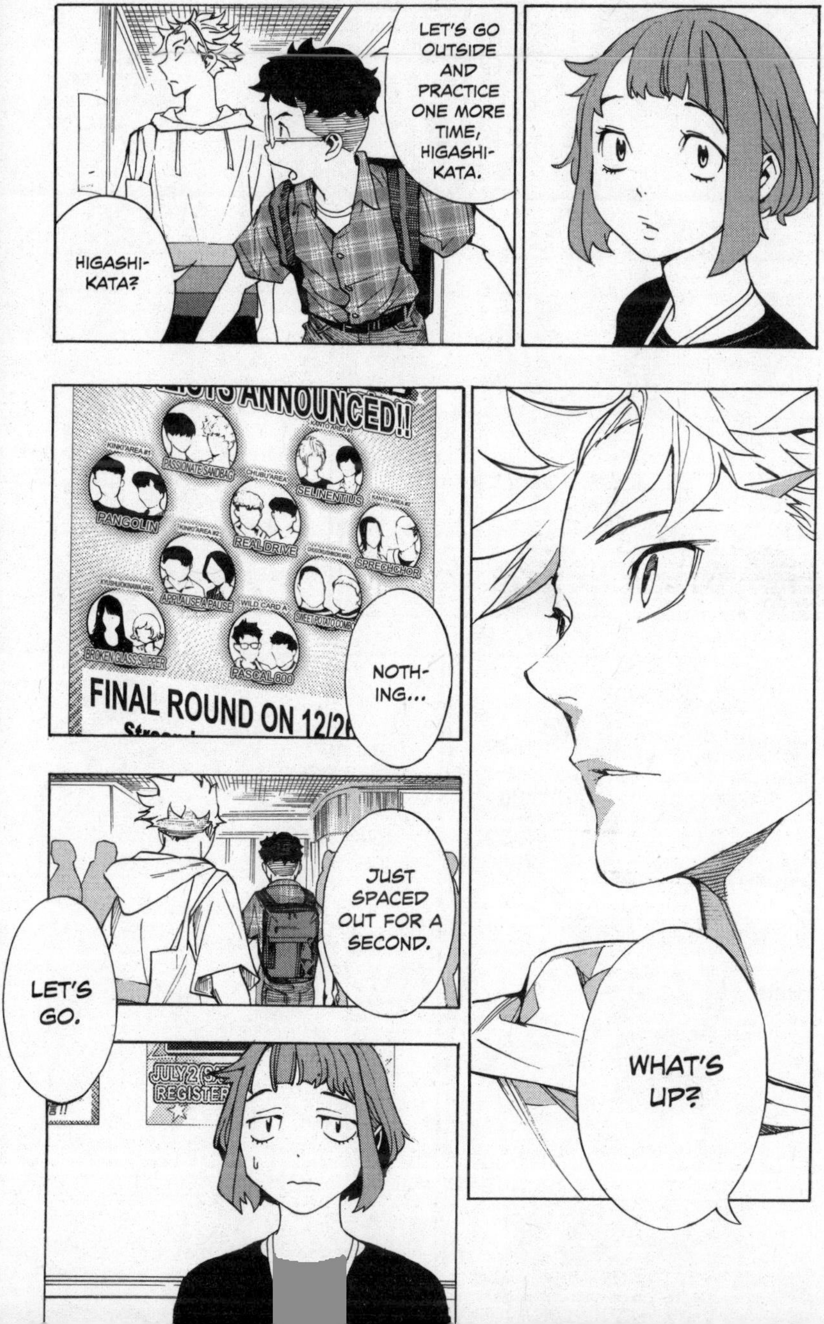
LET'S GO OUTSIDE AND PRACTICE ONE MORE TIME, HIGASHI-KATA.
HIGASHI-KATA?
WHAT'S UP?
ANNOUNCED!!
PASSIONATE SANDBAG
SELINENTIUS
PANGOLIN
REAL DRIVE
SPRECHCHOR
APPLAUSE A PAUSE
SWEET POTATO COMBO
BROKEN GLASS SLIPPER
PASCAL 800
FINAL ROUND ON 12/2
NOTH-ING...
JUST SPACED OUT FOR A SECOND.
LET'S GO.

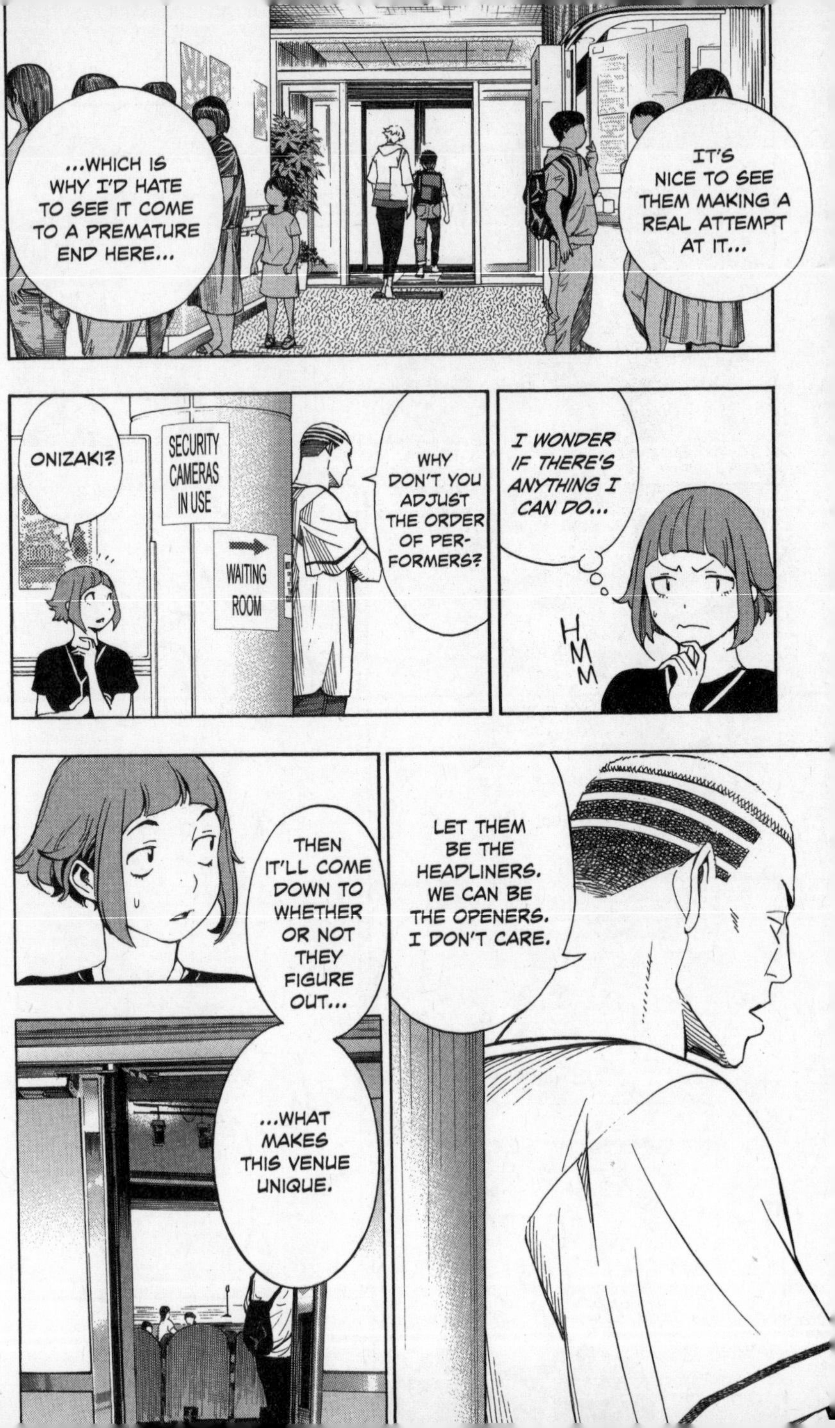
IT'S NICE TO SEE THEM MAKING A REAL ATTEMPT AT IT...
...WHICH IS WHY I'D HATE TO SEE IT COME TO A PREMATURE END HERE...
I WONDER IF THERE'S ANYTHING I CAN DO...
HMM
WHY DON'T YOU ADJUST THE ORDER OF PER-FORMERS?
SECURITY CAMERAS IN USE
WAITING ROOM
ONIZAKI?
LET THEM BE THE HEADLINERS. WE CAN BE THE OPENERS. I DON'T CARE.
THEN IT'LL COME DOWN TO WHETHER OR NOT THEY FIGURE OUT...
...WHAT MAKES THIS VENUE UNIQUE.

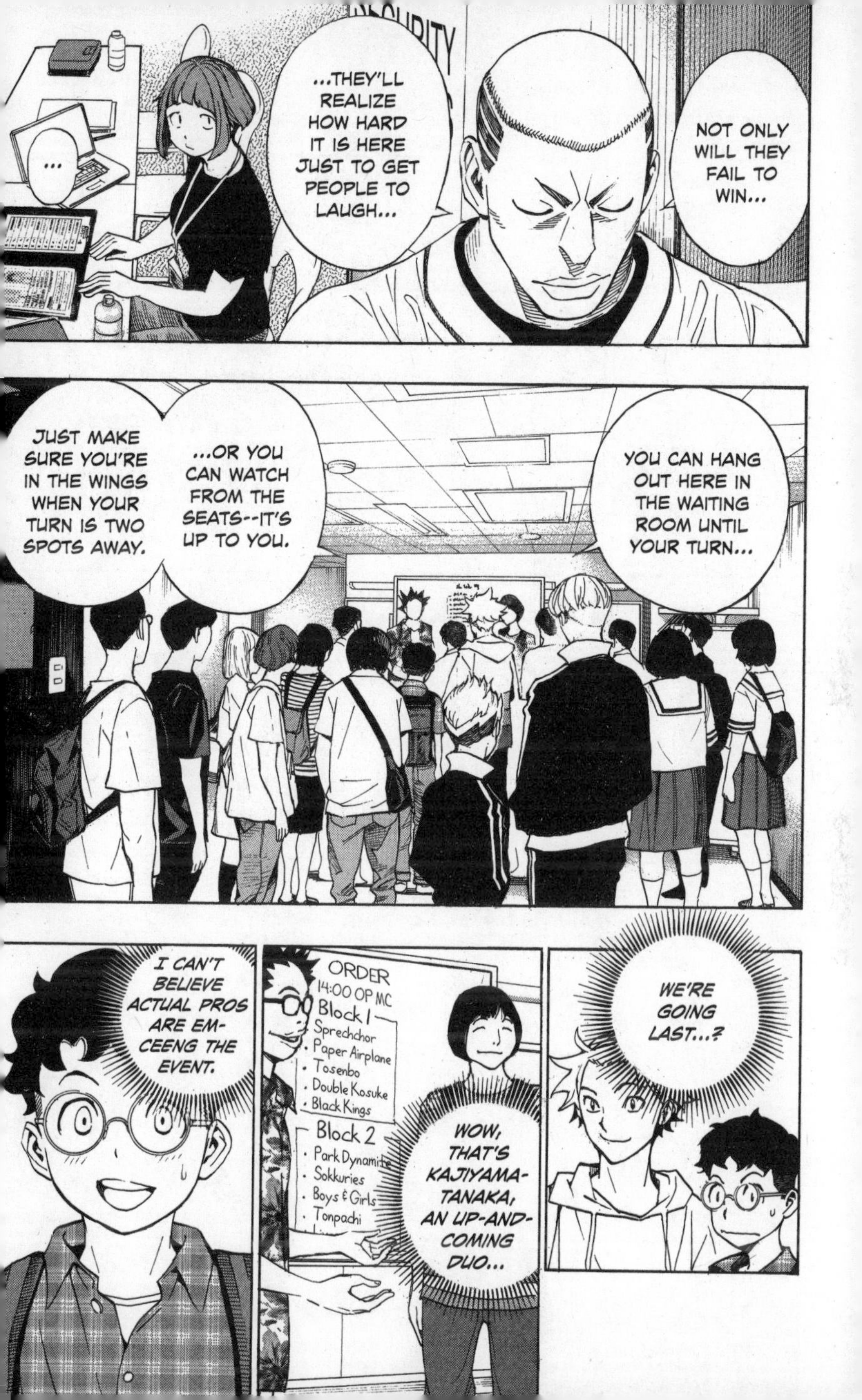
NOT ONLY WILL THEY FAIL TO WIN...
...THEY'LL REALIZE HOW HARD IT IS HERE JUST TO GET PEOPLE TO LAUGH...
...
YOU CAN HANG OUT HERE IN THE WAITING ROOM UNTIL YOUR TURN...
...OR YOU CAN WATCH FROM THE SEATS--IT'S UP TO YOU.
JUST MAKE SURE YOU'RE IN THE WINGS WHEN YOUR TURN IS TWO SPOTS AWAY.
WE'RE GOING LAST...?
ORDER
14:00 OP MC
Block 1
· Sprechchor
· Paper Airplane
· Tosenbo
· Double Kosuke
· Black Kings
Block 2
· Park Dynamite
· Sokkuries
· Boys & Girls
· Tonpachi
WOW, THAT'S KAJIYAMA-TANAKA, AN UP-AND-COMING DUO...
I CAN'T BELIEVE ACTUAL PROS ARE EM-CEENG THE EVENT.

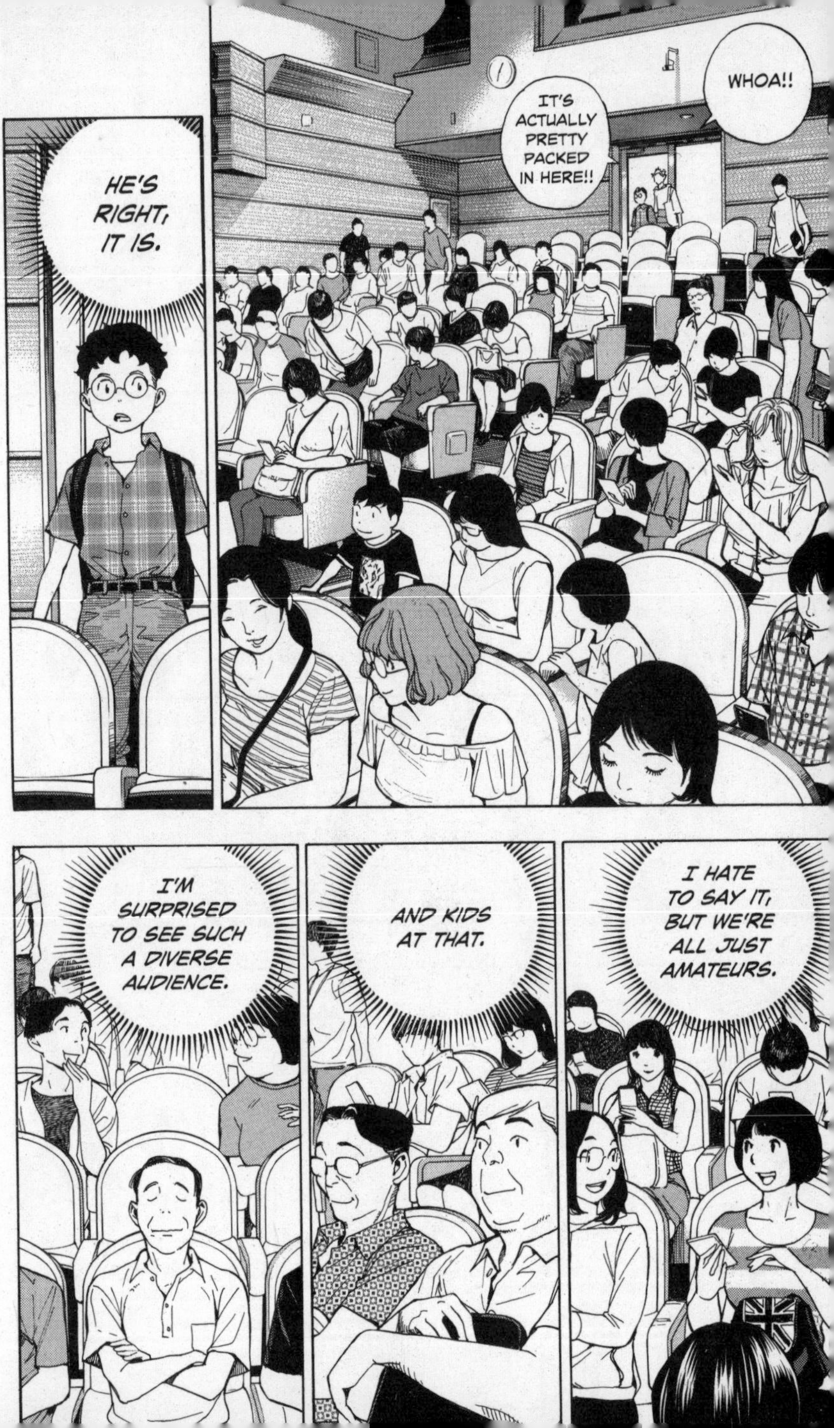
WHOA!!
IT'S ACTUALLY PRETTY PACKED IN HERE!!
HE'S RIGHT, IT IS.
I HATE TO SAY IT, BUT WE'RE ALL JUST AMATEURS.
AND KIDS AT THAT.
I'M SURPRISED TO SEE SUCH A DIVERSE AUDIENCE.

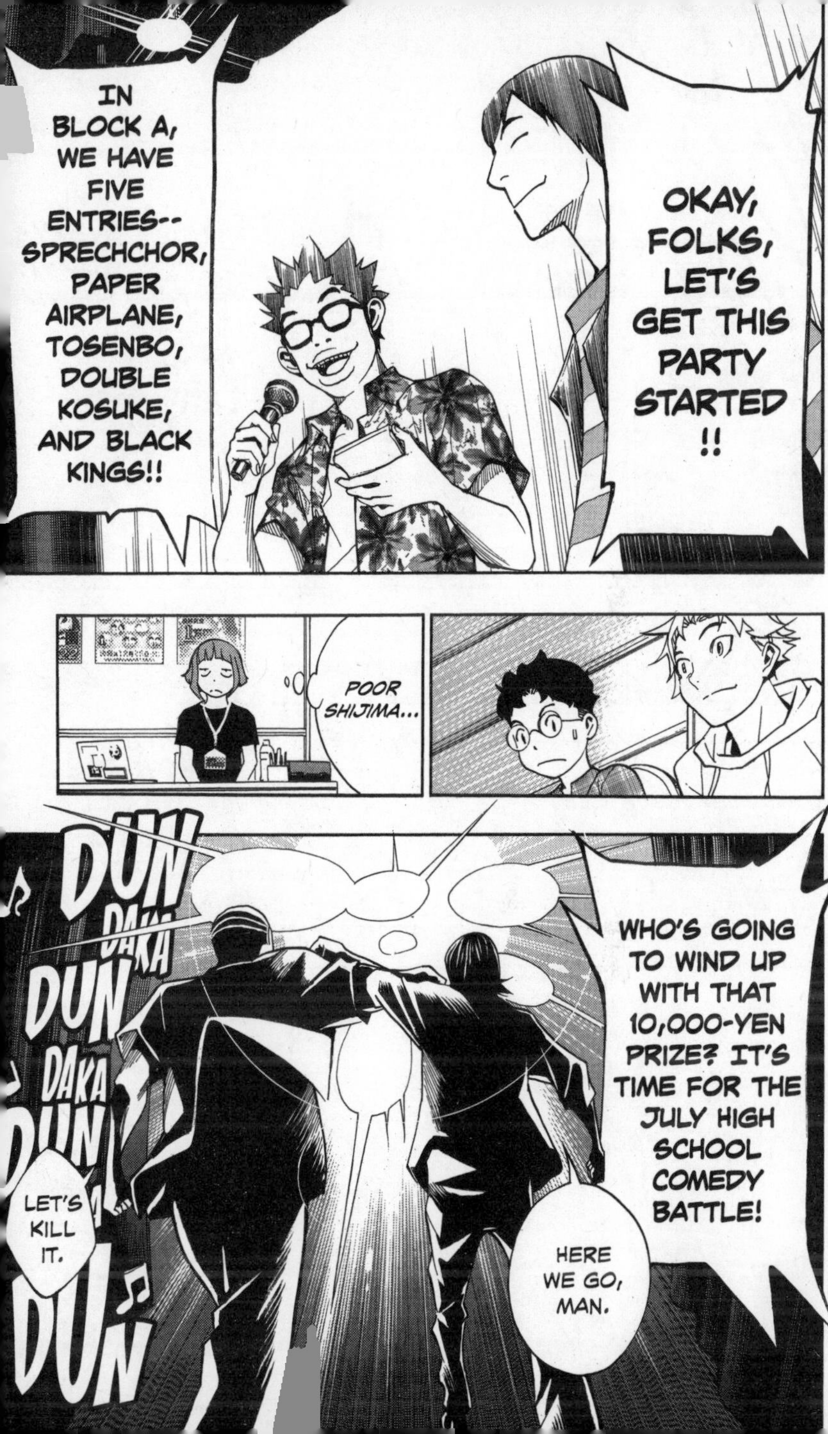
OKAY, FOLKS, LET'S GET THIS PARTY STARTED!!
IN BLOCK A, WE HAVE FIVE ENTRIES--SPRECHCHOR, PAPER AIRPLANE, TOSENBO, DOUBLE KOSUKE, AND BLACK KINGS!!
POOR SHIJIMA...
WHO'S GOING TO WIND UP WITH THAT 10,000-YEN PRIZE? IT'S TIME FOR THE JULY HIGH SCHOOL COMEDY BATTLE!
DUN DAKA DUN DAKA DUN
HERE WE GO, MAN.
LET'S KILL IT.
DUN

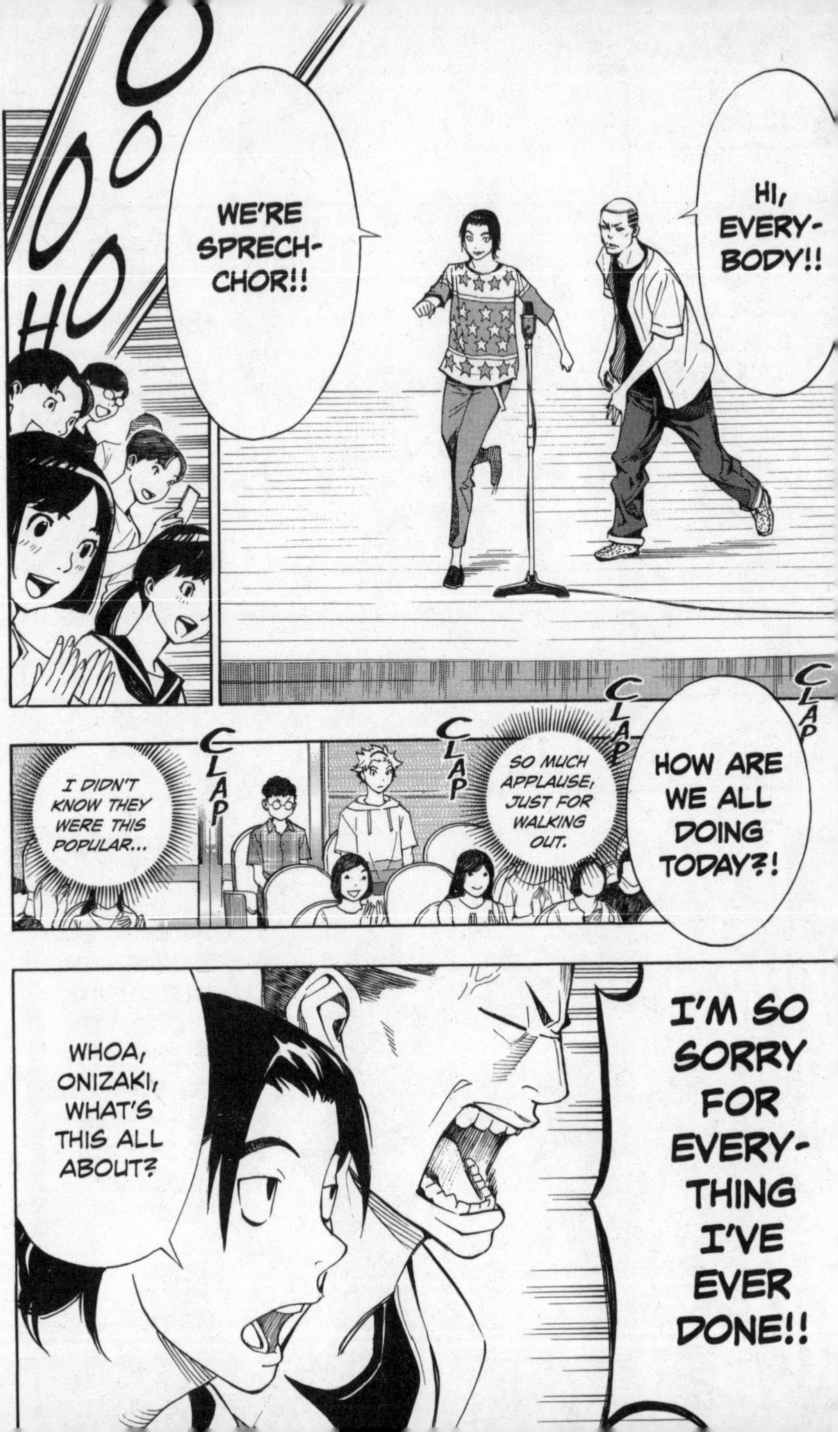
HI, EVERYBODY!!
WE'RE SPRECHCHOR!!
HOOOOO
HOW ARE WE ALL DOING TODAY?!
CLAP CLAP
SO MUCH APPLAUSE, JUST FOR WALKING OUT.
CLAP CLAP
I DIDN'T KNOW THEY WERE THIS POPULAR...
I'M SO SORRY FOR EVERYTHING I'VE EVER DONE!!
WHOA, ONIZAKI, WHAT'S THIS ALL ABOUT?

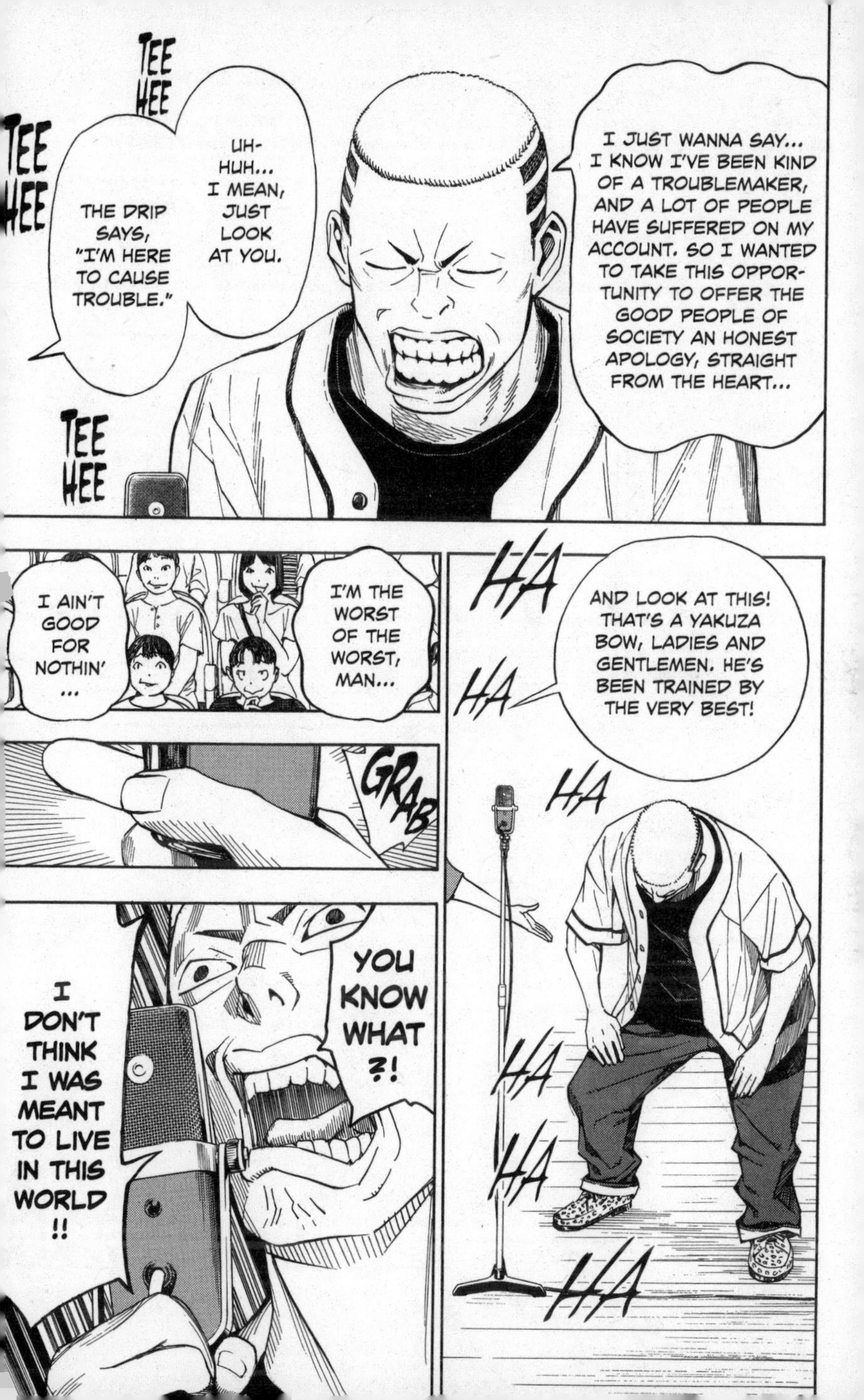
I JUST WANNA SAY... I KNOW I'VE BEEN KIND OF A TROUBLEMAKER, AND A LOT OF PEOPLE HAVE SUFFERED ON MY ACCOUNT. SO I WANTED TO TAKE THIS OPPORTUNITY TO OFFER THE GOOD PEOPLE OF SOCIETY AN HONEST APOLOGY, STRAIGHT FROM THE HEART...
TEE HEE
UH-HUH... I MEAN, JUST LOOK AT YOU.
TEE HEE
THE DRIP SAYS, "I'M HERE TO CAUSE TROUBLE."
TEE HEE
HA HA
AND LOOK AT THIS! THAT'S A YAKUZA BOW, LADIES AND GENTLEMEN. HE'S BEEN TRAINED BY THE VERY BEST!
HA
HA HA HA
I'M THE WORST OF THE WORST, MAN...
I AIN'T GOOD FOR NOTHIN'...
GRAB
YOU KNOW WHAT?!
I DON'T THINK I WAS MEANT TO LIVE IN THIS WORLD!!

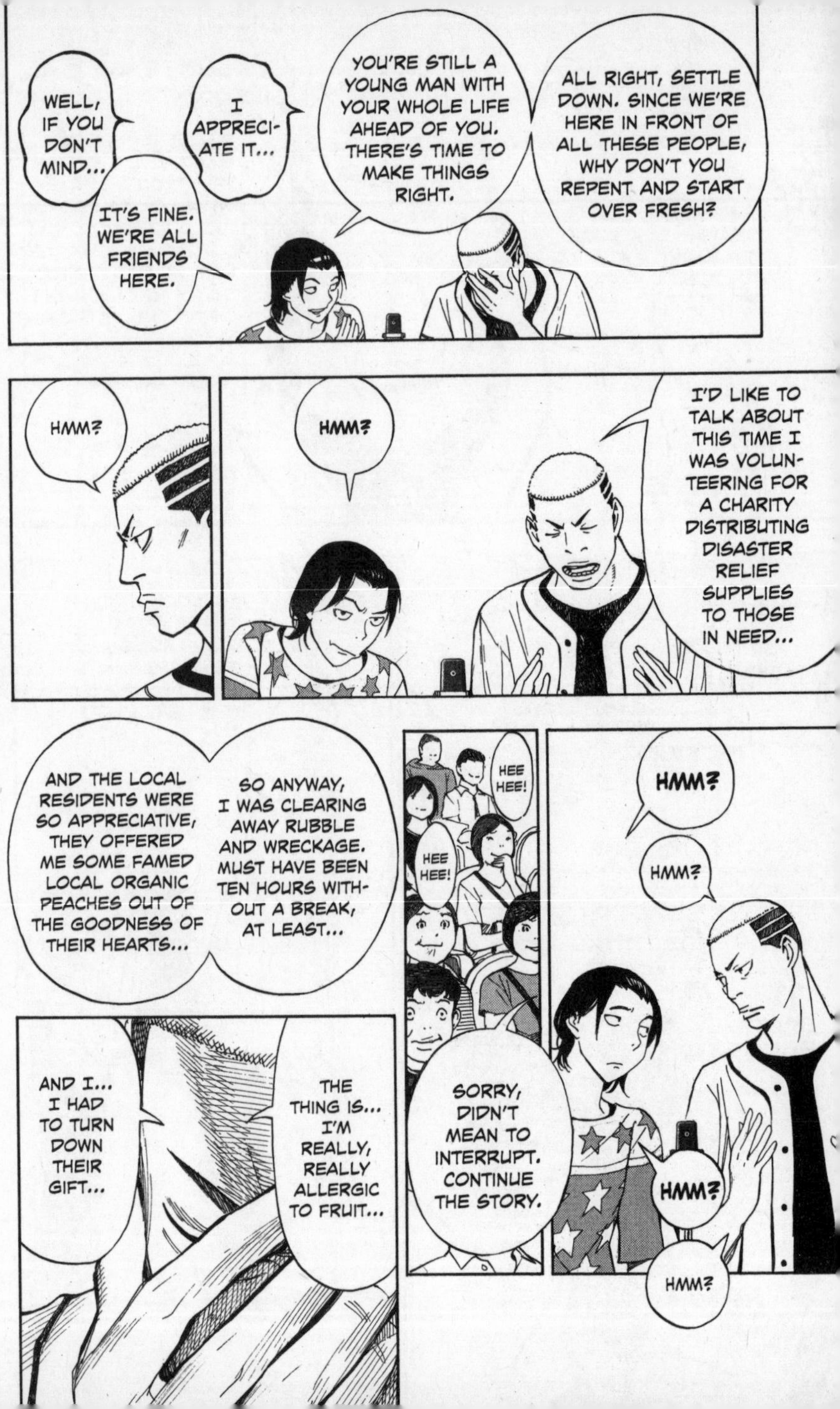
ALL RIGHT, SETTLE DOWN. SINCE WE'RE HERE IN FRONT OF ALL THESE PEOPLE, WHY DON'T YOU REPENT AND START OVER FRESH?
YOU'RE STILL A YOUNG MAN WITH YOUR WHOLE LIFE AHEAD OF YOU. THERE'S TIME TO MAKE THINGS RIGHT.
I APPRECIATE IT...
WELL, IF YOU DON'T MIND...
IT'S FINE. WE'RE ALL FRIENDS HERE.
I'D LIKE TO TALK ABOUT THIS TIME I WAS VOLUNTEERING FOR A CHARITY DISTRIBUTING DISASTER RELIEF SUPPLIES TO THOSE IN NEED...
HMM?
HMM?
HMM?
HMM?
SORRY, DIDN'T MEAN TO INTERRUPT. CONTINUE THE STORY.
HMM?
HMM?
HEE HEE!
HEE HEE!
SO ANYWAY, I WAS CLEARING AWAY RUBBLE AND WRECKAGE. MUST HAVE BEEN TEN HOURS WITHOUT A BREAK, AT LEAST...
AND THE LOCAL RESIDENTS WERE SO APPRECIATIVE, THEY OFFERED ME SOME FAMED LOCAL ORGANIC PEACHES OUT OF THE GOODNESS OF THEIR HEARTS...
THE THING IS... I'M REALLY, REALLY ALLERGIC TO FRUIT...
AND I... I HAD TO TURN DOWN THEIR GIFT...

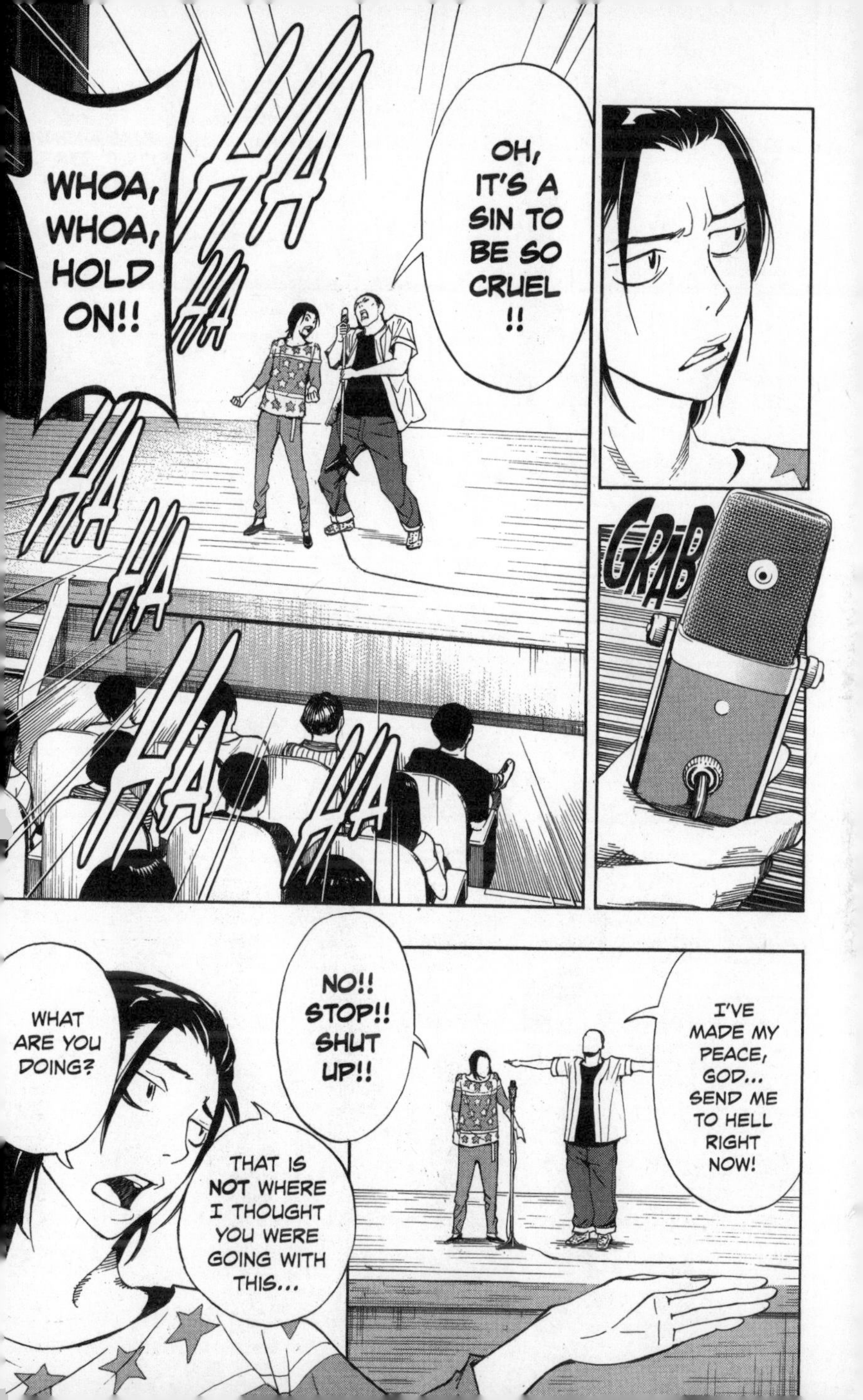
GRAB
OH, IT'S A SIN TO BE SO CRUEL!!
HA HA
HA
WHOA, WHOA, HOLD ON!!
HA HA HA
HA HA HA
I'VE MADE MY PEACE, GOD... SEND ME TO HELL RIGHT NOW!
NO!! STOP!! SHUT UP!!
WHAT ARE YOU DOING?
THAT IS NOT WHERE I THOUGHT YOU WERE GOING WITH THIS...

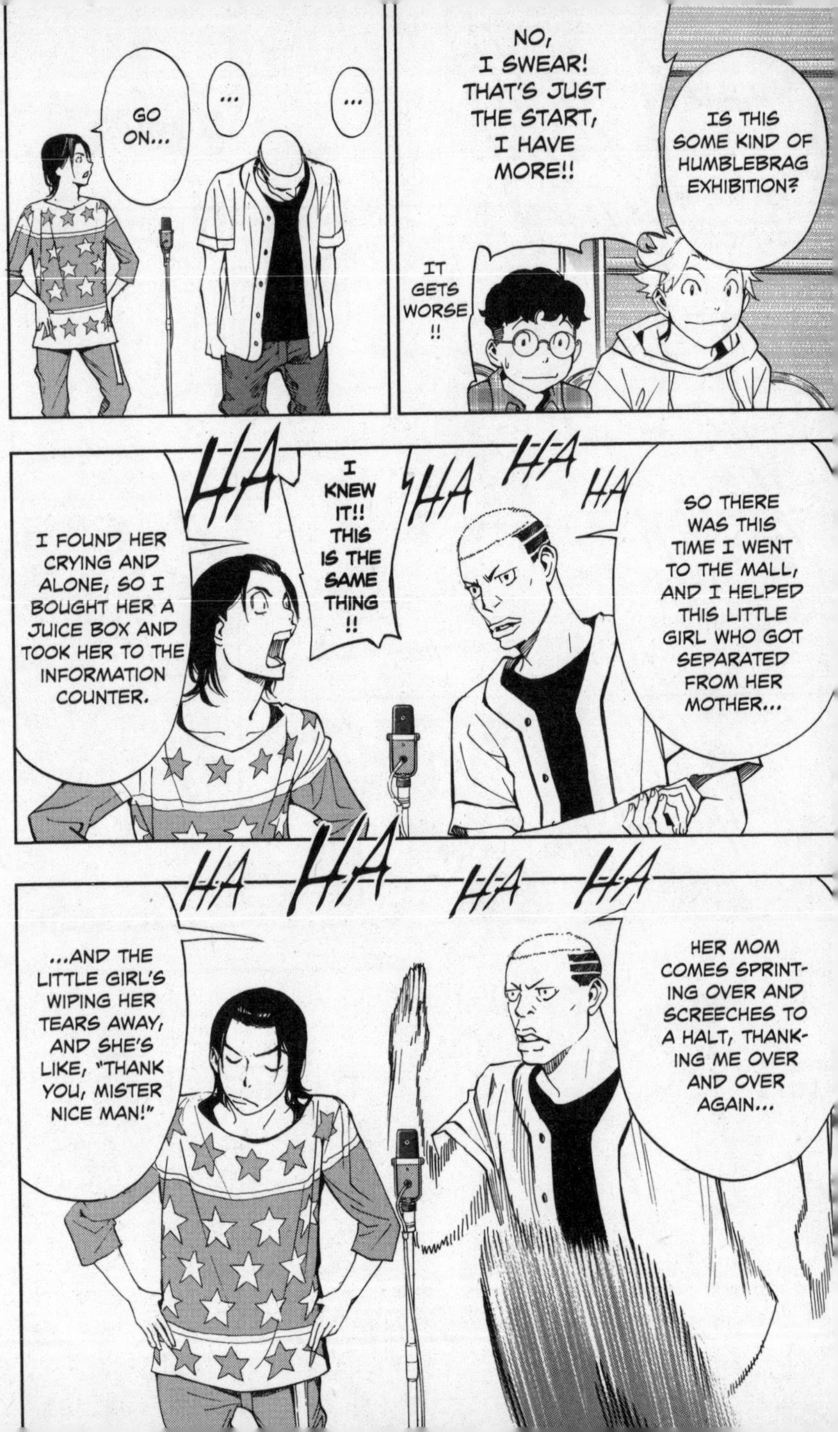
IS THIS SOME KIND OF HUMBLEBRAG EXHIBITION?
NO, I SWEAR! THAT'S JUST THE START, I HAVE MORE!!
IT GETS WORSE!!
...
...
GO ON...
SO THERE WAS THIS TIME I WENT TO THE MALL, AND I HELPED THIS LITTLE GIRL WHO GOT SEPARATED FROM HER MOTHER...
HA HA HA HA
I KNEW IT!! THIS IS THE SAME THING!!
I FOUND HER CRYING AND ALONE, SO I BOUGHT HER A JUICE BOX AND TOOK HER TO THE INFORMATION COUNTER.
HA HA HA HA
HER MOM COMES SPRINTING OVER AND SCREECHES TO A HALT, THANKING ME OVER AND OVER AGAIN...
...AND THE LITTLE GIRL'S WIPING HER TEARS AWAY, AND SHE'S LIKE, "THANK YOU, MISTER NICE MAN!"

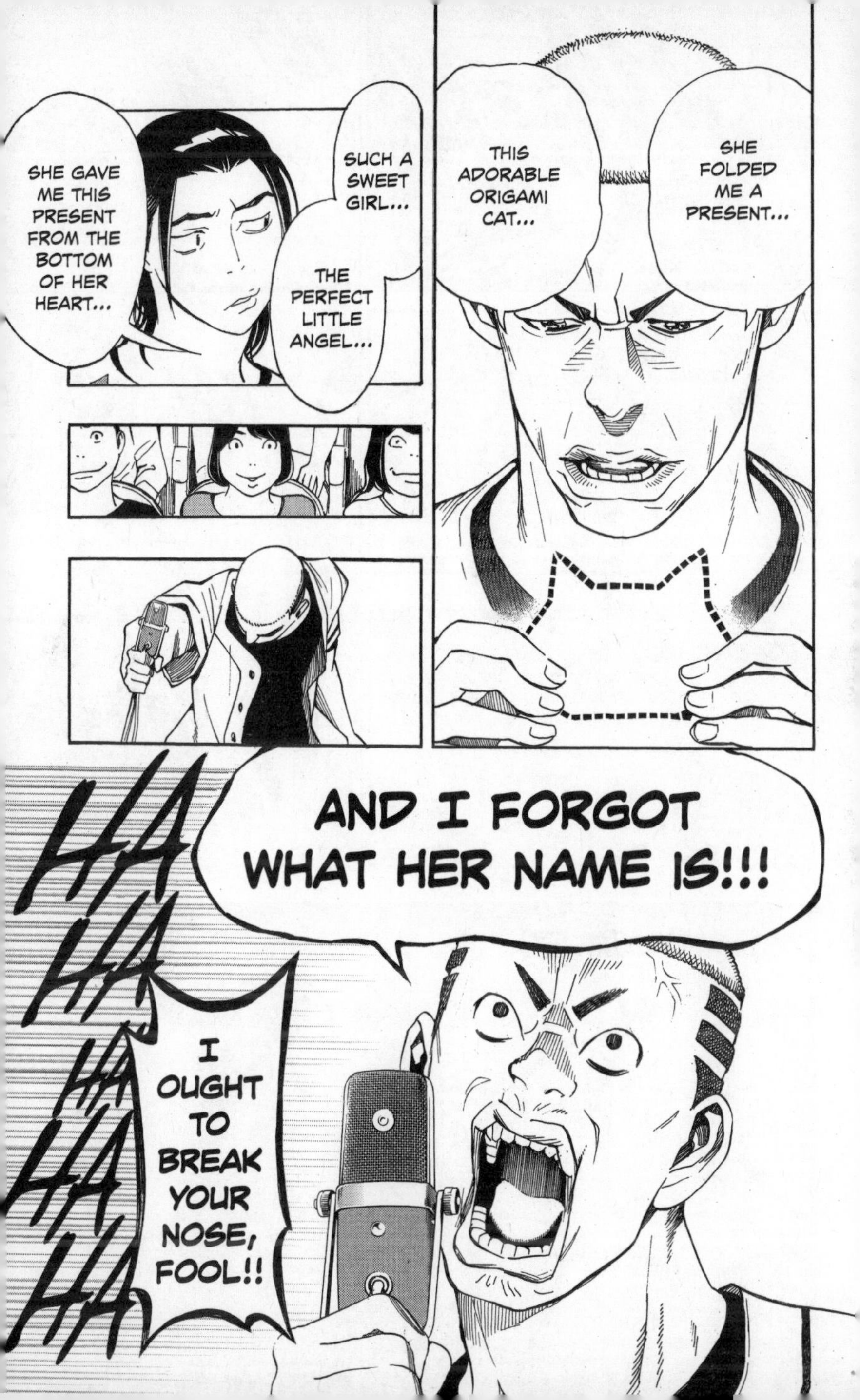

SHE FOLDED ME A PRESENT...
THIS ADORABLE ORIGAMI CAT...
SUCH A SWEET GIRL...
THE PERFECT LITTLE ANGEL...
SHE GAVE ME THIS PRESENT FROM THE BOTTOM OF HER HEART...
AND I FORGOT WHAT HER NAME IS!!!
I OUGHT TO BREAK YOUR NOSE, FOOL!!
HA HA HA HA HA

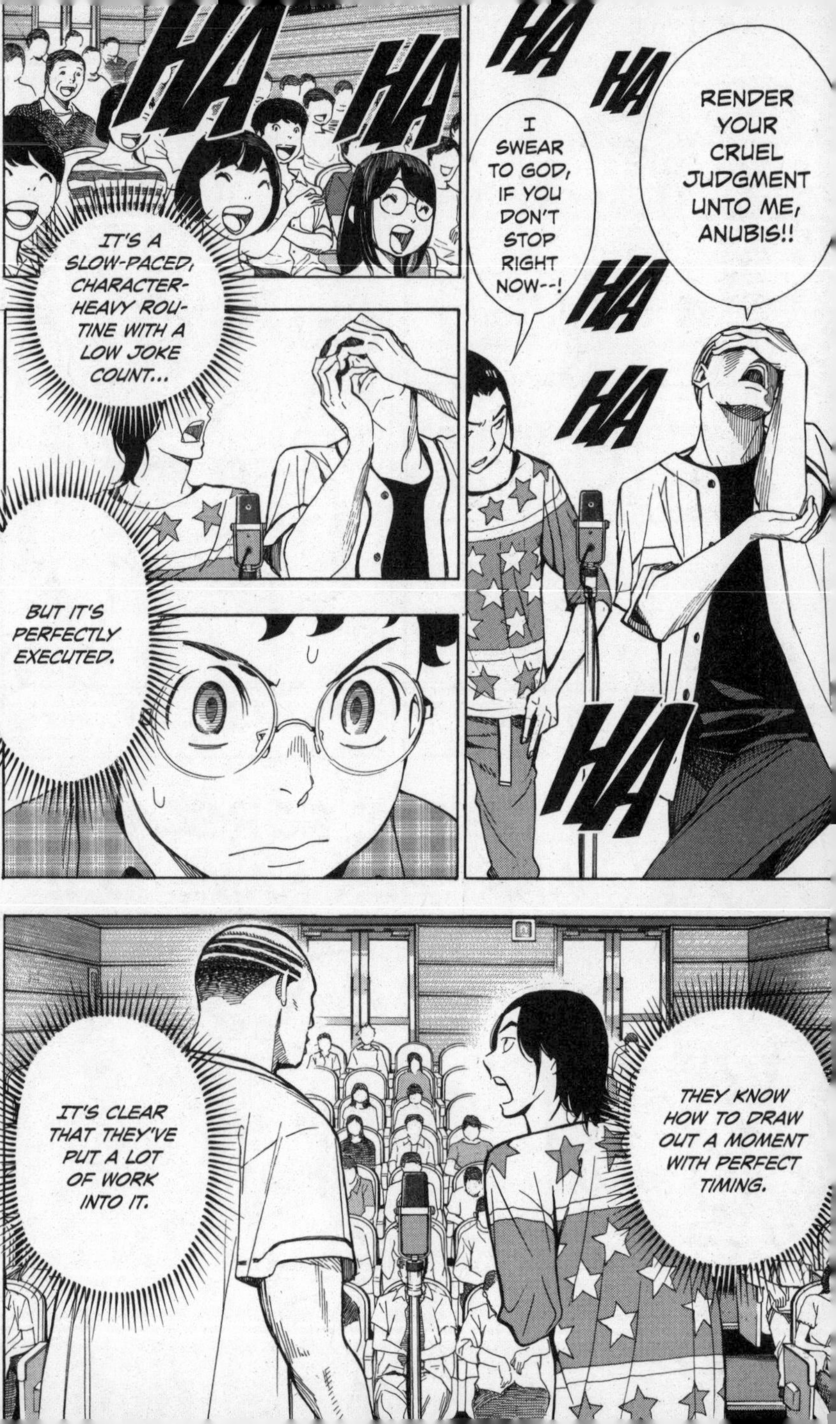
HA HA
RENDER YOUR CRUEL JUDGMENT UNTO ME, ANUBIS!!
I SWEAR TO GOD, IF YOU DON'T STOP RIGHT NOW--!
HA
HA
HA
HA HA
IT'S A SLOW-PACED, CHARACTER-HEAVY ROU-TINE WITH A LOW JOKE COUNT...
BUT IT'S PERFECTLY EXECUTED.
THEY KNOW HOW TO DRAW OUT A MOMENT WITH PERFECT TIMING.
IT'S CLEAR THAT THEY'VE PUT A LOT OF WORK INTO IT.

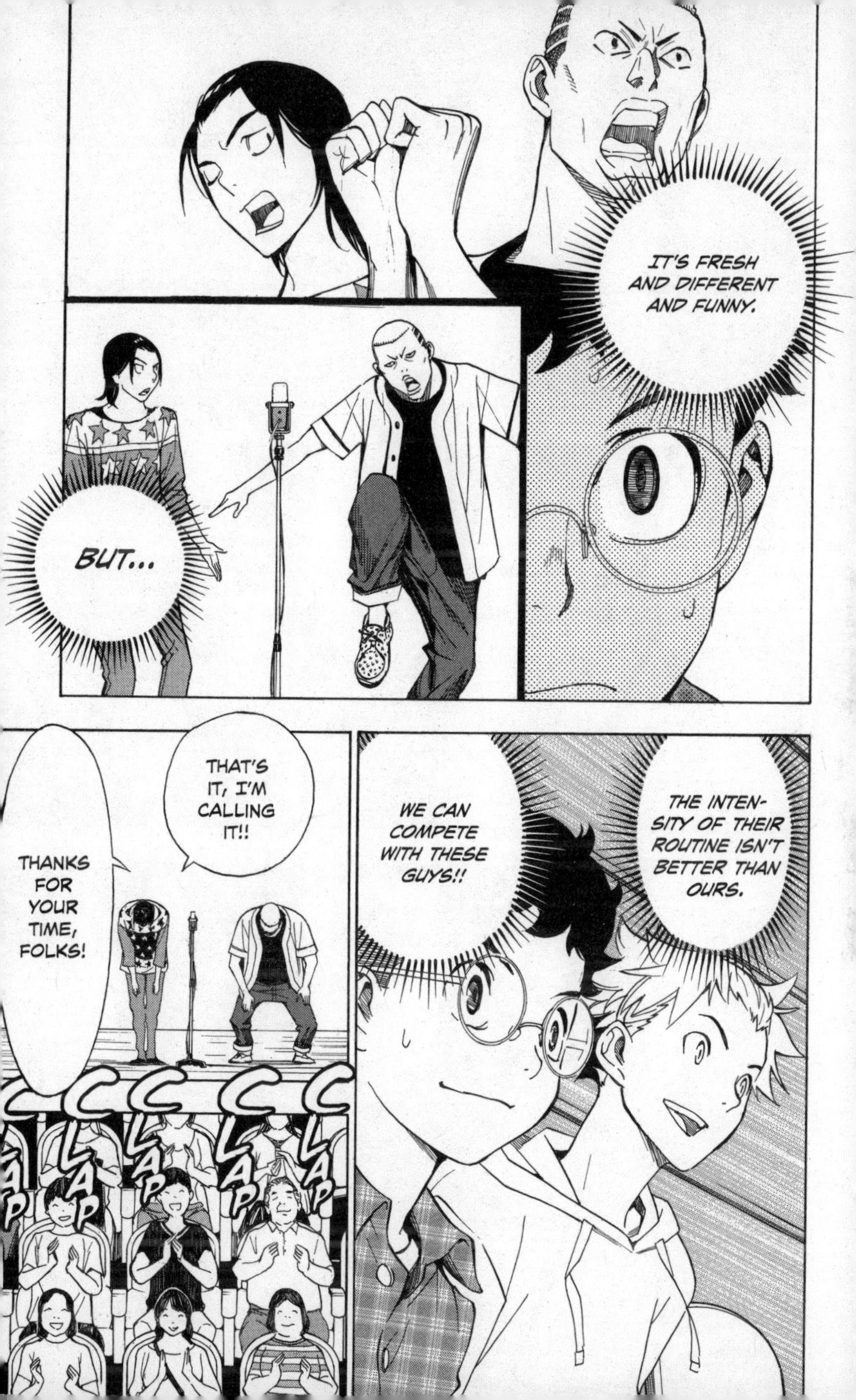
IT'S FRESH AND DIFFERENT AND FUNNY.
BUT...
THE INTEN-SITY OF THEIR ROUTINE ISN'T BETTER THAN OURS.
WE CAN COMPETE WITH THESE GUYS!!
THAT'S IT, I'M CALLING IT!!
THANKS FOR YOUR TIME, FOLKS!
CLAP CLAP CLAP CLAP

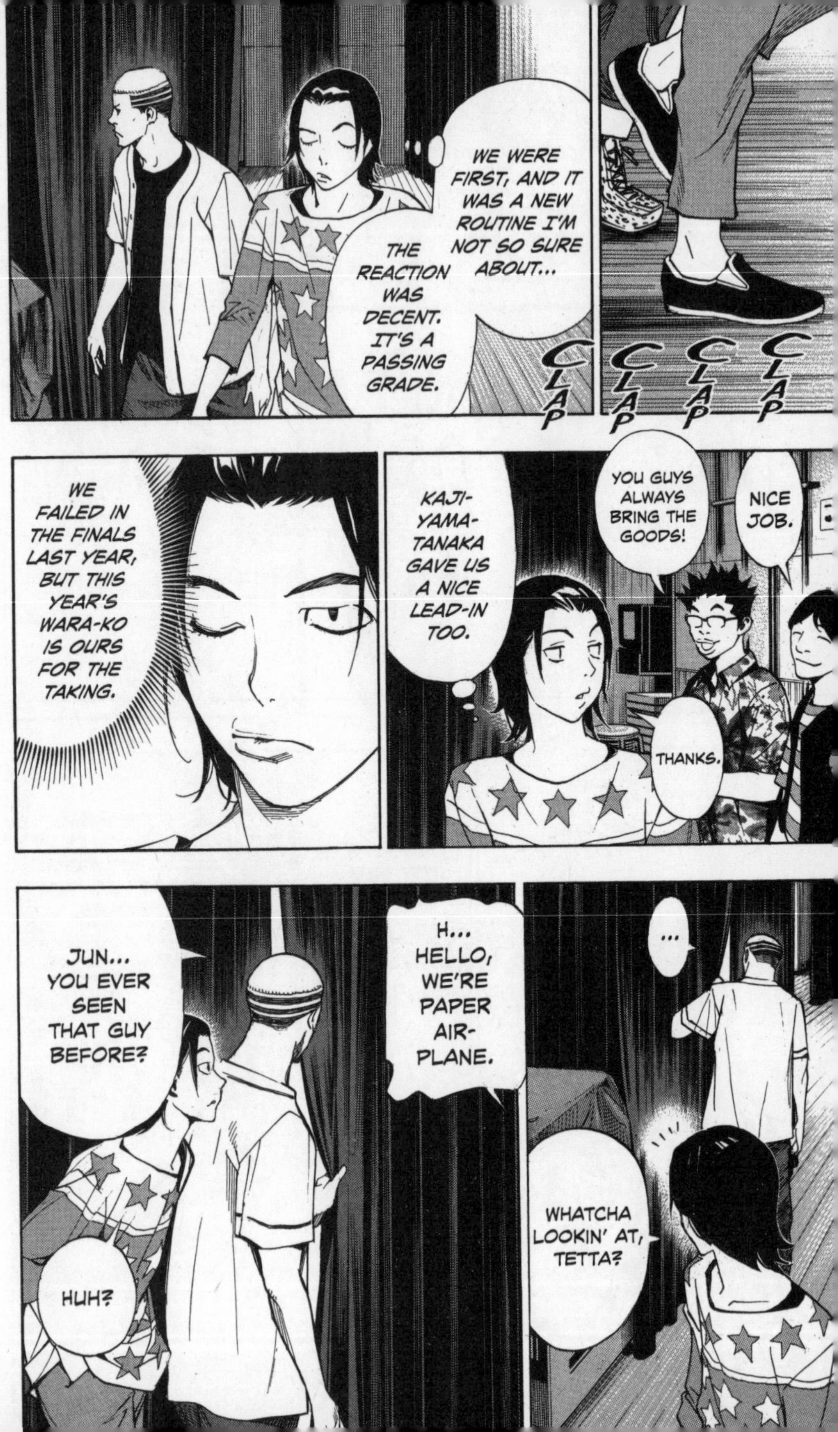
CLAP CLAP CLAP CLAP
WE WERE FIRST, AND IT WAS A NEW ROUTINE I'M NOT SO SURE ABOUT...
THE REACTION WAS DECENT. IT'S A PASSING GRADE.
NICE JOB.
YOU GUYS ALWAYS BRING THE GOODS!
KAJI-YAMA-TANAKA GAVE US A NICE LEAD-IN TOO.
THANKS.
WE FAILED IN THE FINALS LAST YEAR, BUT THIS YEAR'S WARA-KO IS OURS FOR THE TAKING.
...
WHATCHA LOOKIN' AT, TETTA?
H... HELLO, WE'RE PAPER AIR-PLANE.
JUN... YOU EVER SEEN THAT GUY BEFORE?
HUH?

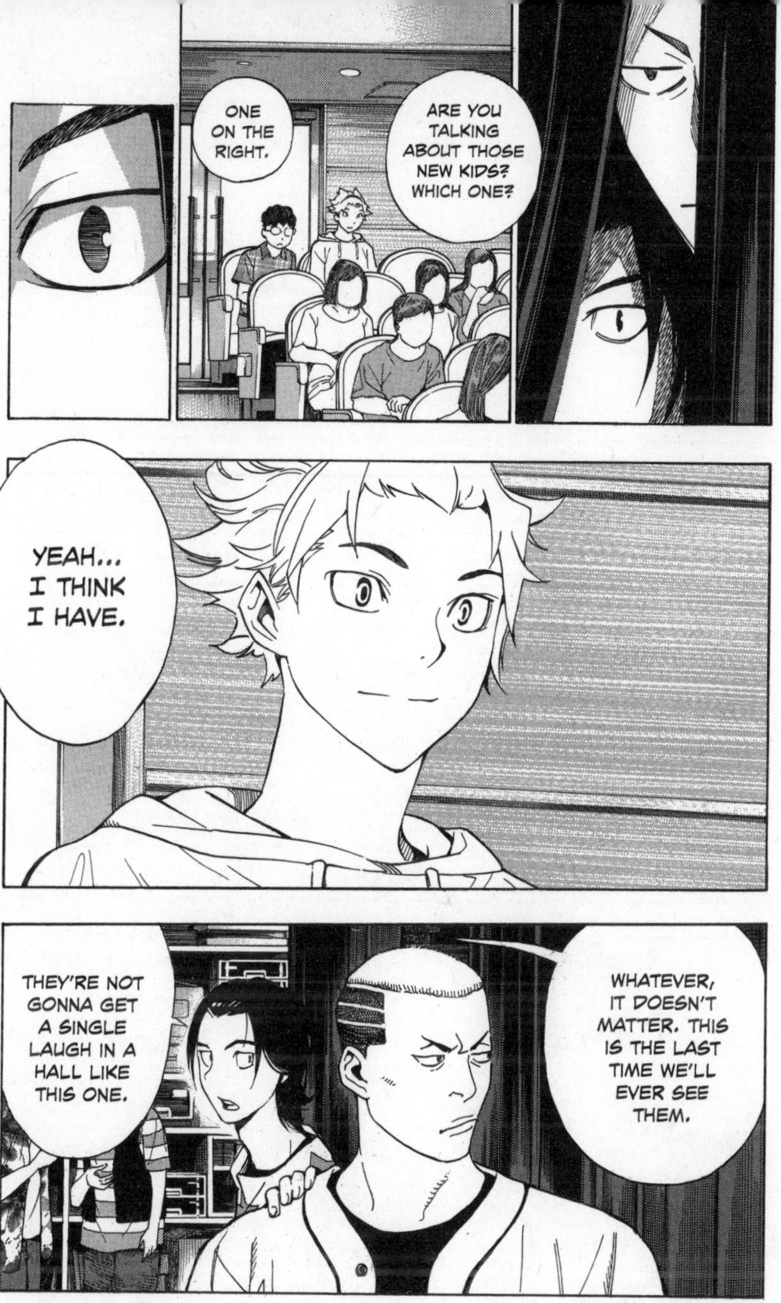
ARE YOU TALKING ABOUT THOSE NEW KIDS? WHICH ONE?
ONE ON THE RIGHT.
YEAH... I THINK I HAVE.
WHATEVER, IT DOESN'T MATTER. THIS IS THE LAST TIME WE'LL EVER SEE THEM.
THEY'RE NOT GONNA GET A SINGLE LAUGH IN A HALL LIKE THIS ONE.

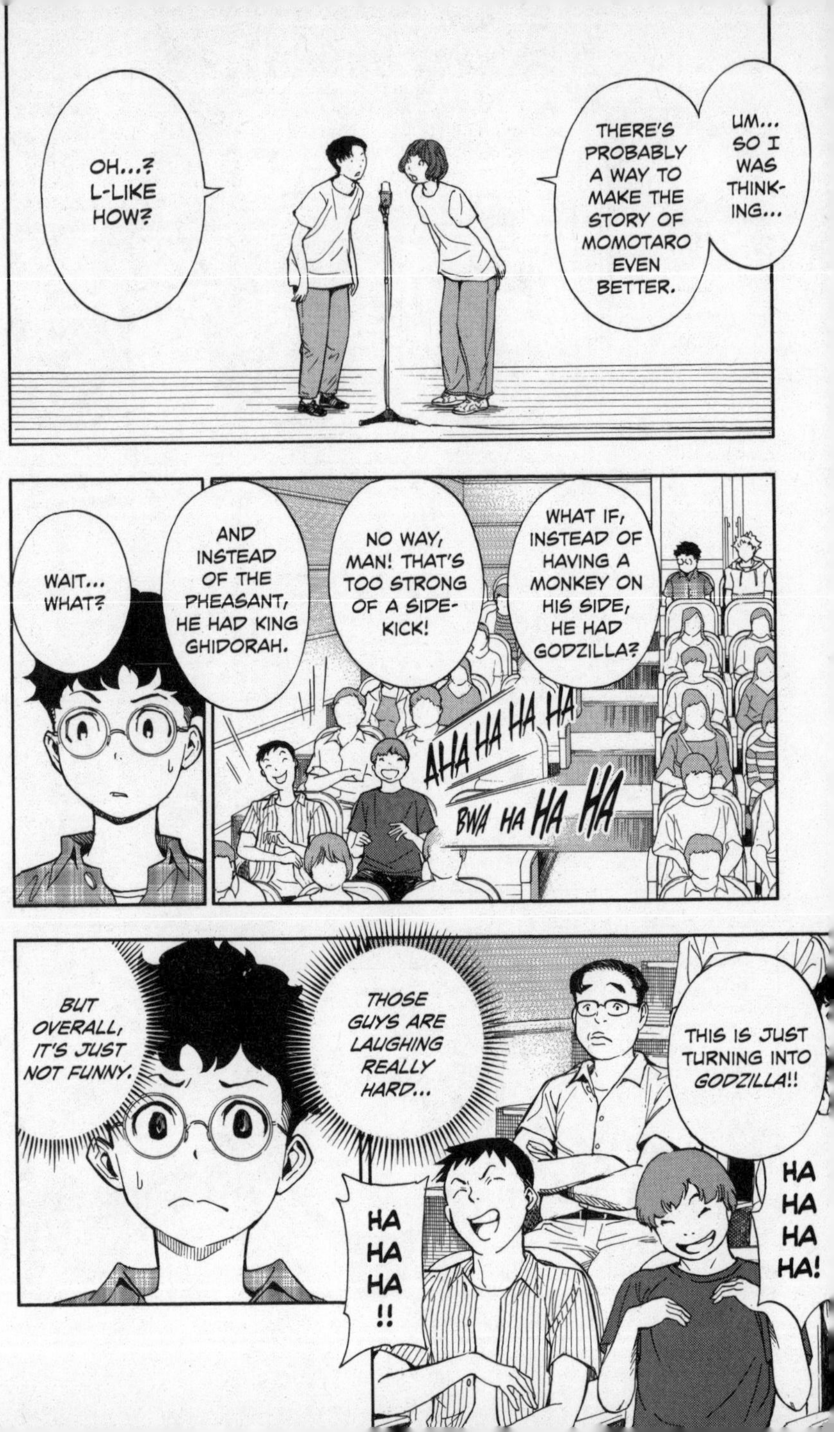
UM... SO I WAS THINKING...
THERE'S PROBABLY A WAY TO MAKE THE STORY OF MOMOTARO EVEN BETTER.
OH...? L-LIKE HOW?
WHAT IF, INSTEAD OF HAVING A MONKEY ON HIS SIDE, HE HAD GODZILLA?
NO WAY, MAN! THAT'S TOO STRONG OF A SIDE-KICK!
AND INSTEAD OF THE PHEASANT, HE HAD KING GHIDORAH.
AHA HA HA HA
BWA HA HA HA
WAIT... WHAT?
THIS IS JUST TURNING INTO *GODZILLA*!!
HA HA HA HA!
HA HA HA !!
THOSE GUYS ARE LAUGHING REALLY HARD...
BUT OVERALL, IT'S JUST NOT FUNNY.

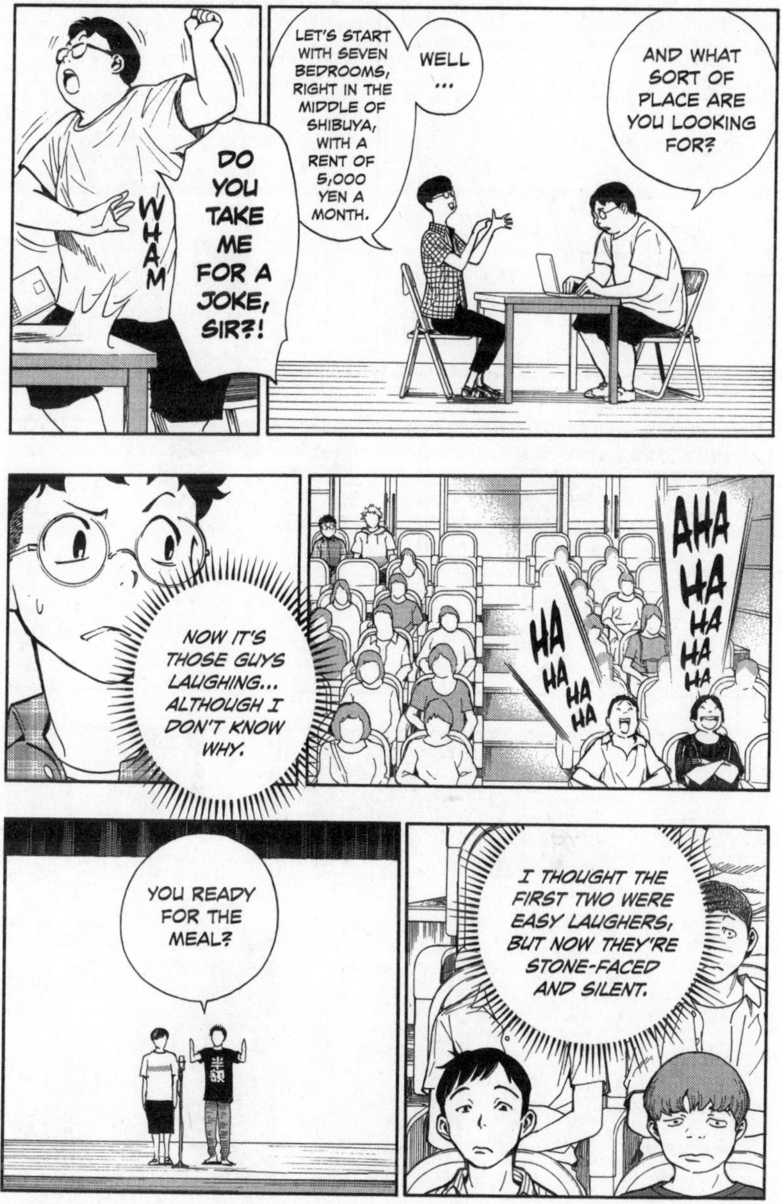
AND WHAT SORT OF PLACE ARE YOU LOOKING FOR?
WELL ...
LET'S START WITH SEVEN BEDROOMS, RIGHT IN THE MIDDLE OF SHIBUYA, WITH A RENT OF 5,000 YEN A MONTH.
DO YOU TAKE ME FOR A JOKE, SIR?!
WHAM
AHA HA HA HA HA
HA HA HA HA
NOW IT'S THOSE GUYS LAUGHING... ALTHOUGH I DON'T KNOW WHY.
I THOUGHT THE FIRST TWO WERE EASY LAUGHERS, BUT NOW THEY'RE STONE-FACED AND SILENT.
YOU READY FOR THE MEAL?

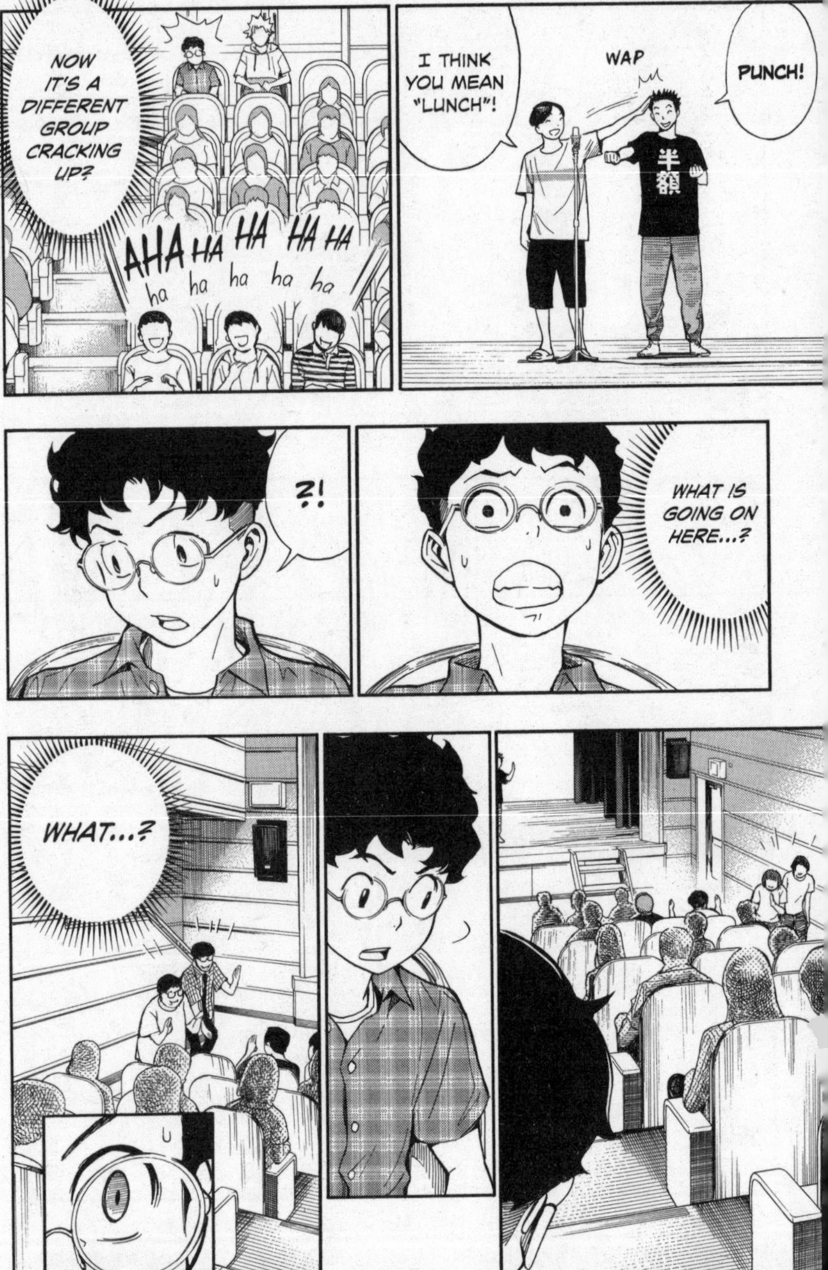
PUNCH!
WAP
I THINK YOU MEAN "LUNCH"!
NOW IT'S A DIFFERENT GROUP CRACKING UP?
AHA HA HA HA HA HA
ha ha ha ha ha
WHAT IS GOING ON HERE...?
?!
WHAT...?

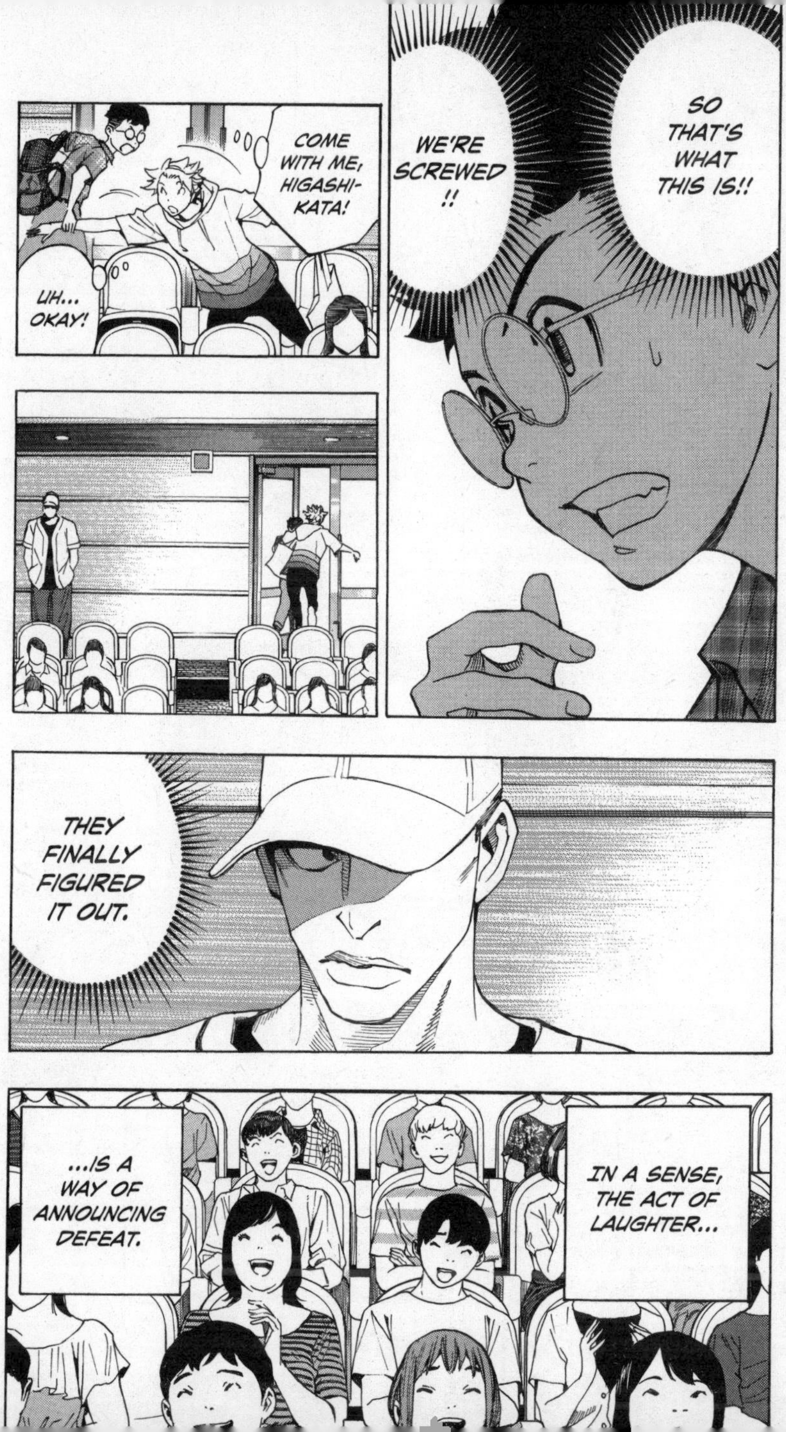
SO THAT'S WHAT THIS IS!!
WE'RE SCREWED!!
COME WITH ME, HIGASHI-KATA!
UH... OKAY!
THEY FINALLY FIGURED IT OUT.
IN A SENSE, THE ACT OF LAUGHTER...
...IS A WAY OF ANNOUNCING DEFEAT.

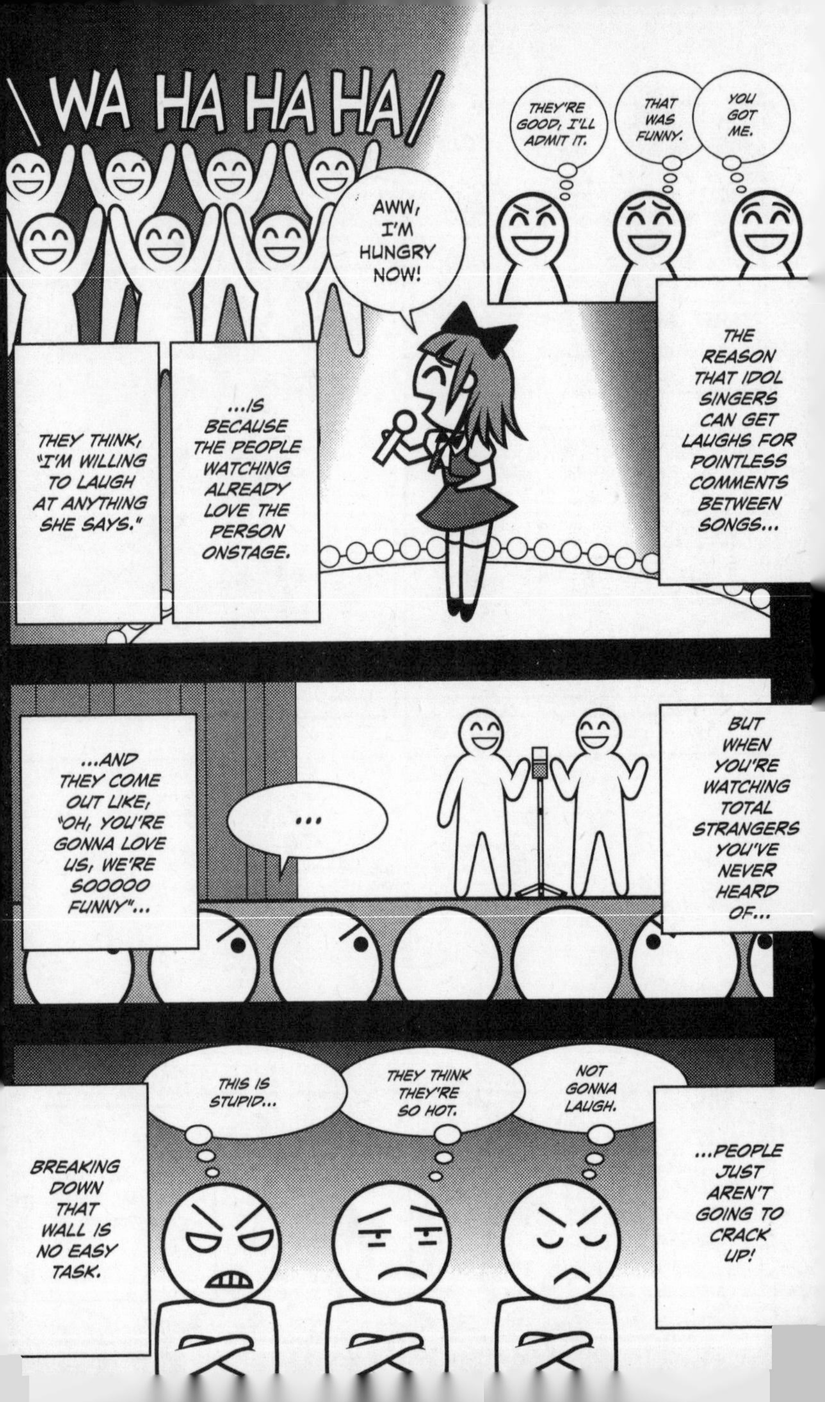
YOU GOT ME.
THAT WAS FUNNY.
THEY'RE GOOD, I'LL ADMIT IT.
THE REASON THAT IDOL SINGERS CAN GET LAUGHS FOR POINTLESS COMMENTS BETWEEN SONGS...
AWW, I'M HUNGRY NOW!
WA HA HA HA
...IS BECAUSE THE PEOPLE WATCHING ALREADY LOVE THE PERSON ONSTAGE.
THEY THINK, "I'M WILLING TO LAUGH AT ANYTHING SHE SAYS."
BUT WHEN YOU'RE WATCHING TOTAL STRANGERS YOU'VE NEVER HEARD OF...
...
...AND THEY COME OUT LIKE, "OH, YOU'RE GONNA LOVE US, WE'RE SOOOOO FUNNY"...
...PEOPLE JUST AREN'T GOING TO CRACK UP!
NOT GONNA LAUGH.
THEY THINK THEY'RE SO HOT.
THIS IS STUPID...
BREAKING DOWN THAT WALL IS NO EASY TASK.

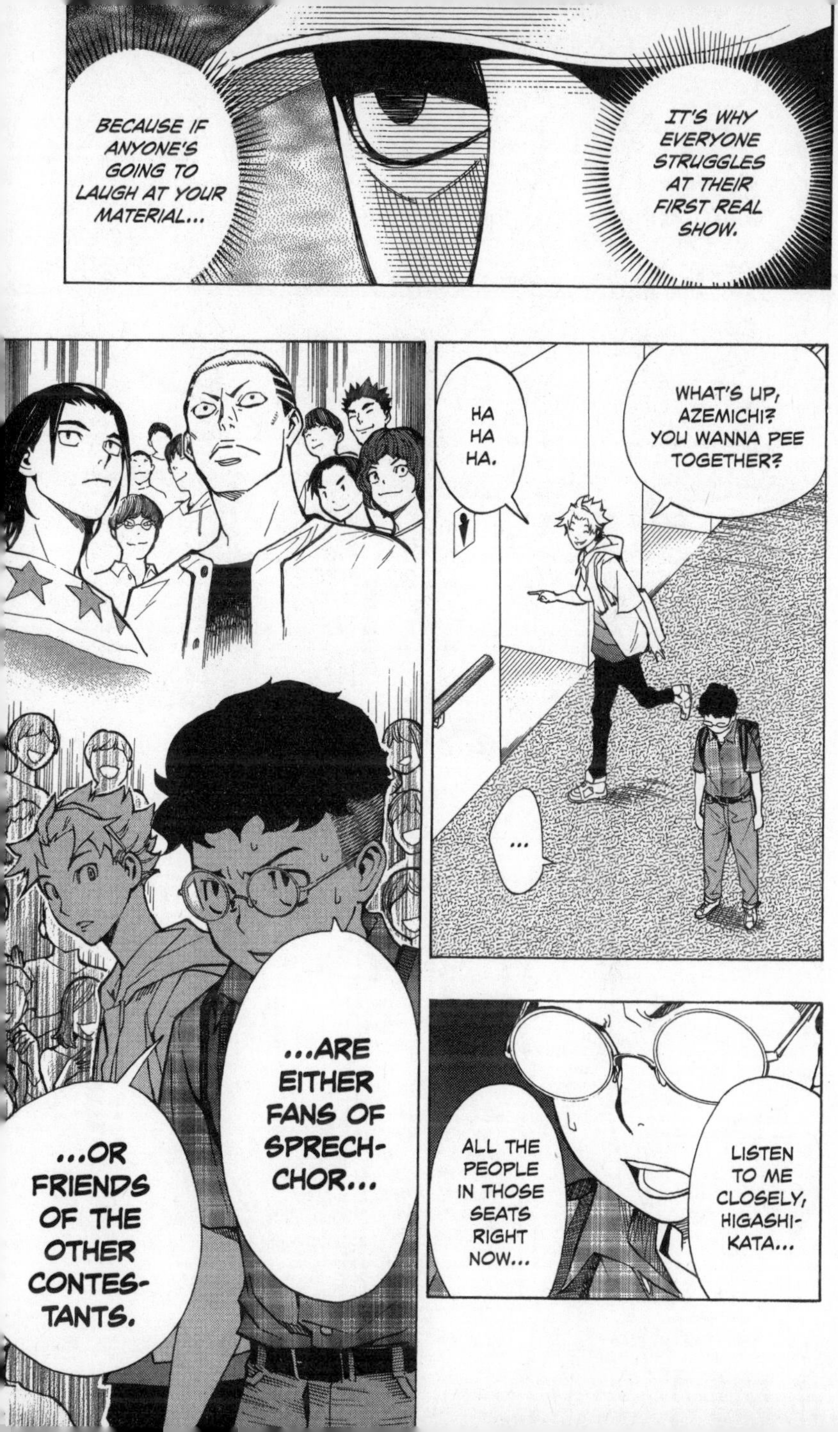
IT'S WHY EVERYONE STRUGGLES AT THEIR FIRST REAL SHOW.
BECAUSE IF ANYONE'S GOING TO LAUGH AT YOUR MATERIAL...
WHAT'S UP, AZEMICHI? YOU WANNA PEE TOGETHER?
HA HA HA.
...
LISTEN TO ME CLOSELY, HIGASHI-KATA...
ALL THE PEOPLE IN THOSE SEATS RIGHT NOW...
...ARE EITHER FANS OF SPRECH-CHOR...
...OR FRIENDS OF THE OTHER CONTES-TANTS.

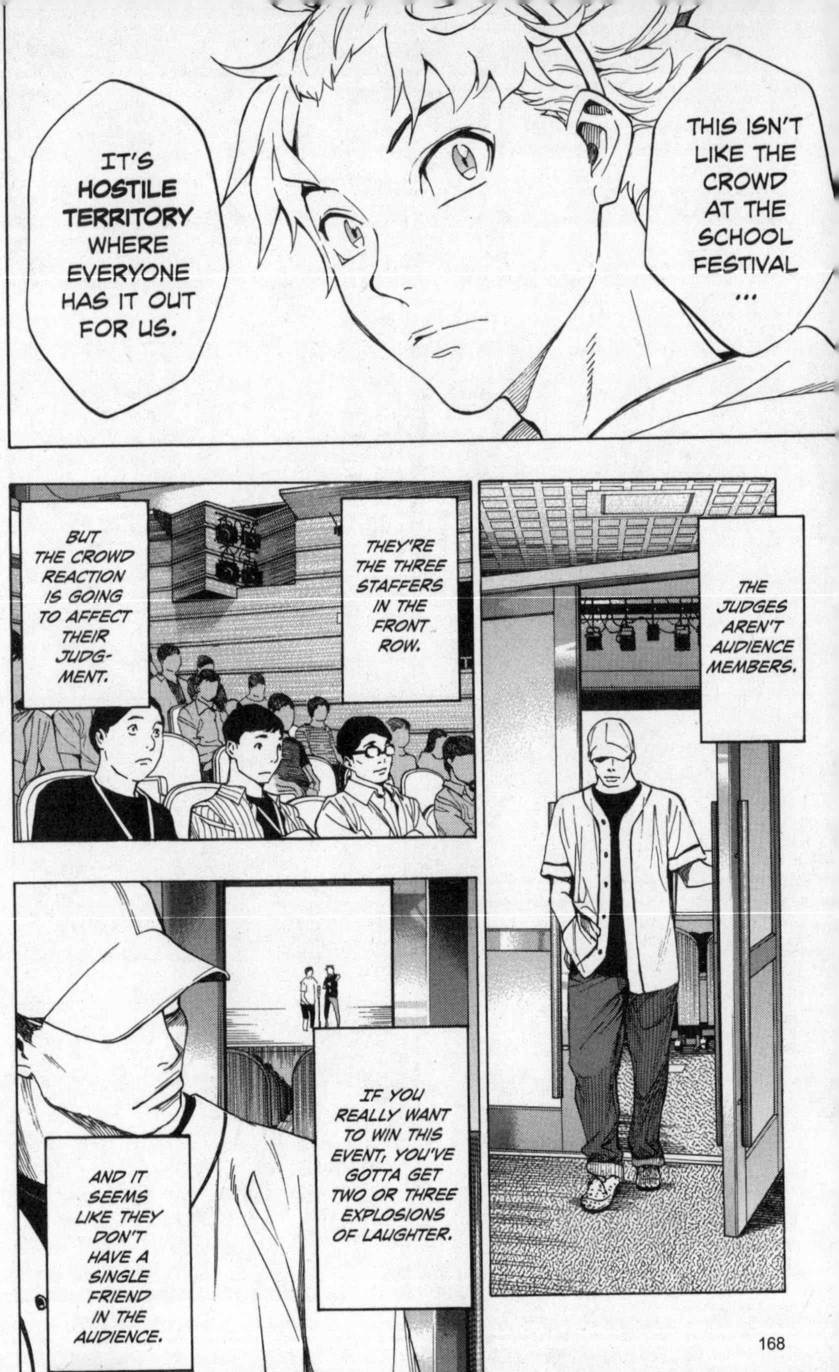
THIS ISN'T LIKE THE CROWD AT THE SCHOOL FESTIVAL...
IT'S **HOSTILE TERRITORY** WHERE EVERYONE HAS IT OUT FOR US.
THE JUDGES AREN'T AUDIENCE MEMBERS.
THEY'RE THE THREE STAFFERS IN THE FRONT ROW.
BUT THE CROWD REACTION IS GOING TO AFFECT THEIR JUDGMENT.
IF YOU REALLY WANT TO WIN THIS EVENT, YOU'VE GOTTA GET TWO OR THREE EXPLOSIONS OF LAUGHTER.
AND IT SEEMS LIKE THEY DON'T HAVE A SINGLE FRIEND IN THE AUDIENCE.

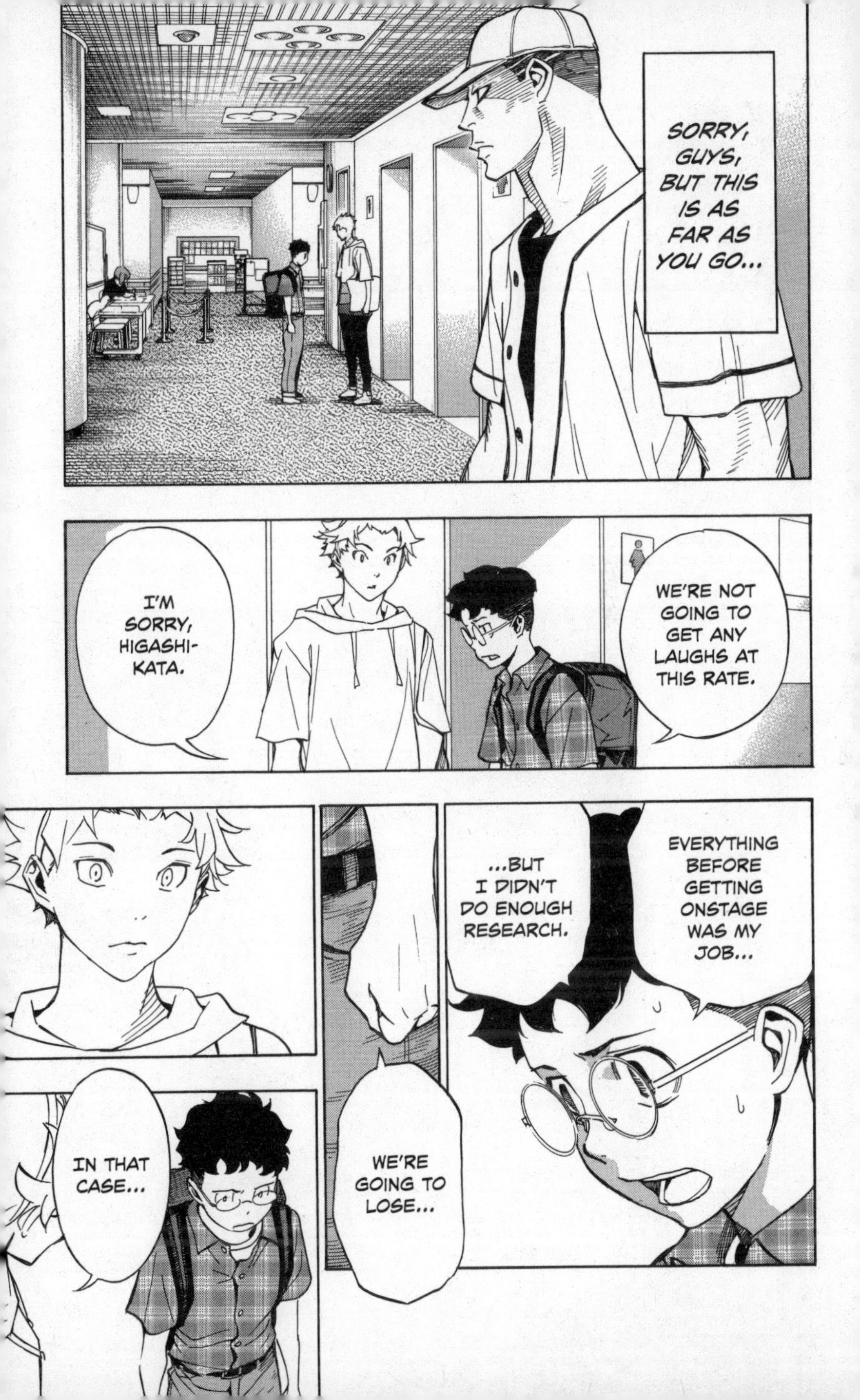
SORRY, GUYS, BUT THIS IS AS FAR AS YOU GO...
WE'RE NOT GOING TO GET ANY LAUGHS AT THIS RATE.
I'M SORRY, HIGASHIKATA.
EVERYTHING BEFORE GETTING ONSTAGE WAS MY JOB...
...BUT I DIDN'T DO ENOUGH RESEARCH.
WE'RE GOING TO LOSE...
IN THAT CASE...

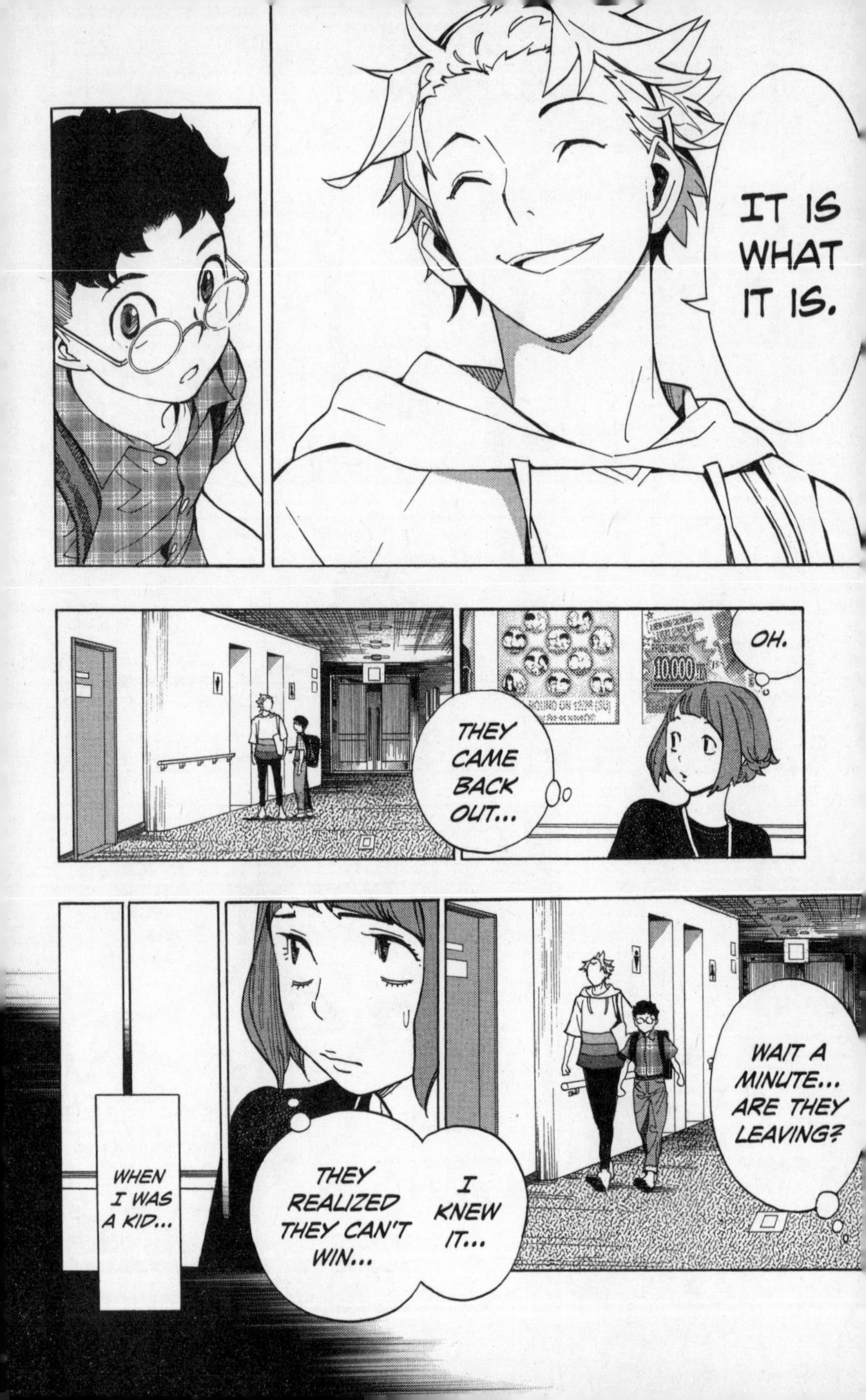
IT IS WHAT IT IS.
OH.
THEY CAME BACK OUT...
WAIT A MINUTE... ARE THEY LEAVING?
I KNEW IT...
THEY REALIZED THEY CAN'T WIN...
WHEN I WAS A KID...

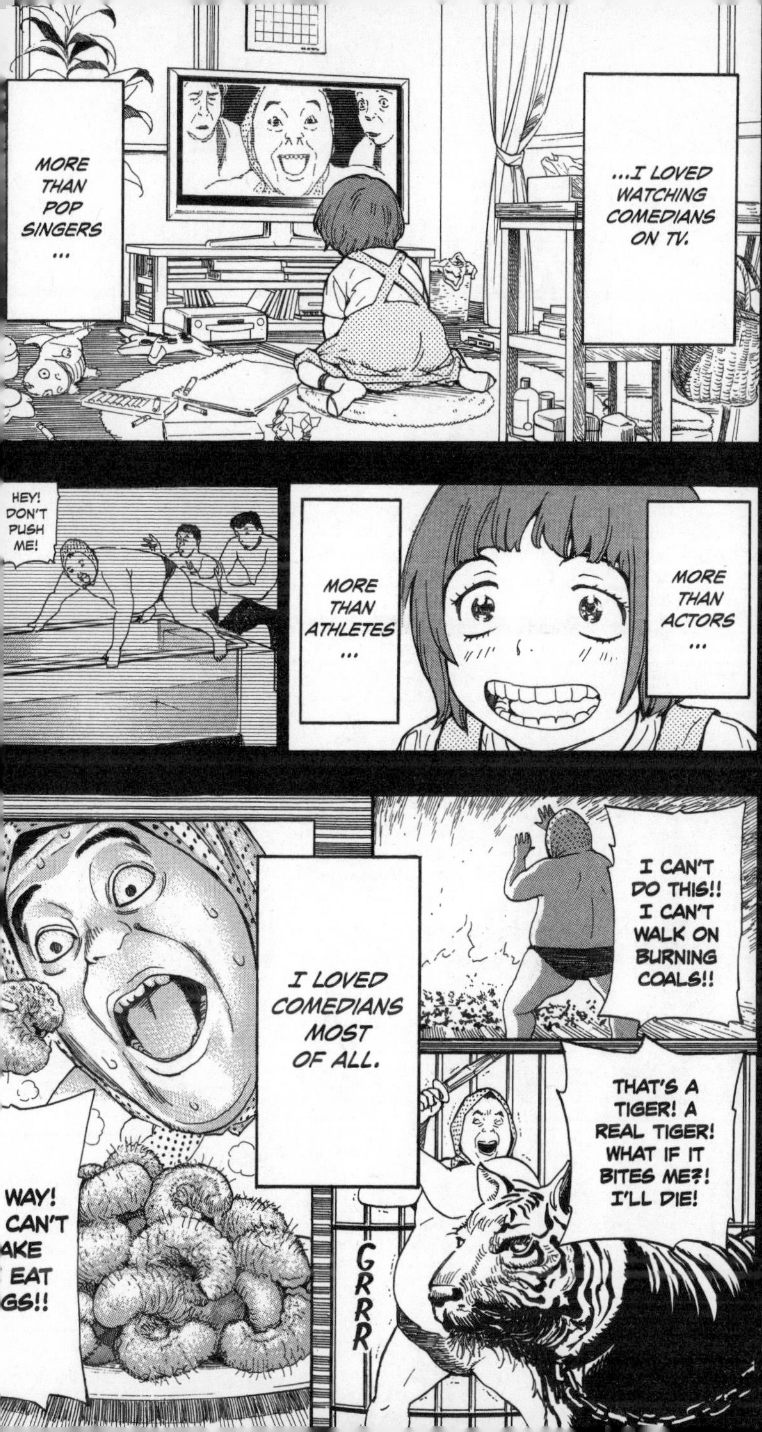
...I LOVED WATCHING COMEDIANS ON TV.
MORE THAN POP SINGERS...
MORE THAN ACTORS...
MORE THAN ATHLETES...
HEY! DON'T PUSH ME!
I CAN'T DO THIS!! I CAN'T WALK ON BURNING COALS!!
THAT'S A TIGER! A REAL TIGER! WHAT IF IT BITES ME?! I'LL DIE!
GRRR
I LOVED COMEDIANS MOST OF ALL.
WAY! CAN'T AKE EAT GS!!

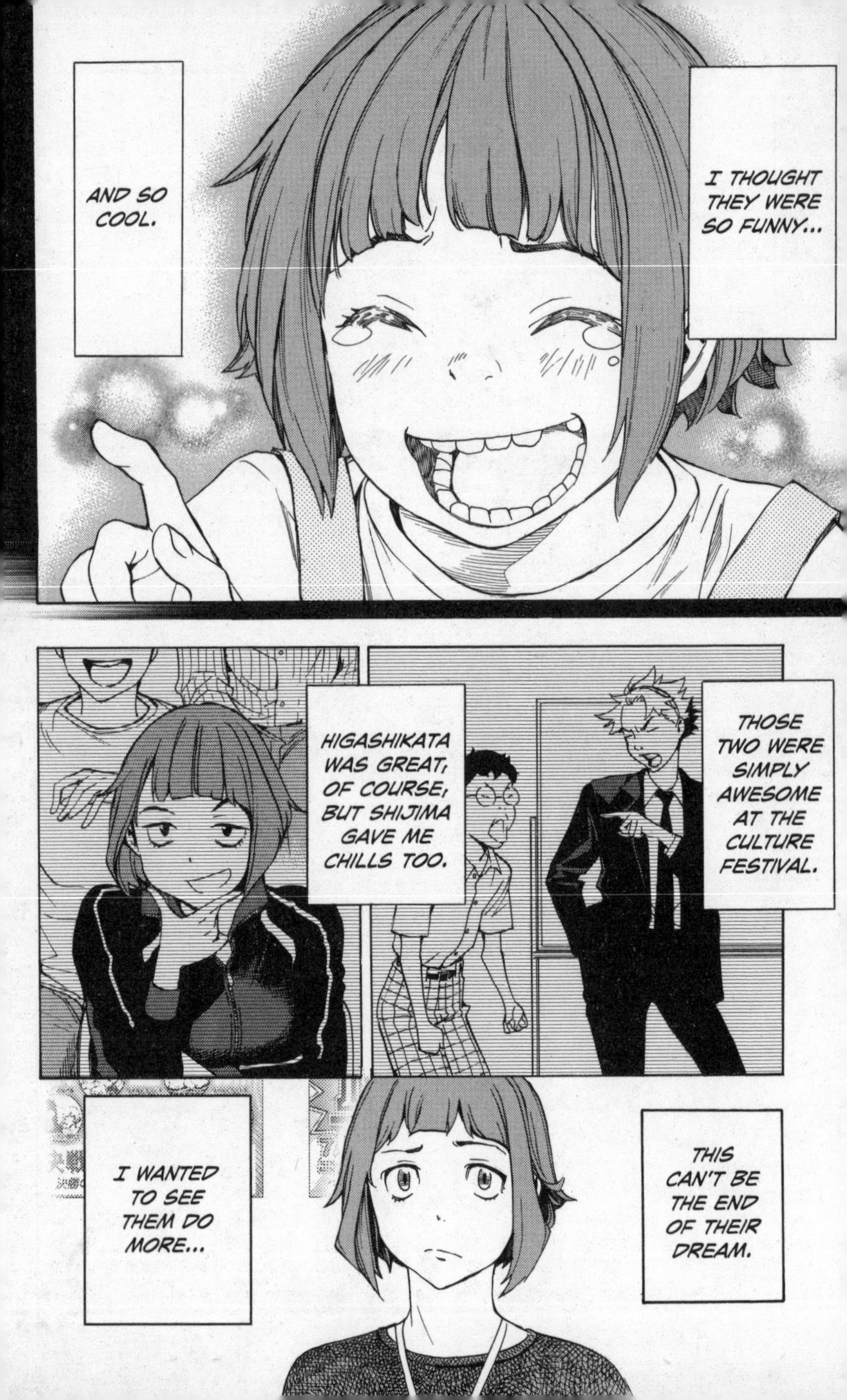
I THOUGHT THEY WERE SO FUNNY...
AND SO COOL.
THOSE TWO WERE SIMPLY AWESOME AT THE CULTURE FESTIVAL.
HIGASHIKATA WAS GREAT, OF COURSE, BUT SHIJIMA GAVE ME CHILLS TOO.
THIS CAN'T BE THE END OF THEIR DREAM.
I WANTED TO SEE THEM DO MORE...

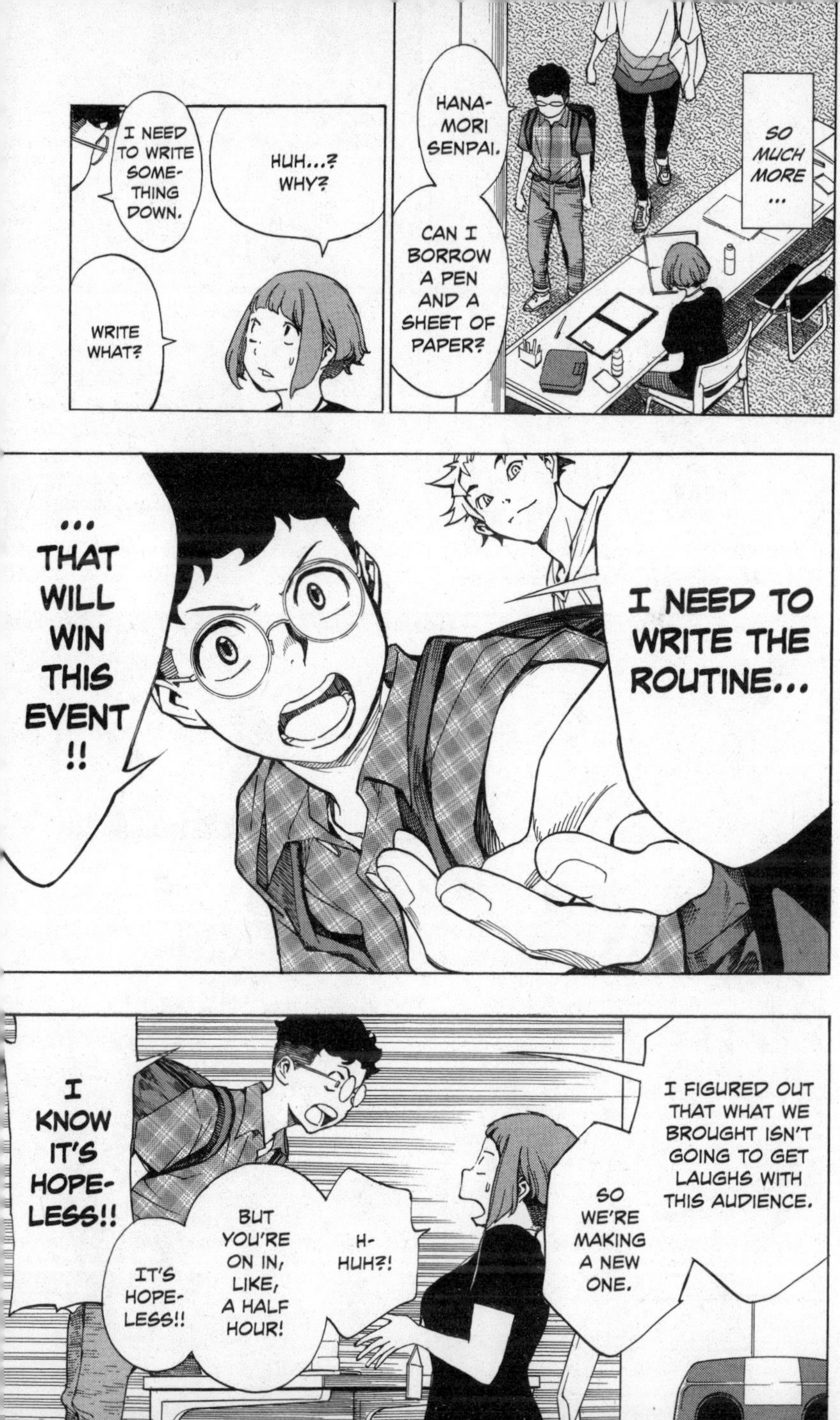
SO MUCH MORE...
HANA-MORI SENPAI.
CAN I BORROW A PEN AND A SHEET OF PAPER?
HUH...? WHY?
I NEED TO WRITE SOME-THING DOWN.
WRITE WHAT?
I NEED TO WRITE THE ROUTINE...
...THAT WILL WIN THIS EVENT!!
I FIGURED OUT THAT WHAT WE BROUGHT ISN'T GOING TO GET LAUGHS WITH THIS AUDIENCE.
SO WE'RE MAKING A NEW ONE.
H-HUH?!
BUT YOU'RE ON IN, LIKE, A HALF HOUR!
I KNOW IT'S HOPE-LESS!!
IT'S HOPE-LESS!!

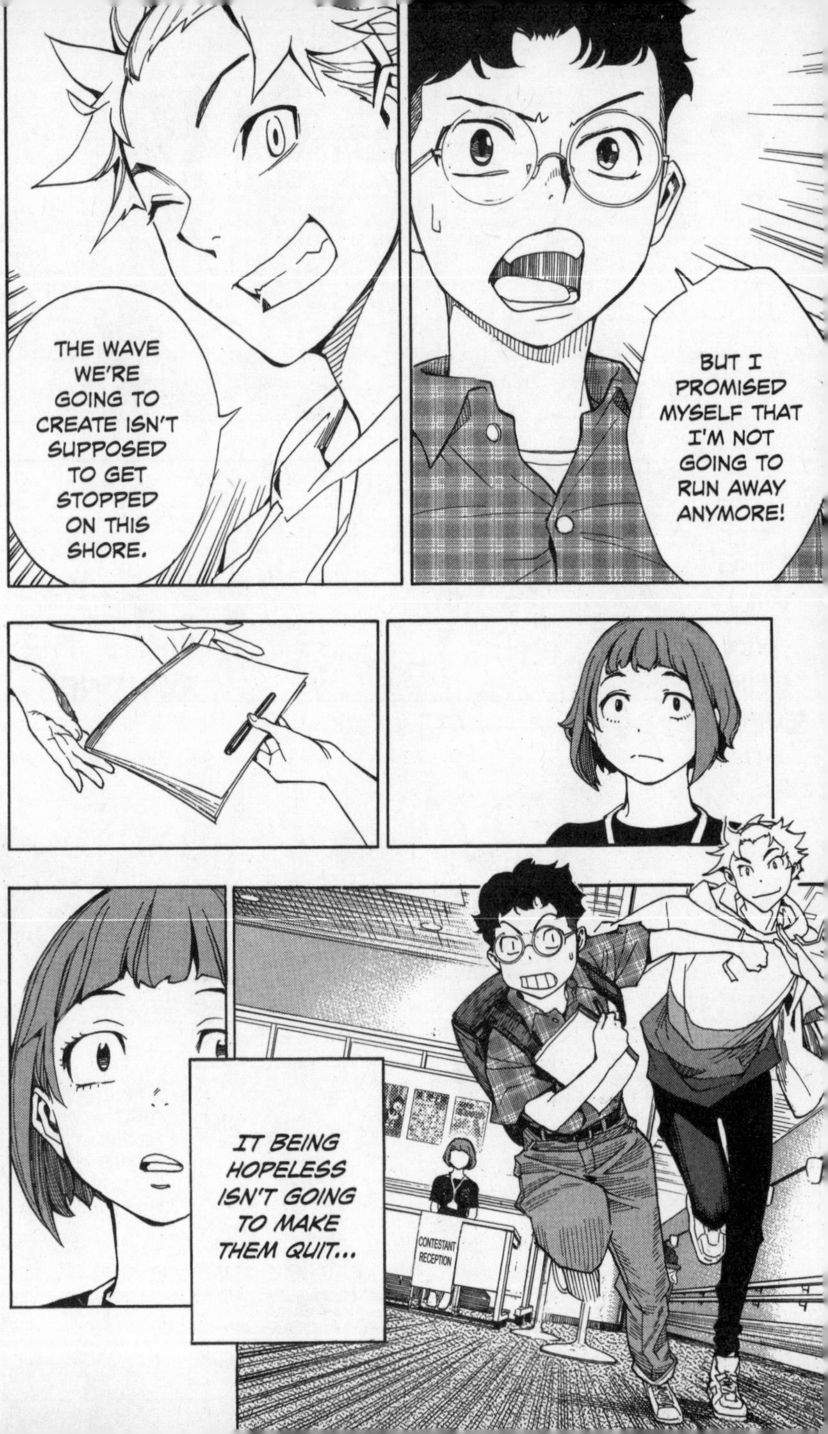
BUT I PROMISED MYSELF THAT I'M NOT GOING TO RUN AWAY ANYMORE!
THE WAVE WE'RE GOING TO CREATE ISN'T SUPPOSED TO GET STOPPED ON THIS SHORE.
CONTESTANT RECEPTION
IT BEING HOPELESS ISN'T GOING TO MAKE THEM QUIT...

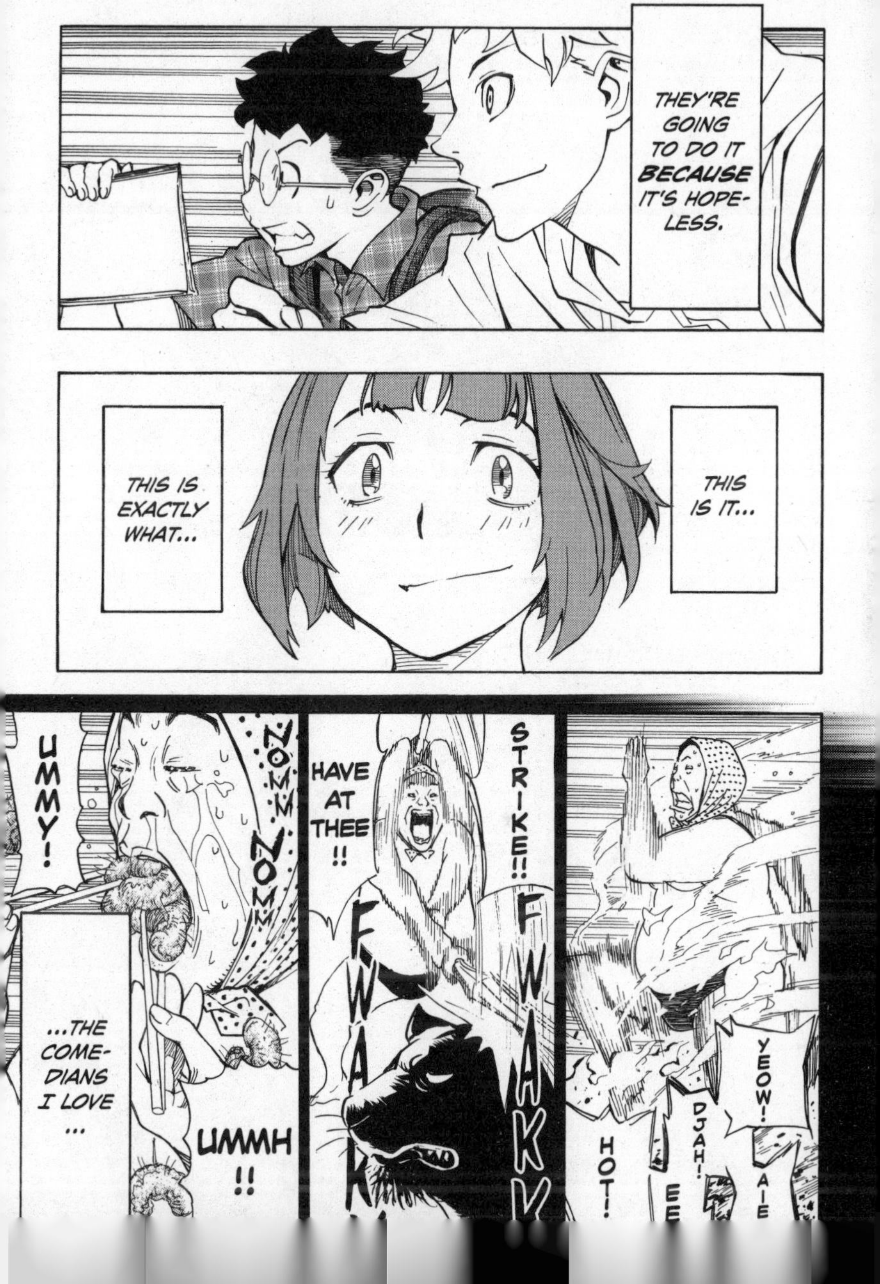
THEY'RE GOING TO DO IT BECAUSE IT'S HOPE-LESS.
THIS IS IT...
THIS IS EXACTLY WHAT...
YEOW!
AIE
DJAH!
EE
HOT!
STRIKE!!
HAVE AT THEE!!
FWAK
FWAK
NOMM NOMM
UMMY!
UMMH!!
...THE COME-DIANS I LOVE...

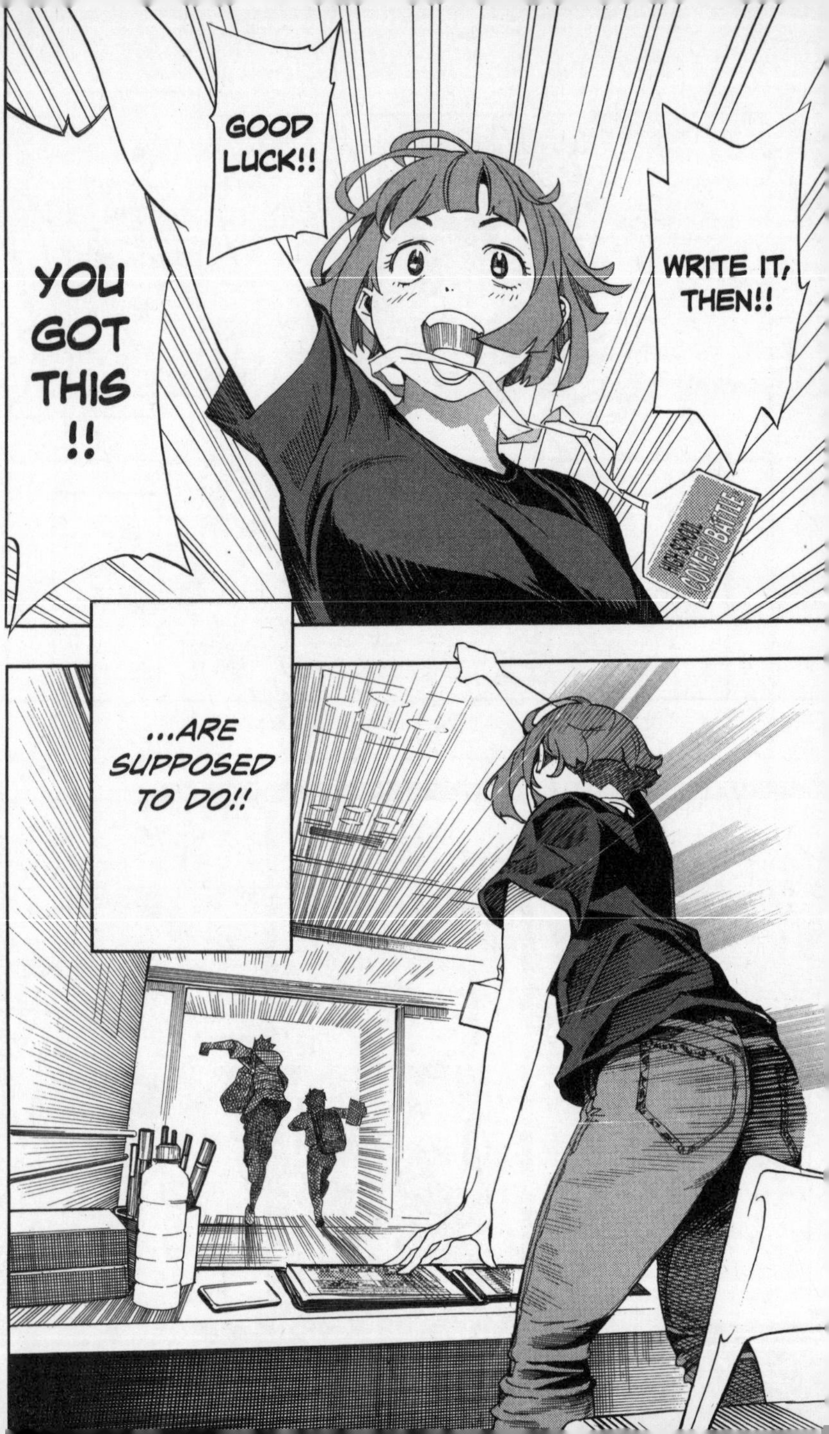
WRITE IT, THEN!!
GOOD LUCK!!
YOU GOT THIS!!
HIGH SCHOOL COMEDY BATTLE
...ARE SUPPOSED TO DO!!

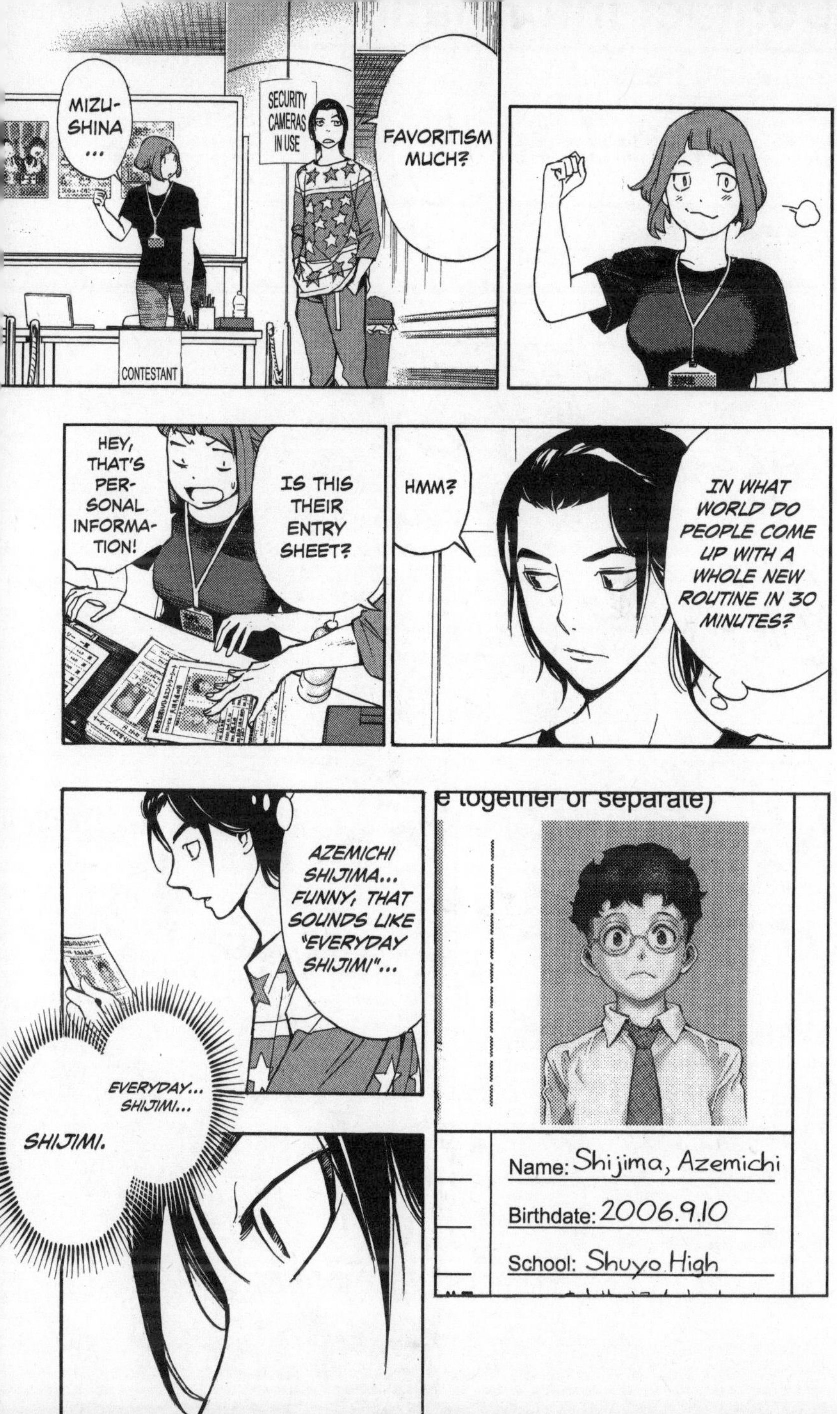
FAVORITISM MUCH?
MIZU-SHINA ...
SECURITY CAMERAS IN USE
CONTESTANT
IN WHAT WORLD DO PEOPLE COME UP WITH A WHOLE NEW ROUTINE IN 30 MINUTES?
HMM?
IS THIS THEIR ENTRY SHEET?
HEY, THAT'S PER-SONAL INFORMA-TION!
e together or separate)
Name: Shijima, Azemichi
Birthdate: 2006.9.10
School: Shuyo High
AZEMICHI SHIJIMA... FUNNY, THAT SOUNDS LIKE "EVERYDAY SHIJIMI"...
EVERYDAY... SHIJIMI...
SHIJIMI.

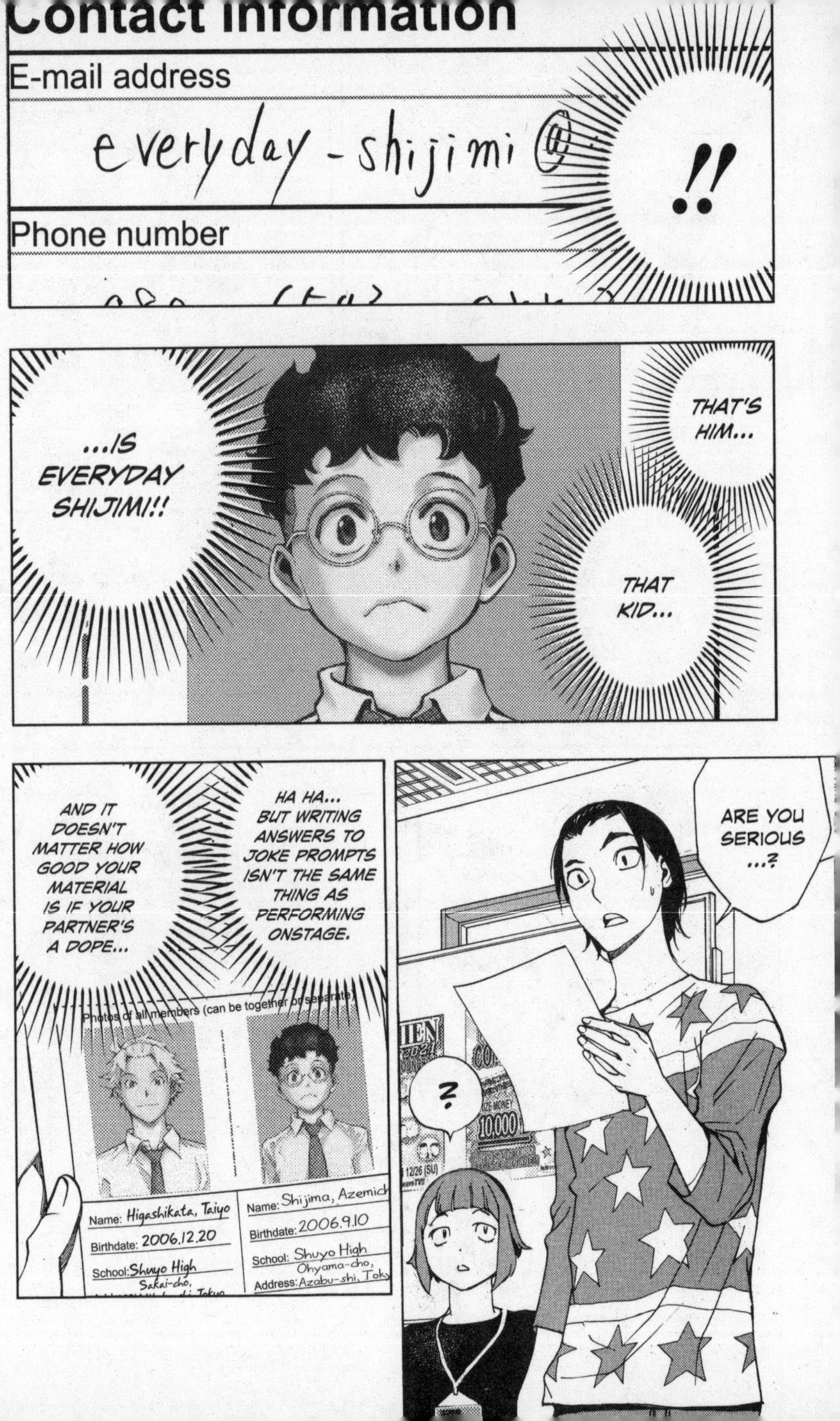
Contact information
E-mail address
everyday-shijimi@
Phone number
!!
THAT'S HIM...
THAT KID...
...IS EVERYDAY SHIJIMI!!
ARE YOU SERIOUS ...?
?
HA HA... BUT WRITING ANSWERS TO JOKE PROMPTS ISN'T THE SAME THING AS PERFORMING ONSTAGE.
AND IT DOESN'T MATTER HOW GOOD YOUR MATERIAL IS IF YOUR PARTNER'S A DOPE...
Photos of all members (can be together or separate)
Name: Higashikata, Taiyo
Birthdate: 2006.12.20
School: Shuyo High
Sakai-cho,
Name: Shijima, Azemich
Birthdate: 2006.9.10
School: Shuyo High
Ohyama-cho,
Address: Azabu-shi, Toky

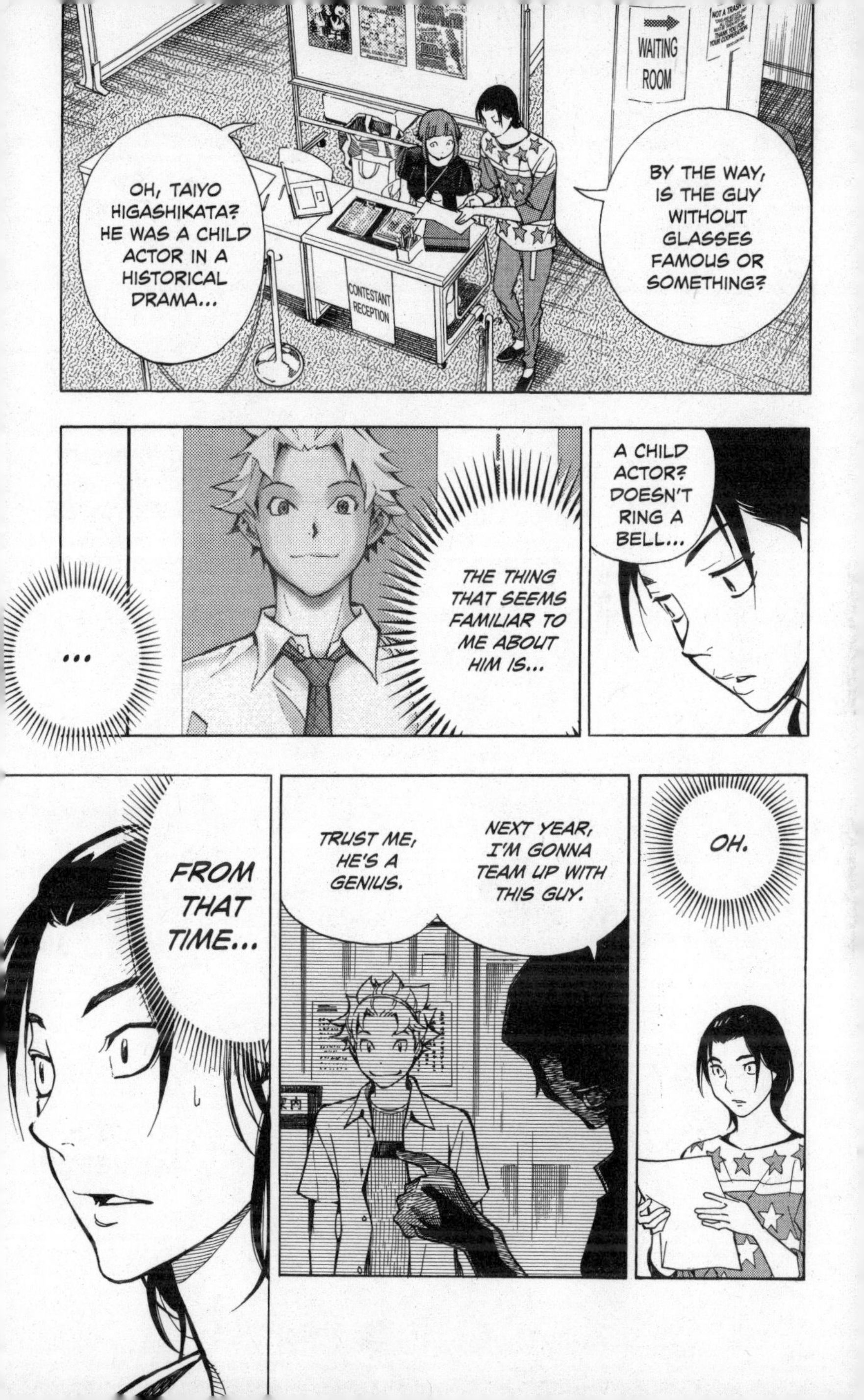
WAITING ROOM
BY THE WAY, IS THE GUY WITHOUT GLASSES FAMOUS OR SOMETHING?
CONTESTANT RECEPTION
OH, TAIYO HIGASHIKATA? HE WAS A CHILD ACTOR IN A HISTORICAL DRAMA...
A CHILD ACTOR? DOESN'T RING A BELL...
THE THING THAT SEEMS FAMILIAR TO ME ABOUT HIM IS...
...
OH.
NEXT YEAR, I'M GONNA TEAM UP WITH THIS GUY.
TRUST ME, HE'S A GENIUS.
FROM THAT TIME...

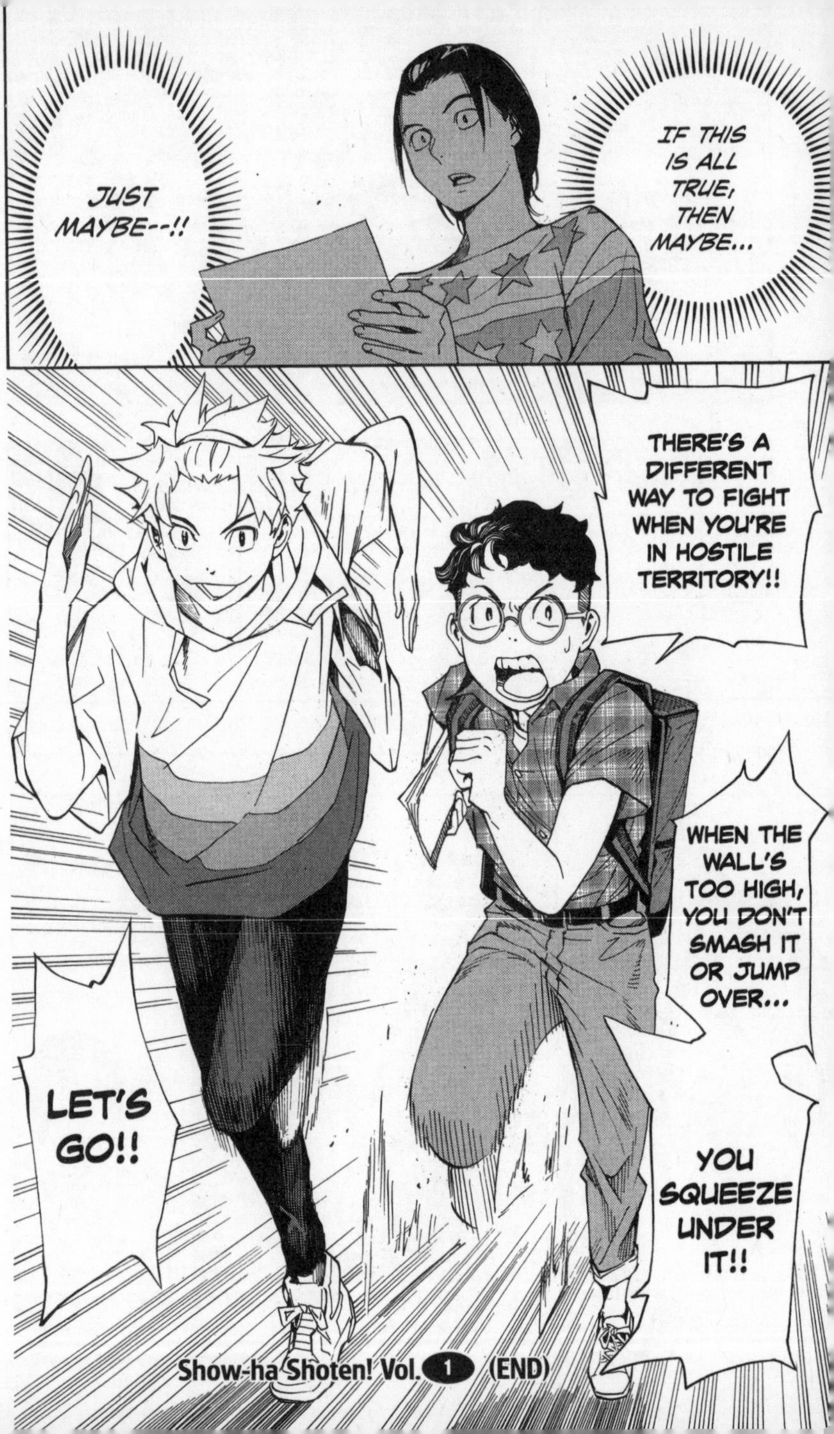
IF THIS IS ALL TRUE, THEN MAYBE...
JUST MAYBE--!!
THERE'S A DIFFERENT WAY TO FIGHT WHEN YOU'RE IN HOSTILE TERRITORY!!
WHEN THE WALL'S TOO HIGH, YOU DON'T SMASH IT OR JUMP OVER...
YOU SQUEEZE UNDER IT!!
LET'S GO!!

Show-ha Shoten! Vol. 1 (END)

Hello. I'm Akinari Asakura, the writer of this manga. Thank you very much for checking it out. When I was young, my dream was to be either a manga creator or a comedian. I'm overjoyed that I've been able to merge those passions into one creation! My first time performing onstage was in sixth grade, when I did a routine with my classmate Jicchan about someone suffering from a mysterious disease called "gyoza."

We performed it during the school fair to a small audience (in a classroom). Whether it was a hit or not is beside the point—we couldn't even finish because the first-graders in the classroom were going berserk. It was a painful way to make your comedy debut, but it's a fond memory to me now.

Jicchan and I didn't learn our lesson, and we wrote another routine for middle school...but that's a story for next volume.

I don't remember the details of the routine. Was it even funny?

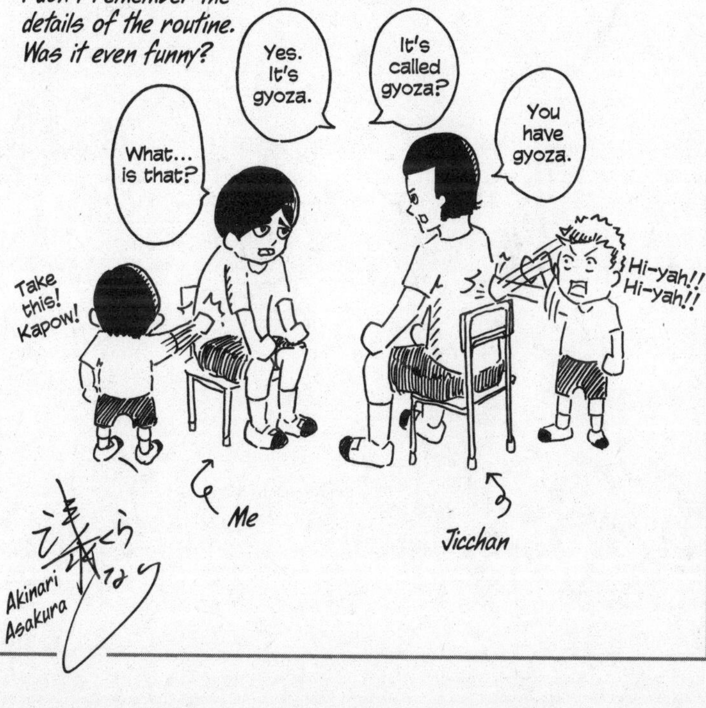
You have gyoza.
It's called gyoza?
Yes. It's gyoza.
What... is that?
Hi-yah!! Hi-yah!!
Take this! Kapow!
Jicchan
Me
Akinari Asakura

Initial Designs

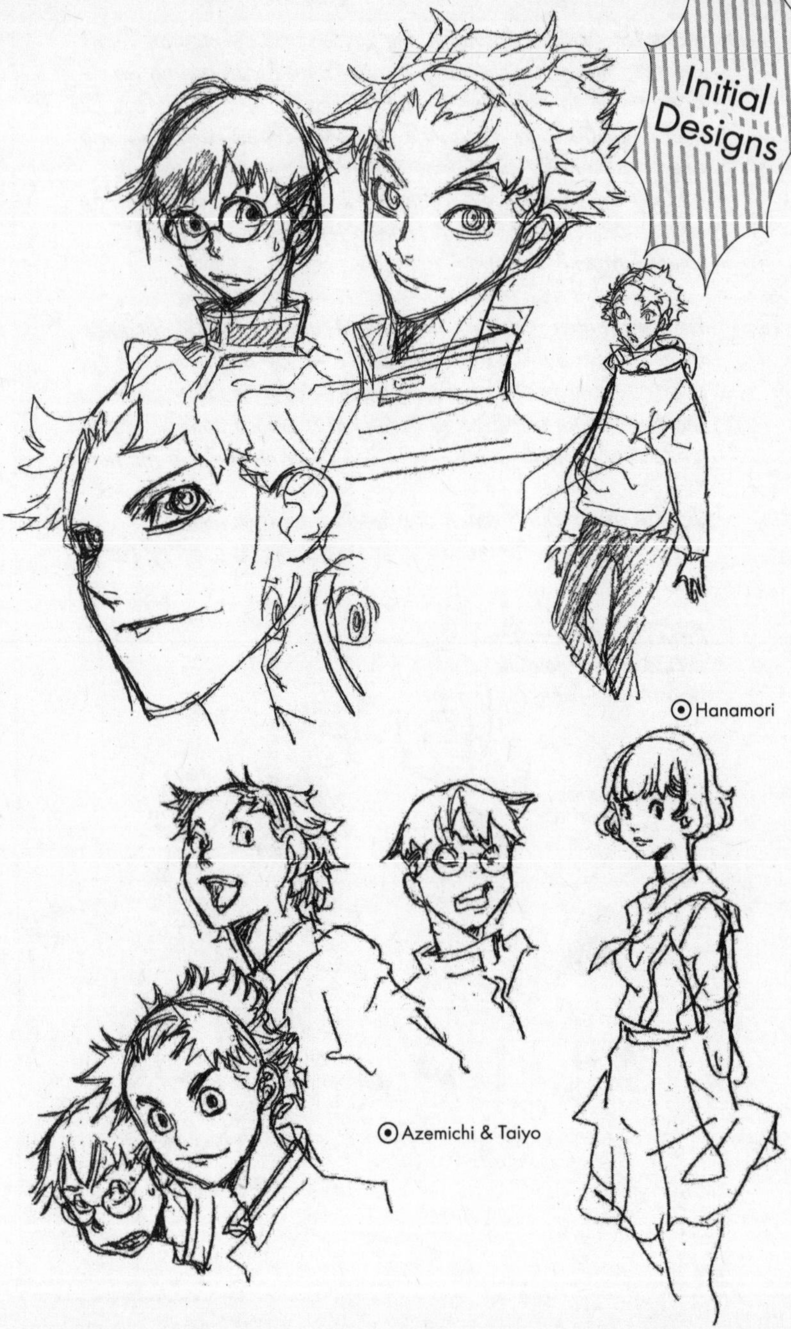

Hanamori

Azemichi & Taiyo

Chapter 1, pg. 53–54

Asakura's Draft

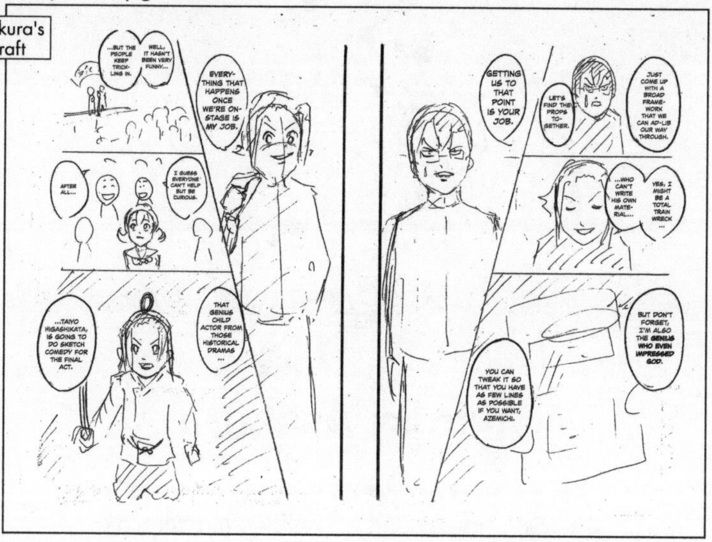
WELL, IT HASN'T BEEN VERY FUNNY...
...BUT THE PEOPLE KEEP TRICK-LING IN.
I GUESS EVERYONE CAN'T HELP BUT BE CURIOUS.
AFTER ALL...
THAT GENIUS CHILD ACTOR FROM THOSE HISTORICAL DRAMAS...
...TAIYO HIGASHIKATA, IS GOING TO DO SKETCH COMEDY FOR THE FINAL ACT.
EVERY-THING THAT HAPPENS ONCE WE'RE ON-STAGE IS MY JOB.
GETTING US TO THAT POINT IS YOUR JOB.
JUST COME UP WITH A BROAD FRAME-WORK THAT WE CAN AD-LIB OUR WAY THROUGH.
LET'S FIND THE PROPS TO-GETHER.
YES, I MIGHT BE A TOTAL TRAIN WRECK...
...WHO CAN'T WRITE HIS OWN MATE-RIAL...
BUT DON'T FORGET, I'M ALSO THE GENIUS WHO EVEN IMPRESSED GOD.
YOU CAN TWEAK IT SO THAT YOU HAVE AS FEW LINES AS POSSIBLE IF YOU WANT, AZEMICHI.

Obata's Draft

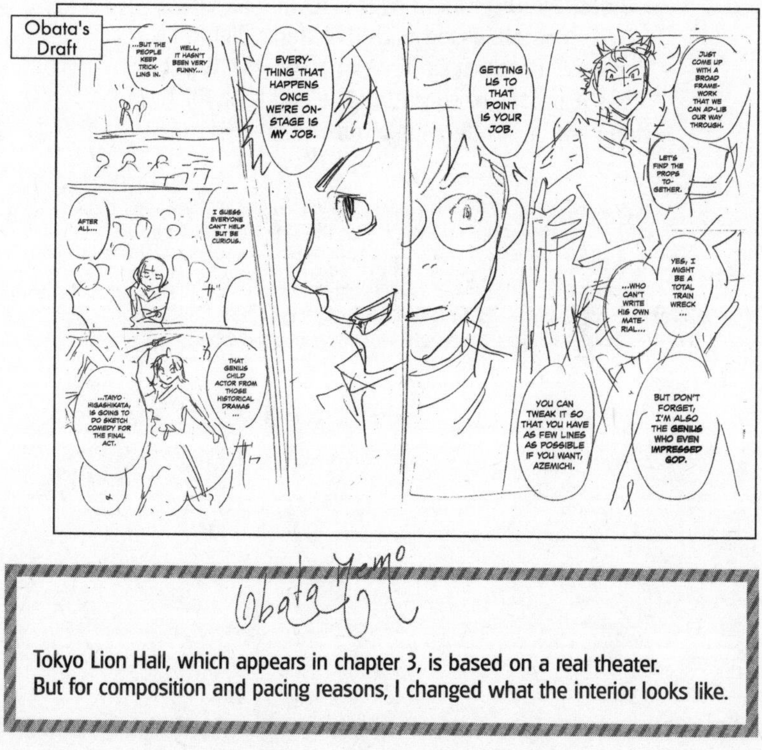
WELL, IT HASN'T BEEN VERY FUNNY...
...BUT THE PEOPLE KEEP TRICK-LING IN.
I GUESS EVERYONE CAN'T HELP BUT BE CURIOUS.
AFTER ALL...
THAT GENIUS CHILD ACTOR FROM THOSE HISTORICAL DRAMAS...
...TAIYO HIGASHIKATA, IS GOING TO DO SKETCH COMEDY FOR THE FINAL ACT.
EVERY-THING THAT HAPPENS ONCE WE'RE ON-STAGE IS MY JOB.
GETTING US TO THAT POINT IS YOUR JOB.
JUST COME UP WITH A BROAD FRAME-WORK THAT WE CAN AD-LIB OUR WAY THROUGH.
LET'S FIND THE PROPS TO-GETHER.
YES, I MIGHT BE A TOTAL TRAIN WRECK...
...WHO CAN'T WRITE HIS OWN MATE-RIAL...
BUT DON'T FORGET, I'M ALSO THE GENIUS WHO EVEN IMPRESSED GOD.
YOU CAN TWEAK IT SO THAT YOU HAVE AS FEW LINES AS POSSIBLE IF YOU WANT, AZEMICHI.

Obata Memo

Tokyo Lion Hall, which appears in chapter 3, is based on a real theater.
But for composition and pacing reasons, I changed what the interior looks like.

About the Writer

Akinari Asakura

story

I'm a logical person, so I usually try to find the reasoning behind everything, but comedy is the one thing I can never fully grasp. That's why I'm so obsessed with it, I think. What is comedy? What does it mean to laugh? What does it mean for something to be "funny"? I hope you'll ponder these questions with me.

Akinari Asakura is a novelist whose previous works include the mysteries *Ore de wa nai Enjou* (I'm Not the One Being Flamed), *Kyoushitsu ga, Hitori ni naru made* (Until I'm Alone in the Classroom), *Noir Revenant*, and the critically acclaimed *Rokunin no Usotsuki na Daigakusei* (Six Lying College Students). This is his first full-length work as a manga writer.

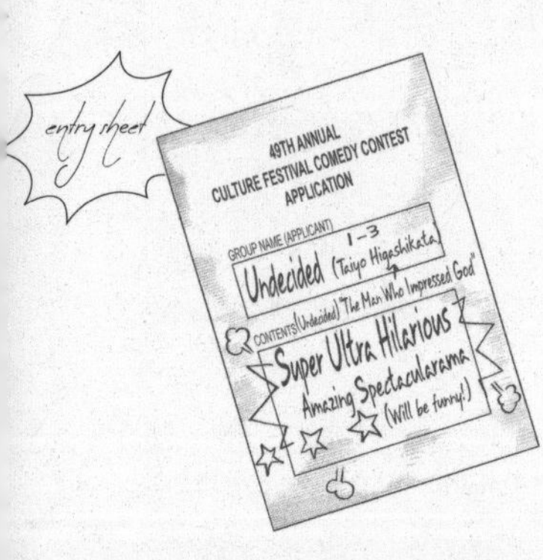
entry sheet
49TH ANNUAL
CULTURE FESTIVAL COMEDY CONTEST
APPLICATION
GROUP NAME (APPLICANT)
1-3
Undecided (Taiyo Higashikata)
CONTENTS (Undecided) "The Man Who Impressed God"
Super Ultra Hilarious
Amazing Spectacularama
(Will be funny!)

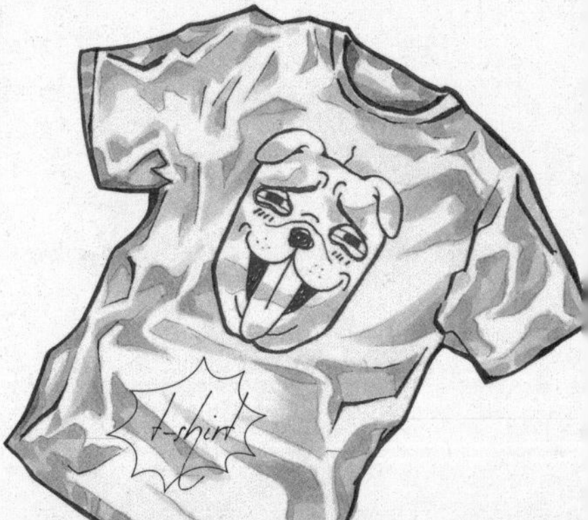
t-shirt

About the Artist

Takeshi Obata

Everyone laughs differently. It must be because everyone's throat has a different shape. I like laughter that starts off sharp and then gets husky. I wish I could laugh that way someday, but I tend to inhale as I laugh.

Takeshi Obata was born in 1969 in Niigata, Japan, and first achieved international recognition as the artist of the wildly popular Shonen Jump title *Hikaru no Go*, which won the 2003 Tezuka Osamu Cultural Prize: Shinsei "New Hope" Award and the 2000 Shogakukan Manga Award. He went on to illustrate the smash hit *Death Note* as well as the hugely successful manga *Bakuman。* and *All You Need Is Kill.*

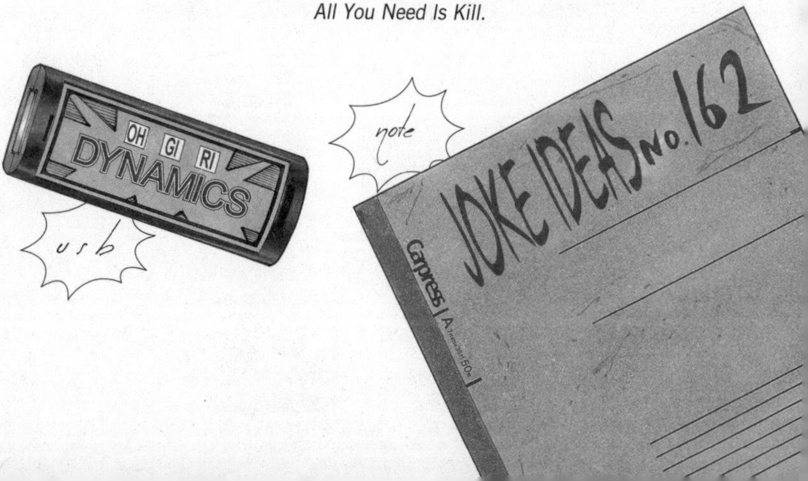
OH GI RI
DYNAMICS
usb
note
JOKE IDEAS NO.162
Campress

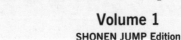

SHOW-HA SHOTEN!

Volume 1
SHONEN JUMP Edition

STORY BY AKINARI ASAKURA
ART BY TAKESHI OBATA

Translation / **Stephen Paul**
Touch-Up Art & Lettering / **James Gaubatz**
Designer / **Kam Li**
Shonen Jump Editor / **Alexis Kirsch**
Graphic Novel Editor / **Hope Donovan**

Printed in the U.S.A.

Published by VIZ Media, LLC
P.O. Box 77010
San Francisco, CA 94107

10 9 8 7 6 5 4 3 2 1
First printing, February 2023

ratings.viz.com RATED T TEEN

PARENTAL ADVISORY
SHOW-HA SHOTEN! is rated T for Teen and is recommended for ages 13 and up. This volume contains mild language.

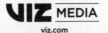

VIZ MEDIA
viz.com

SHONEN JUMP

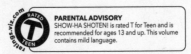

SHOYO HINATA IS OUT TO PROVE THAT IN VOLLEYBALL YOU DON'T NEED TO BE TALL TO FLY!

HAIKYU!!

Story and Art by **HARUICHI FURUDATE**

Ever since he saw the legendary player known as the "Little Giant" compete at the national volleyball finals, Shoyo Hinata has been aiming to be the best volleyball player ever! He decides to join the team at the high school the Little Giant went to—and then surpass him. Who says you need to be tall to play volleyball when you can jump higher than anyone else?

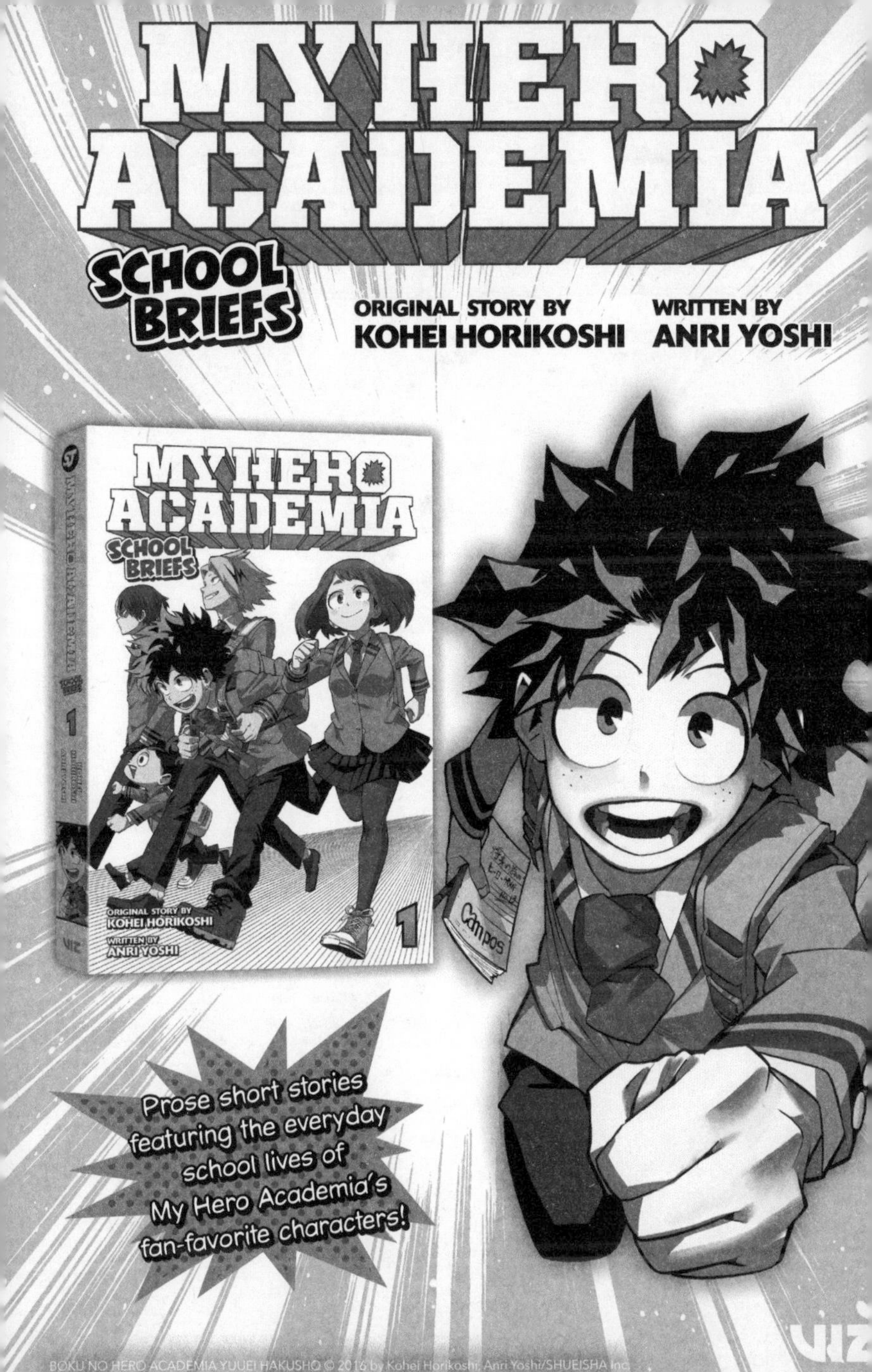
MY HERO ACADEMIA
SCHOOL BRIEFS
ORIGINAL STORY BY
KOHEI HORIKOSHI
WRITTEN BY
ANRI YOSHI
MY HERO ACADEMIA
SCHOOL BRIEFS
1
ORIGINAL STORY BY
KOHEI HORIKOSHI
WRITTEN BY
ANRI YOSHI
Campos
Prose short stories featuring the everyday school lives of My Hero Academia's fan-favorite characters!
VIZ

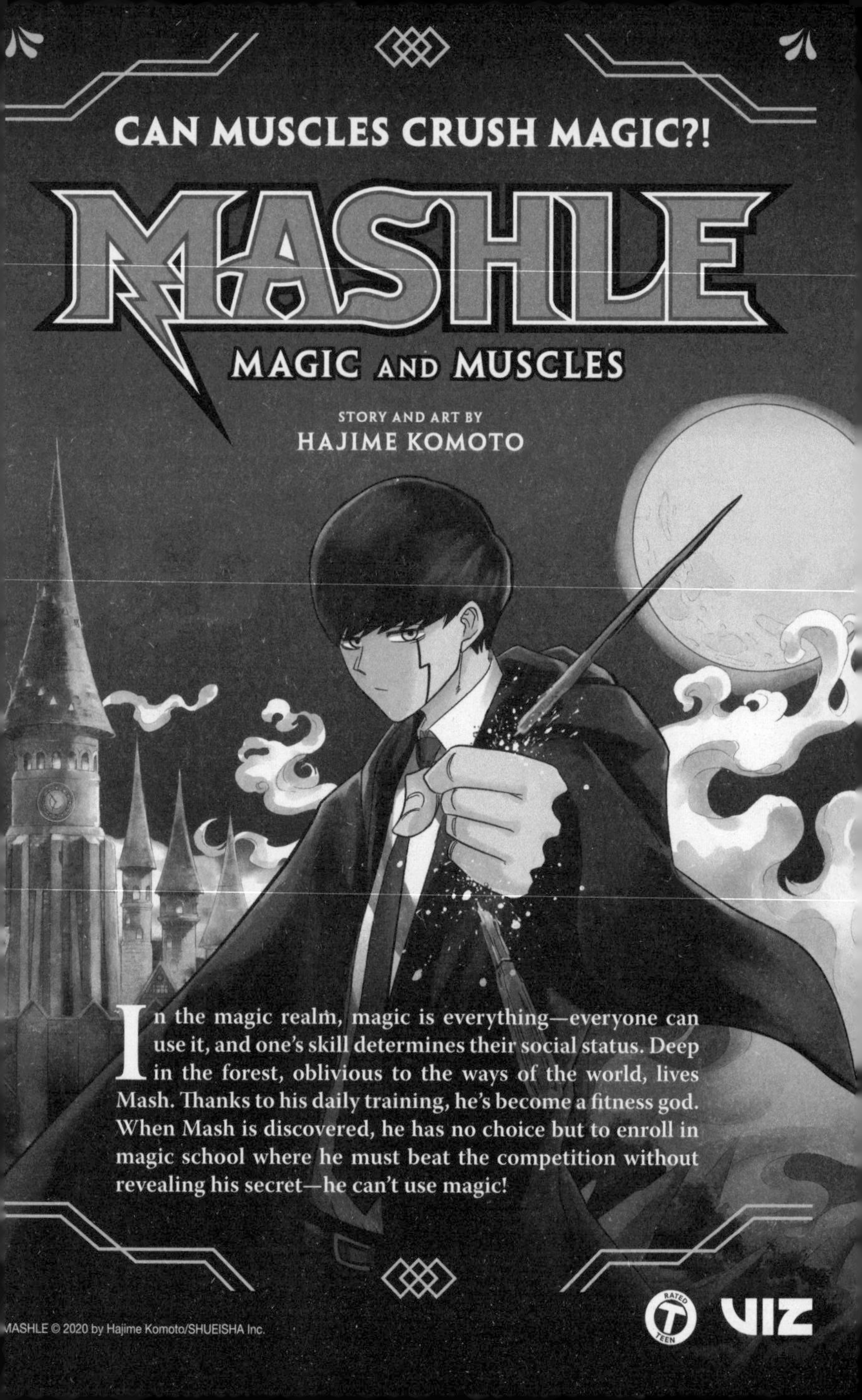
CAN MUSCLES CRUSH MAGIC?!
MASHLE
MAGIC AND MUSCLES
STORY AND ART BY
HAJIME KOMOTO
In the magic realm, magic is everything—everyone can use it, and one's skill determines their social status. Deep in the forest, oblivious to the ways of the world, lives Mash. Thanks to his daily training, he's become a fitness god. When Mash is discovered, he has no choice but to enroll in magic school where he must beat the competition without revealing his secret—he can't use magic!
MASHLE © 2020 by Hajime Komoto/SHUEISHA Inc.
RATED T TEEN
VIZ

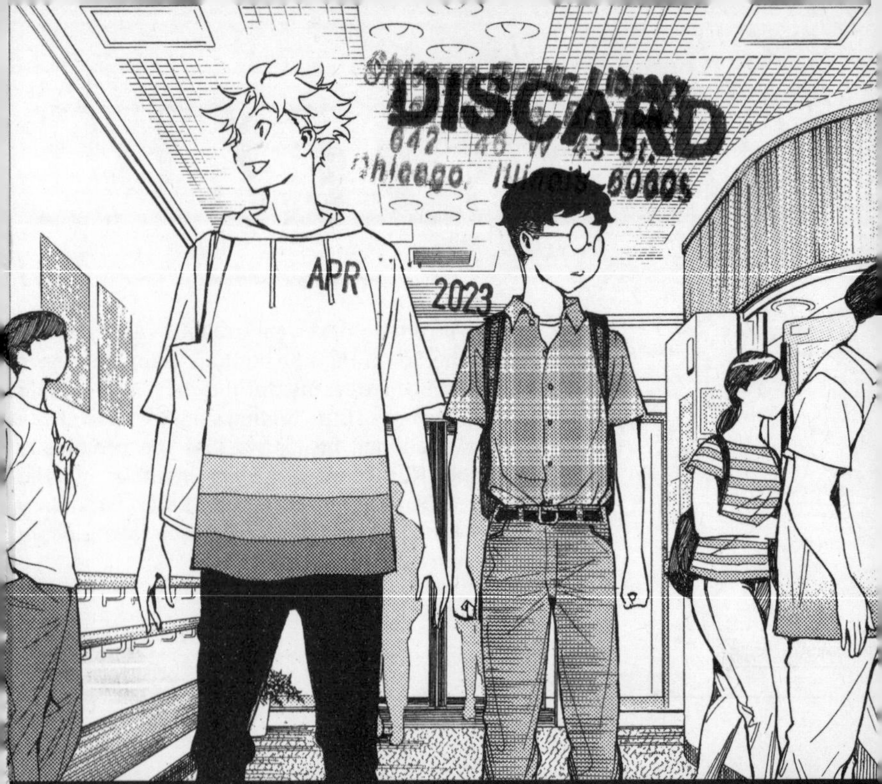

YOU'RE READING THE WRONG WAY!

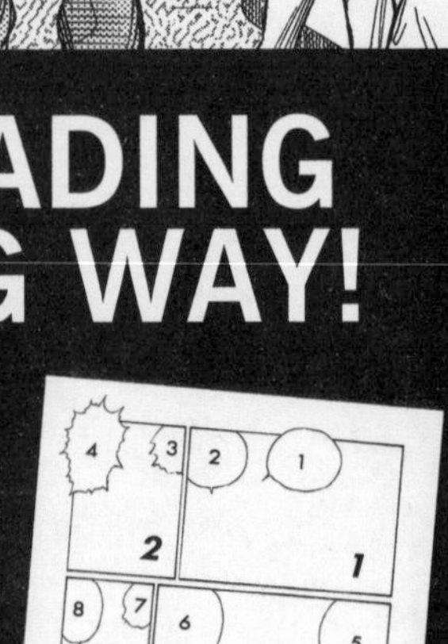
4
3
2
1
2
1
8
7
6
5
4
3
9
5
142

Show-ha Shoten!
reads right to left, starting in the upper-right corner. Japanese is read right to left, meaning that action, sound effects, and word balloon order are completely reversed from English order. Check out the diagram shown here to get the hang of things, and then turn to the [illegible] of the book to get started!

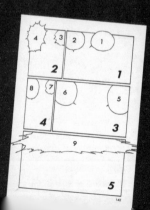